Praise for

Who Needs Gay Bars?

"In *Who Needs Gay Bars?* [Mattson] paints a vivid and nearly comprehensive portrait of the current state of gay bars as an institution and as an important component of the LGBTQ community in all its unwieldy diversity. He also paints a personal journey that many LGBTQ readers will relate to."

—Gary L. Day, *Philadelphia Gay News*

"Mattson does his best to survey as many of the myriad issues as possible, faced by an equally myriad number of bars of a dazzling variety. It's also a personal journey by the author that many LGBTQ readers will identify with."

—*Booklist*

"[One of] the best queer American travelogues since Edmund White's *States of Desire* was published way back in 1980."

—*Passport*

"Riveting . . . provokes a perhaps more existential question: who is the 'we' who needs gay bars?"

—*them Magazine*

"*Who Needs Gay Bars?* is a carefully researched and assembled look at the gay bar as a place of connection in a time when they're in danger of vanishing, erasing a vital part of queer history. With intelligent and easily accessible writing, this account stands as a testament to our community's resilience."

—Alex Espinoza, author of *Cruising*

Who Needs Gay Bars?

Bar-Hopping through America's Endangered LGBTQ+ Places

GREGGOR MATTSON

REDWOOD PRESS
Stanford, California

Redwood Press
Stanford, California

Printed in the United States of America on acid-free, archival-quality paper

ISBN 9781503640139

First paperback printing 2024

The Library of Congress has cataloged the hardcover edition as follows:
Names: Mattson, Greggor, author.
Title: Who needs gay bars? : bar-hopping through America's endangered
    LGBTQ+ places / Greggor Mattson.
Description: Stanford, California : Redwood Press, 2023. | Includes
    bibliographical references and index.
Identifiers: LCCN 2022036724 (print) | LCCN 2022036725 (ebook) | ISBN
    9781503629202 (cloth) | ISBN 9781503635876 (ebook)
Subjects: LCSH: Gay bars—United States. | Sexual minority
    community—United States. | Sexual minorities—United States—Social
    life and customs.
Classification: LCC HQ73.3.U6 M36 2023 (print) | LCC HQ73.3.U6 (ebook) |
    DDC 307.760973—dc23/eng/20220802
LC record available at https://lccn.loc.gov/2022036724
LC ebook record available at https://lccn.loc.gov/2022036725

Cover design: Zoe Norvell
Front cover photograph: Minu Han. "Found in Chaos," 2022. After the loss of so many people and places, a moment of abandon as we continue towards dawn. Hell's Kitchen, New York City.
Back cover photograph: Juan Figeroa for the *Dallas Morning News*
Text design: Elliott Beard

To friends—
Phillip has been there since it started

and lovers—
Jesse was there until the end

"Having recently moved to Macon from Atlanta I felt like I was in a gay desert. I hated driving 100 miles to find a gay bar. Then one day a friend told me about The Mill . . ."

—INTERNET REVIEWER

"A watering hole doesn't make the desert safe; it just makes it habitable."

—SAMANTHA ALLEN

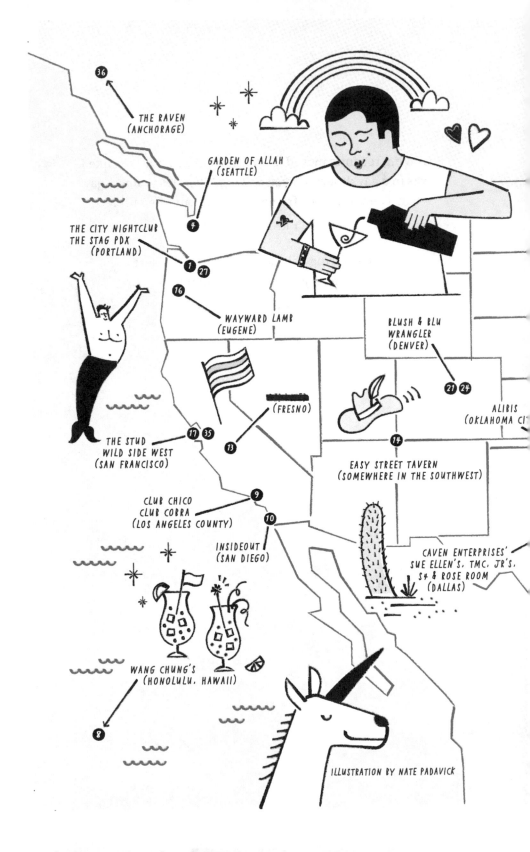

THE RAVEN
(ANCHORAGE)
36

GARDEN OF ALLAH
(SEATTLE)
4

THE CITY NIGHTCLUB
THE STAG PDX
(PORTLAND)
1 27

16
WAYWARD LAMB
(EUGENE)

BLUSH & BLU
WRANGLER
(DENVER)
21 24

(FRESNO)
13

ALIBIS
(OKLAHOMA CI)

THE STUD
WILD SIDE WEST
(SAN FRANCISCO)
17 35

14
EASY STREET TAVERN
(SOMEWHERE IN THE SOUTHWEST)

CLUB CHICO
CLUB COBRA
(LOS ANGELES COUNTY)
9

INSIDEOUT
(SAN DIEGO)
10

CAVEN ENTERPRISES'
SUE ELLEN'S, TMC, JR'S,
S4 & ROSE ROOM
(DALLAS)

WANG CHUNG'S
(HONOLULU, HAWAII)
8

ILLUSTRATION BY NATE PADAVICK

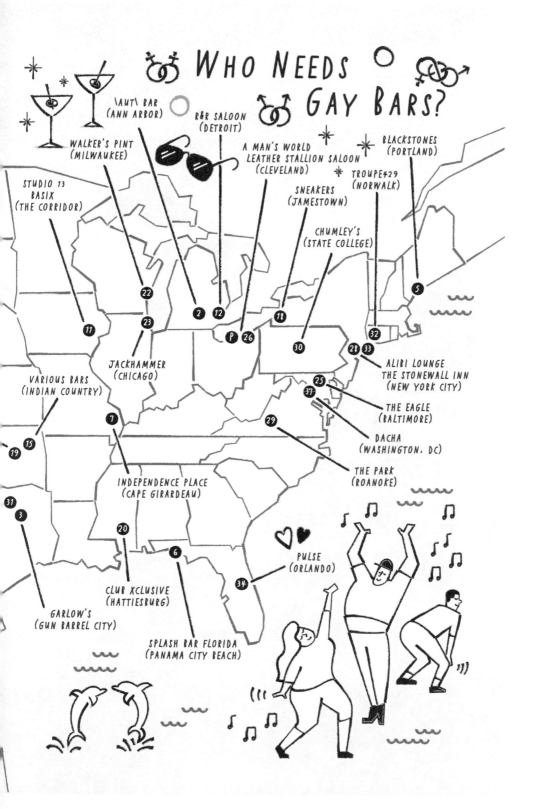

WHO NEEDS GAY BARS?

\AUT\ BAR
(ANN ARBOR)

R&R SALOON
(DETROIT)

WALKER'S PINT
(MILWAUKEE)

A MAN'S WORLD
LEATHER STALLION SALOON
(CLEVELAND)

BLACKSTONES
(PORTLAND)

STUDIO 13
BASIX
(THE CORRIDOR)

SNEAKERS
(JAMESTOWN)

TROUPE#29
(NORWALK)

CHUMLEY'S
(STATE COLLEGE)

JACKHAMMER
(CHICAGO)

ALIBI LOUNGE
THE STONEWALL INN
(NEW YORK CITY)

VARIOUS BARS
(INDIAN COUNTRY)

THE EAGLE
(BALTIMORE)

DACHA
(WASHINGTON, DC)

INDEPENDENCE PLACE
(CAPE GIRARDEAU)

THE PARK
(ROANOKE)

PULSE
(ORLANDO)

GARLOW'S
(GUN BARREL CITY)

CLUB XCLUSIVE
(HATTIESBURG)

SPLASH BAR FLORIDA
(PANAMA CITY BEACH)

22 23 2 12 11 P 26 30 32 21 33 25 37 29 34 11 5 7 19 15 31 3 20 6

Contents

Part Three
Safe Spaces for Whom

Part Four
Lesbian-Owned Bars

Part Five
Cruisy Men's Bars

Part Six
How to Save a Gay Bar

Part Seven
National Monuments

Who Needs Gay Bars?

The interior of A Man's World of Cleveland, Ohio, the bar whose 2013 closure started the investigations that became this book. Photo courtesy of Douglas Jay Sandstrom. Used with permission.

A Sociologist Walks into a Bar

A Man's World
CLEVELAND, OHIO

My favorite gay bar died in 2013, and journalists and real estate developers danced on its grave. A Man's World had been a well-worn bar in Cleveland across the street from my best friend's apartment.[1] A Man's World was the kind of old-school gay bar with blacked-out windows that you had to be buzzed into. The kind with extravagant decorations for every holiday and a free spread on Thanksgiving and Easter for the queers separated from their families of origin, whether by choice or estrangement. The kind where some of the patrons seemed unhoused, and the bouncer had elaborate job-stopper facial tattoos. The kind where the patrons reflected the racial diversity of a Black-majority city with a significant Puerto Rican population. The kind where a man celebrated his first union job by buying a round of drinks for the strangers at the bar—the most touching thing that has ever happened to me at a gay bar. The kind where occasional violence trailed men to their upstairs apartments or cars. The kind with sidewalk planters that sported pansies and little American flags. The kind that was the last place I saw a good friend two hours before he died in a car accident leaving the bar—RIP Trey.

Since 1995, A Man's World had anchored a complex of three gay bars that shared one owner, internal doorways, and a courtyard patio. The Tool Shed on the corner was ostensibly separate from A Man's World, while the basement bar Crossover only opened on weekends and for occasional leather/kink events. In their heyday, these three bars, often collectively called Man's World, crowned Cleveland's Mr. Leather. They also hosted dances by the Rainbow Wranglers, the gay and lesbian country/western dance group, puppet shows in the courtyard (everyone loves puppets!), pool league tournaments, reunions of friends, and anniversaries of lovers. Hundreds of fundraisers in the bars provided a lifeline for HIV/AIDS charities, gay sports leagues, political campaigns, and direct-action funds to help people pay for their rent, medications, utilities, or funeral expenses. The building that housed A Man's World was the first home of what became the Cleveland LGBT Center, and it hosted the first Cleveland Leather Awareness Weekend, now a multistate charity with a million dollars in fundraising to its name.

The bar complex also anchored what was, for much of the early 2000s, the only gay hub in Cleveland, the closest thing to a gayborhood the city had seen before or since. A couple blocks down Detroit Shoreway was Club Cleveland, one of the few purpose-built gay bathhouses in the United States, and the city's prime palace of promiscuity until a rival opened in 2006. A couple blocks up the street was Bounce, at the time the only gay dance club in the county open to people who were 18 to 20 and the primary stage for Cleveland's vibrant drag scene.[2] The Tool Shed's immediate neighbor was Burton's Soul Food and the Ohio City Café, where you could grab an inexpensive bite while you sobered up. The Dean Rufus House of Fun, described by a journalist as an "upscale gay boutique," but by online reviewers as a "gay-friendly variety store" and "a gay porn shop with a large selection of soul records," was open until early morning for casual purchases of designer underwear, stationery, wigs, or lube.[3] On weekend mornings after last call, men streamed along Detroit Shoreway, pausing for one last smoke, taking one last glance, chancing to slip their phone numbers into someone's hand, making tomorrow's plans with friends, wandering down Detroit Shoreway to where Black and Brown hustlers lingered, or slinking off between cars to make out—or more.

New owners bought the Man's World's building in early 2013, evicted the gay men who lived in the run-down apartments upstairs, and began massive renovations. During the bar's last call, flyers thanked the longtime owner, Rick Husarick, for providing "an oasis for the gay community in Cleveland; where customers, employees and tenants alike could gather together to build friendships, celebrate diversity and support the community." These goals were echoed by the new owners, who described theirs as "inclusive," "responsible" development.[4]

These continuities were nowhere to be found in myriad journalist accounts that invariably described the intersection outside A Man's World as "decrepit," "toxic," "nowhere."[5] The newcomers looked back upon a curious frontier that was at once empty and populated, a "vacant" "no man's land" where "no one would want to walk here at night," yet with sidewalks full of "drug dealers and prostitutes."[6]

The queer past of the building that housed A Man's World had grim resonance in the words newcomers used. Journalists thought they were denigrating the old scene when they called it a "complex of debauchery" or a "smorgasbord of vice."[7] Upscale businesses like Harness Cycling Studio and Ohio City Dog Haven took the spaces where men in leather harnesses and dog collars once cruised each other.

Many gay men celebrated the new order in that corner of the neighborhood. For Dean Rufus, whose business was the only one to survive the transition, the change was "good for everybody, it's great for Ohio city."[8] Getting a "more safe, upscale atmosphere" was one goal of patrons who organized a boycott of the bar back in 2008 after a longtime AIDS activist was mugged outside A Man's World.[9] Demands for safety accompanied racist dog whistles that the bar's troubles were caused by "lowball street rats" and "thugs," or descriptions that linked the "seediness" of the bars to the nearby public housing.[10] A white former bartender from A Man's World heralded a kind of post-gay reality, reporting "I don't think there's a need for a gay scene in Cleveland anymore. I go wherever I want with my friends. Every bar is a gay bar."[11] Yet the parts of the queer scene that were racially and economically diverse were absent from the neighborhood's new tony boutiques and art galleries.

If A Man's World presided over a "decaying" corner of poverty, it is because Cleveland's LGBTQ+ people are also poor.[12] If we stood in the vacant lots described by cheerleaders as "missing teeth," they reflected our own smiles.[13] Because it was our gay village, we looked askance at the redeveloper's claims to have founded a village of his own.[14] If we did not shun drug dealers, it's because we knew that middle-class folks got their ecstasy and pot from "friends." We knew all the reasons why a man on the street locks eyes with you for longer than is necessary, and why that can be so threatening to white people if he is not. And we knew that a transgender woman would be arrested for selling sex whether or not she ever had, in a city where her safety was an afterthought.[15]

When A Man's World closed, there was very little hard data about gay bar closures. But it was clear that gay bars were in trouble. Mainstream news outlets began sounding the alarm that "The gay bar is dying" and openly asking, "Do gay people still need gay bars?"[16] Rising LGBTQ+ acceptance has liberated gay bar patrons to visit any old straight bar, goes the story. Smartphone dating apps like Grindr and Tinder have eliminated gay bars' role in helping us meet.[17] Gentrification has pushed these bars out of the neighborhoods they helped make hip. By my count, 37 percent of gay bars closed between 2007 and 2019, and that was before COVID-19 brought the nation's nightlife to its knees and shuttered an additional 16 percent by 2021.[18] Fully 45 percent of gay bars closed in the twenty years between 2002 and 2023.

How that 50 percent hits depends on where you stand. In big-city gay neighborhoods, it might mean a couple fewer choices out of many similar bars for a night out. But it might mean the loss of all the bars for people of color, as happened in San Francisco, or the only club for 18-year-olds, as happened in Cleveland.[19] In rural counties, it might mean that the only public LGBTQ+ space within 100 miles has winked out of existence, as happened when Equality Rocks closed in Joplin, Missouri, in 2018. These media reports, however, were coming only from the coasts where big cities have gayborhoods and a gay press to advertise their goings-on.[20] The question "Who needs gay bars?" is very different if you're sitting in Manhattan, New York, or Manhattan, Kansas—the difference between a city with the most gay bars in the country versus a city that has zero.

And gentrification didn't jibe with what was going on in Cleveland—I should have known better about using the g-word in my diatribe about A Man's World that was published in a local magazine, much of which you have just read. Firstly, it was an unnecessary red flag to the bull of a developer who sent threatening emails to my dean and college president demanding my head. Secondly, I'm an urban sociologist who teaches a class on American cities. Although what happened to A Man's World certainly *looked* like the redevelopment and displacement that you see on the coasts, the situation here in the rust belt is different: Our problem is disinvestment. We have a half-century of population declines and a national banking market that sends our saving accounts sloshing toward the coasts in search of returns. There, mega-condos sell for multimillions, and this fleeing capital sweeps along our young people and the patrons of our gay bars as well. The developer of the Man's World complex asserted that the building had already gone into foreclosure when he acquired it, absolving him of responsibility for its demise. But the response to my Man's World essay convinced me that people really cared about gay bars: LGBTQ+ people, yes, but straight neighbors and allies and journalists cared as well, or were at least *very* curious.

As my then-partner Jesse could have told you, however, I am not the perfect person for this project. I go to bed early, the product of chronic fatigue that has not abated despite getting my severe depression under control and acquiring that most essential life accessory for a gay bear, a CPAP night breathing machine. I am a white, settler, cisgender man, lacking direct access to the experiences of the vast majority of LGBTQ+ people. There are no gay bars in my county west of Cleveland. My hearing loss means I struggle to hear what people are saying when Britney is blasting. And I struggle to separate my life and my work, an unfairness to Jesse who could never tell whether we were out on the town or whether he was an unwitting sidekick to my research.

In other ways, I'm perfect for this project. From my first book, I'm well practiced in conducting interviews. I'm a published expert on gay bars. I was trained in bar observation by a federally funded research project in grad school that first introduced me to the long tradition of sociologists chasing "deviants" in bars.[21] That I was hired precisely as one of those deviants—the gay man working for straight women—was an irony lost on me until much later, after I was fired for fraternizing with the "subjects."

I plotted a two-prong strategy. To track the change in the number of gay bars in the United States, I would count them in old, printed business directories. For this, I grabbed the *Damron Guide*, the longest-running and only national guidebook of LGBTQ+ places. It was once compared to the *Negro Motorist Green Book* for locating safe places in a homophobic world, a false equation of race and sexuality but one that gestured at printed media's role in knitting together a gay nation of travelers.[22] Luckily I owned a *Damron*, purchased from the Lambda Rising bookstore in 1997 as a gift to myself upon graduating from college in Washington, DC: Oh the places I wanted to go, and the men I wanted to do! A quick purchase of the 2017 guide—it was still in print, in a Yelp world!—meant I could calculate changes in the number of gay bars over time. It turned out that the pundits were right. Gay bars *were* closing, but not everywhere. And given the uneven geography of LGBTQ+ acceptance—South Carolina and South Dakota are not California and Connecticut—this didn't surprise me, even as it raised more questions than it answered.[23]

Next, I'd go see for myself and talk to the people who were best positioned to know what was happening in their hyper-local corners of the United States: the gay bar owners and managers and drag queens and DJs who'd been in them over the decades. I planned my first 4,000-mile road trip through 17 states and the District of Columbia, taking my little mutt Blanche in my boxy car my neighbor calls the "plum mini-hearse." I swooped down the Eastern Seaboard with dog as my co-pilot. In Louisiana I met up with just-graduated research assistant Tory Sparks, a queer femme to offset my cis-male energy and to be an extra pair of ears in the clubs, fingers on the laptop, and eyes on the road.

I augmented my *Damron* page-turning with some deep googling, plotting a route to encounter gay bars serving women, people of color, and lone gay bars more than an hour's drive from another: I suspected that not all gay bars were equal. My trip took me through gayborhoods in Washington, DC, and Dallas; big-city bars in Atlanta and Philadelphia; lone roadhouses in Spartanburg, South Carolina, and Macalester, Oklahoma; and downtown small-city bars in Muncie, Indiana, and Springfield, Massachusetts. I piggybacked bar visits onto my occasional business trips and holidays in western states.

I learned that there is great diversity in the way gay bar professionals identify their establishments: gay bars and lesbian bars, yes, but also queer bars, "women's bars," and "everybody" or "alternative lifestyle" bars. I started distinguishing between gay bars and men's bars: Gay bars have often been a literal "Man's World"—if those men were cisgender.[24] "Queer" here is not an umbrella term for LGBTQ+ people but denotes an embrace of radical politics that centers anti-capitalism, racial justice, and a rejection of binaries. I also learned that it's difficult—though not impossible—to operate a radical queer business in a workaday regulatory world, but what constitutes being radical varies wildly in the suburbs or rural areas, or in different regions of the country.[25] Some of the queerest things happen in some very overlooked places in the United States, a country that forgets that it is only part of the continent that is also America.

When giving talks about my early findings, my friends were enthusiastic, but other academics could be disdainful. "Your data only describes the Midwest," one sniffed. Embarrassed by his provincialism, I replied, "And the South. And Appalachia. And the Mid-Atlantic." "Yes, but you don't have bars in big cities," said another. "DC and Dallas are big cities," I replied. Exasperated with me, he snapped, "but you don't have bars in New York and Los Angeles, and that's where most gay bars are." He wasn't wrong—those two metropolitan regions do host the most gay bars, not surprising as they're the two largest cities in the country.

But he wasn't right, either. There are *eight times* more cities with one gay bar than there are cities with gayborhoods: The most common way that gay bars occur is alone in their town. And in any case, the vast majority of gay bars are not in the four big coastal cities that attract most of the national attention.[26] Small cities like Morgantown (West Virginia), Pocatello (Idaho), or Waterloo (Iowa) may feature far fewer consumer choices than big cities, but you can still get microbrews and craft kombucha, visit farmer's markets and farm-to-table restaurants, listen to NPR, take the bus, and hit up a gay bar.[27] You don't need a coast to be cosmopolitan.[28] And besides, plenty of people were writing about big-city gay bars where only a small fraction of LGBTQ+ people live. What about the rest of us?

So I planned a second, more modest voyage of 2,400 miles from Ohio to Philly up to Maine and back across Pennsylvania, stopping in every state of New England and the Mid-Atlantic except Vermont, which at the time had no gay bars. And when my meager research funds couldn't send me to Wisconsin, Nebraska, Nevada, or Los Angeles, standout undergraduate research students Tory Sparks and Jack Spector-Bishop filled in for me. Added to other regional road trips, we racked up more than 135 interviews from 39 states and the District of Columbia, visited over 300 gay bars in 6 years, and put nearly 10,000 miles on my car. It was random which bars responded to my invitations—phones in gay bars are often disconnected or their voicemail is full. Their websites are often out of commission: "404 not found." Their emails often bounce. Facebook proved to be the most reliable way to get a response, though often from a drag queen or bartender rather than an owner. A couple of times I was stood up after driving more than two hours out of my way; nightlife schedules do not always align with a work trip that was planned to the hour.

My strategy was geographic breadth and diversity in the kinds of bars and the patrons they serve. This allowed me to look for patterns across the country. The stories I can tell are thick on reminiscences but thin on day-to-day detail because I was rarely in a bar for more than a couple of hours. And while gay bar professionals are unique sources on recent changes, their reports warrant skepticism. Owners are cheerleaders for their businesses and may be reluctant to share discrediting details to a drive-by stranger, and managers are beholden to their bosses. And yet, my practiced interviewing skills yielded many moments where owners confided things off the record, expressed fears for the future, or told me "I didn't expect to have so much to say" or "I've never told anyone this before, but . . ."

Patterns were hard to detect in the hyper-local world of the nation's diverse gay bars. For every owner who said smartphone apps like Grindr had decimated business, there were others who claimed Grindr brought business in. For every owner who blamed millennials for abandoning gay bars, there was another who bemoaned the older crowd for staying home. And for every gay bar squeezed by economic redevelopment and gentrification, there were more squeezed by local economic collapses, the changing landscape of marijuana legalization, regional population declines, or an inability to serve new populations who demand racial justice and equality for transgender and gender-nonconforming patrons.

Gay bars aren't closing everywhere, they aren't closing for the same reasons, and they are changing in surprising ways that serve old audiences and cultivate new ones. There is no one answer to the question "Who needs gay bars?" because there is no one "who," no one set of "needs," and no one kind of "gay bar." Many of the bars I featured have since closed. But new ones opened. This book is not a eulogy: Gay bars are not dying, they're evolving. It's not a love letter, either, except as tough love, a gimlet-eyed scrutiny of gay bars' flaws and joys.

Since "queer things cannot have straight histories," the structure of this book invites you to hop from bar to bar, chapter order be damned, to wend your own path through the thirst-quenching queerness of gay bars in the United States.[29] Together, these bars reflect an American mosaic as glittering and elusive as a rotating disco ball. On my travels I encountered many Americas, such as the time I stood in the lobby of a cheap motel, eager to get on the road to Asheville, North Carolina, to see an episode of *RuPaul's Drag Race* at O.Henry's with my people. A sporty white man interrupted my reverie to ask me, "Are you here for the drag race?" I was confused. How did this straight man know what I was thinking? Oh. I was near the Bristol Motor Speedway. The *other* drag race. I smiled and said that I was.

This book is organized into sections, some exploring special types of gay bars, others exploring important issues facing gay bars. Each chapter profiles a bar that exemplifies these themes, though bars are not strictly segregated: There are lesbian bars scattered throughout the book, and gay bars for Black, Indigenous, and people of color are not corralled into chapters just on that topic.

Although the American flag still flies from the corner of the building where A Man's World once reigned, the rainbow flag that fluttered beneath has been replaced by the gentrifiers' standard of the neighborhood development corporation. Ten years later, I still miss that bar, a longing more perverse than anything that happened inside it. Journalists eulogized the racially and economically mixed queer scenes as the "inevitable casualties" of the neighborhood's redevelopment.[30] The entrepreneurs did succeed in "curating" a corner of Cleveland that does not "suck."[31]

But for us queers, not sucking is not only no fun, it's not fair.

Part One
Ambivalence

Manager Carl Currie stands in the newly installed window of Blackstones in Portland, Maine. The bar's interior had been boarded up to the street for decades after vandals repeatedly smashed the glass. Both Carl and some queer folks are ambivalent about his pivotal role at the front of the region's only gay bar, but straight people like him have long been pillars of the LGBTQ+ community. Photo courtesy of Joel Page. Used with permission.

One

Ambivalence about Gay Bars

The City Nightclub
PORTLAND, OREGON

LGBTQ+ Americans are surprisingly ambivalent about the decline in their gay bars. Not ambivalent as in apathetic or indecisive, but ambi-valent: being of two minds, having strong feelings that run in opposite directions, of desiring in simultaneous electric contradiction.[1] A former party boy and longtime husband of a gay colleague laughed when I told him I was writing a book on gay bars: "They still have those?" An internet commentor on an article about gay nightlife dying said, "I am glad we don't have to rely on bars and nightclubs," citing churches and restaurants and homes as better places to socialize.[2] A 2022 Pride month story about racial discrimination in gay bars was headlined, "Gay Bars Have Been Closing En Masse. Maybe That's a Good Thing."[3] And some white gay bar owners even falsely equate LGBTQ+ -only spaces to the segregation of African Americans during Jim Crow, welcoming the new era of "integrated" gay–straight socializing. As Clare Forstie concluded, "Ambivalence in queer nightlife spaces means a desire for queer-specific spaces alongside a desire for their absence."[4] If Walt Whitman contained multitudes all by himself, imagine how vastly diverse are queer people, with our infinite vacillating feelings!

Ambivalence is the main thread in these stories because it addresses the double meanings of the question, "Who needs gay bars?" Gay bars—these days, who needs 'em now that we can go to all the bars? But in all seriousness, who really *does* need gay bars? The newly out or newly widowed? The LGBTQ+ people who have rarely found a welcome in bars? We LGBTQ+ people are ambivalent about gay bars because we're divided about what it means to be LGBTQ+. Is it a life-changing, soul-defining call to arms? Or is it a minor, often-irrelevant detail whom we fuck (or not)? This is only one of the many essential, intrinsic ambiguities at the heart of queerness itself, ones I explore here through the stories of forty-two of the nation's gay bars.

My own ambivalence about gay bars runs back to my baby gay beginnings.

It was 1993, and the brick alley was lit by streetlight in the Industrial Triangle of Portland, Oregon. The smell of cafeteria green beans from the Henry Weinhard's brewery was in the air as were the wafts of clove cigarettes. Clammy hands and fluttering heart and the distant thump-thump-thump as we approached the door. Paying five sweaty dollars and up the stairs and into the lights. Gay bar, first time. With my only ever girlfriend. That first song as I walked through the door is so embarrassing today, marred as it is by *Saturday Night Live* skits, but then so touching, so apt, wailing:

"What is love? Baby don't hurt me."[5]

Everyone has a first-time story in a gay bar. Like losing your virginity, it was probably awkward, fear-soaked, and unforgettable. Most are also anticlimactic. The buildup of shrieking anxiety was driven by the fact that at 18, the only gay people my age I had ever seen were on the daytime talk show *Geraldo* when I was home sick with an asthma attack.[6] New York Club Kid Michael Alig and his co-conspirators were on the television stage. I thought all gay people wore wigs and horns and were terrible and eccentric with eye makeup and unashamed faggy voices. Stepping into the cavernous City Nightclub in Portland, Oregon, that first night, the lights and the music were dazzling, but the crowd was just kids. No batwings, no shadowed eyes. Just kids. Like me.

How disappointing.

What a relief.

What I didn't know at the time was how special The City Nightclub was: the nation's only all-ages, alcohol-free, gay nightclub a mere thirty minutes from my small-town hometown of Camas, Washington![7] I certainly didn't know about its struggles with the homophobic Portland police, nor owner Lanny Swerdlow's longtime activist mission to provide places for LGBTQ+ teens to socialize.[8] Nor did I know about the club's outrageously over-the-top stage shows on Saturday at midnight: Heather and I only went on the Fridays-that-became-Saturdays because early Sunday mornings were for church with our families. All I "knew" was that the club was owned by a pedophile who liked to date 16-year-olds— rumors that formed the basis of an indictment that was never sustained, a homophobic smear campaign that was actually orchestrated by city hall and that reached far beyond the outer suburbs. When authorities finally managed to close The City, teens organized a 1996 march on city hall that received national coverage by MTV.[9]

The City Nightclub captures its own ambiguities about gay bars: Do nightclubs count as bars? What about LGBTQ+ restaurants that also serve liquor, or ostensibly straight bars that are teeming with gay people? Are lesbian bars gay bars or something different? In what possible world does The City, an all-ages dance club that doesn't even serve alcohol, even count as a bar? These days, online business listings from Google and Yelp don't register the nuances that we might make between the gay-friendly straight bar or the gay-owned restaurant that attracts gay-friendly straight people. To the algorithms, a bar is either gay or it isn't, a straight definitiveness that doesn't capture the deliciously messy realities of queer ambiguity.

When bad things happen to gay bars, however—a shooting, a pandemic—plenty of LGBTQ+ people rush to celebrate them as safe spaces. Patrons rally to save them, community historians rush to preserve memories, artists stage grand gestures, and op-eds decry the loss of our queer national heritage.[10] So we're not *all* ambivalent about gay bars, *all* of the time.

What premature eulogies miss is that gay bars were never *all* things to *all* LGBTQ+ people—caring about gay bars means reckoning with their histories of exclusion. Scholars once described them as the "primary social institution" and "most important social spaces" of gay and lesbian life, but they haven't been that for years, even for the white cisgender gay men they have often primarily served.[11] There are long histories of gay bars discriminating against people of color and women, and plenty of us queer folks never felt welcome in them due to body size or disability or gender identity.[12] Many LGBTQ+ people are explicitly excluded from them, such as the under-21 crowd, not to mention others without government-issued ID—the poor, the undocumented—who often can't enter gay bars at all.[13] And then there's those of us in recovery from alcoholism, the anxious and depressed, and the introverts. Gay bars were never for all of us.

Staid, middle-class white cis gay men may feel free to go anywhere because every bar feels like a gay bar to them, but for many LGBTQ+ people, recent changes have made them feel welcome in gay bars for the first time. The purported "transgender tipping point" in the 2010s highlighted new challenges to bars that had long made trans people unwelcome in gay bars, not to mention other queer identities like gender nonbinary, agender, or asexual.[14] This was especially a challenge for lesbian bars trying to provide a women's-only space, or cruisy men's bars that had trouble adapting to younger patrons' new kinks and demands for gender inclusivity.

Besides, some of the most vibrant innovations in queer community happen outside the bars: in LGBTQ+ bookstores, direct-action organizations, kickball leagues, reading clubs, and nonprofits.[15] Queer pop-up parties and house parties sprang up to explicitly counter gay bars' histories of racism, transgender exclusion, and misogyny.[16] LGBTQ+ youth have often flocked to coffeeshops and late-night diners to find their community: What region doesn't have a gay Denny's or a queer Waffle House? For years I organized a LGBTQ+ happy hour in my little town, an alternative to the bars forty-five minutes away, and one that was accessible to the retirement community up the road and locals without cars. Bars have never been the be-all and end-all of LGBTQ+ life.

Do we still need gay bars, then?

Are "we" even a we?

Ambivalence is home turf for queer people: We push away the things we want because we want things that we shouldn't, not because we are confused but because we are deprived of role models for joy. We want to hide for our safety, and we want to be visible at the same time, seen for who we really are or noticed by the cute person over there. We want to push through the pull of respectable, heterosexual tides, and we want a place and time just to rest. We want to be special. We want to be normal. For F. Scott Fitzgerald, that inveterate partier, "The test of a first-rate intelligence is the ability to hold two opposed ideas in the mind at the same time, and still retain the ability to function."[17] Understanding gay bars today requires this ability: to see them as cherished institutions *and* as places that have not welcomed everyone in the LGBTQ+ community, historic places that must change to secure their place in the future.

Gay bars fascinate and exhaust me. They are places of desires—that burning glance, that perfect moment—and hours wasted, waiting for something or somebody to happen. Some of my favorite memories happened in them: dancing in the snow on the back deck of Tracks in DC! A cowgirl projectile vomiting in Denver! Two drag queens clawing at each other's wigs in a parking lot!

But I live in a world that doesn't *need* gay bars, perhaps. I am one of those white, middle-class cisgender men who *can* go everywhere, when I emerge from clinical depression or bother to go *anywhere*. From my rollicking urban 20s I've settled into my small-town 40s with a partner, a mortgage, and the disposable income to take weekends out of state. I love gay bars in theory, but I rarely go out. I might show my face in Cleveland's bars eight times a year, which doesn't make me a customer on which anyone could base a business model. I love a good cocktail, but I can get those in town without driving forty-five minutes to the nearest gay bar—it's especially tedious to ration the fun and the drinks for a safe drive home. I am a fair-weather gay whose friends and workplace are mostly straight and whose radical queer credentials are largely academic at this point.

When I go out in my small midwestern college town (Oberlin, Ohio), it's to The Feve (pronounced, naturally, in the French way, as "fehv"). This pub is a short walk from my house. When I stroll there from my campus office, I pass the rainbow flag flying on the town square of my small blue bubble in a sea of red.[18] It's on the edge of the campus of a college whose students are famously queer and for whom this is not just *a* bar in town but *the* bar. The Feve is owned by two brothers with wives and kids, but it's long been so gay friendly that a member of the Lorain County LGBTQ+ Task Force described it to me as "a gay bar that's straight friendly." The staff are queer and queer friendly, and the bar has long sold t-shirts that show modified bathroom icons with two women holding hands, two men side by side, and a man and a woman. When I asked co-owner Jason Adelman about them, he replied "Being gay friendly was just always important to us." Graffiti in the upstairs bathroom proclaims "Gay Bar Yay!" And on Friday nights when classes are in session, the upstairs heaves with dazzle-eyed young people, including genderqueer groups and same-sex couples. The majority of the patrons are straight or straight passing, but the bar exemplifies a kind of post-gay existence, an acceptance that exceeds the lukewarm tolerance of "live and let live."[19] And alongside the vegan-friendly menu, it serves the best brunch in Ohio, that iconically gay meal.[20]

I still *want* gay bars, though. I want to watch the finals of *RuPaul's Drag Race* surrounded by a quivering crowd. I want to see the out-of-towners in their fetish gear at CLAW, the annual Cleveland Leather Awareness Weekend (now that I've told you, you're aware). And I want to live in a world where the queer burlesque troupe takes the stage to raise money for their local Planned Parenthood clinic. Those things get lost when gay bars close, and so does the community feeling of being in the physical presence of other humans who are like you in a sea of often well-meaning straight people, a feeling that, as we learned during the COVID-19 pandemic, can't really be replaced by the virtual realm.

Sometimes I wonder if my spotty middle-aged patronage is robbing younger folks of the establishments in which I reveled in my 20s. Were those bars supported by the $20s dropped by the middle-aged gays who came out in the 90s to watch *Ellen* and the lesbian *Friends'* wedding on the bulky cathode-ray tube TVs lashed to the walls? Did their top-shelf martinis keep the lights on so I could ration my budget Miller Lites?[21] I couldn't afford to put dollars in the jukebox if I wanted to tip the bartender, so someone else must have kept the music playing.

Yet if I'm honest, bars—all bars, not just gay ones—are often a big waste of time. To quote an ex: "Nothing happens. Everyone is ugly. The music is bad." It's often hardly worth the bus ride, the taxi fare, the wait in line, the cover charge, the ironed shirt, the time spent shaving, the wasted adrenaline rush. And yet: He and I still went out every weekend of our long, glorious summer, including to the gay nightclub in which we'd met, DTM. And yet: Twenty years later, he was on Facebook bemoaning the disappearance of gay bars:

> These places were really important to me in the past, a place where I belong, a place to be normal. . . . Maybe today's youth don't miss gay bars, maybe they're no longer traumatized by their differences, maybe I'm already a man from the past.

We who enjoyed them in our youth are sad that they're going away, but I find that my students are fascinated by gay bars, even as they're too young to attend them—legally.

So why do we go out?[22] There's always the promise of those perfect moments, the outrageous and sexy and shocking memories that keep us coming back, the serendipitous "art of finding what was not being sought."[23] The new friend who offered you E. The dyke with the shaved head who sidled up to the urinal next to you, grinned, and let loose. The drag queen who won't let go of your hand. The blow job behind the ATM machine. Having a surreal conversation with a raspy-voiced man who called himself Uncle Jody. Laughing so hard you nearly peed and crying on the sidewalk like you'd never been happy. The scales of ambivalence can be tipped into desire by the promise of these possibilities. With Jeremy Atherton Lin, author of *Gay Bar*, I agree: "If my experiences in gay bars have been disappointing, what I wouldn't want to lose is the expectation of a better night."[24]

There's this mistaken belief that we mainly go out to hook up, but unless we're real sluts we usually go home with the ones who brought us. We go out mainly to be with friends, to see what's going on, to escape our room, to not be physically alone even if we're still technically lonely. In the era before home video game consoles and streaming TV services and endless smartphone scrolling, bars only had to compete with VHS rentals and cable TV for our eyeballs and pocket money. Now our phones can summon an endless stream of queer Tik-Toks, and a drag show is only a TV streaming service away. It's not just Grindr and Tinder and Lex and Scruff that've got us captivated: Our screens compete with gay bars for our attention.

I am ambivalent about whether these online pleasures can replace being co-present with other people in a physical place, even as I met a partner on an app ten years before. I'm mindful of the fact that most cities didn't have a City Nightclub for queer teens. For me, The City's physicality was a revelation even in its Friday-night conventionality. Gay people—I presumed they were gay, my gaydar had not yet been installed then—seemed happy, had friends, had access to cool music, were dancing boldly with swiveled hips and raised arms, brushing against me. And yet: I only ever talked to one person there. I don't even remember his name. But when he invited me to a suburban hot tub party that I knew I would never attend out of fear and self-loathing, his handshake kindled in me the possibility that life contained more than it had only moments before.

I grew into that moment over time, but The City's days were numbered. In 1998, while I was living in England pursuing a master's degree on *very* gay topics with my hard-won but youthful confidence, the FBI raided Lanny Swerdlow's home and his teen-saving nightclub. As his "Queer Heroes 2020" commendation states, "Swerdlow claimed the warrants were obtained with perjured testimony, but he gave up and sold the business. The FBI kept the evidence they had seized for four years and then returned it without bringing charges."[25] Portland-area teens would have to find someplace else to find each other in real life.

Today, the back alley industrial building that was The City Nightclub is a Danish furniture showroom, around the corner from an indie record store, a Whole Foods, and a Lululemon yoga apparel boutique. The neighborhood I knew as the Industrial Triangle was rebranded by real estate developers as the Pearl District. The giant brick brewery whose exhalations perfumed the area is now upscale office space and street-level retail anchoring luxury condos. In 1992 when I was on the cusp of visiting The City, Portland had twelve gay bars. By 2022, as pundits pronounced gay bars dead, the city had thirteen.[26] If this was extinction, it sure looks like a party. It seems the promise of that perfect moment keeps us going out, at least sometimes, at least when we're not tired of life or feeling introverted or content with the sofa, Netflix, and chilling with a box of wine and a bag of chips. At times like these, ambivalence about gay bars seems purely practical.

Two

Changing Bars and Aging Bodies

aut\ BAR
ANN ARBOR, MICHIGAN

Did the bars change, or did we? We only go through life in one body, and that makes it hard to figure out if we've changed or the bars have—or if the world has changed around us. Are people really worse at small talk today because they're staring at their smartphones, or did the adrenaline of youth just compensate for the awkwardness? Are there more drag queens than there used to be, or was I just not friends with them? Did I age out of going out, or was I always a boring misanthrope? Are bars going away because they're bad, or did we get out of the habit of going out while we were quarantined? Are bars less cruisy, or are ageist beauty standards rendering me invisible? Such questions have trailed after me through the bars I've been visiting for the entirety of my career—half spent in gay bars and the other in sociology. If accounting for change were easy, we wouldn't need social science and memoirists. My experiences in one gay bar twenty-one years apart dramatized, for me, that *everything* had changed.

I first visited \aut\ BAR in Ann Arbor in 1996, mere months after turning 21. My friend Chris Moody and I drove nine hours in a rental car to Michigan from Washington, DC, to see two cute boys. They were University of Michigan students on spring break who had car-avanned to the nation's capital, volunteering at the National Gay and Lesbian Task Force. I was the social coordinator of the Lesbian Gay Bisexual Alliance (which the university president mistook for the LPGA—the Ladies Professional Golf Association). Over the screening of a new documentary about Audre Lorde, I wooed a handsome poli sci student. Two months later, after the long drive, Chris and I found ourselves with our beaus in \aut\ BAR, then only one year old. Despite the sweet liberation of making out in public, it couldn't drown out bitter memories of the co-op's vegan oatmeal bricks we had for dinner and the humiliation of being dumped that same weekend, reportedly for being bad at sex.

When I returned to Ann Arbor in 2017 to interview \aut\ BAR's owners, I was delighted to find that the bar had changed hardly at all. Its walls were still painted the primary colors of Keith Haring's art. They were still lined with framed black-and-white Herb Ritts photos of lesbian icon k. d. lang, anonymous muscled bodies, and interracial couples locked in embrace. The bathroom still featured vintage saf-er-sex campaigns of groups of multiethnic men smiling arm in arm, their t-shirt sleeves cuffed charmingly. The foyer of this one-time sin-gle-family house still stocked stacks of gay and lesbian newspapers, free condoms, and flyers for health services, community meetings, support groups, and arts events. The time capsule was completed by the adjacent Common Language Bookstore, run basically as a charity by the bar owners, then one of the last ten surviving LGBTQ+ book-stores in the United States and Canada.[1]

The bar hadn't changed, but I had, and so had the world. Back in 1996—freshly 21 years old—I was a slender twink who appreciated the upstairs bar for late-night drinking and loud music. By my 40s, how-ever, I was a fat, bearded bear who appreciated the dog-friendly patio for a drink in the daylight, the full-service menu to dodge home cook-ing and dirty dishes, and the casual joy of being gay in the daylight and in bed by ten. Back then, gay bars held the promise of making out in public; now it was for meeting friends after popping into the deli around the corner and browsing the nonfiction books for sale in the house next door. In 1996 it was a doomed long-distance affair. By 2017, Chris and his Michigan beau Ryan LaLonde were celebrating twenty-one years together, now with a teenager of their own and little time for gay bar frivolities.

It's impossible to be ambivalent about the dramatic changes in LGBTQ+ life over those twenty-one years. In 1996, LGBTQ+ people were still banned from the U.S. military by the three-year-old Don't Ask, Don't Tell policy. By 2017, the ban's repeal was five years old. In 1996, AIDS still seemed like a death sentence, and the newly introduced highly active antiretroviral therapy (HAART) wasn't readily available. In 2017, the same drugs were advertised to HIV-negative people to prevent infection altogether as part of pre-exposure prophylaxis (PrEP). In 1996, queer sex was still illegal in twenty-three states, and a commitment ceremony meant a rented hall amongst friends; by 2017, the Supreme Court had overturned sodomy bans and legalized same-sex marriage in every town hall in the land. In 1996, I traveled with my physical copy of the *Damron Guide*, a one-pound brick of a national guide to LGBTQ+ travel; by 2017, Yelp and other smartphone apps had taken its place, and 35 percent of gay bars had closed with more on the verge.[2]

When I talked to co-owners and life partners Keith Orr and Martin Contreras, they reflected on the changes since opening \aut\ BAR in 1995. The bar and its sister enterprises were in single-family houses that opened onto a courtyard festooned with fairy lights that served as a queer town square with an adjoining parking lot that was the site of innumerable Ann Arbor Pride celebrations. The courtyard was framed by the two-story gay bar, the bookstore, a performance space, and the Jim Toy LGBT Community Center, named after Michigan's titan of queer liberation.[3] Keith, a white man who was once a professional musician, proudly recounted how author and *Sister Spit* co-founder Michelle Tea had dubbed their cluster of buildings the "homoplex." The \aut\ BAR's space had been first a Mexican restaurant that Martin started with his mom Lupe, but as he told me, "It was an easy transition from a gay-owned restaurant that identifies as gay-owned to a gay bar and café."

The couple described the AIDS crisis as their prompt to get into the gay bar business. The previous gay bar in town was "dark and dingy," and the straight owner reportedly barred a collection for the local AIDS charity with the dismissal, "AIDS is depressing." As co-owner Keith Orr recalled,

Having seen so many friends and lovers succumb to the disease, it became depressing that it was our community space. So that became one of the motivations for us to open a place. To us, it wasn't just about being a bar, it was about being part of the community.

The bar was a business, yes, but it was never just about business.

They never wanted a bar just for gay men, or even just for LGBTQ+ people. "We envisioned our community as a place to bring co-workers, family, friends, allies, straight friends. That was unheard of at the time," Keith explained. Of their famous brunches, they advertised: "'Discover what gay Ann Arbor already knows.' We put that in the straight press. We make it clear we're not a *gay*-friendly place, we're a *straight*-friendly place." And of their welcome to the entire LGBTQ+ community,

> It was part of what we envisioned as sort of a modern-day gay bar, not just a men's bar, or a lesbian bar, or a suit bar, or a leather bar. Big cities have those, they have a huge community and can subdivide like that. We're just a little town and this is the gathering place.

Straight people have thus long been welcomed in small-city gay bars, although perhaps more by owners than patrons. I'm reminded of the time I was visiting The Zone in Erie, Pennsylvania, when a straight woman at the bar welcomed my gay male friend Kazim by telling him he was a beautiful transgender woman. Then she earnestly extended her hand, "I'm your Goodwill Ambassador!" Slow your roll, girl, we thought to ourselves: This particular bar may be new to us, but it's still *our* home turf.

Keith and Martin's ambivalence about a liquor-serving bar being the sole site of the community spurred the creation of the other enterprises. The community center, Keith described, "more or less stands on its own," though he conceded, "our rent to them is below market rate," and "we do a lot of fundraisers for them." Of the bookstore, Martin said, "We try to build the synergy between both businesses," but Keith expressed disappointment that "our most avid buyers are out-of-towners. They come into town and discover, 'Oh my god, there's a gay bookstore here!' And for good reason: There's only like twelve left!" While many bar patrons don't realize there's a bookstore next door, Keith said wryly, "Everyone who goes to the bookstore knows there's a gay bar next door." They envisioned the bookstore's stock of personal lubricant as a source of synergy. Keith described a campaign they'd tried in the past: "Take your receipt from here and get 10 percent off next door, even to buy lube." Laughing, he continued,

> We do a "lube for literacy" campaign as well. Just in this town, with the number of gay men and women who need lube, if they all bought it at the bookstore, we would have a healthy and thriving bookstore, we could keep the literature going!

As Keith said of bargoers generally, "Over the years, it's adapted that people seem to want to be entertained all the time. It's not just enough to sit down with friends and have a conversation or play pool and listen to music." This prompted some changes that would have seemed outré when they opened:

> We got a TV—we acquiesced. Never needed that before, but now we can turn Oscar night into an event. Started doing a DJ upstairs on Saturdays. Would never have done that ten years ago. We've done live music on the patio for the last two summers, jazz on Tuesdays, women's music on Wednesday.

Noting their recent foray into offering what they called "alt-drag," Keith explained, "One of the challenges of being a small business owner is you have to respond to the needs of your clientele. Young drag performers who say, 'We need a space where we're welcomed.'" The duo had to talk it over: "We've never done drag, there's other venues that do drag. Do we really need to do that as well? Should we? And how can we?" Keith and Martin laughed, noting that the queens dressed in the bookstore at night before tromping through the snowy Michigan courtyard and up the outdoor steps to reach the upstairs dance floor. Serving the community, Keith explained, meant adapting to the fact that now, "People need constant stimulus. When we first opened, it was enough to be a neighborhood bar. . . . Now that's not enough."

These pivots brought in a younger crowd and kept them engaged. As Keith laughed, "We're not as good as the 20-somethings at social media, but we could do no advertising for a drag show and we could fill the bar. In that respect it's been a win-win situation." This pivot to connect with young bargoers implicated another change, one Keith volunteered: "We didn't even touch base on the whole generation that can't separate themselves from their phone." He laughed, recalling bartender and trivia host Terry McClymonds's assertion: "As long as you can't get a drink on the internet, my job here is safe!" Keith noted that along with the drink or the food, "You have to provide an experience. That's the only way to get people to go out."

Smartphone cruising apps, Keith averred, had not dented their local business, describing them as "one of the things that's actually helped us out—because I know a lot of gay bars closing because you don't have to go to a bar to hook up—but there's also more and more people who want to meet the person before they commit to . . ." he raised his eyebrows knowingly. As he continued, "because we're looked at as a safe space, you see people who are clearly meeting up here for the first time in person."

Their mission for the homoplex always went beyond service industry imperatives. As Keith said, "While we certainly want to serve good food and drink, the mission statement is about a safe space." He noted that this was self-evident when they started, but that the LGBTQ+ community had questioned it in the Obama era. As he continued, noting the turn during the Trump era:

> People would look at me, "Oh, isn't that quaint" in the last couple of years, what with gays in the military and marriage equality. It's like, "safe space?" But after November 2016 there was a resurgence: "Oh, we do need safe spaces, don't we?"

This presaged another resurgence of interest in safe spaces in 2022 when the Supreme Court smashed through the constitutional right to privacy.

Keith ended our 2017 interview on a pessimistic note, commenting that the couple had not had a vacation in over five years. Martin stated, "I don't wanna die on my feet in the kitchen after thirty-one years," noting that fetching items from storage in the basement was hard on aging legs. "I don't think we're going to have success finding somebody who wants to take over the \aut\ BAR. Whether we sell the building, business, or property, we *have* to be able to retire," groaned Keith. The safe space must survive, but we must have rest. Talk about ambivalence.

In 2020 a miracle occurred: A local nightlife conglomerate stepped in to buy \aut\ BAR, one of the ways that gay bars can be saved these days. The couple had already shuttered the bookstore in 2018 in preparation for the sale of the buildings, recognizing that a new owner would not run a charity literature shop.

But then came COVID-19.

The new owners pulled out, announcing \aut\'s closure. They did return the bar's signage, intellectual property, and social media accounts to Keith and Martin, who hoped someone else would step forward and continue their legacy.[4] Terry continued his trivia Thursdays on Zoom for a while during 2020's pandemic summer, but events dwindled to nothing in the fall. The Jim Toy Community Center moved out of the homoplex, its building sold from under it, and it was still without a permanent home when Jim Toy himself died in 2022.

To date, the bar exists in limbo: a brand without a building, owned but without any operators, no willing bodies to bring the ice up out of the basement and the bar out of exile. A longtime restaurant in neighboring Ypsilanti announced plans in 2022 to open a franchise of the nation's only LGBTQ+ restaurant and bar group, Hamburger Mary's. But in Ann Arbor, \aut\'s longtime patrons continue to age, while every fall, new fresh-faced students at the University of Michigan continue to arrive to a town that once, until only recently, had a gay bar of its own.

Three

Outpost Bars Put Assumptions under Scrutiny

Garlow's
GUN BARREL CITY, TEXAS

Who are the "we" who don't need gay bars anymore? Embedded in the stories we tell about gay bar closures are some stark assumptions that don't hold up to scrutiny. Online and face-to-face aren't zero-sum opposites—we use Facebook and Twitter to plan lunches and political protests, after all. The gentrification blamed for the rising rents of big-city clubs is only a dream for struggling manufacturing towns or the depopulating farm regions of the American interior. The idea that all bars are gay bars now is suspect given the uneven geography of LGBTQ+ acceptance, whether in Idaho or Indiana or Arkansas, or the less gay-friendly neighborhoods of our gay-friendliest metropolises: You can't tell me that every bar in Staten Island is a gay bar. LGBTQ+ acceptance may be as much of a business opportunity as a threat, as onetime gay-only spaces can attract straight people to their drag shows and cabaret performances. The Great Recession and Grindr may have killed gay bars in 2009, but many have opened since then and thrived. And gay bars may be for-profit enterprises, but they are also nonprofit fundraising powerhouses that often operate, ambivalently, like community centers. Consider the only gay bar in one of the reddest counties in the country, which challenged many of my preconceptions about the possibilities for gay bars in the United States today: Garlow's in Gun Barrel City, Texas.

Red Garlow did not live to see the gay bar that now bears his name. There was already one gay bar in Gun Barrel City, but "It smelt bad and it was seedy. He just didn't like it, so the plan was to be the opposite of what that bar was," Michael Slingerland, his partner, explained. Michael, a white man with graying temples, sat and slowly smoked a cigarette in his no-smoking bar while a baseball game aired on a TV in the corner. Michael explained that "Garlow," as he was known, fell ill with cancer before his "grandiose ideas" could be realized. Michael cared for Red for two-and-a-half years until he passed, "and then I opened up the bar he wanted to open" in 2010. A gay bar can be a living memorial.

The bar was easy to spot when researcher Tory, fluffy-dog Blanche, and I rolled into town from Longview, Texas. From the outside, the bar looks like the plumbing warehouse it used to be, marked by a sign sporting the bar's logo with its signature rainbow swirl and the tagline "Where Friends Become Family." Leaving the little pup under a large tree with a bowl of water and a bone, we entered. Murals depicted silhouettes of classic Hollywood: Top-hatted dancers were framed by unspooled film reels, the effect interrupted by small wooden signs. One read "Drink Til He's Cute," another "Pony Express: Young, Wiry Boys Wanted," and "Not Everyone Can Be the Queen: Someone Needs to Stand and Applaud When I Enter the Room." Above the door to the patio one was simply "Red."

Today, Garlow's is the only gay bar in Gun Barrel City, Texas, a growing town of 6,190 people a little over an hour southeast of Dallas—so named because its main drag is as straight as a gun's barrel. It may sound like an Old West frontier town, but it was incorporated in 1969—the same year as the Stonewall riots in faraway New York City. On the banks of the recently built Cedar Creek Reservoir sprang up a little town attuned to lakeside recreation. Garlow's is the only gay bar in Henderson County (population: 75,532), a deep-red county in a red state: 79 percent of voters chose Donald Trump in 2020.

Michael assesses Gun Barrel City with a businessman's gimlet eye. The town has nine bars, and of the residents, "Half drink and half don't, so you're fighting for everybody's entertainment dollar and to struggle to get enough people to get in here to pay your damn bills." He answered with folksy wordplay in response to my question about why own a gay bar in the age of Grindr and gay marriage: "You have to have a conjugating place, and this here is the conjugating place for all the locals."

Not only is Garlow's the only gay bar in Henderson County, it's also the only one in any of the eight counties that border it. Gun Barrel City may be only an hour's drive from the big-city gayborhood of Oak Lawn in Dallas, but for most folks in these other counties, Garlow's is the closest gay bar by more than an hour's drive. I call these bars "outposts," part of an archipelago of queerness, a constellation of LGBTQ+ sites connected to one another by sentiment, a sense of shared fate, and the peregrinations of drag queens.[1] Garlow's, by being in the local lake and leisure town, is intimately connected to the Dallas gayborhood of Oak Lawn, just as Provincetown is connected to Boston or Fire Island to New York City. Michael explained to me, "On the weekends we have a good Dallas crowd. A lot of Dallas people, they have houses out on the lake, so they come in on Saturday and Sunday after they've been on the lake. Our Friday and Saturday night crowd is 70 percent Dallas and 30 percent local."

Garlow's is part of the local LGBTQ+ community but isn't the entirety of it. Michael estimates that the town is one-third gay. "The [straight] shopkeepers, they don't mind it because we pay well so they shut up!" Michael admits that the weekend crowd doesn't have so many lesbians, but this isn't true during weekdays: "We get a lot of lesbians, the locals. The Dallas lesbians, they don't own houses out here like the men do." Lesbians, weighed down by sexist and homophobic pay gaps, don't earn enough to frolic as much as gay men do—or to buy second homes.[2]

Like all outpost bars, straight people are a significant portion of patrons: Concerns that straight people are invading gay bars are a thing of the big cities.[3] In small cities, straight people are drawn to gay bars in part by the safety they offer. As Michael explains,

First it was the little girls who wanted to get away from their boys in the big pickups, and they weren't going to be seen in a queer bar! But then they realized if they wanted to see their girls they'd best get over it! So now all the young kids come in and nobody gives a shit anymore.

He explains why: "We're the only bar with a doorman, so you can feel all right by yourself and see what's going on in a gay bar."

Originally, this security was put in place to comply with regulations allowing 18-year-olds to be in Garlow's. This hassle and expense mean that most bars don't bother, but having an 18-and-up door policy was important to Michael, both from a moral sense and a business sense: "That's your next customer base." He continued:

We nurtured the young crowd coming here because they won't get chastised or be made fun of or be put down or bullied, so when they become of age they came here. Why would you go to [another bar in town], which is a redneck bar? This is the only bar they *should* go to!

When I asked whether the underage patrons spend enough to make it worth the bar's while, Michael replies with the long-term perspective of a successful businessman: "The old crowd may have money, the young crowd not so much, but they will *eventually* have money, they will be the old crowd someday. That's just business." The fact that the bar is now one of the most popular for straight kids in town? He told me, sweeping his arm across the interior:

You have to adapt: You're in a small town. On a steady night you can see two guys kissing, two gals kissing, and a guy and a gal. It's an everybody, no-drama bar. We haven't had a fight in years. We don't have any troubles from anybody.

In addition to the drag shows, the bar has a series of weekly events, including live music. As Keith of Ann Arbor's \aut\ BAR discovered of today's gay bar patrons. they need to be entertained. The Thursday that Tory and I visited was going to be poker night—Texas Hold 'Em, naturally—"and there won't be a gay person here," laughed Michael. "And the queers will come in later and the queers will be over here," he gestured across the bar, "and the straights will be over there," he waved to the pool tables. Of hosting events that feature and attract straight people, Michael claims: "If we didn't do that, we wouldn't have survived. When we opened up in 2010 it's like there was no water in the lake, we were on the Obama economy. It's a very food-stamp-oriented town." The regional economy may have improved with the national one—despite that president's best efforts—but that doesn't mean Michael didn't put his shoulder to the wheel.

Michael is well known in town, and this was part of his marketing strategy for Garlow's:

> I'm on the city council, I'm on the economic development council, I'm on the zoning council. I know everyone in this town. I thought, if I got involved in politics, everyone would know who the hell we were. And they do.

Becoming a civic fixture bemuses him, because it stands in stark contrast to his childhood and young adulthood: "I'm more popular than in my entire life!" Growing up, he describes himself as getting bullied until he went to college to "get out of that damn town. Now that I opened up this bar, Christ! Everybody knows me but I don't know anybody! I've got 6,000 friends on Facebook, but I couldn't tell you much about any one of them." While Michael clearly enjoys this turn of events, it's also good for business: "You have to keep the name out there, the name Garlow's has got to be out there all the time. I go to many city council events, and so when I'm getting my picture took, I always say, 'Local faggot makes good!'"[4]

Inspired by another city councilor who invited the council to meet in their place of business, Michael conducts official business at Garlow's as well:

> When I'm on committee meetings I won't have them at city hall. I make them come in here! And everybody likes to smoke and drink and so we do the committee work here, so the city of Gun Barrel is sitting in the gay bar.

With evident pride, Michael reports that "the mayor's been in lots of times."

Like every small-city gay bar I've visited, drag shows are a big draw. On the day we visited, manager Glen Robison was in a rush to drive to Dallas to pick up Onyx, a performer for that Saturday's show. "All of them have drama dripping the fuck off them," Michael said good-naturedly as Glen hurried away. Hosting out-of-town drag queens brings in patrons, but also incurs expenses for the bar that boost the local economy. "Anytime we bring in outside talent we put them in a hotel room, we get a deal with the La Quinta so we give them rooms. Not their own room mind you, we stack them in there like cord wood." Small-city gay bars have surprisingly vast visiting rosters, and some have ties to real drag royalty, but few of them are as close to a major drag talent center as small-town "GBC" is to Dallas, home to the Davenport dynasty familiar to fans of *RuPaul's Drag Race*.

Garlow's is also a significant source of charity in town, Michael boasted:

> This bar gave $57,000 to charity last year—that's more than most families make around here. Anyone who knows us knows we're the number one charity bar in the county. Toys for Tots, ASPCA [American Society for the Prevention of Cruelty to Animals], the [Social Services] Resource Center . . . we do shows so they can give money to help people with their rent or for their electric, they help take care of people.

As Michael reported about a recent benefit for the volunteer fire department to buy hoses, I interrupted him: "Are you telling me your volunteer fire department has gay hoses?" He laughed, "I don't know about that, but they sure as hell bought them with my damn gay beer!"

Michael continued, describing how the bar facilitates the charity of others more than giving of its own resources. Describing a $12,000 haul for Toys for Tots that allowed them to buy 37 bicycles in a town of under 6,000 people, he describes how the bar donates the stage and the drag queens donate their tips—another way that drag queens are true influencers in the analog realm as well as the social one:

> We didn't give away a fucking nickel. The people of this town came in here and started tipping the queens so everybody in this town did—they didn't consciously know that they gave away $57,000. That brings the whole town together, to help a charity.

If Garlow's is a "conjugating place for all the locals," this is in no small part because Michael has local concerns and has embedded his bar in them: "That's how we became a household name, because we became the number one charity in the world. When you do that in a small community, you get to be very well known, very quick."

Small-town life suits Michael, and he wouldn't have opened a gay bar anyplace else. "Being a rural bar has its advantages. If you want to be going to a gay bar, well, we're the pick of the litter!" He knows many of the bar owners in the Metroplex and does not envy them:

> I would hate to have to compete in Dallas with all the major bars for their entertainment dollars. There's a lot of people in Dallas but I would hate to be a chickenshit little bar, getting only the scraps from when the others are full.

Michael grew up in small-town life and measures the quality of his current living against his childhood in a town of 1,500 with 28 people in his graduating class:

> If you were gay everybody knew it, and it was terrible. I didn't go to a gay bar until I was 21 because I was scared to death someone would see me, but it doesn't dawn on you then that the stark raving terror of being found out is the most terrible part. I had a friend of mine that hung himself because he was gay. He couldn't quite get over it.

Or, I thought, he couldn't get over the fucked-up homophobia of that time and place. Michael attributes the positive changes in the world since then to the youths who congregate in his bar on week-end nights: "Nowadays it's a lot better because the *kids* have made it a lot better. We made it better together, maybe. Being gay now is not a stigma, and people are lot more forgiving and easier on gays I guess, so it's a lot better than it was."

Looking around the bar, he summarizes his later-in-life turn of events. Echoing other owners, he was emphatic: "There's no money in gay bars. You have to really like this or really like queers. It's a tough job. I wouldn't wish this fucker on anybody." But he clearly loves the place. "It's got the good, laid-back vibe when you walk in. That was Garlow. I know that Garlow is in here, and I know that he's in heaven, and I knew when I opened this that I wouldn't fail because he's watching."

So even Michael Slingerland is a little bit ambivalent about gay bars. But even if Garlow's were the only bar of its kind in the United States, Michael's story complicates conventional wisdom about the decline of gay bars. He opened a successful one, in a place that seems unlikely to those steeped in the big-city provincialism that scholars have critiqued as "metronormativity": The assumption that queer equals metropolitan erases the suburbs and the rural.[5] Michael opened a successful gay bar just as news stories announced that gay bars were failing during the "Obama economy" of the Great Recession. Garlow's is in a rural hamlet but is intimately tied to a cosmopolitan gay neighborhood, albeit one in Dallas, Texas, and not some more famous coastal city. Garlow's is a bar that has welcomed straight patrons from the beginning without experiencing them as invaders, and it embraces the young patrons blamed for "ruining" other markets. It is deeply rooted in its red-state community but fosters openly LGBTQ+ identities.[6]

But Garlow's is *not* alone. In 2019 there were ninety-three gay bars in the United States that were alone in their city, lone outposts of LGBTQ+ culture that were far from coastal gay neighborhoods but intimately tied to them through our shared culture. Taken together, there were more of these outpost bars than there were gay bars in the cities of San Francisco, Chicago, and Los Angeles *combined*.[7]

If we only imagine gay bars in gay neighborhoods, we miss out on their most common form. The "we" who don't need gay bars don't all live near a gayborhood, and we may not like it even if we did. Gentrification may be squeezing gay bars on the coasts, but not in the American interior. Gay bars aren't just the creatures of blue-state cities, nor do queer people in red counties cower in them in fear. Straight people in gay bars may be new in big cities. But they've long been a welcome norm in the parts of the country where most LGBTQ+ people live. And focusing just on the interiors of bars ignores the ways that they can be as connected to local institutions as they are to their sidewalks, the way that bars spill out onto the streets and their local economies shows how queerness cannot be contained so easily.[8] Our representations of gay bars don't match their reality, not until our imagination expands to contain our queer multitudes.

Four

Gay Bar History

Garden of Allah
SEATTLE, WASHINGTON

For good or ill, contemporary LGBTQ+ politics come from gay bars, although ambivalence about this fact runs deep.[1] The "classic" gay bar as we expect it to be today—a 24/7 place exclusively by and for LGBTQ+ people—is a surprisingly recent invention, dating to the middle of the twentieth century.[2] But from the moment that gay bars emerged, we queer people have been looking for alternatives to escape them—first because they were disreputable, later because they weren't radical, and now because they're not digital. When I read the history of Seattle's long-shuttered Garden of Allah, one of the nation's first gay-owned gay bars, I was surprised at how fresh it seemed, and how different it was from the classic gay bar that many people expect.[3] The Garden of Allah taught me that contemporary gay bars, lashed by change though they may be, have more in common with a bar that closed in 1956 than with the classic gay bar than I could ever have guessed.

Why bars at all? Other communities are grounded by places of worship, restaurants and food stores, barber shops and hair salons, bookstores and colleges, and the natal family itself. For LGBTQ+ people, it was only away from the domestic sphere and the workplace that a LGBTQ+ public sphere could form.[4] As Lucas Hilderbrand has written, "We came out by going out."[5]

Before World War II, there had been hangouts where LGBTQ+ people gathered, of course, and not always surreptitiously. These were in spaces shared with straight people. Some of them were non-commercial: YMCAs and YWCAs, boarding houses, and certain parts of beaches, parks, boulevards, and bathhouses. Many others were commercial, like restaurants and bars: queer public life flourished in privately owned businesses.[6] These early queer businesses came in two flavors: scandalous ones in which patrons were openly sexual or defied gender norms, and virtuous others in which covert homosexuals socialized under the cover of respectability. Low-rent automats and red-light district dance halls might accept "bulldaggers" openly courting other women or the campy antics of "nelly" "nances"; such displays were not permitted at "classy" hotel bars or restaurants that might develop an underground reputation for covert, gender-normative LGBTQ+ people. As one gay man told a historian of the 1990s about Seattle's gay life back in the 1940s, "I have a friend who was a teacher, who was a snob, still is, and he would only go to hotel bars, never would go to the other bars."[7] Of course avoiding gay bars was not always about snobbery: Bars were frequently raided by police, and patrons' names were published in local newspapers. If you had a reputation, you could lose it utterly.[8]

In Seattle, the disreputable places that permitted gender deviance were concentrated around Pioneer Square, the city's raucous "original neighborhood," a mile and a half from today's Capitol Hill gayborhood.[9] By 1930, one habitué described it as "twenty blocks of honky-tonk taverns, restaurants, all-night theaters, pawn shops, army surplus stores, cheap hotels, and peep shows."[10] Respectable LGBTQ+ people shunned these risqué neighborhoods, but they proved a beacon to those who dared to risk their reputations.

It was in these commercial establishments that a queer, all-gender community took shape alongside straight patrons. Some straight people came because they, too, felt like outcasts: artists, sex workers, and those in interracial relationships. Others, the slummers, came to gawk.[11] Some of these places facilitated only gawking—stage shows where homosexuality was put on parade for straight society.[12] These and other nightclubs may have fostered the beginnings of an LGBTQ+ culture, but they were still owned by, and largely depended on the patronage of, straight people.

Things began to change with the end of Prohibition in 1933. In cities like Seattle, some aboveboard taverns joined the underground clubs in permitting gender deviance, but audiences were still all-gender and mixed with straight people. In New York City, however, the increased policing of alcohol had the perverse effect of encouraging gay-only spaces. With their alcohol licenses on the line to prevent indecency, respectable bars and restaurants increasingly shunned anyone who seemed homosexual or gender deviant. The businesses that sprang up to serve queers, especially those who weren't white, were often backed by crime syndicates or protected by paying off corrupt policemen or liquor inspectors.[13] Even so, such clubs were invariably short-lived due to police harassment, but these transient few were majority-LGBTQ+ spaces.[14]

World War II brought millions of LGBTQ+ people out of the American interior and put them in close contact with each other, both in tight quarters overseas and on the domestic military training bases that were built around the country. Having now found each other, groups of gay people could be bold. A group of gay servicemen in Denver adopted Mary's Tavern and kept returning after being thrown out or arrested, eventually driving the straight patrons away.[15] Military police began keeping track of establishments near bases where homosexuals gathered, inadvertently publicizing them by telling soldiers and sailors to stay away. Perhaps it was experiences with such establishments that servicemembers took with them after the war when they demobilized to cities across the land, leading to the spread of a previously uncommon kind of business: gay bars just for gay people (even lesbians largely referred to their establishments as gay bars during this time).[16]

Seattle's Garden of Allah opened in 1946, one of the first gay-owned gay bars in the country. It was named after a film from 1936 that starred queer icon Marlene Dietrich, based on a novel steeped in offensive stereotypes about the permissive sexual mores of the Orient.[17] It was a theater with cabaret seating and a stage that doubled as a dance floor between shows, the dancing propelled by a mighty

Wurlitzer pipe organ. It featured burlesque and female imperson-ation—"drag" was not yet the term of art, and indeed was derogatory, referring to unskilled impersonators who lip-synched. These were professional artists, *darling,* who sang live and were represented by a union! The bar was modeled off a club in San Francisco, Finocchio's, to which it was linked by the to-and-fro migrations of performers who worked at these and other clubs all around the country.[18] These es-tablishments catered to mixed crowds of straight and LGBTQ+ people drawn to a twilight world of risqué humor and illicit experiences. "Straights and gays," argued community historian Don Paulson, "could mix and even learn about each other with no strings attached." But among the queer folk who attended the club, strings *were* knitting them together, uniting them into the kinship that bound strangers into a community.[19]

For the ten years that the club operated, until 1956, it was beloved by Ls, Gs, Bs, Ts, and Qs. Gay men were the majority of the non-straight patrons, but they mingled happily with lesbians. "There was not the animosity then between the men and the women," recalled one lesbian, a sentiment echoed by her gay male contemporaries.[20] "Butches" who said they wished they could be men and "queens" who lived their lives as women mingled with people who moved among the genders throughout their lives, prompting headline performer and emcee Billy DeVoe to routinely greet the gender-diverse crowds with, "Good evening, Ladies and Gentlemen and the rest of you."[21]

Such a world was not welcomed by LGBTQ+ people who treasured their reputations; they preferred to socialize in private, including one gay man who recalled of the Garden, "I was totally disgusted. It was all cock and sex jokes—looking up and reaching up each other's dresses—just dirty." And middle-class lesbians—especially lesbians of color and those in committed couples—often preferred house parties.[22]

Though the Garden of Allah thus bore many continuities with the queer-straight clubs of the prewar period, it was part of a new national trend of gay bars owned by gay people, ones that were in-creasingly just for gay people. Café Lafitte in Exile of New Orleans, sometimes claimed as the oldest gay bar in the country, became the region's "first predominantly gay bar" only in 1953.[23] Oklahoma City got the Mayflower Lounge in 1958, a year before the state repealed its late-ending liquor prohibition.[24] Greater Memphis had to wait until 1962, for Frank's Show Bar Lounge, to have an exclusively gay bar.[25] In 1966, the Mafia bought a dumpy bar known as The Stonewall Inn in New York City and turned it into a popular gay bar by having a jukebox and dance floor at a time when same-sex dancing was grounds for losing your liquor license.[26]

Cisgender gay people welcomed these new gay-only bars for the "aura of respectability" they offered in comparison to cruising in public or mixed-gender cabarets like the Garden of Allah. Bars were dangerous and discreet, suspicious of strangers, and ever wary that undercover cops had infiltrated their twilight world, and yet they offered a lifeline to a world beyond isolation.[27] As one gay man wrote of classic gay bars in 1951, "One need not hide one's head as an acquaintance walks by; one does not deny encounters, but on the contrary makes appointments, utilizes the meeting-place for social convenience."[28] This community effect could be temporary for others, however; one lesbian argued, "The beneficial effects wear off quickly, leaving the hard facts of the Lesbian's isolation unchanged."[29]

These postwar gay bars offered a sense of community that previous institutions hadn't, in part because of the safety garnered from the assumption that everyone else inside was gay as well. "Public cruising can be dangerous," a gay man told a Denver reporter in 1965. "This is why you see so many fellows patronizing the gay bars. They're safe there. They're among their own kind."[30] Being among one's own kind engendered the kinship that helped create a common feeling, of similarity, among erstwhile strangers.

After World War II, the bars themselves were the social networks that helped create a broadly accessible gay and lesbian culture with its own lingo, norms, and sense of collective struggle. As prominent LGBTQ+ historian John D'Emilio wrote, "Of all the changes set in motion by the war, the spread of the gay bar contained the greatest potential for reshaping the consciousness of homosexuals and lesbians. Alone among the expressions of gay life, the bar fostered an identity that was both public and collective."[31] In other words, it was in these new gay-only bars that the isolating closet fell away, replaced by a sense of shared fate under the dim lights.

Shared fate, that is, for gender-normative LGBTQ+ people. Increasingly, gay bars attracted "conventional" folks who happened to be gay, wanted to be with others like themselves, and disdained the gender deviance of butches and queens.[32] It also brought LGBTQ+ people of different classes into close contact with each other, although many places were still fiercely racially segregated. And increasingly, gay bars were gender segregated, attracting only men or only women, perhaps due to rising feminist sentiment and more economic opportunities for lesbians. Of this gender, class, and racial homogenization, you could say that it was this postwar, "classic" gay bar culture that, for good or ill, put the "same" into "same sex," the "homo" into "homosexual."

As classic bars spread to new cities, this insider LGBTQ+ culture spread, transmitting information and ideas. If gay bars "were seedbeds for a collective consciousness that might one day flower politically," as D'Emilio described them, they were seeds watered by the pressure of the closet, police raids, and public condemnation.[33] In the conservate climate of the 1950s, police stepped up actions against homosexuality, and the government went on witch hunts for homosexuals in the ranks of the civil service, targeting them in part through their patronage of LGBTQ+ spaces.[34] This policing was ambivalent. Gay bars were sites of stings and raids, but they were also sometimes tolerated by city officials as a way to corral LGBTQ+ people into one place.[35] Gay bars serving gender-normative gays still spread, though, and increasingly diversified to serve subgroups of the LGBTQ+ community.[36] By 1979, sociologist Martin Levine was surprised at how open they had become: "Gay bars are not what they used to be—clandestine hideaways where a few of the more brazen gay people sought one another out in secret."[37]

It was a 1969 police raid on a gay bar that is mythologized as sparking the LGBTQ+ rights movement, of course, changing American history in the process.[38] The story is well known: LGBTQ+ people fought back when police raided a Mafia-owned bar in New York City's Greenwich Village. The one-year anniversary of that Stonewall Inn uprising was marked by marches in three cities around the country—the first Pride parades—that soon spread around the world.[39]

It has become conventional to date LGBTQ+ history into "before" and "after" Stonewall. It is similarly conventional to treat New York

City as the lone wellspring of LGBTQ+ history, but like most cities in the country, Seattle also had pre-Stonewall activism.[40] In 1958, Madison Pub owner MacIver "Mac" Wells won a court injunction against police harassment of gay bars. Less than a decade later, he collaborated with the FBI to bring down the police protection racket, sinking the police commissioner's career along with it. Ironically, perhaps, it was this protection racket that had allowed gay bars to flourish during this period of Seattle's history, with police quoting fixed prices for overlooking illegal activities like drag shows and same-sex dancing. This act of early gay heroism goes unremarked on Madison Pub's website: A bar by that name still exists in Seattle!

The Dorian Society, Seattle's first gay civil rights organization, incorporated in 1967, receiving a high-profile cover story in the city magazine that same year.[41] Before Stonewall, it helped establish the Seattle Counseling Services for Sexual Minorities, the nation's first LGBTQ+ counseling center.[42] The Dorian Society, like many new organizations in the 1950s and 60s, was formed as an alternative to the bars, emphasizing respectability as "a direct effort to push against the bar culture."[43] And Seattle wasn't particularly special: Many cities of all sizes have proud traditions of pre-Stonewall activism, with national organizations like Mattachine forming chapters around the country. The Daughters of Bilitis and ONE, Inc. used technology no more sophisticated than the typewriter and the postal service to spread information about homosexuality to anyone with a mailbox, or who had a friend who could discreetly pass along copies by hand.[44]

The flowering of gay liberation after Stonewall included both conservative assimilationist groups like the Dorian Society, but also radical organizations influenced by feminist, antiwar, and Black revolutionaries. These radicals rejected bars with the slogan "out of the bars and into the streets!" Some objected to bars as parasites on community, such as lesbian activist Felice Newman who described the gay community as "weakened by alcoholism and exploited economically" by gay bars and their owners.[45] In Philadelphia, the Gay Activists Alliance picketed gay bars that used dress codes and carding policies to discriminate against women and African Americans.[46] Meanwhile, more assimilationist groups increasingly used bars for politicking and as places to recruit petition signers and voters.

For good or ill, and to the radicals' chagrin, gay bar politics became mainstream lesbian and gay politics—moderate, incremental, working for respectability in alliance with the establishment and not devoted to smashing the patriarchy or overthrowing capitalism. Tavern Guilds were some of the first gay organizations: alliances of gay bar owners to protect their patrons from police and show community leaders that they were not just making money off of LGBTQ+ people.[47] But bar owners also policed their patrons, stopping things from getting too out of hand, enforcing rules about gender presentation, and maintaining racial segregation so as to not fall afoul of local officials.[48] Most of the early gay civil rights cases were brought by gay bars arguing for freedom of assembly against morals clauses that defined the presence of homosexuals as immoral. California was the first, in 1951; Virginia was the last, in 1991.[49] Property rights were the first gay rights: freedom to buy and sell, not freedom to *be*.[50]

And yet, the bars became "a kind of politicized community center," if politicization meant making public claims on behalf of gay equality or living an openly LGBTQ+ life among family and co-workers.[51] Everyday life is a form of politics, although one that may not have been recognized by political radicals. It was from the bars that the first openly gay electoral candidate launched his campaign—José Sarria of San Francisco, the Latinx female impersonator known as the Nightingale of Montgomery Street. Harvey Milk, one of the country's first openly LGBTQ+ elected officials, campaigned in the bars (mistaken claims that Milk was the first erase the election of out lesbian Kathy Kozachenko in Michigan). Gay bars are thus institutions that represent the origins of a national LGBTQ+ political consciousness, one that was largely assimilationist, not necessarily radical.

The ambivalent community relationship to bars continues because the "we" of the queer community are of many minds and political persuasions. Some radical queers disdain bars for being "notoriously misogynist and racist," for excluding homeless people "so they don't get in the way of business," and for mindless patriotism in their display of "Amerikan" flags next to Pride flags.[52] Mainstream gay rights organizations ignored them, perhaps for being too frivolous or banal, at least they did until the COVID-19 pandemic threw their very survival into question. And yet, more people go to gay bars on any random weekend than attend protests in an entire year, or than donate to political causes.

When it closed in 1956, the Garden of Allah was less like the gender-segregated gay bars that we now regard as classic and more like the pre-Prohibition queer-straight nightclubs. But from the vantage point of today, the Garden looks more like contemporary LGBTQ+ clubs than those classic gay bars of the post-Stonewall years. Today's clubs increasingly focus on live entertainment, especially drag but also the burlesque, comedians, and live music that were common at the Garden.[53] As at the Garden, contemporary gay-owned clubs cater to mixed crowds of straight and LGBTQ+ people, with drag queens heckling bemused straight men. Armed force members again socialize openly in their uniforms. Straight people are again key consumers.

The Garden's decline was blamed on trends familiar today. Today, marijuana legalization has disrupted the gay bar business in many states, and gay bars increasingly face competition from straight ones for clientele. Then, the legalization of liquor by the glass meant that illicit clubs now had legal, reputable, non-queer competition.[54] As with today, technology was blamed for pulling away patrons. As one former female impersonator claimed, "I like television but because of it, all those places are gone."[55] These days, smartphone apps get blamed as the entertainment that keeps us at home. And to stem flagging revenues, the Garden pulled a tactic common today: It started offering drag brunches.[56]

There are differences, of course. Racial segregation is no longer *de jure*, while it still often remains *de facto*. Today, there is a lively world of LGBTQ+ people in the daylight. As one Garden queen reminisced, "Back in the Garden days we didn't have the freedom that came later. If you want to walk down the street in drag today, you can. Back then you had to hide those things."[57] DJs have replaced the old pipe organ (can you even imagine boogying to a Wurlitzer?).

On a visit to Seattle, near where my sister lives and where I was visiting a dying friend, I walked past the Garden of Allah's old address at 1213 First Avenue. What once was a raucous, low-rent honky-tonk district is now catty-corner from the Seattle Art Museum. The bar used to be in the basement of a hotel that is long gone, replaced by a towering glass building of apartments and a four-star hotel. The historic buildings nearby still contain cafés, but since they serve mainly businesspeople from bedroom communities, they're not open past 7 pm to serve their delicate toasts topped with piparras relish or mushroom escabeche (I don't even know what those are). There are still bars and a liquor store nearby, but also an art gallery, a luxury French furniture store, and a Tesla electric car charging station. The last of the Pioneer Square neighborhood gay bars, the Double Header, long the oldest gay bar in the country, closed in 2015. Years ago the gay bar scene had moved a mile or so, ensconced in the gayborhood of Capitol Hill. There, the drag and burlesque and all-gender dancing continue, in bars like Pony and Queer/Bar.

But if today's young people appreciate the resurgence of burlesque and drag artistry, we forget that today's youth enjoy them "as much as their parents and grandparents did" back in the 1950s.[58] If today, gender-diverse people find a new welcome in gay bars that were classically gender segregated, we forget that gender diversity was the norm in early twentieth-century clubs. If the Garden of Allah was built "on the fantasy that someday there will be a world of comfort, support, and love," it is a fantasy from the 1940s that we recognize today.[59] It is a fantasy that gay bars have only ever imperfectly— ambivalently— addressed. Perhaps the dream's materialization only ever exists in the future.[60] Or perhaps we'd need to look up from our little screens for it to manifest.

Five

Not-Quite-for-Profit, Privately-Owned Community Assets

Blackstones
PORTLAND, MAINE

Gay bars are private businesses, but we often treat them—and sometimes they function—as nonprofit community centers. I describe them as not-*quite*-for-profits. This is driven in no small part by gay bar professionals themselves who uniformly report that they could make more money running a straight bar. Angst over the role of gay bars in the broader community—even when there is only one—illustrates our ambivalent desire for inclusive community centers, but where someone else bears all the risks.[1]

A controversy over flags at the 2018 Pride parade in Portland, Maine, encapsulates the inseparability of its only gay bar, Blackstones, from the city's especially fractious queer identity politics.[2] Portland is Maine's largest city: 70,000 souls anchoring a metropolitan area of half a million, a seaport town that has shifted to the gentrification-inducing creative economy and tourism, including from day-tripping Bostonians. Blackstones transitioned from its former reputations as a gentlemen's club, a leather/kink bar, and then a bear bar, into "a community gay bar for the pansexual, queer, bisexual, and transgender community," in the vision of manager Carl Currie. This was a necessary shift due to the 2016 closure of Styxx, the only other gay club in the city, but a change that came with all the intractable contradictions of trying to reconcile unruly queerness with the workaday rules of running a private for-profit business.[3]

When I sat down with Carl in June of 2018, a volunteer was packing what looked like acres of rainbow bunting into large duffel bags. This was, I learned, the famous River of Pride, a 900-foot Pride flag that would go on to be featured at 2019's World Pride in New York City that celebrated the fiftieth anniversary of the Stonewall uprising. The massive flag was the brainchild of a onetime-Blackstones's bartender who had actually sewed the flag on the bar's pool table.[4]

This year, for the first time since its creation in 2006, the flag would not be permitted in Portland's parade. The River of Pride was being carefully packed away, a casualty of the shift toward direct action and away from corporate—and gay bar—participation in the June festivities. As Carl explained, without apparent bitterness, "We had a long Pride flag that walked through the city, but we didn't feel like it was inclusive enough." The River of Pride was the "classic" gay Pride flag with six colors, not the original with eight, nor the 2017 City of Philadelphia flag that added Black and Brown stripes for racial justice, nor Daniel Quasar's Progress Pride flag to which the transgender flag colors were added as well.[5] Traditionalists wanted the River of Pride in the parade, while others who were focused on righting exclusionary wrongs felt the classic flag sent the wrong message. "It's really dividing the community," Carl reported.

Gesturing to the four LGBTQ+ flags flying outside the bar, "These flags are up there and I'm trying to make it known to people that it's okay to come in." Outside the bar alongside the classic Pride flag were flags celebrating transgender, bear, and pansexual Prides. "The younger generations have been showing so much more diversity, you can't just fly a Pride flag and have them come in," Carl explained in reference to the younger generation's embrace of queerness, suspicion of traditional gay politics, and opposition to the gender binary.

But indeed, you can't just fly a classic Pride flag and honor the bar's old-timers either, many of whom felt shoved aside by Blackstones's move towards inclusivity in the same way their beloved pool table was shoved aside so that younger patrons could dance. Inside the bar, alongside the signs for many of Portland's past gay bars, were many small iterations of the leather Pride flag, with its black, blue, and white stripes under a red heart. The leather Pride flag makes visible the longtime association between Blackstones and the Harbor Masters of Maine, the oldest leather/Levi social club in the state, whose name plays both on Portland's maritime heritage (a harbor master is the official who ensures that Coast Guard rules are followed) and BDSM, where the "master/slave" dynamic is but one of many kinky possibilities. Leather/Levi clubs are fraternal organizations for men who celebrate sex, sometimes kinky sex, and who traditionally looked askance at women and drag and wore hypermasculine clothes that recalled motorbikes, laborers, and cowboys. For many years Blackstones was co-owned and run by Ralph Cusack, who had also cofounded the Harbor Masters back in 1984. But the leather scene, an important community for some cis men, was not enough to sustain a bar of its own, so now it had to share the space with the broader community.

Blackstones hosts the Harbor Masters monthly meetings and occasional pajama parties and auctions of leather gear like harnesses and jackets. Their paraphernalia decorated its walls, including plaques, a framed black leather biker jacket, and a ship's wheel encircled by a metal chain. Harbor Masters survives as the only leather club in Maine after its brother club disbanded in 2015 because "membership is hard to maintain without the aid of a host bar," indicating the importance of Blackstones, even a changed Blackstones, for maintaining the historic men's club.[6]

Carl said of the bar's previous role in the community, "Blackstones had a debaucherous reputation in the 90s as a leather bar and like a private club." This was somewhat at odds with how previous owner Ralph remembered it, telling a community historian that Blackstones had "a leather crowd, a transgender crowd, a straight crowd, a neighborhood crowd."[7] Nevertheless, Carl noted that when the new owner Matt Pekins took over from Ralph in 2014, "He tried to run it as a bear bar, a gay men's bar." With that idea not working, Matt promoted Carl from fill-in bartender to manager in 2017 based on his experience in the bar industry, and somewhat reluctantly accepted Carl's sweeping changes. Under his vision, he said, Blackstones needed to "get away from being an old men's party leather bar" and instead be turned "into a place where anyone can come in."

Inclusivity was his primary goal, but his method of achieving it surprised me: "The initial thing for inclusion was stocking better liquor," describing this issue as so crucial "it was like a bar rescue." As he explained of local LGBTQ+ folks' preference for higher-quality spirits on contrast to Blackstones's previously limited offerings, "Portland is so inclusive for all of its bars, they have the choice of going to twenty other bars, and if all they can get is this, then they don't want to hang out here." Even as Portland embraces radical queer politics, at least some queers prefer top-shelf imported liquor, a class privilege sometimes at odds with radical politics. Or not. Even radicals want something that's not well, sometimes!

Carl recounted that some of the controversies that swirled around the bar were because "people are so sensitive and immediately jump on the internet." For example, he recounted one instance when "the place was packed and someone bumped into a customer—we witnessed it—the person spilled their drink, but they came to me and said, 'Someone attacked me!' and burst into tears." While being consoled, the person asked Carl, "Are you going to throw them out?" This wasn't a rare occurrence; Carl described patrons so accustomed to hostility in the outside world that they expected it at Blackstones as well. An eavesdropping patron leaned forward and said to Carl, "and you're a straight white male so you can't go and tell them, 'You're acting like a fucking asshole,'" to which Carl affirmed, "I can't do that." Carl's identity makes him especially vulnerable to criticism as the heterosexual custodian of Portland's only gay bar and preeminent LGBTQ+ space. Recalling a time he kicked someone out of the bar, that person said "you're telling me to do that because you're privileged," and yet, Carl added, "You have to fear the repercussions of them going on Facebook."

Facebook was a regular topic in the interview, in part because Carl administers both a public-facing Facebook business page and also a private group of more than 1,300 members that shares announcements, bar conversations, and—inevitably—drama. As Carl described, "If I wake up and see something at the Blackstones page I will contact

them immediately." Brushing away my question about economic business challenges, he answered as if the only challenges were digital:
"I don't want that negativity written on Facebook because that's the
most negative thing affecting the bar."

Carl's assiduous Facebook messaging allowed me to monitor
Blackstones from afar over the years, and one of the things that consistently impressed me was how seemingly every segment of the
LGBTQ+ community showed ownership of the bar by organizing its
diverse regular programming. Sure, Blackstones screened weekly episodes of *RuPaul's Drag Race* and Patriots football games, and hosted
karaoke contests and trivia nights emceed by drag mother Danielle
Dior. And yes, it had a Beer Bear Bash, a monthly potluck brunch,
reminders about the Dyke March, a fundraiser for the local center
for adults with disabilities, and discounted beer on Election Day to
accompany multiple reminders to vote. But it also hosted special
parties organized by MaineTransNet and events by a group called
the Superhero Lady Arm Wrestlers of Portland. The bar had earlier
hosted a Thirsty Thursday Q&A on pre-exposure prophylaxis (PrEP)
by the local HIV/AIDS resource center, the Frannie Peabody Center ,
a public health contribution to gay bars' not-quite-for-profit missions.
And while the bar's monthly movie screenings included the usual suspects of *Priscilla, Queen of the Desert* and *Judy,* it also included Korean
film *Parasite* and the documentary *Paris Is Burning* for Black History
Month. This preceded a Melanin Magic Dance Party celebrating Black
artists—impressive for a bar in a metropolitan region that is 2 percent
African American.

The year 2018 also saw the return of the Miss Blackstones pageant
after an eight-year hiatus, cementing the former leather bar's engagement with the state's drag community and starting an event that
quickly outgrew the bar. The 2020 pageant, held before COVID shuttered nightlife, was so massive that it required multiple preliminary
contests at the bar before a final affair at a sold-out 600-seat music
hall several blocks away. This event, made accessible by the venue
and ASL interpretation, also featured boylesque troupe Boxer Briefs,
drag king Lou Zér, and local burlesque celebrity Kinky Slippers. The
Miss Blackstones 2020 pageant, in peripheral Maine, was as plugged
in as any city anywhere to the trend of burlesque and king inclusion,

and as much a part of the national embrace of drag by bars that had previously been cruisy men's bars.

Consent was a regular feature of conversations on the bar's Facebook community group and in their events. A screening of risqué cult film *The Rocky Horror Picture Show*, announced regarding the show's audience participation antics, proclaimed that "consent beads will be used to signify willingness to participate." A patron's Facebook group exhortation against nonconsensual touching prompted a lively community conversation about what was acceptable in a bar. In this discussion, Kevin Norsworthy recounted an occasion where a bartender supported their complaint about a harassing patron, asserting "screw those 'it's a bar' people. It's not just a bar. It's Blackstones."[8] Carl also alerted patrons to suspected incidents of drugging in the bar, a level of transparency I have never seen from any other bars. The bar subsequently posted "Guidelines for Consensual Contact" and planned to train "bar guardians" who could monitor special events, help patrons who had perhaps had one too many, and keep an eye out for potential druggings.

Unlike bars that merely acknowledge LGBTQ+ days of remembrance with memes on their Facebook pages, Blackstones patrons put it at the center of broader LGBTQ+ community events. For example, during Transgender Day of Remembrance 2019, the bar hosted a brief program that included local trans community members reading the names of those lost to violence and reflecting on their own experiences in Portland. The event had ASL interpretation, and all happy hour tips were matched by the bar and given to MaineTransNet.

Similarly, for World AIDS Day in 2019, the bar hosted a Red Ribbon Wall that was carried to the civic vigil at Congress Square Park to represent members of the community who had died. This was part of a program that included a Night of 100 Stars (which raised over $500 for the local AIDS service organization), a screening of the AIDS film *The Normal Heart*, and a group karaoke tribute to AIDS martyr Freddie Mercury.

These programs reflect two different but intertwined gay bar trends—the standards to which a contemporary LGBTQ+ bar should be held, and the way a bar can fill a community center role that in other cities might be performed by a nonprofit. While nearly all bars do some community-minded things, few bars in the entire country do as much as Blackstones. But even for bars that do none, it is the standards to which we hold them that allow them to function as places for *all* of our diverse community—or not.

Blackstones and its staff were regularly accused of racism and transphobia. One patron dubbed the bar "Whitestones" on Facebook, while another described it as dangerous for Black transgender women. There have been occasional demands that members be blocked from the private Blackstones group over things posted on their personal feeds that others deemed exclusionary, and some activist members have been removed for being disruptive or not following community guidelines. Controversy about misgendering also erupted when Carl used "you guys" to refer to a gender-diverse group of people.

Yet, Black and transgender patrons often defended the bar and Carl for his transparency, responsiveness, and sincerity. One community member wrote that while they had personally had bad experiences at the bar in the past, bad behavior had been significantly curtailed since Carl was put in charge. The patron continued with praise about the bar's emphasis on consent and at crafting consensus among a diverse LGBTQ+ community. Quinn Gormley agreed, addressing Carl on Facebook: "A few years ago I'd tell trans folks to stay away. It might not be perfect now, but you've put in the right work and carved out space for us, space that simply hasn't existed anywhere else."[9]

Blackstones gives me pause and offers several lessons. Carl's role as the *de facto* "face" of Blackstones is a reminder that straight people have always been key figures in the LGBTQ+ community, as Carl himself intimated when he casually talked about how "we" didn't want the River of Pride.[10] True, he was vulnerable to having his identity weaponized against him, but it was also a virtue for community organizing. Black sociologist and Blackstones DJ Theo Greene told me,

Carl's greatest strength is his ability to say, "I don't know, help me understand." There is a vulnerability to say, "I need community to make this happen." Somehow that vulnerability is what allows the community to feel invested in Blackstones and his success.

On the one hand, I know of no other gay bar in the United States that is as transparent and responsive to critique as is Blackstones. On the other hand, even this bar is unable to represent all members of the local LGBTQ+ community. Whether this is due to deep intersectional lapses in bar management or run-of-the-mill personality conflicts depends on where you sit. Do you believe, as hurled by one patron on Facebook, that Carl is using Black and trans patrons and staff as a shield for his privilege? Or would any bar manager also be caught in the unavoidable clash of queer politics, capitalism, and diversity where inclusion is not a destination but a process?[11]

A 2021 news article carried charges by patron and performer Jake Boyce calling on Carl to resign and arguing that the bar should be turned over to an advisory board of "diverse queer people who aren't directly affiliated with Blackstones."[12] Jake displayed what Theo calls "vicarious citizenship" when he asserted ownership over the bar that he had earlier called to boycott, emphasizing the tight relationship between the bar and the city's LGBTQ+ community: "I'm still a family member of Blackstones just by being a queer person."[13] Even for those critical of Blackstones, they regard it and its patrons as kin.

Such a move to install a diverse board might be routine for a community nonprofit, but it's unclear what it would mean for a private business to be turned over to people who aren't "directly affiliated" with it. While it's possible that this outside pressure pushes the bar's programming to be as intersectional as it is, the inclusive offerings are also a measure of how diverse patrons have taken their talents into the space and remade it in their image.

In 2019, Pride Portland issued a press release announcing the return of the 900-foot River of Pride flag, describing its 2018 absence as a "misstep."[14] After 2019's Pride, regional straight newspapers took note when Blackstones removed the plywood from the front of the bar and replaced the giant plate-glass windows that had been repeatedly smashed in the 1980s and early 1990s. This opened up the bar to the street and allowed the fluttering flags on the façade to be glimpsed from inside the bar.[15]

The return of the River of Pride and the positive press did not surprise the unflappable Carl, who only one year earlier had calmly insisted to me that Blackstones would be involved in the 2018 Pride parade no matter the queer desires of some to exclude gay bars: "We're the last flag-flying gay bar in Portland. We should be involved." Some community members may be ambivalent about Blackstones's for-profit realities, but Carl manages to successfully run the not-quite-for-profit enterprise that is treated as a community asset even by its critics. Community involvement may look different in other cities, but understanding gay bars means understanding their business funda-mentals, the theme that unites the next section of this book.

Part Two

Gay Bar Fundamentals

Research assistant and co-author Tory Sparks, Blanche Dubois, and author Greggor Mattson in the oldest gay bar in Missouri: Cape Girardeau's Independence Place. Drag queens like Blanche are fundamental to gay bars' culture and economies but especially in outpost bars that serve entire regions. Photo courtesy of Tory Sparks. Used with permission.

Six

Mom and Moms and Pop and Pops

Splash Bar Florida
PANAMA CITY BEACH, FLORIDA

To understand gay bars, you have to understand their fundamentals: what they offer, how they're run, where they're located, their vast variety. Gay bars may be hailed as safe spaces, historic queer heritage sites, and as places of ambivalent politics, but at the end of the day, gay bars are just small businesses. Unlike other communities anchored by institutions of faith, families, or foodways, the LGBTQ+ community has, uniquely, depended upon privately owned spaces that serve alcohol to have public squares of our own. And in a world of liquored-up corporate chain restaurants, almost all gay bars are mom-and-pop businesses, or mom-and-mom and pop-and-pop businesses, as it were. And most of these small business owners have day jobs or other sources of income because gay bars are not big money-makers anymore: Jon Pepe told me that to keep Chez Est (Hartford, Connecticut) afloat, "I work prolly fifty hours a week at my day job and about thirty-five hours a week here, Tuesday through Saturday nights and Sunday for our beer bashes and tea dances." Justin Menard of Bolt (Lafayette, Louisiana) admitted, "People don't realize that I'm bartending now because I can't afford to pay myself." As one reader exclaimed upon finishing the book, "You have to be bananas to open a gay bar!" And perhaps like all "bananas" small business owners, they assume risks, assess customers, and cut deals on the fly.

"Shit, there's gonna be a cover charge," reported the polo shirt–wearing bro to a dozen clean-cut millennials trailing him to the podium in front of Splash Bar in Panama City Beach. It is one of the coastal communities along the Florida Panhandle that rebranded themselves as Florida's Emerald Coast, trying to get away from the Redneck Riviera reputation it received from aggressively heterosexual TV coverage of countless *MTV Spring Breaks* and, more recently, the MTV reality show *Floribama Shore*.[1]

I was interviewing Splash Bar's owner Tony Boswell while he worked the door at his own bar, a staffing strategy to keep costs down. While he negotiated with the muscled leader of the group, a sun-kissed bro in Oakley sunglasses enthusiastically shot the shit with me.

"Man, have you been in there yet?" he asked.

"Not yet," I replied from my perch beside the greeter's podium.

"Man, you gotta go in there—this place is the best time in Panama City!"

"What's so good about it?" I asked.

The bro replied, giving a remarkably sweet answer for why a straight man might enjoy a gay bar:

> the vibe, the atmosphere. Everyone is here just to have fun, man. There's no assholes bumping into you who think they're better than everybody else. You can go to other places for fun, but when you really want to have a good time, you come to Splash.

Toxic masculinity is toxic for everybody it seems, and appearances can be deceiving.

While we chatted, Tony cut a deal with the group's leader to let them all in for half the $10 cover charge, forgoing $5 a head in order to get a herd into the bar early in the night. As the leader stood outside the bar calling friends on his mobile phone, Tony murmured, "That one guy brought me thirty people."

Embracing straight people has, of course, long been a business practice of small-city gay bar owners,[2] who overwhelmingly framed this as reciprocal acceptance of tolerance and diversity. But it is more and more a business necessity now that LGBTQ+ people increasingly take their business to non-gay establishments. For straight young adults today, Tony explained, "They could care less whether we're a gay bar. They want to know what our beer price is and your cover charge is." To my question about one of the scourges of many big-city gay bars, Tony smiled: "Bachelorette parties? We get lots and lots, and I like them."[3] This welcome to groups of straight women stood in stark contrast to New York City's Flaming Saddles, famous for their wooden sign reading, "STRAIGHT WOMEN NO WOOHOOING," a complaint common at big-city bars about ways of showing appreciation that detract from the LGBTQ+ ambiance.[4] Mark Hurst of the bear bar Diesel (Seattle, Washington), rehearsed his incredulous reply to men's hostility to women in his space: "The same people who brought a woman last week are now all like, 'Why are there all these fucking women here?' Because you bring them here!" And, bars that try to shoo away groups of women invariably end up turning away bisexual and pansexual women, and even groups of lesbians as well.

But haggling over the cover charge touches a nerve that many bar owners complain about when asked what patrons don't understand about running a gay bar: costs. Almost every one of the 130 managers and owners I talked to said that patrons didn't understand how much it costs to run a bar: the hidden fees of insurance, credit card fees, cable TV and internet fees, liquor licenses, business licenses, and taxes. But bar owners reserved special frustration for resistance to cover charges. Cover charges, the cost just to enter the door, *cover* the extra costs of entertainment, explained owners. As Tony says, "They think they pay for it out of the drink price," but drinks alone don't generate the profits to pay thousands of dollars for the one-night appearances by name-brand DJs or *RuPaul's Drag Race* (RPDR) alums. "People are very hesitant to cover charges," Tony says ruefully, echoing scores of other owners. "It's a rough sell."

I asked Tony about recent changes in the business, and he said that today's patrons are "going out smarter, to get the most value for the dollar and not going out intentionally every day the way *I* used to." Of today's wiser customer, he was conciliatory: "I think it's healthier if people go out less than they did ten years ago. I think that ten years ago, the gay people were in an unhealthy extreme: The drinking, drugs, sex, were done to the extremes." In contrast, it was Tony's impression that "the gay community is getting smarter. I think they're getting more educated, and learning how to use their money, so to tie two of your questions together, I think the part they don't get is the expense to fully entertain them."

Entertainment is key to Splash Bar Florida's business model, as it is for most contemporary gay bars that have increasingly embraced creative strategies to provide an experience rather than just a barstool.[5] "We had to aim to a younger crowd that came out more. We had to change the entertainment value," Tony asserted, though this was not a sentiment shared by all owners: Just as many depended on older patrons and wondered where the younger ones were. With pride, Tony noted that here in the Florida Panhandle, each June, you can see the same LGBTQ+ performers that you do in New York, Atlanta, or New Orleans. He does this because he wants locals to "be proud of their local Pride." As he notes "we had to change our entertainment practices to make sure they were up to the expectations of the tourists as well as the locals." Success has meant that people now plan their visits and vacations around the big stars that come in.

This means, as Tony explains, that "pricing for entertainment, that's one of the biggest expenses we have." He boasts that his bar features the most RPDR girls in a year of any bar in the country, artists who can command appearance fees north of $4,000 even before expenses are accounted for. The night after I was in town, Nina Bo'nina Brown was performing on the very night of the season finale in which she appeared. "We're flying her in from New York. The finale, it's live, and she's there, and then they're flying her straight to here." As he noted, "The handler fees and all that adds on to the contract: the champagne, the food service, it's astronomical." He continued, "We *have* to—" before catching himself and editing, "we *want* to offer our patrons the best entertainment." True, this was June, Pride month, but Nina wasn't the only entertainment on offer:

We have porn stars and go-go dancers coming for Pride, airfare that's paid for, our hotel rooms are $200 to $300 per night with a minimum of two nights even if they only use them for one night, and the customers don't see that you can't absorb those costs any-more.

Hence cover charges, no matter how despised and misunderstood.

And of course, being on Panama City Beach with its bombastic roadside attractions means that nightlife operators have to offer something big: "Here you have to have drag queens and strippers and roller coasters, you have to offer so much to catch the gay dollar." Tony's hardly exaggerating: Driving in Panama City Beach means seeing go kart tracks, water slides, and oceanfront nightclubs that can admit thousands of MTV spring breakers. And yet, not all of the new entertainment offerings are strippers and Ru girls. Incredulously, Tony reported: "We added bingo here. I never imagined my bar having bingo! It's a big night for us! But it would not have worked here five years ago, so the gay community is morphing."

This morphing necessitates a constantly updated and adaptive business model. He gives an example of the elaborate lighting his bar installed. "Now, this bar was the first to have LED lights. My business partner had gone to a light show and came back and said, 'We need to get those.'" Installing them offered another opportunity for a shrewd deal, however.

> We made a deal with the guy who had them: He said if you'll put them in here, I'll put them in at my cost. And as soon as we got them, people started taking pictures, and now everyone in town has them.

As Tony modestly concluded, "We try to stay ahead of the curve."

When I asked whether smartphone apps like Grindr or Tinder had affected business, Tony said yes but not in the way I expected. "Our Wi-Fi bill is outrageous, but we have to have high-end Wi-Fi: Everyone is on the phone. They're using our Wi-Fi to download everything." With pride, he notes of Splash Bar's free high-speed Wi-Fi: "When we first did it, it was just us and McDonald's." But, Tony growled, "They just increased the charges because of the usage; people are using it so much. It just goes higher and higher. It's a business expense that most gay bars wouldn't anticipate." As he explained, Grindr might have affected his outpost bar less than those in big cities: "When you're the only gay bar for 350 miles around, all those people who are not out may not be able to download Grindr because it's a work phone or on a family plan." A family plan prevents some LGBTQ+ people from being with their *other* family, at least via smartphone.

If Wi-Fi is essential because of social media, it's also because social media is the most important source of the bar's advertising. "We've used social media to get those young people into the bar. It's *the* tool." Tony explained how the bar had been very successful early on with MySpace but was caught off guard when that platform collapsed. "We weren't embedded into Facebook. Now, anything new that comes out, we grab it, and if it doesn't develop, we don't develop it. Then, it was Snapchat that devastated Facebook." While pundits blame smartphone apps for devastating gay bars, several owners found it a plus, including Michael of Garlow's and Keith of \aut\ BAR. Tony described the queerly ambivalent relationship between the physical and the virtual realms: "Social media is a tool that works for us and against us, but if you do it the right way, it's a net win."[6]

Tony continued, describing his mission as "get the phone out of their hands! If you can do that, even for a small amount of time, you do it. Force them into interaction with each other!" Characterizing smartphones as an "addiction," he explained how he and some of his bartenders take people's phones away and put them in the tip jar and don't give them back until they talk to their neighbor. It's so successful, he claims, that "they forget to get their phones back!" He explained one consequence of the addiction of phones: "People have lost the ability to meet other people and that's why you come out to the bars! It's to meet people!" Tony's impressions are validated by sociologists: Contact online doesn't readily lead to contact face to face even when you're in the same room.[7]

Being in a tourist town means that Splash Bar's income is highly seasonal—something common to the gay bars in resort communities like Rehoboth Beach (Delaware), Saugatuck (Michigan), Eureka Springs (Arkansas), or Guerneville (California). As Tony spelled it out, "We do have those people who come year after year during the season, but if we didn't have the young people who live right here year-round . . ." he trailed off. Splash Bar's pivot to social media wasn't to let out-of-towners know about the bars, however: "Originally, it was for the locals—if you like our page, we'd give you a free drink and bam! We had 6,000 followers." The pop-and-pop gay bar has to be plugged into its local community, even as it innovates, claims Tony: "Each gay community is different from the next city's"—something echoed by the rare owners who owned bars in different cities.

Only after we had been talking for almost ninety minutes did Tony confess, "This bar would be more profitable if it was a straight bar. I do 20 percent of the business that my competitors do—I ran those bars so I know." This was also a common theme from owners: Running a bar more is for the community than to maximize income. One owner, off the record, confessed that they'd repaired the bar's roof using their personal credit card. Another, also privately, noted that they'd been slowly liquidating their retirement to make payroll while they hoped business would pick up, and this was before coronavirus clobbered the nightlife industry. This choice to maintain LGBTQ+ spaces despite meager profits and frequent losses made me ask Tony whether gay bars were not-*quite*-for-profits.

"But that's what we are," Tony agreed, noting that he made a living off Splash even if it didn't provide the income it used to. Still, "We provide for a segment of the market that's underserved, but that's a big job." Lots of bars did all sorts of things, including by hosting community theater productions of queer musicals, as did Trevi Lounge of Fairfield, Connecticut (*Xanadu*) or the Club Cabaret in Hickory, North Carolina (*Rent*).

When I asked if he'd considered leaving the business, Tony shook his head. But he said of other gay bar owners, "We know each other on the Gulf Coast and a lot are ready to retire." As he explained, "You give up every holiday, every Christmas, that everyone else in your family gets to enjoy and at some point say 'I want to live life.' They put ten or twenty years in, and want to cash in." When I asked what he meant, he said, "This liquor license is our retirement."

I asked how that worked, and he said his ability to retire was predicated upon "protecting that piece of paper. We don't play around with underage, or drugs. We're very restrictive on those things." Tony clarified that restaurant liquor licenses cost less than a third of the cost of liquor-only licenses, which perhaps explains why there has been a proliferation around the country of liquored-up restaurants that compete with bars—including chain restaurants like Chili's whose corporations can help individual franchisees weather tough times and whose buying power can make bargain cocktails profitable.

The costs of liquor licenses are also expenses that patrons don't see, and they must be paid even before a business can open, often at the cost of significant debt. "To issue a new liquor license, there are only those people who compete and pay all the background checks and it's always a lottery." The winner, he explained, almost always sells them: "They're $380–400,000." When I gasped, he pitied my ignorance: "In Key West, it's $2 million!" Tony explained that this meant investment groups were often necessary to open a club now: "A lot of the mom and pops have closed, and now there's a moratorium on nightclubs. They'll give you a restaurant license, but you won't get a nightclub license." Of nightclubs like Splash that served only liquor, not food, he reported of Panama City Beach, "We're all grandfathered in but they're not going to let any new ones in. We can all sell our licenses." But, he added ominously, "The ones that close down don't re-open."

Tony explained, after greeting a few more patrons by name, that liquor licenses had recently become more plentiful for restaurants. "Now, they compete with us—even Applebee's has a license!" This is a change because "before, in the South, churches wouldn't do business with someone who had a liquor license," adding "now, food and liquor are family friendly." When I noted that fast casual restaurants are located nearer peoples' suburban homes than gay bars, he said, "You hit it on the head. Those places are a bigger threat to the gay bar industry than Grindr is," a point the pundits have missed in their diagnoses of gay bar travails. Every bar may not be a gay bar, but a strip mall cocktail is still a cocktail.

Given gay bars' not-quite-for-profit moneymaking limitations, I asked why Tony kept the bar open as a gay bar, and he waxed passionate about being an outpost: "Gay bars have a really important place for the community. They're not a thing of the past in the rural South, or even on the outskirts of every big city. They're necessary." The downside, however, is that "it's really time-consuming, the bar business." Tony explained that in the old days he could hire things out and spend weeks of the year away on vacation. "Now, if it breaks, I fix it. If it gets dirty, we clean it. We're the ones running these shifts. Our business model is to keep costs down." Hence Tony at the door on a balmy June night while a mix of straight and LGBTQ+ 20-somethings sailed into the bar.

I asked if the decline in gay bars on the Emerald Coast had meant queer pop-ups at straight bars, and he shook his head. "I don't think in the South they'll allow you to do a gay night."[8] I asked if he could pioneer that segment of the population, and he frowned: "I don't think we could become a straight bar with a gay night." I asked why. He answered that safety wasn't really possible in a straight bar:

> I want people to be safe, to have a safe haven, especially in the South. We have people who live on Highway 79 and 231 who have never been around another gay *person,* much less the gay *community.*

I asked if he could spot these people when they visited, and he nodded. "We see them here at the door. They'll walk through the parking lot and stand here. Then they'll walk away. I know what they're doing. They're trying to find a way to come here."

Another reason to keep Splash a gay bar was the public health services it can offer to the community.

> We've provided support for them to be tested for STDs and HIV, and it's nonjudgmental. The guys who are living up these roads, these highways in the middle of nowhere, their chance sexual encounters are high risk. They can't get tested in their hometown because of the stigma there, so we find that we get a lot of people from the rural areas come here.

As he concluded of public health interventions, "It's a very important part of what gay bars serve. I ran straight bars for years, and I never saw any straight bars do that." Splash Bar isn't alone; many owners discussed their offerings, and I bumped into gay bar HIV testing in big-city Detroit and in small-college-town Morgantown, West Virginia.

I realized that we had been talking for nearly ninety minutes, and I hadn't asked any pointed questions about numerical profits, gross income, or monthly receipts. I'll happily ask someone where they put their junk last night, but I can't bear to ask how much money they made last month, at least not on the rapport that can be earned in a one-off interview at someone's place of work. Before I could screw up the courage, Tony explained he had to go help his bartender serve the herd that Oakley bro's friend had brought: "Wednesdays are dollar drinks night and he's really busy here all by himself—he just got thirty people at the bar."

I appreciated his strategy of meeting the new patrons where they are rather than blaming old ones for staying home, and I couldn't help admiring the passion and hard work it takes to keep a mom-and-mom-pop-and-pop business afloat. "I hope that gay bars can morph into what the community needs from us," Tony said as he moved toward the door, adding "I don't foresee gay bars closing down until straight bars have drag shows!" Which Rockin' Rodeo did after Denton, Texas's gay bar closed: the incomparably named Mabel Peabody's Beauty Supply and Chainsaw Repair. Drag shows popped up at Whiskey Dick's in Joplin, Missouri, after Equality Rocks closed, too.[9] But the straight bars on the Redneck Riviera don't have drag shows—yet.

Seven

The Training Grounds of America's Next Drag Superstars

Independence Place
CAPE GIRARDEAU, MISSOURI

Drag performance is fundamental to gay bars, and vice versa: As José Esteban Muñoz declared, queerness is not a stage to get over but a stage to get on.[1] I had finished my interview at the Southside Speakeasy in Salem, Oregon, when Ardina slid next to me at the bar and talked my ear off about the challenges of being a drag queen.[2] "There are times, if I'm being completely honest, that I'm relegated to a non-sexual role. I'm here as an accessory for your girlfriend or your ego." Describing the distance she'd come from her deer-hunting childhood, Ardina confessed, "I drank the blood of my first kill at 12 years old. That's what you did in the West." Gasping, I asked, "How much?" Touching her drink to her lips, she replied with a dreamy smile, "Just a sip. I bawled and cried and threw up!"

I have had zany experiences like this all over the country, a constant reminder that drag artists are some of the most vibrant nightlife personalities and signal that a place might, just might, be a gay bar. Drag queens were among the first "professional homosexuals," people able to make a full-time living off LGBTQ+ culture.[3] Drag performers are also activists, both in and out of their gender-bending garb, some-times just for existing in public as queer touchstones, and other times as the political vanguard of diverse LGBTQ+ movements.[4]

Drag is a vast artform that defies easy generalizations and has struggled to acknowledge its formative debt to transgender origina-tors when it is cisgender gay men who receive most of the shine. In a common drag show, a lineup might be three or so queens and one king, each taking turns to lip-sync a song while performing a gen-der-bending persona in a one-of-a-kind outfit. One queen often acts as the "show director" for a bar, managing the lineup by mixing local talent with out-of-towners, some of whom drive from *their* local bars more than four hours away to perform. These networks of friend-ship—and sometimes rivalry—form a connective tissue of living liga-ments or neurotransmitters that knit individual gay bars into one vast body that spans state lines and communicates business innovations, activism, and also, always, *tea,* that essential information of the queer world.[5]

Audience interaction is key, with fans approaching the stage to hold outstretched bills for the artist to collect. Artists typically receive only a small fee from the bars for performing, sometimes less than $100, so these tips can be key to recouping the costs of the wigs and the makeup and the lashes, much less the elaborate outfits that are sometimes worn only once before being reworked for a future show. Sometimes these tips are collected perfunctorily, with the performer sweeping through the crowd. More often, however, the queen or king holds your hand much longer than is necessary, looks deep into your eyes, and for a long moment, the club and the crowd fade away and the song is only for you.

Drag is a primary engine of gay bars' considerable fundraising power, and it continually generates a feeling of community in gay bars. As a queer cultural form, it delves the archives of past pain and camp humor, mixing it with of-the-moment pop culture and theatrics that can be simultaneously shameless, tragic, smutty, elegant, and sublime. Shows can range from glamorous female illusionism to edgy performance art to the folksy: At one show in Detroit, a queen from the House of Chanel was selling her home-canned pickles at the desk, and in the South, I heard more than one rendition of Dolly Parton's

"A Lil' Ole Bitty Pissant Country Place," the brothel anthem from the musical *The Best Little Whorehouse in Texas*.

Recently there has been a drag explosion in America, around the world even, in part due to the success of a certain reality TV show that debuted in 2009 and grew into an international media empire.[6] But *RuPaul's Drag Race*? Queens are sure ambivalent about it. As bartender and "true Cajun girl at heart" Keisha Wright of Crystal's Downtown of Lake Charles, Louisiana, exclaimed, "Drag is big again. Thank you, RuPaul!" Meanwhile, Blanche DuBois of Independence Place in Cape Girardeau, Missouri, said of the show: "HATE IT."

Nobody keeps track of how many drag artists there are: There is no Who's Who of kings, queens, and others. Increasingly drag shows feature burlesque and artists whose gender-bending moves exceed mere kinging or queening. This makes it impossible to quantify the contemporary drag explosion or to compare it with the previous one that occurred around 1970.[7] But everyone I spoke to said there were more drag performers now than ever in their living memory, and that included queens who would never admit their obvious seniority to a stranger.

This drag proliferation means that gay bars that shunned drag now feature it. This included men's bars such as Blackstones in Portland, Maine, which transitioned away from a "seedy" men's bar into reviving the Miss Blackstones pageant, or the Leather Stallion Saloon in Cleveland, Ohio, where leathermen who disdained drag now flock to drag bingo.[8] But it also includes lesbian bars that embrace drag in all its forms, such as My Sister's Room in Atlanta that moved to a larger location in part to feature shows helmed by owner and sometime drag king Chase Daniels.[9] Crush in Portland, Oregon, expanded their space to accommodate three monthly drag variety shows and the entertainment that current owners say is key to keeping a gay bar open: burlesque, boylesque, and the self-explanatory Pants Off Dance Off.

Longtime drag bars have added new weekly shows and new *types* of shows. Several bars reported adding programming to help baby drag queens grow up big and strong, like the Drag Survivor program that helped launch the second gay bar in Hattiesburg, Mississippi, Black Sheep's Café & Speakeasy, by general manager Gary May as "a weekly competition on Thursday nights for people who want to get into drag. They can come and hone their skills." Out and About (Pasco, Washington) added an all-ages show that attracted "mom, dad, kids—none of them gay—who just wanted to watch a show," in addition to Wednesday night shows that allow performers "to get yourself together and practice your makeup," said manager Jay Chavez. Here, queens may have been following the lead of drag kings, whose troupes have to continually replenish their memberships, whereas queens often functioned as independent contractors whose "mothers" bring up "daughters."[10] It is partially because straight people don't come to king shows that management may limit their performance time and pay them less: Only R House of Toledo, Ohio, reported having a show director who was a king, Justin Case. Because kings aren't given performance time—particularly in marquee venues like *RuPaul's Drag Race*—they are trapped in a cycle of marginality.

At one of these all-ages shows, Russ from the Rainbow Members Club in Longview, Texas, recalled the craziest thing he ever saw: "A little boy was 9 maybe and in full-blown drag. His mom and dad were both there supporting him. I thought it was fantastic, really special. Yeah, he stole the show." "Did he get tips?" I asked with my mouth open. "I didn't pay attention. I was too busy crying."

New gay bars have opened up specifically to feature drag. Chris Newell, owner of Trade ("LGBTQ fetish & kink bar") in Denver, Colorado, opened the nearby Gladys, The Nosy Neighbor to feature drag, burlesque, and out-there performance art. Cabaret Club Dothan in Alabama originally opened for drag shows that were displaced by the closure of the Wiregrass region's only gay bar, with owner Ron Devane explaining, "I try to make sure I always have a drag king." Fat Mary's in McAlester, Oklahoma, had no trouble booking queens from hours away because of their purpose-built drag dressing room in their former goat barn that featured a rare high-powered air conditioner to keep makeup from melting away; it is plastered with a handwritten sign that reads: "DO NOT touch thermostat. If you are skinny, move away, eat a chicken leg & get a coat. Thanks!"

RuPaul's Drag Race may always feature queens from New York City, Los Angeles, and Chicago, but these cities draw upon the talent nurtured in the heartland. Many small-town queens migrated to gay metropolises to become America's Next Drag Superstar™—Alaska

Thunderfuck 5000 is from near Erie, Pennsylvania; Bob the Drag Queen is from Columbus, Georgia; Bianca del Rio is from Gretna, Louisiana; and Sasha Velour is from Urbana, Illinois. Having a Ru girl from your hometown can even save a gay bar: All Star–winner Trixie Mattel became a co-owner of Milwaukee's This Is It! when it nearly closed in the COVID-19 pandemic.[11] Thus to understand the titanic changes in the relationship between gay bars and drag artistry, there was no better place to go than the oldest gay bar in Missouri, Independence Place in Cape Girardeau.

"I have not had eyebrows since 1998," drawled Blanche DuBois as she sipped a drink and explained her commitment to her art. We were speaking to Miss Independence Place 1990–91 in the only gay bar in the town of 41,000 perched above the Mississippi River north of its confluence with the Ohio River. Blanche was the show director of the Missouri bar at the time that we spoke. An Illinois resident, she commuted across state lines to run Independence Place's popular drag shows. The bar, like many gay places, is completely unassuming and hardly visible from the street, marked only by a worn vinyl banner. Its front door is in the back of the building, up sun-bleached wooden steps leading from a weedy yard full of junk framed by a chain-link fence. The bar is a survivor, having weathered several fires—one of them arson—since its founding in the late 1980s. Inside is a glittering palace with a drop ceiling of tinsel, rainbow bunting, and various LGBTQ+ Pride flags with framed posters recording the proud lineages of former Miss and Mister Independence Places going back to the regnal year of 1988–89.

Many bar professionals remarked on queens' prowess at promoting themselves on Facebook and Instagram, drawing in new patrons. When I asked Independence Place's bartender JT about patrons at his outpost bar, he named regulars who traveled from more than an hour away to see the shows, "some from Carbondale, Poplar Bluff, up to St. Louis. This is the only bar still open in the area."

St. Louis might be an hour and forty-five away by car, but it's not the only city that sends queens to Independence Place. As local drag celebrity Sasha Moore (Miss Independence Place 1996–97 *and* 2006–07) explained, "A lot of queens start out here in this bar, and then they'll go to St. Louis or Kansas City or New York or Chicago," returning from time to time with skills and tricks honed in the big city. Blanche herself travels all over, giving her a perspective on the gay bar business at large: "Bigger cities keeping their bars going, it's easier for them. It's a lot harder for the small towns. That's what I've seen because I've been to Chicago, St. Louis, New York, Virginia." She described Independence Place as the "localized safe spot" that helped retain LGBTQ+ people in the region, but not always queens, because "when they make their name in the big city, they'll stay there." Shaking her head, Blanche said:

> It saddens me a little bit that you never get to see what the small towns bring at all. It's sad to say that when I was in New York, I met a bunch of people who came to the big cities because there wasn't community back home.

Community, she implied, that bars like Independence Place help foster.

Drag has long brought straight people to gay bars.[12] Now, they're increasingly replacing lost LGBTQ+ patronage, both trends part of the rising tides of both LGBTQ+ acceptance and straight folks' drag fandom. "Straight crowds keep the bar open," Blanche declared flatly. This was a common refrain at other bars as well. As the bartender at Kinkead's in Fort Smith, Arkansas, noted, "It's always had drag shows and straight folks come," but he added that "now a few straights come in even when there's not a show." Jerry Ehlen of B-Bobs in Mobile, Alabama, concurred, noting "It's more accepted by the straight community to come, convinced by *RuPaul's Drag Race* to come watch the shows." This may explain part of the inordinate attention that Ru girls attract as part of a show that envelops diverse viewers into an earnestly campy and occasionally catty world of shared catchphrases, shocking stunts, and gag-worthy wig reveals. Straight people may be getting their first taste of the drag world from RPDR, but plenty of gay men only come out to see a celebrity drag performer, too: Most people can name more Ru girls than local drag artists, an indication that drag has become "celebrified."[13]

Nevertheless, Independence Place bartender JT echoed these sentiments:

> I think a lot of the gay bars now are turning more straight than gay. It's more alternative now because there are more straight people

now. They'll do the whole gay Pride thing, all the gay things like that, but there's no point in separating anymore. That's the great thing about it.

By JT's reckoning, the college night drag show is more than 95 percent straight, as students from the nearby Southeast Missouri State University "absolutely love it." Such a comment called into question journalists' reports from big cities that straight people had only recently invaded gay bars, or that straight acceptance was only a factor in coastal blue-state metropolises.

Queens weren't ambivalent about their straight patronage at all, not even the straight men whose potential aggression was feared until recently. They're more than welcome, JT explains, because "they interact, they tip well. They have fun if you mess with them, they don't care if you call them out or hit on them. Back of their mind, they know it's a joke. It makes it more interesting."

This was echoed by other owners. Shane Shumaker, the straight manager The Blue Lite in Sheboygan, Wisconsin, said of straight men, "They know it's a joke, they know it's all fun and games. I do too." And besides, noted Cody Koch of Faces in Reno, Nevada, "Straight men find it flattering to be hit on. Not all of them, but a lot of them." LGBTQ+ patrons do not always find straight people in their midst to be so delightful, however, and sometimes resent the ways management is perceived to cater to straight audiences who are increasingly drawn to drag performances—and on whom management often depends to balance the bottom line.[14]

Drag brunches, in particular, are cited for allowing straight folks who might not feel comfortable in a nightclub environment to experience live drag shows, not to mention the access to queer culture they give to LGBTQ+ folks with kids, who are sober, or disabled. As Jason Gilmore in Roanoke, Virginia, said of the weekend morning drag brunches at his bar The Park, "It's typically not a gay crowd. It's a lot of straight clientele that brings their grandmothers, brothers, sisters, wives. The grandmothers are the most fun, the absolute best. Why?" Cackling, he continued, "When you ask what she wants to drink? She wanted a blow job!"

Straight people may adore *RuPaul's Drag Race,* but academics are as ambivalent about it as are some queens. The Emmy-winning pro-duction has been critiqued for policing the boundaries of drag and thus changing what drag is.[15] The show explicitly limits what kinds of queens can compete: It long barred transgender people, cisgender women, and drag queens with facial hair. It still bars drag kings, who have their own distinct queer aesthetics,[16] and queens whose alt-drag styles are too far beyond those approved by the show's producers.[17] Queens and managers also noted that a televised drag show teaches patrons to be passive spectators and to expect more for less, and that girls who came up on Instagram don't embody the interactivity of a seasoned "show bar" performer.

Blanche was unequivocal about the show when she asked me "do you watch *RuPaul*? I HATE IT." Critiquing the stand-and-look-pretty attitude of girls raised on Instagram, she explained, "Our drag is not really that style of drag. That's great for TV, it's not great for a show bar. It's not interactive." With perhaps a touch of jealousy, she continued:

> Some of these queens that have won it were no-name queens when some of us have had to work our asses off! When I first start-ed working here, I worked two years for zero dollars. On the stage I earned $25 a show!

As she said, the easy fame has affected the hardworking queens' path-way to fame: "If you're not on *RuPaul's Drag Race*, it's a lot harder."

Many bar owners complained—some of them off the record—about the skyrocketing fees commanded by Ru girls to make appearances at their bars. To this I can attest as the faculty advisor of my college's undergraduate drag ball committee, which frequently brings two or more to small-town Ohio. The $6,000 invoices make my eyes water, and every year I ask the students, "Do you know how many Cleve-land queens you could get for that kind of money? All of them!"[18] This means that for many bars, such as C4 in Fayetteville, Arkansas, bring-ing in Ru girls is a once-a-year splurge even as other bars make them a staple of their lineups.

The show's politics have also been criticized for their treatment of Indigenous queens, fat contestants, and contestants of color, par-ticularly those who are Spanish speaking or Asian.[19] The show has contributed to a "celebrification" of drag that glamorizes individualistic commercialism over do-it-yourself craft,[20] garnering a fan base that often crosses over into cyberbullying, particularly of Black and Latinx queens.[21] This celebrification, and the ubiquity of Ru girl performances, prompt an ambivalent response from a gay bar lover in Los Angeles: "You can't go to any bar without one of them being there. It's difficult. I love it and hate it."

Missouri's Blanche DuBois shares with *RuPaul's Drag Race* a belief that there are positives to having boundaries for drag. She is disdainful of the alt-drag aesthetics that are uncommonly seen in the television show: "They're not illusionists, nuh-uh," describing with incredulity one local queen by comparing her to me: "She was as hairy as your bearded face in a dress and armpit hair as long as the hair on my head." Bearded queens are common in clubs but have not yet been seen on *RuPaul's Drag Race*.

Mikey, the drag show director of Lucy's in Johnstown, Pennsylvania, contrasted the impact of the show for the bar versus its impact on queens. "In terms of the business, it's positive," he claimed, but noted that "as an entertainer I think it's horrible. *RuPaul's Drag Race* is filmed ahead of time, they have filters, producers saying, 'Turn your head sideways.' I don't have those luxuries." As he continued "it puts out unrealistic expectations. I don't have $7,000 to drop on Swarovski crystals. I have $45 at Joann's Fabrics."

Several show directors also noted that newcomers to the drag scene sometimes expect too much, too soon based on expectations nurtured by the high-flying lives of Ru girls. Blanche emphasized that the point of drag should be gender illusion:

> Any person thinks they can do it now. Not everyone can do it! I had a brand-new queen who did not wear tights, no hose. Transsexual. She knocked on the bar door asking for $225! . . . Nooo. Not gonna happen.

The new queen asked, "What do you mean? I can charge whatever I want." Blanche acted out her reply, "Look in the mirror, baby! Do you know what this is? Right now you look like a boy in makeup." Cissexism is often rife, claims former gay bartender Alicia Randolph from

North Carolina, lambasting "all the gender dynamics, all the trans exclusion. Every person is a drag queen whether or not they are trans or actually in drag." But for Carl's the Saloon in Reno, Nevada, adding drag performance was interpreted as a welcome to the transgender community. "We got a lot of thank-yous," reported owner Ron "Bear" Swasek.

Changing attitudes have brought the broader straight community closer to the bar in other ways. As Blanche gathered up her things to prepare for her show, she remarked,

> I know this is kind of a sad note but it's a good note: When Orlando happened, the TV here, the newspaper here, bigger businesses here, got more interest into this bar, into the gay community here, to see what we're like. They talk to us more than they used to.

Indeed, for the local newspaper, the interviews with the staff of Independence Place after Pulse were the first times it had ever published the phrase "gay bar." Sailing off to the dressing room, Blanche declared, "Now they see us as part of the community. They see *this bar* as part of the community." Drag is fundamental to community in gay bars, and community is integral to gay bars. Increasingly, drag is a bridge between gay bars and the straight world on whose patronage they increasingly depend. And yet—people love drag but don't keep the bars that nourish them open. Talk about ambivalence.

Eight

Bars for People of Color and the Ambivalence of Racial Camp

Wang Chung's
HONOLULU, HAWAII

Certain forms of irreverent joy only flourish in spaces by and for queer people of color. There, racist tropes can be simultaneously mocked and mimicked, while at the same time anti-queer sentiments among communities of birth can be resisted. One way to name this razor-edged humor is *racial camp*.[1] Camp, that queerly excessive humor that delights in kitsch and bad taste, is usually assumed to be white despite people of color's foundational command of the aesthetic.[2] Building upon the argument that "Camp contains an explicit commentary on feats of *survival* in a world dominated by the taste, interests, and definitions of others," film scholar Susan Gubar writes that, "Racial camp hints that feats of survival occur through inauthentic mimicry that affronts the blatantly suspect arbiters of good taste."[3] Gay bars that allow these "feats of survival" to take center stage are thus special to racialized communities; gay bars that serve people of color are a fundamental type of gay bar. But such bars are also in peril, closing at a much faster clip than bars that serve white LGBTQ+ people—more than 60 percent faster—emphasizing their vulnerability even amidst their rarity. There were only forty-five of them in the whole country in 2021.[4]

One bar that illustrates both the pleasures and perils of racial camp is Wang Chung's of Honolulu, Hawaii, a metropolitan area of more than 800,000 people, the majority of them with Asian American and Pacific Islander (AAPI) heritage. Every bar here might be an Asian bar, unlike on the mainland with the rare gay bar maybe known pejoratively as a "rice" bar where white men fetishistically pursue AAPI gay men.[5] But few Asian bars are gay, even in Honolulu. So as an "Asian-inspired" karaoke bar, Wang Chung's celebrates an AAPI queerness usually erased or belittled in LGBTQ+ life, whether in liberal talk of "equality" or online cruising apps where "no Asians" is a commonly expressed racist "preference."[6]

In spoofing white racism, however, Wang Chung's may give permission to white patrons to reproduce anti-AAPI racism when they parrot its jokes out of context. Racial camp can also homogenize Asianness in ways that some might see as cultural appropriation of one Asian group by another. But then, the AAPI acronym itself homogenizes, lumping together groups with disparate histories: The experiences of immigrants from Asia are quite different from those of the colonized Native Hawaiian peoples, whose traditional respect for sexual and gender diversity often goes unrecognized.[7] Racial camp does the opposite of homogenization, however, exploding the differences between and among AAPI people, building bridges among them across diverse peoples through mutual insider understanding.[8] This raises the question of whether I, your white interviewer, can even get the joke—or whether you can either, if you're not AAPI.

Honolulu's diverse residents have propelled Wang Chung's to the top of lists of the state's best karaoke bars. Chinese American owner Danny Chang intended the bar to cater to visiting Japanese tourists when he opened in 2009. He hadn't considered opening a gay bar, he explained, because they were no longer essential: "I grew up in a generation when it was already okay to go out and mingle in non-gay spaces." The problem was that visiting Japanese tourists didn't want to visit a bar in America that reminded them of Japan.

Instead, Danny quickly realized that locals, tourists, and transient military personnel and flight crews made up the majority of his clientele, and they were the ones who gave his bar its reputation. As he recalled those early days, "Some of the bartenders were LGBT, but we never fully committed or labeled ourselves a gay bar." And besides, he recounted, "It was the mixed crowd that came in, that kept us going, though we did advertise back then in some gay magazines." Their reviews were gushing, as he remembered: "Oh my god, it's an Asian-inspired bar!"

Danny's Chinese family was against him opening the bar, and particularly his Vietnam-born mother. Laughing, he recounted,

> I was telling one of my cousins I was going to open a bar business, and *her* parents called *my* parents and my mom called me crying. The Asian guilt: "I raised you! I sacrificed!" I have a big extended family and they read about my bar on Yelp and it says, "Gay this" and "Gay that" but the reviews don't say anything about Chinese people.

Danny recalled what his brother had imparted at the time: "Yelp outed you long, long ago!"

The bar got its name in an irreverent application of Hawaiian slang:

> I didn't have a name for the bar when I was building it initially. When I was applying for the liquor license and building it out, I was texting my mainland friends, "Who's going out to wang chung tonight?" and they were like, "What's that?"

As Danny explained, the phrase comes from the name of an English new wave band famous in the United States for their song, "Everybody Have Fun Tonight": "I was born in the 80s, I love the 80s, it's become a verb here in Hawaii: 'Let's wang,' 'Everybody wang chung, everybody have fun tonight.' That's the inspiration." I asked if there'd been any legal issues of using a white-guy one-hit-wonder 80s band name as the name of his Asian-inspired gay bar, and Danny's eyes twinkled: "I *look* like a Wang Chung, right?" Danny thus delights in the campy humor of appropriating a white band's Chinese-language name and flirting with the way that non-Asian folks confuse AAPI people with each other, as mocked by the #wrongasian hashtag.

The logo for the bar, and much of its iconography inside the bar, draws upon Japanese culture, a choice that might be appropriative from a white owner but not, apparently, by a Chinese millennial, given that online reviews of the decor are unfailingly gushing. The bar's logo of a wide-cheeked Asian woman is an adaptation of a logo from a brand of *natto*, the fermented soybean snack that is popular in Japan but polarizing outside it. The wall features a large cut-out of the 1950s manga character Astro Boy augmented with a rainbow cape. The bar has also given out "misfortune cookies," with the little message inside reading "you will never be enough," mocking both the faux-Confuscian platitudes that charm white people and the harshness attributed to Asian parents. Beer coasters and giant wall prints feature a *maneki-neko*, the little white cat with red ears that signifies good luck in Japan, what Danny calls his "kitties." But here, instead of the traditional upraised paw, Wang Chung's kitties give the surfers' "hang loose" sign of an upraised fist with thumb and pinkie extended.

Where one gay Asian American man complained that white gay men have "neatly packed gay Asians into stereotypical takeout boxes," in 2018 for the Pride march, Danny dressed his staff up as literal walking Chinese takeout boxes that spelled out the bar's name.[9] And when I was there in 2019, an advertisement for Drag Brunch featured a gender-bending drag performer who appeared samurai from the neck down and geisha from the eyes up. The geisha/samurai advertisement playfully confronts two stereotypes often leveraged against AAPI people, addressing what C. Winter Han describes as the quandary facing LGBTQ+ Asian and Pacific Islander men: They are often seen as *either* gay *or* Asian, but not as both.[10] AAPI women often face the same quandary, a racist frame that presumes queerness is only white.[11] No one would mistake the geisha/samurai as anything but Asian *and* queer.

Some of the decor is edgier and wouldn't fly outside an AAPI-majority city where Japanese Americans are one of the most influential groups in the state: This humor is not punching down, at least in today's Honolulu.[12] A rainbow neon sign features the logo from Japanese snack Pocky, a running man with arms outraised in victory, but here he holds up a sign with the phrase "Aroha, beaches!" The phrase is in "Engrish," a usually racist slang term for the variations in pronunciation and word usage of English by East Asians. The neon sign plays off the difficulty of Japanese speakers in distinguishing between the "r" and "l" sounds and the way that they pronounce "i" with the long "ee" sound, warping "bitches." The neon sign is not a one-off: Wang Chung's used to sell t-shirts with the phrase on it.

"Aroha beaches" gave me pause. If Danny says it, it comes off as a loving ribbing of his relatives' accents. If a non-AAPI person like me says it, it sounds wildly racist. And then there are the Instagram selfies of white people grinning under the sign who are perhaps not fully aware of what they are endorsing: Loving queer AAPI people can itself be a sign of racism.[13] Danny described his identification with the people who speak in Engrish, explaining of the sign, "We do little things to put the Asian twist and make fun of ourselves. In Hawaii, that's what you do, it's such a big melting pot of different cultures, especially from the plantation days," citing the turn of the twentieth century in which agricultural laborers were imported to Hawaii, especially from Japan.[14] Danny quoted the song "Mr. Sun Cho Lee," called a "Hawaiian classic" on many blogs, which includes the line in Hawaiian Creole English: "One thing, I wen notice about dis place, all us guys we tease da other race."[15]

By making it clear that "aloha" is being said with an accent ("aroha"), it disrupts the tourist industry's commercialization of a Native Hawaiian concept that has been used to colonize their islands. Native Hawaiians are often coerced into "performing aloha" to make a living on land that was once theirs, taken by a country that does not recognize them.[16] "Aroha beaches" may then be mocking the U.S. appropriation of Native Hawaiian *aloha*. Or not. It may just be funny to Danny and his patrons.

Where I would worry about cultural appropriation when a Chinese American warps Japanese cultural objects, racial camp problematizes *me*, the good white progressive, as a "blatantly suspect" arbiter of good taste.[17] Under the sign of racial camp, "aroha beaches" is just an Asian twist upon the racist conflations that all Asians are the same, especially when it is so clear that it is "inauthentic mimicry" at play in Wang Chung's flamboyant, "Asian-inspired" decorations and its reclaiming name from an 80s pop band. If racial camp describes cultural practices that decenter whiteness, then it is also a reminder that the joke is not for white people to get—so they should probably steer clear of repeating it.

Another example of this edgy racial camp is in the sign at the door giving the rules for Wang Chung's. The rules themselves are perfunctory—21-and-over only, one-drink minimum, no outside food or drink—with flair only coming from the last one: "Drink, sing, be gay, be maarrry." But the poster is labeled "Mama san's rules," using the term American servicemen gave to the madam of a brothel, in a city that was a major staging point for U.S. military interventions in the Pacific. This continues a general gay male identification with—and sometime misogynist mocking of—female sex workers (such as calling each other "whores"). But here, the Asian twist adds a racialized sense of humor that might be seen as sexist on the mainland, or in a context where Japanese tourists aren't such an important part of the economy: Honolulu's public buses sport digital signs in Japanese. Indeed, when I asked Danny if he could be as playful with his branding if the bar was in the San Francisco Bay Area, a place he spends a lot of time, his answer was quick: "No way!" But, he concludes, "In Hawaii it works really well." Camp is not just historically situated, but geographically as well.[18]

Such geographically bound camp doesn't always translate to the broader patronage of the bar. Danny described an earlier menu themed around "*hanabada* days," the Hawaiian Creole English phrase for "back when we were snotty-nosed kids." As Danny explained the cocktails, "We did the flavors of what people were growing up with: green river drinks, and liquid passion fruit Lilikoi drink. There was salted plum, we did cocktails with that, and with pickled mango chili pepper water." I asked how it went and he shook his head:

> It was one of my worst-selling menus because even the people who live here didn't grow up with it, [and] the transplants didn't know. Turned out we were trying to target such a small niche. Locals and tourists will not buy any of that, it was nothing familiar. Just because I like it doesn't mean other people will like that. You always think that people will try things off the menu, but they order things that are familiar to them: Moscow Mule, Mai Tai, that's safe.

So while the Asian camp of "Aroha, bitches!" launched a line of t-shirts, some things, like flavors of drinks, can actually be *too* campy.

Danny attributed some of his business practices to emulating the owner-proprietor of Uncle Clay's House of Pure Aloha, a shaved ice stand. "When I first met him, everyone, he would greet you, talk to you, introduce you to someone else." This inspired Danny: "That's what I did at the old bar all the time. With anybody that came in, I would greet them, hug them, try to find something in common with them and introduce them to someone else." Indeed, Danny gave me a big hug upon meeting me and threw a beautiful orchid lei—my first ever—over my head. I was torn. I generally refused freebies from bar owners, despite their consistent generosity, but how to refuse such a welcome without seeming culturally offensive? While an earnest gesture of performing *aloha*, I'm sure, it was also an extravagant one.[19] Danny had me over a barrel, and the lei was already around my neck.

This was the bar's second location, but Danny was already plotting for his third move because the small bar was often at capacity. And in his edgy, self-deprecating way, when he drafted an expansion proposal, the title of his award-winning business pitch was "I want a bigger Wang." Danny's racial camp thus played with stereotypes about Asian penis size, one of the "failures" of white masculinity that haunt Asian American men.[20] Danny's racial camp thus takes racist tropes that constrain queer AAPI men and remixes them for humorous—and remunerative—purposes, creating a possibility for a partnership between straight white dollars and Asian gay lives.

Racial camp made me think of how unique it is to have a place like Wang Chung's, and how the famous gay bars that served AAPI people on the mainland had long since closed: N'Touch in San Francisco closed in 2006, and The Web in New York City closed around 2013.[21] It made me think of how special it is that there are Black-owned bars like the Jeffery Pub on the South Side of Chicago or the Latinx-owned New Jalisco Bar in downtown Los Angeles—places where drag queens can speak the way they do at home, in neighborhoods that *are* home.[22]

Glancing at his watch, Danny jumped up to run to another appointment. Without allowing me to ask him to spell out what he meant by "a bigger Wang," he gave me a very Wang Chung's, very ambiguous, and somewhat campy one-off: "Gay bars as we know them are dying because they're evolving. Bye!"

But surely, I can hear many white readers asking: Haven't we left behind those days when Black patrons were asked for multiple forms of identification, or when bars refused to accept Latinx patrons' documents issued by foreign governments?[23] The occasional headlines documenting these continuing practices testify that no, we haven't, and illustrate the protective reason why people of color need their own queer spaces beyond letting their unique cultural forms flourish.[24] While nearly all of the white bar professionals told me their patronages were racially diverse, white people are notoriously bad at estimating the racial climate of a room.[25] Of all my interviewees, Todd Howard of Escafé (Charlottesville, Virginia) confessed, "Candidly, the people that we have the most trouble with are white people. Those are the ones that have some sense of entitlement." Many white owners looked at me blankly when I asked how many of their staff—besides security—were people of color. Even among bars that claim a kind of colorblind racial neutrality, DJs continue to refuse to play reggaeton or hip hop, and bouncers look askance at headscarves and do-rags— what Reuben Buford May calls "velvet rope racism."[26]

Because they are populated by white people, bars facilitate experiences for people of color that are often unwelcoming at best—when they're not downright hostile. I'm thinking of the drunken white man who kept throwing gang signs at my Black partner from across what had been, until that evening, my favorite gay bar: The bartender dismissed it as harmless. Or it brings to mind the bar that basically encouraged blackface by handing out masks with Rihanna's face on them for its majority-white patrons. Then there's the bar owner I interviewed who called her Indigenous bartender "my little Indian princess," or the time when a conversation with an Asian American friend at A Man's World was interrupted by a passing white gay man singing, "ching-chong, ching-chong!" These are the racist things that I witnessed in the presence of racialized people; I'm not even counting the racist conversations that white people have in their absence, which I describe elsewhere in this book.

Gay bars that center Latinx and Black folks likely employ their own forms of racial or ethnic camp, their own ways of dancing and moving and humor and politics. My undergraduate research assistants only identified forty-five gay bars serving primarily people of color in the entire country in 2021. And some of those bars, identified as they are in guidebooks that mainly serve white readers, are no doubt less celebratory spaces than sexual marketplaces that facilitate hookups between white people and people of color. This means those places that can celebrate racial camp are rare and special indeed.

Gay bars by and for folks of color are rare and becoming rarer; this explains the special pleasures, for LGBTQ+ people of color, of the occasional parties or monthly events that feature Black or Latin or Bollywood music.[27] Such queer pop-up parties may seem new to some observers, but they have long been among the only moments of public queer communion for LGBTQ+ people of color.[28] But even in big cities, you're lucky if there's more than one night a month to let loose and let go in a space that feels safe.

Such club nights and bars, describes Ramón Rivera-Servera, offer

a space to experience what freedom from homophobia, and sometimes from racism, feels like. The club also provides me with spaces where experiences of discrimination can be addressed and exorcised in the company of others who, like me, understand the at times difficult and pleasurable path of being a queer of color.[29]

At Wang Chung's, Danny's racial camp both refuses and embraces those two stereotypes that haunt Asian American—those of being forever foreigners or model minorities—posing a future without such preconceptions by staging something new and edgy in the present.[30]

Certain things only become possible when there is a critical mass of *your* people: the head nods of acknowledgment and the sense that someone might have your back if things go sour, a flirty conversation with someone who doesn't ask "What are you?" or "Where are you *from*?" and instead wants to know where you're going. The importance of those particular moments, those ruptures, where one of *your* songs plays. And people like you rush the floor and suddenly, for a moment, the club has become *for* people like you.[31] Then certain kinds of humor and resistance and celebration and glamor become possible, and the world is made that much more livable.[32]

Nine

There Are Easier Ways to Make a Buck in the Big City than a Big Nightclub

Club Cobra and Club Chico
LOS ANGELES, CALIFORNIA

By 2018 I had interviewed over forty gay bar owners and managers, getting a handle on their business realities and hopes and dreams. But I hadn't interviewed the owner of a big nightclub in a coastal city with a big dance floor: Dancing is a queer survival strategy and is fundamental to understanding gay bars.[1] Nor had I been to many bars that served the queer and trans BIPOC community. And I couldn't forget the skepticism leveled at me by my academic colleagues who doubted that the business models of bars and clubs in the "great cities" of New York, San Francisco, Chicago, and Los Angeles would bear any relation to those in small cities in the American interior.[2] So in Greater Los Angeles, my research assistant Jack Spector-Bishop found the perfect places: one bar and one nightclub that shared the same ownership and staff and that were regionally famous for serving Latinx patrons. The insights of these owners and staff were echoed by those of other dance clubs, whether Club FAB in Fresno, California, or Paradise in Asbury Park, New Jersey.

What I learned was that there are more continuities in the business models than divergences between big-city and small-city bars. Gay bars in big cities are still small businesses, ones that few people recognize are not rational investments: owners derive as much meaning from providing community as they do from any profits. I also learned that running a big dance club brings special risks and considerations. But whether in cities big or small, to keep the party going and the safer spaces open, owners have to keep an eye on the bottom line, train and manage their staff, and keep their finger to the stiff winds of change.

Why own a small gay bar or a big nightclub when you can own one of each, especially if they're the kind of special clubs that cater to queer people of color? Marty Sokol and Julio Licón are titans of Los Angeles nightlife, childhood friends who became business partners. Club Chico came first in 1999. It was the first, and was long the only, gay bar in Latinx-dominated East Los Angeles—the bar, in the suburb of Montebello, was just outside LA city limits.[3] Chico drew a mix of neighborhood "cholos," "homies," and "queerdos," especially to the long-running monthly punk-drag sCUM party that garnered national attention for its unique Latinx queer aesthetic and politics, the "Spanish-language queer punk party of your dreams."[4]

Marty and Julio opened Club Cobra in 2006 in North Hollywood, making it the oldest (and, for many years, the only) gay Latinx nightclub in the region, famous for its sexy go-go boys, celebrity sightings, and "drag show en Español."[5] The bars, separated by twenty-two miles and on either side of traffic-snarled downtown Los Angeles, both feature the Spanish-language music so rare in LGBTQ+ spaces, ranging from reggaeton to bachata to rock.[6] Both also offer an alternative to the more homogeneous scene in West Hollywood, the famous gayborhood that is also famously white.[7] Club Cobra also hosts Transfix, the longest running and only trans-run party for transgender people and their admirers in Southern California, "a one-of-a-kind event that gave transgender people a space to earn a living, be celebrated, and grow."[8]

My assistant Jack Spector-Bishop sat down with Marty in 2018 to reflect on his two decades in the nightlife business:

> We've had a lot of things that have happened here over twenty years, and it's a good business, an honest business. But I'll be

honest with you. I could've taken the money and made a lot more money doing other things with it.

This echoed what other owners reported, including those who had direct experience managing straight bars as well: Gay bars make less money, so rather than maximizing profit, owners also place a personal value on the creation of community. As Marty remarked, "Yes, I make a nice living, but it's wonderful to have other sources of income; however, there are easier ways to make a buck is what I'm trying to say."

Marty described a "night and day" transformation from when he and business partner Julio Licón had opened Chico in East Los Angeles back in the late 90s, recalling getting eggs and epithets hurled at him on a regular basis: "That hasn't happened in fifteen, twenty years." Marty recalled other signs of the changing times: the police harassment the club faced over its transgender night eleven years earlier that targeted the women for suspected prostitution or nudity, scrutiny that was not leveled at straight clubs during that time. Marty said such persecution was "unimaginable" today. Shaking his head, he said "to me, there's very little difference between 2007 and 2018, but there actually is a huge difference. Things have changed in such a short amount of time."

These changes had only accelerated recently. "The gay bar business has changed radically in the last ten years," Marty asserted. "Gay people don't need to go to a gay bar anymore. The world has changed." They may not *need* gay bars, but they still *want* Cobra (a nightclub that provides Latinx dancing culture) and Chico (a bar with a stage for edgy Latinx performance art) in a vast county that is nearly one-half Latinx. But these were only strategies of the moment, with Marty explaining, "We are malleable to the times, we've had to be fluid." As Marty stated firmly, "There's room in our community for gay nightlife."

Marty was emphatic that the changes have not dented business—it was just that "people don't look at a gay bar anymore the way they used to." Part of this was an influx of straight people: "It has not gotten worse, it has gotten better, it's just less gay." He contrasted the market for gay bars with the "tense" market for straight bars, given virtual alternatives to physical socializing. As he noted, "People are not coming here to drink. It's cheap to stay home, with a six pack, or a bottle of whatever, and put on Netflix." Here he was explicit: The screens that have captivated our attention are not just Grindr and Lex, but the golden age of streaming television as well.

According to Marty, smartphone dating apps had clobbered the club business upon their debut, an effect that seemed to have waned: "It was a noticeable drop-off difference. That has since changed." It was hard to disentangle apps' effects from the lingering Great Recession of 2008–09, the same year Grindr debuted, the first of the smartphone hookup apps. Marty recalled, "We hung on and white-knuckled it through," citing a severe dip in business until 2014. He observed that a change in patrons' smartphone behavior coincided with an economic upturn by around 2015: "I don't even see people using their apps in the clubs the way I used to." Miming a zombie staring down at a screen, he continued, "I used to see people walking around doing this, right? But now I don't even see it anymore." He speculated that this may be because of a change in the popularity of various platforms that allow more personal interactions through content and direct messages (DMs). "I think it's moving away from the hookup apps and maybe finding a happy medium on, say, Instagram, with people DMing, right?" Here Marty may have been verifying his speculations with the young person at hand, an undergraduate whom he presumed was a "digital native" to the world of DMs and hookup apps—in this case correctly, as Jack was conducting his own research on gay men's sexual experiences that became a bang-up honors thesis.

The changing world has changed Chico and Cobra:

A gay nightclub now needs to be more diverse for a number of reasons. Back in the day you would never see straight people in a gay bar. Now you always see straight people in the gay bar. And that's fine. It's not our core business, but we have to make room for it because it really could, does, make up 20 percent of the night.

These new straight patrons were surprisingly indistinguishable from the old gay ones: "Maybe their sexual preferences and maybe their sexual fluidity has changed. I don't believe the patrons themselves have changed." All the patrons came for the same upbeat, safe, fun time, regardless of sexual orientation.

This meant that although there were no problems with straight men in the club, he did see things that concerned him regarding straight women.

> When the lights come up at 3 am, nine nights out of ten there's gonna be a girl, a straight girl, standing right in the middle of the dance floor, holding her shoes, drunk. She's come with her friends, but they've all ditched her.

The problem? "I can tell you there are one, two, three, four, five guys, not gay, who are watching her and waiting for her." He was quick to qualify:

> I'm not saying we're known for that 'cause we're not, but I'm watching at the end of the night, and we'll usually have security escort these girls out, because it's not a place to be alone drunk at the end of the night.

Nodding thoughtfully, he added, "And you know, you'd think guys can take care of themselves too, but trust me they get in trouble too. Not often, but it happens." There are predatory men everywhere, one of the ways in which masculinity is toxic.

Increased diversity at Cobra and Chico was also racialized. "Our brand was always core Latino. That was our brand. We were the first Latino gay club in LA." The increased patronage by non-Latinx white, Black, and Asian revelers, Marty explained, "is more a sign of the times than through design." As he explained, "We would have been happy to stay closer to the brand, but that's not what happened with our community." In the nightlife industry of a big city where competition abounds, the bar for queer and trans people of color is a "brand," a word I had previously associated with mercenary exploitation but, in Marty's hands, was interchangeable with the warm feeling of community. Whether "brand" or "community" or both, however, at Club Chico and Club Cobra, every night was Latin Night, celebrating the bodies and aesthetics of the people who make up about half of LA's population but who have very few 24/7 gay bars of their own—maybe five out of twenty-two.

The rise of apps and virtual businesses have disadvantaged brick-and-mortar ones. Marty said that patrons didn't understand "the high cost of running a high-risk business," arguing that "if you took a half a million dollars and invested it into a virtual business with no brick and mortar and no overhead, you'd make a lot, you'd do a lot better with no risk, right?" Marty explained, "This is a high-risk business. You have alcohol, you have dark, and you have movement all at once. And none of those are a good combination." These engendered costs patrons never see directly: "We spend hundreds of thousands of dollars per year on liability insurance. They don't understand that the state levies, for example, we pay a dance floor tax, and a cabaret tax." That didn't count sales taxes:

> In California we're at a 10.5 percent sales tax, which means I'm paying almost 25 percent before I've done anything to the state just for the right to be in business. Forget the Feds, you're at almost 50 percent before you put a key in the door, that is, before you pay rent, before you've paid the federal. So if your Fed taxes you 50 percent, and the state taxes 50 percent, what's left?

Such costs vary by city and state, making running gay bars across jurisdictions a challenge and giving deep-pocketed chain restaurants an edge in providing cocktails in the suburbs ringing a big city like LA. Marty didn't begrudge patrons' blissful ignorance, however: "It's not their responsibility to see it. It's our responsibility to make sure that we are giving them, the customer, an experience that makes them see that $10 cover is worthwhile to them." Unseen expenses are part of any business' sleight-of-hand of providing seamless products and services, but they are perhaps even more invisible—because more resented—in places that patrons describe as "home" or a "safe space."

Like other owners, Marty described plentiful, trained staff as key to managing these risks. Chico and Cobra share a pool of over thirty employees, meaning one person's mistake puts many livelihoods in jeopardy: Let in one underage kid or permit one patron to get out of hand, and a liquor license suspension puts everyone out of work.[9] As Marty explained, "We're very fortunate and we have a great security staff. But it's a lot of keeping your tabs on a hundred thousand different moving parts at the same time." Marty noted that many of his staff have been with them from the beginning, something relatively uncommon in the nightlife business. Being an old hand doesn't mean not needing to stay updated on new trends, however:

> Your staff better be fresh, your team better be on point. You ask what's difficult? Security, being present but not being in your face, very important. It's really caring for the customer with white gloves. That's the most difficult thing to do.

Longtime business principles still hold, despite changes in the gay bar market, because "people are pretty much people." Switching into teacher mode, he asked Jack, "You know the Pareto rule, right? It's called the 80–20 rule: In business, 80 percent of your business comes from 20 percent of your customers." Who are Cobra's 20 percent then? asked Jack. Marty replied, "They're here, present, two to three times a week," adding, "Those are the people you really want to take care of, that's your bread and butter right there."

Cultivating a community feeling among the 80 percent is a way to draw them in, too: "It's not just a party. It's about community," Marty averred.[10] Marty cited the public health mission of being a not-quite-for-profit enterprise: "We have free HIV testing; if you get HIV tested outside you get in for free." Another promotion aimed to reduce drinking and driving: "If you take an Uber or a Lyft, we give you ten bucks back at the door to spend at the bar." Jack asked what it was that drew these people to the clubs, even occasionally. Marty was matter-of-fact:

> Humanity. I don't even think it's the gay humanity, it's just humanity. Because again, anywhere you wanna drink it's cheaper to drink, certainly cheaper than at a nightclub. So you must be coming here for another reason than alcohol.

Keeping patrons connected to the "greater us" is part of Chico and Cobra's virtual offerings. Marty and Julio employ a staff photographer to populate their Instagram feeds with pictures of revelers and sexy dancers. The clubs launched a podcast in 2019, *Homo Homie*, to "be an extension of his clubs and provide a voice for Gay Latinos particularly from neighborhoods that were traditionally underrepresented."[11]

These digital offerings proved prescient during the COVID-19 pandemic. Drawing upon the "greater us" of the Chico–Cobra family, the bars launched a non-nude variety show on OnlyFans to be what Marty called a "party in a box."[12] It showcased the gyrations of their dancers and showgirls, updates from their bartenders, and drag queen performances. This allowed staff to make some money during the decimation of the nightlife industry, but it also kept patrons engaged—the channel was in the top 10 percent of OnlyFans pages.[13]

When Marty and Julio announced that the clubs would not reopen due to the pandemic, there was an outpouring of grief and support, with patrons and journalists decrying the loss of two of Greater LA's only Latinx clubs. Unexpectedly, the duo reversed their decision. As Marty told a journalist, "Our backs were against the wall. We were forced into collapsing or building, and we built."[14] Club Cobra reopened on its main site with a complete remodel, meaning North Hollywood's big Latinx nightclub survived. Chico left its permanent home in East LA, on the other hand, to take up residence as a once-a-week party in a gayborhood nightclub—the kind of pop-up party that LGBTQ+ people of color have long had to settle for.[15] This represented a loss of gay bars in Latinx-majority East LA and their concentration in the West Hollywood gayborhood. Club Cobra's success shows that Latinx people still need a big nightclub, a place to dance and be free in the metropolis. The survival of the Club Chico "brand," but only as a once-weekly party in the gayborhood, illustrates the possibilities that gay neighborhoods offer for gay bar community—but also their limitations, and it is to gay bars in the gayborhood that we now turn.

Ten

Queer Spaces in the Gayborhood

insideOUT
SAN DIEGO, CALIFORNIA

Gay bars are fundamental anchors of gay neighborhoods, and no tour of gay bars would be complete without gay bars in the gayborhoods that are often assumed to be their natural habitat.[1] To explore how gayborhood bars were different from outposts and others, I wangled an invitation to a conference tangential to my profession just to have an excuse to visit San Diego, the country's eighth-largest city and home to Hillcrest, one of California's gayborhoods. What I found is that gayborhoods permit a specialization of gay bars—by fostering lesbian bars, bars for older LGBTQ+ folks, and unabashedly "queer" spaces that refuse categorization even as bars.

On Halloween evening 2021, I sat on the outdoor patio of Barrel & Board, Hillcrest's new "woman-forward" wine bar and restaurant recently opened by employees of Gossip Grill, the only lesbian bar in Southern California. For an Ohioan, sitting outdoors on the cusp of November was a luxury, but the outdoor heaters were welcome if not strictly necessary. The costumed revelers streaming down the sidewalk at dusk marked the gayborhood as the epicenter of the city's public festivities. Halloween is *the* gay high holy day. It's long been a gateway to drag and was historically the only day that crossdressing wasn't punished by law—San Diego's ordinance was only repealed in 1998.[2] As I picked at my charcuterie, a muscled white man in a skin-tight Green Arrow superhero costume solicited "hey boyyyys" as he passed in a costume that left little, including his religious leanings, to the imagination. A gaggle of white men wearing sexy cow outfits stumbled past, their abs gleaming behind Holstein spots. One caught my eye and shrieked at me and the butch lesbians on the patio: "Happy Halloween! Welcome to Hillcrest!"

Hillcrest is an LGBTQ+ village for its diverse residents, yes, but also suburban day-trippers, crosstown partygoers, gawkers, and tourists alike.[3] It is a middle-class residential neighborhood cut through by a one-mile east–west commercial strip along University Avenue that trails south down Fifth Avenue. It is anchored on the east by the nonprofit LGBT center and a plaza flying a giant rainbow flag; the western edge is Urban MO's, a longtime gay bar and restaurant whose business model of drag and grilled food belies its origins as a onetime location of Hamburger Mary's, the nation's only gay bar/restaurant chain. Hillcrest includes massive gay nightclubs like Rich's, youthful karaoke spots like Flick's, and The Merrow—a not-strictly-gay live-music club that hosts queer pop-up events that include goth nights, queer kink demonstrations, and karaoke ranging "from Sinatra to Dua Lipa." While the gayborhood streetscape is fairly diverse, the clientele of most of the bars was, like the Holstein twinks on Halloween, mostly white non-Latinx gay men, despite San Diego's role as a border city and gateway to the United States for many Mexican LGBTQ+ people.[4]

The gayborhood may not be as welcoming to all as its promoters believe. Friend-of-a-friend T.J. Tallie agreed to describe their hometown to me as a longtime local and fellow academic. They described the gayborhood as a place where being fat and Black means always being out of place and in the way. They recalled a party that celebrated "Dads I'd like to fuck," or DILFs: "I was at the Rail and it was some sort of night, a DILF night or a daddy night, and there was some sort of comment about how it was open for everybody." While this might be true for some older guys, T.J. scoffed:

Everybody at the bar who was dancing all looked the same, the same version of a white man you would see in porn. They were all muscled, they had the same mustache, and they were allowed five pounds of fat.

I asked T.J. why go to Hillcrest then, and they replied: "It is a space that can be useful. It is nice to have access to things, queer spaces to go, but at the same time it's nowhere as liberatory or frankly as interesting as its prominent boosters imagine."

My conversation with T.J. took place in North Park, a more affordable and racially diverse neighborhood, a vision of what a gayborhood might look like if it wasn't mostly white. We had breakfast at The Mission, only one mile due east of insideOUT, but a world away. North Park is not awash in rainbow flags, but Héctor Carrillo described it as having an "emerging, vibrant, and distinctive Latino gay ethnic culture."[5] This emerged amid businesses that testified to the diversity of people who shared North Park—from Black beauty stores advertising lace-front wigs and Chinese medicine emporiums to signs of gentrification, including slick cafés, a "canine country club," and an advertisement exhorting passersby to build tiny homes in their backyards. Such racial and economic diversity meant white people had trouble recognizing it as a nascent gayborhood, a term that is basically only deployed when it is white LGBTQ+ people who congregate.[6]

Hillcrest also includes insideOUT, the only gay bar in the city helmed by a transgender woman of color, general manager Paris Quion. Except don't call insideOUT a gay bar: "It's a queer space," explained Paris, citing the term preferred by many as an explicit welcome to transgender people and a signal of progressive politics. As she continued, she rejected the bar designation as well:

I didn't want to get pigeonholed as a bar or as a restaurant. It's a multispace. Yes, you can come in for drinks. Yes, for dinner. Yes, for your board meeting, totally. It's got that flexibility. I took away the words "bar" or "restaurant."

She swept a graceful braceleted arm across the elegant space. "Wording is really important," she affirmed, for creating a broadly inclusive space.

insideOUT occupies the first floor and interior open-sky atrium of an über-modern cluster of red-towered condos that are directly around the corner from the San Diego LGBT Community Center, which anchors the eastern edge of the gayborhood. The interior is a stylish, glittering space of polished concrete and designer light fixtures that seamlessly give way to the courtyard adorned with a pond, patio umbrellas, and lush tropical foliage. Tables are scattered along a switchback walkway up to a patio area that looks down on it all, dotted with outdoor space heaters. The multiracial, tattooed staff wear sexy brown leather harnesses over their crisp shirts, and the menu is a fusion of Californian, Mediterranean, and Asian flavors.

insideOUT is part of a gay bar hospitality group (MO's) of six gay-owned-and-run restaurants, bars, and clubs. Banding together and specializing is one way to save gay bars. Mo's holdings included my Halloween dining perch Barrel & Board and its then-neighbor, Salad To-Go-Go, both proudly flying LGBTQ+ flags.[7] Urban MO's is the mothership, a "hetero-friendly" restaurant that serves up cocktails, *RuPaul's Drag Race* watch parties, and live performances.[8] The group also includes Baja Betty's: a Mexican restaurant open to queer people of all ages that proved a revelation to a gay Mexican friend when he was 19 years old, too young for the bar scene but agog at an interior that was "So gay, full of gay people." Like Baja Betty's, insideOUT thus illustrates the importance of restaurants, and cafés, to providing LGBTQ+ spaces for underage queer folks and their friends and families. Down the street, the Hillcrest Brewing Company (another MO's holding) advertises itself as the "first gay brewery in the world," and its freezers provide storage space for Gossip Grill, whose pink neon "Welcome home, beautiful" sign is only a block away, beckoning patrons of one of the country's last twenty-odd lesbian bars.

This kind of specialization among gay bars is only possible in bigger cities, but especially in gayborhoods where individual clubs can attract enough patrons from slices of the LGBTQ+ community to be viable. Some of these slices are demographic: Most lesbian bars are in cities with gayborhoods, including San Diego's own Gossip Grill (though owner Moe Girton will correct you—it's a "women's bar"). Cruisy men's bars usually only happen in cities with multiple gay bars, even if the bars themselves are often outside the gayborhood, as San

Diego's Pecs and The Eagle are beyond Hillcrest. And self-identified and unabashed "queer spaces" like insideOUT similarly only appear in big cities and never as outposts.

The gay bars outside gayborhoods draw attention to the many other LGBTQ+ scenes that have always been beyond the gayborhood, especially the house parties and rented halls that often constitute the most vibrant social scenes for LGBTQ+ people of color.[9] And bars can serve different groups throughout the day.[10] I went to another bar, The Loft, for happy hour, where a spry retiree served me a slice of his birthday cake in the early afternoon before the crowd gave way to guys in their 30s and 40s after work, who were themselves replaced by younger men later in the evening.

In the country at large, however, gay bars are mostly scattered across the landscape in ones and threes, and they are special because they're the only public place you can reliably find other gay people. This isn't true in cities with gayborhoods like Seattle, Oklahoma City, or Wilton Manors, Florida. In these special havens, the entire street-scape becomes queer for those who can read the signals:[11] Hillcrest's hardware store sells "Yaaassss Queen" throw pillows, the streetside garbage cans demand that society "End intersex surgery," and there are rainbow crosswalks. Gay people are in every café, just tapping away on their laptops! Lesbians are in the grocery store, selecting produce! Trans people are laughing on the sidewalk as they chat on their phones! And when LGBTQ+ people are everywhere, just living, then everyone is possibly pansexual: That pastor? The old lady pulling her granny cart? Those teens? That homeless man? Which is to say— people on the sidewalk enliven gay neighborhoods, even as white middle-class gays are often irritated by poor or BIPOC individuals whom they rarely read as queer and thus demand be removed from "their" space.[12]

In gayborhoods, then, bars are anchors, but not the entirety, of the queer scene.[13] Bus shelters feature ads from the FBI about reporting hate crimes. Rainbows are in windows everywhere: in the hardware store, at the sushi restaurant, the mattress discounter, the chain coffee shop. A salon's ad offers "let us blow you," a diner is called Breakfast Bitch, and the independent bookstore is named for the feminist intellectual Bluestockings.

Paris is a formidable presence in San Diego, and not just because she's the general manager of insideOUT. She told me she "flowed into business" from a background in community work and performance, but she was downplaying her community impact. She serves on the board of San Diego LGBT Pride, which reports her biography as a "Drag entertainer, nightlife personality, community activist and business owner."[14] She was one of nine drag queens named "legendary" in an exhibit of the San Diego History Museum, alongside hometown girl RuPaul herself.[15] She is well known for her activism: helming fundraisers, providing gender-identity training for city and county workers, speaking to high school and college students, and liaising with government agencies.[16] Of her vision for insideOUT, Paris recalled, "My personal goal as general manager and partner was I wanted it to be very representative, so that everyone sees themselves in the space."

Paris described public relations as one of the ways she ensures a diverse and queer clientele. "Our marketing is showing every kind of person." Where pundits worry that social media is eroding gay bars, Paris uses it as a tool to curate an inclusive insideOUT:

> If I would scroll through our Instagram, I would think, "I can go here." No matter what ethnicity, gender expression, sexual orientation, anything, that "yes, oh God, our friends are going to be fine, let's go."

Her focus on gender is deliberate: "I wanted to make sure that our lesbian sisters and bulldyke friends know this is your space too, this isn't just for men, but also to let my trans girlfriends know: 'Come, you're very safe here.'" Paris laughed, affirming insideOUT's role as a safe space:

> We look like the perfect commercial that every big business hopes for when they want those very multicultural diverse commercials, and we didn't have to do anything directly. They just came on their own. That was the best outreach we could do, without pandering.

Paris was unambivalent about insideOUT's welcome of straight people: "We do welcome straight people, yes. We're going to have a bachelorette party—but we're also going to buy you shots!" She attributes this welcome of straight allies to the gayborhood itself: "I'm very proud of Hillcrest for that. I've been very grateful to travel the country for entertainment, but a lot of gay neighborhoods weren't as welcoming to allies." She cited allies as key to the longevity of the business, laughing cheekily: "I don't consider you allies. You're family. You just happen to love differently from how we do!"

Without my prompting, however, Paris reported there was community uneasiness about Hillcrest's welcome of straight people. Some customers ask her, "Aren't you afraid of losing our queer spaces?" Shaking her head, Paris countered, "Our allies, they're keeping our queer spaces open with their money and support and presence! The only problems are when they don't respect our spaces, and that's one in three million." Gesturing to the door and deviating from her own "queer space" branding for the space, she continued, "And that gets checked real quick. Move on. Another bar will enjoy your company."

Straight people have long been key to maintaining LGBTQ+ spaces, even more so now that queer people feel comfortable socializing anywhere. Paris shook her head at the very premise of the question of preserving queer space for queers. "I hope that conversation filters out soon. No. I want: 'You love queer people? Come sit right here next to me. All good.'" Her strategy, when LGBTQ+ patrons comment on straight patrons, is to effuse, "Isn't it great?" But, she acknowledges, "They're bringing it up out of concern." This is a concern she does not share because "These people come in knowing full well it's a LGBTQ place. Ninety-five percent of my staff is queer, and they see me right at the front door. I highly doubt they're coming here with ill intent." Thus while gay patrons may fear a straight takeover, owners and managers see a way to thread the needle between profitability and community.

Paris cited hiring practices as one of the ways that a space like insideOUT stays queer. "It's the spirit of the place. It doesn't take 8,000 rainbow flags or saying on the door, 'gay gay gay gay *gay*' that you know it is a gay space." This is probably truer in a gayborhood where the default expectation is that a place is gay, though, and certainly insideOUT's idiosyncratically capitalized name draws attention to the über-gay metaphor of coming out of the closet. Rather than flags, Paris claimed, insideOUT is queer because of the people who staff it: "It's who we are, as people. It's what our staff brings in their personalities." She recounted how one of her employees came from a background in the Black church but had gained self-confidence by working at insideOUT:

> Being a gay person, he was worried that he was being a little too loud or in your face about it, and I'm like, "No, absolutely not. Be as gay as you want. There's no toning it down when you come in here, be the person you want to be today. Let's do it, babe!"

Gay bars thus change their employees as much as their patrons, and indeed offer a key employment opportunity for those who are fabulously camp or butch.

Between the staff and the social media feeds, insideOUT's marketing is itself very queer. As Paris explained,

> Everyone knows our essence and spirit. Our marketing has the spirit of queer people within. You add that extra sparkle, that extra light, that extra laughter. Our guests holding hands or looking into each other's eyes.

She added that she often asks patrons if she can take pictures of them for social media: "That's the only good way to keep it as community-based as possible but also still welcoming to our friends. I feel a little like a paparazzi but don't mind me!" Social media sometimes replaces LGBTQ+ places, but sometimes it advertises them.

insideOUT is defined in relation to its sister businesses in the MO's Universe Restaurant Group. Of her sister establishments, Paris explained, "We have multiple playgrounds—like MO's and Gossip—where the rowdier crowd goes to get wasted, to party, to have the loud DJ music and *go in*." What was missing, both in Hillcrest and in the hospitality group, was

> something for the adults, for the gayborhood. It's nice to have our nightclubs, like Rich's and Uptown, but it was much needed to have a place for queer people who want to have a conversation—or an interview like this—and be able to talk.

Indeed, I myself struggle to hear in places with a lot of ambient noise, one of the reasons I feel isolated in loud nightclubs, so my middle-aged ears appreciate a place that is upbeat but where conversations are audible. Older people, folks with impaired hearing, and those who want a quieter space with food need gay bars too. Given the ageism that is pervasive in LGBTQ+ spaces, and my own graying beard, having a place where the patrons don't care that I don't know how to use Instagram or TikTok is refreshing.[17]

The queer space of insideOUT, Paris noted, "Was crafted. The music is at a certain level, the ambience of the events that we host aren't nightclub events. We'll do cabaret shows but more jazz singers, not so much go-go dancers." As she recalled, "I didn't care to do drag shows because I myself started in entertainment. I didn't want people to think that Paris is opening this restaurant so it's going to be a drag bar." Laughing, she conceded, "But when I started needing the fundraisers in the gay world, well, when you need a fundraiser you call a drag queen!"

insideOUT embodies many of the contemporary trends in gay bars, for all that Paris and her team brand it as a "queer space." It offers a full menu where alcohol isn't the only specialty beverage available. It embraces the breadth and depth of the LGBTQ+ community, reaching far beyond white cisgender gay men. And it embraces straight allies not merely as begrudging contributors to the bottom line but as family.

But it is also a high-end aesthetic experience that is a barrier to poor people. This is not only through the fact that the "simple breakfast" costs over $12. The sleek ambience and solicitous service can make those accustomed to greasy spoons uncomfortable. What is a luxurious comfort to some is an off-putting discomfort to others, even if upscale margins are necessary to pay rents in a marquee location in an expensive neighborhood of one of the nation's most expensive coastal states. The menus and websites are also only in English, in a county that is one-third Hispanic, another possible barrier to broader inclusivity.

A queer space that is also an elegant restaurant may be a hothouse orchid that needs the protective panes of Hillcrest to flourish: a critical mass of LGBTQ+ people, both residents and day-trippers, and the gracious, affluent—and perhaps self-congratulating—allies. Or could a queer-helmed and -staffed "space" flourish anywhere? Certainly, in small cities without gay bars, I occasionally saw restaurants and cafés featuring small rainbow stickers reading "Y'all means all." Every Starbucks and bookstore seemed to have its queer or queer-friendly staff, often the only ones I could see. And in Middle America, where the appetite for high-end cuisine is less capacious, it may be that only in these smaller, more age-accessible establishments can something like queer space flourish.[18] But some smaller cities *do* have gay bars, and it is to those lone outposts of LGBTQ+ space that we turn next.

Eleven

Small-City Gay Bars and the Only Gay in the Village

Studio 13 and Belle's Basix
THE CORRIDOR: IOWA CITY AND
CEDAR RAPIDS, IOWA

Being the only gay in the village is a fundamental state of being for many gay bars, not just in some cities, but many counties and some states as well. We often imagine gay bars clustered in gayborhoods, but the most common type of gay bar is one that's alone in its city. In 2019, for example, there were ninety-three cities with only one gay bar. But these bars are more similar to one another than you might expect given their vast geographic spread. Unlike gayborhood gay bars that can specialize in serving one slice of the community, lone gay bars are generalists, serving all the Ls, Gs, Bs, Ts, and Qs. They are often crucial outposts of LGBTQ+ culture that draw people from all over their often-conservative regions, catalyzing LGBTQ+ activism and celebrations that bring a cosmopolitan flair to their cities and regions but on their own terms, not those dictated by the gay meccas.[1] They are also surprisingly connected to the other gay bars in their regions and deeply integrated with straight people and their broader communities.[2]

* Chapter co-authored with Tory Sparks.

For example, when the 75,000 people of Iowa City celebrate Pride, they do it around the corner from Studio 13, the city's only gay bar. Together with Belle's Basix forty minutes up the highway in Cedar Rapids, the two bars comprise the public queer scene of The Corridor, as that part of eastern Iowa is known. Studio 13 shares a building and business owner with the Yacht Club in a stately red-brick building right downtown near the edge of the University of Iowa's campus. The Yacht Club—a half mile from the nearest water, the just-navigable Iowa River—is a live music venue that dominated the downtown streetscape before ritzy new condos dwarfed it.

Like gay bars of old, to find Studio 13 you have to go around the Yacht Club building and down an alley of cracked pavement lined with dumpsters. What once was a relatively nondescript entrance got a glorious new facelift in 2021, with an artist's mural outlined in neon providing a twenty-first-century entrance to a twentieth-century alley. That door opens into a dazzling space with a stage, table seating, and Instagrammable neon signs including a pink outline of an angel asking viewers to "lose your halo" and a violet neon sign shouting (ironically?) "PLEASE DON'T DO COKE IN THE BATHROOM." When this chapter's co-author Tory visited on a Saturday at noon, there was a full-scale drag photoshoot in process, no doubt part of Studio 13's robust marketing for its near-daily drag shows. The bar might be in a back alley, but unlike gay bars of yore, Studio 13 is out in front of the community at large.

The bar is an integral member of the local business improvement district (BID), which facilitates the Pride festival in a major downtown intersection. The bar's owner, Jason Zeman, is a board member of both the BID and the Iowa City LGBT Pride Organization and is a member of the Partnership for Alcohol Safety Coalition that works with police and alcohol regulatory authorities. Jason is a seasoned business owner with over twenty years of ownership in everything from cell phone stores to kids stores to liquor stores. This ties the bar into the fabric of the local civic and business communities, which was also in evidence during COVID-19 when Studio 13 and the Yacht Club held fundraisers for neighboring bars and restaurants that were closed.

Iowa may be one of the whitest states in the union, but the bar catalyzes diversity beyond gender and sexuality. The Pride march in 2020 was canceled due to COVID, but the virtual events were themed around the Black Lives Matter movement. And during the city's #BLM marches, Studio 13 opened to protestors so they could get some water, get out of the heat, or use the restrooms. As Jason told a journalist, "The first Pride was a riot! It was a transgender African American who started Pride, basically. Everything we have, we owe to that. People have to remember that."[3] This led him to raise money for BLM through a Black Lives Matter drag show, explaining "about 60 percent of our staff are people of color, and I thought it was just really important." This wasn't a first, however: The bar had long featured occasional drag shows just for queens of color, including the Haus of Eden until they decamped for big-city San Antonio, Texas.[4]

Studio 13's 2020 virtual offerings also featured other firsts uncommon on the coasts. Iowa City Pride's reigning Miss Iowa City that year was Hazy Buchanan, who describes herself as both a "faux queen" and a "female female impersonator." She was the first cisgender woman to be crowned in Iowa and one of the few to be crowned in the country. While the presence of cisgender women in drag has been controversial in other places, Hazy told a fan that

> everyone I've met in the Iowa City drag scene has been nothing but supportive. I was a little nervous when I started as a [cisgender] female queen, but I'm happy to say that the community is full of some of the most kind and genuine people I've ever met.[5]

In other words, to find the cutting edge of drag, sometimes you have to go to the middle of the country.

Studio 13 has a packed roster of other events that include trivia, comedy shows, karaoke, fundraisers, burlesque shows, potlucks, screenings of both *Ru Paul's Drag Race* and the University of Iowa football games, and drag shows up to five nights a week. But where some drag bars struggle to field a drag king here and there, Studio 13 is the home bar of the I.C. Kings, probably one of the longest-running drag king troupes in the country; they take the stage in a monthly show. The King Nights not only keep the drag fresh, but they fill the bar with "90 percent lesbian clientele," as Jason reports; the nearest lesbian bar is in Chicago, over 225 miles away.[6] And while some big-city bars bristle at bachelorette parties, Studio 13's website specifically welcomes them. After all, where else can they see local celebrity Sasha Belle, the local alumna of *RuPaul's Drag Race*, host her *own* local drag race?

Studio 13 made a conscious choice to become a 19-year-old-and-up venue when Jason started getting at least one or two emails a week from students wanting to come in, because "what else is there?" For young people who "want to be around 200 gay people on a Saturday night, this is really your option," so Jason got the business reclassified as an entertainment venue, rather than just a bar, in order to lower the minimum age. When young LGBTQ+ people need a gay bar, it takes some business savvy to admit the under-21s and give them those crucial moments of "I'm not the only one" and "it gets better." The threat of underage drinking is a big deterrent to most bars, so big that most bar owners don't even want to deal with it, but Jason happily reports that Studio 13 has "one of the lowest underage drinking ratios in town . . . our GLBT population appreciates it so they don't try to have issues with it." When the community treasures a space and knows how vital it is, they'll go a long way to protect it and ensure it can be accessible to as many as possible.

The club has also been recognized as a disability-friendly business by the local paper, one of the very few gay bars to do such outreach. On Mondays, Studio 13 hosts Studio Mondays, a dance for people with disabilities and their caretakers. As patron Katie Stewart told a journalist, "Me and my friends dance every Monday afternoon. I can dance with my boyfriend there. I like that."[7] Studio also allows patrons to reserve tables next to the stage on busy nights, a critical accommodation that allows people with physical needs to enjoy the drag shows.

Scholars are concerned that gay bars aren't radical and queer because they cater to a straight-emulating, bland "homonormativity,"[8] a term that one critic defined as "the current homogenizing, normalizing, and desexualizing of gay life."[9] But Studio 13 hosts kink parties for Iowa City leather and features another event called Frisbee's Sex Dungeon Strip Club Party, and has "leather invasion gear nights" that draw participants from Kansas, Nebraska, and Minnesota. Bland this club is not when serving the kink communities who don't have their own bars in this vast region.[10]

Small-city gay bars are often blue bubbles in a sea of red. Owner Jason Zeman feels Studio 13 excels because of this blue-bubble advantage: "Iowa City has always been extremely liberal. I think the college is a big part of it," citing the University of Iowa whose campus is two blocks away. But it's not just the students that keep Studio 13 afloat in this little blue pond: Jason notes that during the school year, they see a lot of students but that Studio 13 is "one of the few bars downtown that doesn't take a hit in the summer time because we stay consistent with the townies." With pride, he noted, "We have the second oldest gay Pride in the country, it started a year after Stonewall, because a group of lesbians marched that next year with the university. Iowa City is very unique for the Midwest."

Small-city gay bar owners know each other across the miles, and they all acknowledge there is no one-size-fits-all business model. Jason explained the difficulties of the sister bar thirty-two miles up The Corridor, Belle's Basix, owned by Andrew Harrison aka local drag icon Pretty Belle: "I can see that being a challenge especially in a blue-collar city like Cedar Rapids. It's completely different, it really is. I appreciate that. I feel bad for Pretty Belle sometimes because it is such a different animal." In some cities, like Cedar Rapids, the gay bar *is* the blue bubble, while in others, like Iowa City, the gay bar sits comfortably within a larger blue city. Gay bars provide a cosmopolitan feel to these blue bubbles in conservative areas, anchoring regional Pride celebrations and giving straight allies a place to catch a drag show. As Jack Gieseking commented upon reading this chapter, "What work queers take on!"

Cedar Rapids didn't always have only one gay bar, but Belle's Basix is the last one standing. If Studio 13 is downtown but in a back alley, Basix is right on the edge of town on the "main drag," the meager Cedar Rapids skyline in the distance. The bar has a down-home, homemade feel—nothing flashy, but a roomy drag performance area, a small shrine to the Chicago Cubs, and, in 2017, a politically themed drink special called Moscow's Fool: "Stolichnaya Orange Vodka, Pussy Energy Drink, Mexican lime juice, ginger beer, and *very* simple syrup." As Belle explained, "We used to have like four or five gay bars back in the day. One catered to lesbians, one would cater to the leather crowd, one would cater to the twinks, the drag queens and all that stuff, and I miss that." Belle's Basix exemplifies the complex relationship between a small city's vision of itself and its gay bar. As the bartender, who gave his name only as Damien, explained of Belle's Basix,

> To a certain degree, we're the right-sized city to continue to support it. We're a small enough community where the gay community is exactly that: It's a community. For the most part if you're gay in Cedar Rapids, you know most of the people in the community— that's not the case in New York or Chicago. But, Cedar Rapids isn't so small that it's closed-minded.

Although, it's small enough that your dirty laundry could get aired on Basix's Facebook page if you cross Belle.

Belle's is the only place in town where you can get an after-hours HIV test, one of the many social service offerings found in gay bars that operate as much as community centers as for-profit businesses. As Pretty Belle says, "We're open every day. If there's a blizzard, we're open." Belle cut back on her own drag performances because of the daily stresses of being the owner. "It's hard to perform and have a patron complaining 'oh, my girlfriend's here and she's gonna kick my ass! Like, okay well, I'm performing right now! Just calm down!' Or the bartender comes up, 'We're out of ones!' because people are tipping me ones."

As Damien rhapsodized about Cedar Rapids, he could have been describing any number of small, overlooked cities, little blue islands in the sea of the red Midwest:

> You'd never vacation here—nobody comes to Iowa for vacation. But it's a great city. You *won't* tear it down! But Iowa is wonderful: It's cheap, it's safe, it's quiet. For the asshole of America, it's kind of progressive.

So progressive, in fact, that Pretty Belle bemoaned the descent (or ascent?) into post-gay territory, citing a majority-straight crowd at drag shows and queer gatherings at straight bars. Sometimes the blue bubble means everywhere is gay friendly, and the gay bar gets left behind.

In 2022, it seemed like the music would stop in Cedar Rapids.

On January 9, Belle announced that, with heartache, shame, and embarrassment, the bar would close February 1, describing a "toxic relationship" with the bar for over twenty-four years: "I love her, but I need to let go. The gay community seems to have let go so I need to do the same." Belle continued: "I HOPE and PRAY that with the current political climate that we as a community can be safe without a safe space. We shall see." Calling for no fundraisers or advice on how to make the business busier— "I am done"—there was an outpouring of grief on the bar's Facebook page.

But only two weeks later came a shock announcement that a new owner had been found. Belle reported thinking "no one would want to step up and purchase the bar during this trying time in our history—through a pandemic and the Grindr age." The new buyer? Jason Zeman's Corridor Entertainment Group down in Iowa City. Local media exploded with stories, with Jason telling a local paper, "I've known Andy for 20 years and they're an amazing person who has done so much for the community." Citing the difficulties of COVID-19, Jason continued "the past two years have been incredibly difficult for everyone in the bar and restaurant business, and solo operators were hit the hardest. We're happy that we can carry on the hard work Andy has put into Basix in the past 10 years and hope to nurture and grow it into the future."[11] Pretty Belle, in turn, implored the community to "SUPPORT SUPPORT SUPPORT the bar," promising that "what you put into the community safe spot you can get out of it tenfold." And she got her flowers in the end: Cedar Rapids hosted its first-ever Pride march in 2022 and named Andrew Harrison grand marshal. The commendation reads, "As Pretty Belle, for 25 years, Andrew has entertained, supported, and been a role model for countless other Drag Queens. We want to thank Andrew for being an important part of our community."[12]

Belle's advice to "SUPPORT the bar" is valid beyond Iowa. If you find yourself in a small city with a lone gay bar, drop in. You'll be welcome, whoever you are. You might see a *RuPaul's Drag Race* celebrity: The queens regularly tour the bars of middle America because many of them grew up there—Sasha Belle at Basix and Studio 13 in the Iowa Corridor, while winner Sharon Needles is a native of Newton down the road. Tip your bartender, don't be shy about getting extra one-dollar bills to tip the kings and queens, and ask anyone you meet about their stories. And just like Iowa City's Yacht Club doesn't need water to rock, Studio 13's successful rescue of Basix shows that you don't need a coast to be cosmopolitan. Assuming that there are no cosmopolitan spaces in middle America reveals just how very provincial you are.

Part Three

Safe Spaces for Whom

Twelve

Gay Bars Were Never Safe Spaces

R&R Saloon
DETROIT, MICHIGAN

In the wake of the 2016 massacre at Orlando's Pulse nightclub, at the time the deadliest mass shooting in American history, many writers wrote heartbreakingly about gay bars as liberating sanctuaries, transformative sites of community, as refuges.[1] "The gay bar represents a physical manifestation of safety and desire," wrote one pundit in its wake.[2] Gay bars can be those things, and they deserve to be celebrated and defended. But I, like many others I spoke to, am extremely ambivalent about calling gay bars "safe spaces."[3]

For me, gay bars have also always been dangerous and continue to be. There is a long history of violence at gay bars, and not just from anti-queer and anti-trans terrorism. To be sure, violence, discrimina-

---

Image on opposite page: Gay bars are frequently hailed as safe spaces, and they do offer safety for many. But not everyone can gain access or feels welcome in them, and many gay bars only play the music craved by immigrant patrons one night a month, if that. Photo courtesy of Juan Figueroa for the *Dallas Morning News*. Used with permission.

tion, and side-eye happen at straight bars, but straights can flirt with impunity at work, at church, on the bus, in all bars. Gay bars are practically the only places we have, but they have always been magnets to gay bashers, pickpockets, car break-ins, and arsonists. Gay spaces attract crime, and we have often not been seen as deserving of safety.[4] For me, too, they have been sites of anxiety, disappointment, humiliations, thwarted desires, and body shaming. As much as I've needed gay bars, I would never describe them as "safe."

In 2011, I was in Michigan for a one-year fellowship in Ann Arbor, before this project began, back when I was in my mid-30s. I found Ann Arbor delightfully cosmopolitan compared to small-college-town Oberlin, but I was also eager to explore Detroit forty-three miles away. A car Luddite, I went to the Detroit International Auto Show. I also went to the nineteenth-century brick-covered Eastern Market, to what Yelp told me was the best falafel, and to Dearborn for the best *albiqlawa*. In visiting places beyond the gentrifying midtown, I was mindful that I was a white man in a Black-majority city with famously diverse Arab immigrant communities, things that seemed to make other white people fearful but made me respectfully deferential, perhaps patronizingly so.[5] I also explored the gay bars, with my usual trepidation. I'm nervous anytime I go to a gay bar, because for me they are as much sites of anxiety as desire.

The first time I parked down the street from Detroit's R&R Saloon, I sat in my car to screw up my courage. I scanned the empty street looking for shadows in the dark storefronts or between two vans parked next to each other. As I stepped out of the car, I glanced through the windshield, making sure no jacket or loose change were visible that might cause a thief to smash the glass. As I walked toward the door, my heart raced, my hands went clammy, and I felt self-conscious about my gait.

This ambivalent mix of excitement and dread did not flag when I noticed the security guard in his orange hi-vis security vest at the doorway who scanned the street behind me as he checked my ID. As I stepped through the door into the steaming, thumping din, I shot straight to the bar for a beer. Awkwardly signaling the bartender, I scanned the room for a place to perch that wasn't too close to any of the other men but had a good view of the figures passing from the illuminated bar into the shadows of the dance floor. Finishing my beer too quickly, I tried to look nonchalant as I returned to the bar to get a second—to a different bartender, so I didn't look like a lush. I calmed my beating heart and strategized: Who would find me hot? Who was hot to me? Would I even approach him? How? Second beer finished, I planted myself as a wallflower at the edge of the vacant dance floor, waiting for more than three men to hit it so I could join them and maybe find abandon.

This is what it's like for me to visit any gay bar for the first time, and I'm a big cis white guy who no one fucks with who's been to hundreds. Some mystery and riskiness are part of the attraction of gay bars: of being seen by someone who doesn't know you're gay, the uncertainty from walking in a part of town people call bad. The transgression of being around men making out or having sex in the corner, the possibilities of meeting someone, the temptation to go *too far*. Danger was certainly part of my attraction to the R&R Saloon. It would continue serving alcohol after hours even after they'd covered the liquor bottles with a tarp, ladling "punch" from buckets under the bar. There I once saw someone snort a line of white powder from the edge of the pool table and a man give a blow job behind a broken pinball machine in the basement. Risks have long drawn people to bars, including myself.

It's interesting to consider *who* feels safe in gay bars. For many straight women, gay bars are a welcome haven from pushy, handsy, rapey men. As one woman told the *New York Times*, "We come to have fun and relax without anything sexual."[6] My research assistant Tory benefited from the presumption of safety in gay bars, telling me, "My mom wasn't as worried about me coming with you because she perceived gay bars as safer for a young woman." Even James Bond himself, Daniel Craig, said that he had been going to gay bars "as long as I can remember" because he didn't have to fear fights and could feel safe—and occasionally pick up on the single straight women in attendance as well.[7] To which some gay barhopping sociologist remarked on the "brokenness of straight bars that even a famous, buff guy doesn't feel safe going out."[8]

And of course, as long as straight women have been going to gay bars, some gay men have been complaining about them.[9] But what had long been a trickle apparently became a flood in the last decade, launching a raft of opinion pieces decrying straight women in gay bars.[10] Responders then decried the sexism and misogyny of the gay male complainers.[11] More keen observers have found that gay men often enjoy the presence of straight women in bars, especially when they are their friends or are fellow patrons who amplify the scene with their enthusiasm.[12] When it comes to straight women in gay bars, queer women are, on the whole, much more ambivalent.[13] This is because the presence of many straight women in a space makes lesbian, bisexual, and queer women feel *less* safe, not to mention making it more difficult to find other queer women to hit on in a sea of straight ones.[14] This led one gay woman to growl: "Get out of my gay bar, straight girl."[15] The safety of gay bars depends on who is in them.

I'm not alone in feeling gay bars' push and pull. Justin Torres, whose elegiac "In Praise of Latin Night at the Queer Club" brings tears to my eyes, wrote that "'safe space' is a cliche, overused and exhausted in our discourse, but the fact remains that a sense of safety transforms the body, transforms the spirit."[16] As columnist Dan Savage commented,

> Joy isn't the only thing you'll find in gay bars. You'll also find aggression, judgment, shade, prejudice, side-eye, rejection, and heartbreak. Some bars are welcoming, and some aren't. Some people are assholes, and some aren't. There are good and bad people everywhere, gay bars included.[17]

That formulation is true as far as it goes, but it ignores the inequalities of racism, transphobia, and ableism that mean some of us meet these assholes more often than others do.

Gay bars have never been for everyone in the LGBTQ+ community, including people without government ID, patrons who fall victims of bar owner's bigotries, or those whose communities aren't recognized in them: Not every bar has a Latin Night. Bars are only as safe as the world, a world that is also hostile to disabled, fat, gender-non-conforming, and Indigenous people.[18] Gay bars by and large are also overwhelmingly white spaces, full of microaggressions for LGBTQ+ folks of color who face sexual racism from white people who all too often either dismiss their attractiveness or fetishistically slot them into narrow sexual stereotypes.[19]

Police, too, have historically been agents of violence in gay bars, and not just back in the "bad old Stonewall Inn days."[20] True, off-duty officers are often the helpful hired security guards on deck when you need help at your local gay bar. But you only have to read the lawsuits and hospital reports from two violent 2009 raids in Fort Worth and Atlanta to learn that police terrorism against LGBTQ+ people is a twenty-first-century phenomenon too. Off-duty police officers are often the hired security at gay bars, but this police presence feels very different for Black people, as Black Lives Matter activists remind us, including at our annual Pride marches.[21] Police scrutiny of Black gay bars has long been a constant; the 1984 raid on Manhattan club Blues prompted a multiracial coalition to march in its defense, while police harassment of Black youths on the street in front of Manhattan's Black gay bar Chi Chiz forced its closure in 2011.[22] Most cities don't even have Black gay bars—at least ones recognized by white LGBTQ+ folks. But even showing solidarity with Black lives can have costs: During the 2020 Black Lives Matter uprisings, police raided gay bars in Des Moines and Raleigh because they were offering aid to protestors.[23]

Many of the dangers of gay bars also come from within the LGBTQ+ community. There are the routine hazards of gay bars that happen to nearly everyone: rejection, body shaming, humiliation, indifference, drinking too much. There are the likely ones that will happen to you at some point or to someone you know: blacking out, being pulled over by the police, being mugged while leaving, being roofied, getting in a fight, being groped, or worse. And some of these dangers are invisible: The only time I know I was roofied was because I wasn't drinking that evening, and the funny-tasting Coke given to me by a pushy, generous shorty made me so blackout drunk that I don't remember my friends taking me home, apparently babbling the entire way.

LGBTQ+ people in general experience risks in gay bars, but those dangers are not distributed equally. Queers of color and transgender folks feel less safety because they face more dangers, ones that often get lost in the rosy-eyed talk of safe spaces and community, or the fatalistic claims that *everyone* faces risks in gay bars.[24] The risk of humiliation or worse: of being asked for multiple forms of photo identification at the door; of being turned away at the door for no reason or for showing a passport instead of a driver's license; of waiting at the bar for every possible patron to be served before you; of having your song request from the DJ be dismissed, perhaps with a racist comment about it being "ghetto"; of being ignored by every hot person in the place because of your body. As Corey Antonio Rose said, "How are you supposed to feel welcome in a community if you have to defend your humanity every time you go out?"[25]

This is why gay bars for people of color are so important, and why it is dismaying that they are closing at rates 60 percent greater than gay bars overall.[26] In San Francisco, that ostensible capital of gay America, the only gay bar for African American men closed in 2004. The only gay bar for Asian men closed in 2007. The only gay bar for Latinxs closed in 2014.[27] To be a queer or transgender person of color who visits gay bars is to constantly have to make space in "the community" that may not appreciate you or even want you, in cities where there is no 24/7 place that is truly yours.[28]

Beyond these factors, which we queer folks talk about among ourselves and which occasionally surface in the gay press (itself in danger of disappearing), there are other dangers we pose to each other. We fight each other, attacks that are easily mistaken for hate crimes, what one of my interviewees called "queer on queer violence." There are predators among us, agents of sexual assault and murder. Notorious serial killers have cultivated their prey in gay bars; I will not add to their infamy by naming them here. And there was the little death that was actually a plague. When asked to imagine my own mortality in an undergraduate class on the psychology of death and dying in the early 1990s, it was obvious to me that it would come via HIV/AIDS acquired from a hookup from the club.

A recent book highlighted the 1973 arson at New Orleans's UpStairs Lounge, until then the deadliest attack on an American gay bar.[29] Few mention that the only suspect was a gay man who had been turned away from the bar earlier that night. When Gordo's in Anchorage, Alaska, burned down, it was a rival gay bar owner who committed the crime.[30] When two women were shot outside a lesbian bar in Los Angeles, the shooter was a lesbian who was unhappy that the victim had flirted with her girlfriend. A 2018 shooting outside San Antonio gay bar Pegasus was not a hate crime, explained the police chief, because the shooter was an "angry patron who probably had too much to drink and was kicked out of the club."[31]

Gay bashers sometimes turn out to be queer, attacking others out of fear of being outed, out of shame. These men—and they are almost always men—come along every so often, meeting us in gay bars, taking us home, preying upon us. The brittle, toxic masculinity that is shored up by homophobia is something we all recognize, even when we don't challenge it. For example, sociologist C. J. Pascoe has shown how high school boys use "fag" to police each other's masculinity far more than to target gay classmates.[32]

And these extreme cases are only the most spectacular versions of the ways that we sometimes quietly hurt ourselves: through untreated mental illness, self-harm, alcoholism, drug abuse, suicide. Or even just saying something harmful about other people in the LGBTQ+ community: Calling your best friend a faggot is fine, until some poor queer passerby hears it out of context. After all, we have all heard these words, whether they be from religious figures or childhood bullies—but also from otherwise loving family members, TV pundits, respected politicians, sports heroes, co-workers, and classmates. We also experience the casual exclusions from workplace get-togethers, family holidays, and weddings. And classrooms and religious congregations and workplaces are no safer than gay bars, as the increasing rate of mass shootings attests.

The ways that contemporary commentators use the term "safe space"—such as among my own students—belies its origins. A product of the 1970s mostly-white women's movement, safe spaces were not just about freedom from outside violence, symbolic or otherwise. As Moira Kenney recounts, "Although bars represent one type of space—a momentary respite from oppression—the women's movement sought to create a radically different sort of place": one that would remake the world.[33] As such, safe spaces were not free from conflict, riskiness, or forces like racism. Rather, "Safe space, in the women's movement, was a means rather than an end."[34] In other words, safe space was a temporary zone to bridge differences, formulate plans, change minds, and change *selves* in order to change the world.

But as Black feminist Brittney Cooper reminds us, for Black people, "safe spaces" first means safety for their bodies in public, something they have never been able to take for granted.[35] And as Black gay author Jeffrey DeShawn has written in his memoir *No Safe Space*, "How many times have I shrank or not shown up because of the fear of feeling unsafe or experiencing harm or trauma?"[36]

In life, the most transformative visions of the world are driven not by a fixed definition of what is safe; instead they are motivated by *freedom*, both freedom from violence, at the most basic level, but *freedom to be*.[37] And if becoming is always a process, then the safe space that my students sometimes request—and that gay bar fans want them to be—is one in which multiple becomings, sometimes conflicting ones, are happening simultaneously. This means that ours should be "a quest for safety that is collective rather than individualized,"[38] and it is perhaps inevitable that we feel both support and betrayal in LGBTQ+ spaces.[39] Certainly the R&R Saloon was both an "embarrassment" (called by one white blogger)[40] but also celebrated by Black documentary filmmaker Jordan R, who called it the "dirtiest and most exhilarating bar in Detroit."[41]

When we claim that there is safety in gay bars, we have to interrogate: Safety from what? And for whom? In the past, gay bars promised relative safety in numbers. But that's not community—at least not yet. It is the means to realize it, though. What if gay bars are a means, then, rather than an end? What if we ask of ourselves, this diverse LGBTQ+ community, "What can we do *with* gay bars" rather than "Who needs gay bars"?

In this broader, more expansive definition of safety, then maybe gay bars *can* be safe spaces, but only if we recognize and address the violence within the LGBTQ+ community. Dangers are routine in gay bars and are a part of what makes them exciting. "The gay bar represents a physical manifestation of safety and desire," but queer desires are never safe.[42] Throughout this long project, I still felt anxious every time I entered a new gay bar, and I don't have to fear racist and transphobic shit. I still go because of the possibilities for connection inside, and because whatever dangers gay bars hold, they still sometimes feel safer than the world.

Thirteen

Undocu-Queer Dreaming and Government ID

FRESNO, CALIFORNIA

Bars are legally defined as public houses in common law—it's the origin of the abbreviation "pub." Gay bar fans define them as essential, safe spaces for the whole LGBTQ+ community. But bars, by definition, are highly regulated businesses that deny some members of the public at the door, including those who cannot afford the cover charges.[1] The law requires, for example, that bars ensure that patrons are over the age of 21, and they do this by checking government-issued identification. This means gay bars have never served the entire LGBTQ+ community. In fact, they exclude the people who may need LGBTQ+ space the most: undocumented immigrants, unhoused people without access to identification, or the underaged who are desperate for a taste of community, if perhaps also alcohol. One bar in Fresno, California, a Latinx-majority city, has found a workaround—an illegal one—illustrating that some bars are willing to risk their licenses to serve the people who may need gay bars, but who also dream of better places that don't yet exist.

Early in this project, I visited Fresno to see Kris Clarke, a friend and colleague I'd met while doing research in Finland. An immigrant to Finland herself, she'd gotten me a desperately needed consulting gig at a time when I wasn't permitted to work in Europe on the tourist visa that I'd extended by technically legal means. She helped me out again this time, directing me to Latin Night at a local club. She noted that the police sobriety checks that often surround gay bars, ostensibly as often as they do straight bars, held a more severe implication in Fresno County in the Central Valley of California. Here, in a county that is more than 50 percent Latinx and home to an estimated 68,000 undocumented people, police encounters also ensnare those trying to connect to the LGBTQ+ community.[2]

The identity "undocu-queer," wrote Fresno activist Grisanti Avendaño, "forces people to look at two identities at once. In one breath, in one word, we can confront two things people feel strongly about," as is evident in their defiant chant, "undocumented and unafraid, queer, queer and unashamed."[3] As researchers write of the undocu-queer, "The constant threat of deportability runs parallel to blatant attacks on individuals' sexual orientation and gender identity, as responding to incidents of violence increases undocuqueer immigrants' exposure to local and state agencies."[4] In Fresno, these agencies don't just mean the police, but all people who check for state identification, including the bartenders and bouncers who must follow state law to protect their bars' licenses to serve alcohol.

At ███████████ that night, I approached the stocky dark-haired bouncer wearing a Dickies jacket and ballcap checking IDs. I stepped to the side, telling him I was waiting for someone. This allowed me to observe the short but steadily refreshing line of men waiting to enter the door from which Spanish-language music was blasting, so rare in gay bars.[5] All the men appeared to be Latino, some fidgeting as they produced their IDs. The bouncer held his flashlight overhand and carefully inspected each card that was proffered.

What surprised me was what he inspected. One late-20s looking Latino gave him a Target gift card, which was duly inspected and handed back; the bouncer nodded its bearer inside. A rockabilly man with a slicked back pompadour, wallet chain, and wide-cuffed jeans offered a California state driver's license; it received the same treatment. A third young man in cowboy boots and clean but worn jeans offered what seemed to be a business card bearing the image of a lawnmower, which the bouncer considered for a beat before nodding the landscaper inside. Here, at ████████, the lack of a government ID was no barrier to entry, at least tonight.

Inside the club I took up a perch in the corner to observe the male couples embracing on the dance floor. Some wore the cowboy boots and well-worn jeans that you'd only see on this night at this bar, others wore crisp designer denim and tight-fitting t-shirts that you might see in any gay bar on any night. The rockabilly man stood at the bar, deep in English-language conversation with the bartender, alongside a thin, short man with gelled black hair in his late 20s who kept catching my eye. He slid onto the seat next to me, greeted me in Spanish, and introduced himself as "Richard," the English language version of Ricardo, which I was sure was his given name.[6] "Hablas inglés?" I asked, in my clumsy, informal, twentieth-century Spanish. He shook his head and launched into speech that was both too rapid for my language skills and partially inaudible over the pulsing beat of the music. In the course of our halting conversation, I learned that he had traveled over fifty miles in a borrowed pickup to come to this night at this bar, the only place he knew to find other men into men. He had migrated from Mexico to California seven years previously to work in the *campos*, the fields. I couldn't understand, or he wasn't specific about, what particular work he did, and he was vague about precisely where he lived, but he described living with several other men in a small house. None of them knew he was here or that he was queer.

████████, on this particular night, is the only gay place he goes to because his English is "bad." He doesn't want to feel stupid at the door. Here, the person at the door speaks Spanish, the bartender speaks Spanish, everyone in the bar knows Spanish, so it's comfortable. When I started to describe the other gay bars in Fresno, he waved his hand in front of my face: He didn't know about them, and he didn't want to know about them, or didn't want to know about them from me. This place is *seguro*: safe, but also reliable. Perhaps I was also safe—the only obviously non-Latinx white person in the club and one whose hips barely swivel, perhaps evidence of the way that "colonialism and heteronormativity soak into our erotic proclivities."[7] Richard seemed as eager for connection as for sex, and as my long-ago-college Spanish faltered, he invited me to his pickup *para tener sexo*. I was tempted. Not wanting to waste his time, I bid him goodbye and watched him approach another guy across the room.

I'm told ████████ no longer exists, but I don't name it. No reason to jeopardize anyone for their actions back during the Obama administration. And of course, not all undocumented people are Latinx: In California's Central Valley, many are Indigenous, and some are Sikh. Nor are most immigrants undocumented: The vast majority are authorized. Yet the nervousness of the Latinx patrons at the door who did not present government ID and the illegal actions of the bouncer illustrate how gay bars have never been safe spaces for everyone in the LGBTQ+ community. This Fresno bar also illustrates the creative ways that some bars, or at least some bar workers, ensure that their establishments are accessible spaces, if not safe ones.

The next day, after giving a talk at Fresno State, I sat in an empty classroom with a group of undocu-queer activists. They were all beneficiaries of the program named Deferred Action for Childhood Arrivals, or DACA, a group often called Dreamers after the proposed legislation to grant them citizenship, the DREAM Act. Where Richard had described the unnamed club as safe, Angel Sanchez described it as "on the side of town where almost nobody goes, and also in the street there's a lot of crime, so it's very sketchy." He compared it to a cruisy men's bar in town: "That one's into the hardcore gay scene, and more into leather, bears—you gotta be a certain kind of gay to go in so it doesn't feel safe either."

Luis Ojeda, another of the undocu-queer Dreamers, qualified Angel's assessment, explaining that undocumented doesn't mean foreign in a county that's 50 percent Hispanic—you're not foreign just because you speak Spanish, when half the people around you can, too. He contrasted their activist group's relative comfort in other Fresno gay bars with the discomfort some folks, like Richard, have in the most gay bars:

> Just because there's a room full of Latinos doesn't necessarily mean anything, or can mean different things. Thinking just because everyone in the room is Latinx doesn't mean it's a space open to everyone. For folks in cowboy boots—very Mexican

boots—for Mexicans who just came here, they only have their one night at ███████.

Here Luis described the class differences that create friction within the Latinx community that has never been a monolith, and he talked about the sometimes-shaming of those who had recently arrived for being too "ethnic."[8]

Angel noted that it was natural that the "folks in cowboy boots" wouldn't feel comfortable at the other gay bars in town, including the one co-owned by a man with a Hispanic name: "They play the mainstream Latin music, but they don't play the *corridos,* or the music they like, or the older songs that they might want to hear." Afro-Latin rhythms that permeate contemporary pop music do not resonate with the Latin music of Mexico.[9] Luis disagreed with Angel's assessment that the other bars in Fresno don't play that much Latin music, noting that they "sprinkle in a song or two in a night, they'll have Selena in the mix, but I don't think, 'Oh, they're playing Latin music,'" to which someone said, to much laughter, "Why does it always have to be fucking Selena?"

Luis noted that not all bars accept the *matrícula consular,* the photo ID issued by the Mexican consulate, so "before I had DACA, I would use my passport, my ginormous thing." He recalled a situation when a place in town refused to accept a passport as valid ID. I've seen this myself, having argued with bouncers on more than one occasion that friends' European passports were valid. For many door people, government-issued ID means U.S.-issued ID.

Luis weighed his discomfort at Latin Night at the unnamed club against his critiques of this other gay bar in town: "I don't know where I belong, or if I belong in that space."

Grisanti Avendaño jumped in to assert that this was because they didn't belong in those spaces, that they needed a new one, something that was like a gay bar but more than that: "My dream space, it would be colorful—."

Angel interjected, "—big, spacious—."

Grisanti continued: "—it would be decorated with *papel picado,* the bartenders would be from the queer community, be POC, they would know how to make our drinks and how to serve our beers."

Luis caught their enthusiasm, contributing: "Free entrance! I feel like everyone is welcome even if you're not going to be drinking or just dancing. I feel like it should be more accessible." Referencing the talk I'd given earlier in the day, Luis added:

> I think in your presentation you talked about what role the bars play in the community. Because the dream space would be centered around the needs of people, it would be very political. And open up their space to community events, and not just exist separately from the community.

Angel interjected: "and gender-neutral restrooms, and not the ones for one person. It would have food too."

Luis added, "a kitchen and have food that you can take to the dance floor! To a patio!"

Grisanti: "Tea and coffee!"

Angel: "Open 24/7!"

Luis: "Board games! I love playing the life-size Jenga when you're drunk. Sometimes you don't want to go dance, you want to play Jenga and talk about life, but this sounds like a very nice place that we should go."

I couldn't help but smile and get carried away by their dreams, these Dreamers. It did indeed sound like a place we should go. *All* of us.

Fourteen

Owners Behaving Badly

Easy Street Tavern
SOMEWHERE IN THE SOUTHWEST

Gay bar professionals are *personalities*: people who can spin a yarn, promote their business, and turn visitors into regulars. As you can tell, I like the people I meet and am perhaps too sympathetic to the strangers who took time out of their days to chat with me, a nobody in a car from elsewhere. I was, for example, unperturbed by the owner who, at the conclusion of our interview in his backroom office, offered to show me his dick (my partner, who was waiting for me out at the bar, was not so forgiving). Nor was I surprised, although I was disappointed, by the owner whose social media was a mishmash of new world order conspiracy theories and far-rightwing memes, or the one who spammed me about adopting dogs from a faraway state. I was, however, irritated at the tragic interviewee who I rebuffed for sending me nudes, but who then pestered my partner online in the delusion that he could convince me to put out. But I'm a jaded bitch who's seen it all: One of Tory's young friends who accompanied them to The Max in Omaha, Nebraska, was sexually harassed to his extreme humiliation by employees who hounded him to go shirtless or submit to a blow job in the back.

Nightlife people can be magical and nutso and amazing and problematic all at once—how's that for ambivalent. It was hard to always trust owners when their words were contradicted by my gut—and it was hard to trust my gut knowing that I was bringing urbane sensibilities to down-home lives, as was the case with "Paula" of Easy Street Tavern, whose affection for her customers was accompanied by language I found racist and transphobic.

Easy Street was an especially memorable gay bar, for reasons so vexing that all the proper names in this chapter are pseudonyms, as I'll explain. An outpost bar in a small city in the Southwest, it served a 16-county territory with 300,000 deeply conservative people and its own regional identity but only one gay bar.[1] Easy Street was one of only four out of the hundreds of gay bars I've visited that was a real roadhouse on the edge of town—a lone building bordered by a state highway, railroad tracks, and vast fields to the horizon.

The bar was also the only one—really, the only one!—that reported any troubles with locals that exceeded disputes with the fire marshal over occupancy. Which is to say, bartender "Lady" disavowed any drama, but then suddenly recalled, "There was that one time when kids threw lit firecrackers through the door."[2] It's quiet here on the edge of town, Lady averred, "But there was that one time when someone barricaded the front door with a sofa and set it on fire, but that was no big deal. We just went out the back, came around, and put it out." Smiling, she reiterated, "really, it's very quiet around here." She paused, before remembering, "But there was that one time when kids in a passing pickup shot out the windows with guns, but they didn't hit anyone, and it may not have been from being a gay bar, because the windows of the VFW get shot out too," referencing the Veterans of Foreign Wars Hall that is often a pillar of rural social life. What was no big deal to Lady made me check for the exits.

This was only one of the many contradictions of Easy Street Tavern. My gut said low-key terrorism, Lady said no big deal. In my conversation with owner Paula, my gut said casual racism and transgender exclusion, but she would no doubt disagree—and so might her very diverse clientele. The patrons of outpost bars depend on one individual for their only LGBTQ+ public place, and that person bears a tremendous responsibility both to those patrons and to their own bottom line. Easy Street Tavern made me question my ability to know what is or is not a safe space, and for whom.

Paula was a no-nonsense lesbian: a white, blonde spark plug with a husky voice, easy smile, and a wicked sense of humor. Her Facebook name was a raunchy pseudonym that a drag queen might use, like Anita Dick, but that was funny coming from a lesbian who might own more than one. Paula had acquired the bar less than a year before from its founding owner whose long run made Easy Street the oldest bar—gay or straight—in the county. Asked to describe the bar, Paula was quick to provide options: "We are a gay bar, lesbian, gay, homo, however you wanna hear it."

These terms aren't just words that Paula uses; they are terms passersby hurl from the street. Further contradicting Lady's assertions of acceptance by the locals, Paula said that patrons who are outside Easy Street often receive catcalls from passing cars: "They call the girls nothing but a butch licker babe!" When Paula used "licker" to refer to lesbian cunnilingus, the question mark on my forehead must have been visible. She explained the joke, "They're not even queer! It's kind of funny. We take it with a grain of salt."

As Paula laughed, I pondered her statement. The casual homophobia and misogyny were funny because passersby were misidentifying straight women outside the bar as lesbians. This was only "kind of" funny, however, and required a grain of salt to tolerate. On a more serious note, Paula continued,

> Let's not forget why we have gay bars: We are still not accepted in a lot of places. If I can't hold hands with my girlfriend, kiss her, then I don't wanna be there. It can be so lonely, but sometimes you're out and it feels like home.

Easy Street Tavern is not home, but "like" it. This might explain why I witnessed one young white man going down on his knees in front of another between the cars in the parking lot: because he didn't have privacy at home. When I asked about the difference between a gay bar and home, Paula only replied, "I don't know what it is, but there's a difference."

The male roofing contractors Paula hired also received a taste of what it means to be gay, or perceived so, by passersby as they labored.

As she related, "The straight guys get called qu██r, fa██ot from the street. They're used to it now." Used to it, she implied, like we are. Maybe in such an environment—a red county in a deep-red region—safety is relative.

For Paula, these slang epithets seem less an explicit politics of reclaiming abusive language than a light-hearted way of showing affection. She describes a joking game she plays with some of her straight friends in the bar: "They'll be whispering 'there sure are a lot of fa██ots in here,' and I'll be like 'I know right?'" She cackles and explains the purpose of this "play" in Easy Street: "No one hating on you, we all love you. Colored people call each other n█████s. We love each other, just let it go. We're having a good time." I was unsuccessful at keeping my eyebrows level at the sound of a white person uttering the racist slur, and it made me wonder how safe Black patrons would feel if they overheard Paula. While I wasn't perturbed by her use of a slur to refer to gay men, other readers have objected to the double standard of redacting one and not the other. I come from the generation of edgy gay men that reclaimed "fag," but other generations have other emotional experiences with the word.

Paula would surely describe herself as not racist because she affirmed the importance of socializing across racial lines, albeit in the colorblind language that erases, rather than recognizes, racial difference:[3]

> It's time Americans start looking at people as people, stop worrying about all these labels, and support one another. It's important. There's been a lot of division over race, it doesn't matter what race you are, if you're gay you hang together.

Indeed, on the night I was at the bar, more than one third of patrons were people of color—in a county that is 75 percent white and near a large Indian reservation. Paula introduced me to her night bartender, David, as "her little Indian princess," who scowled but didn't verbally object (David scowled at me all night, so maybe it was me he objected to). When a Black patron walked up and gave Paula a hug, she beamed and said, "Here comes Thomas, he's chocolate, he's an entertainer, a colored boy that put on a huge show," adding "he's going to bring me more of that type of people." Thomas seemed to have genuine affection for Paula; my gut twisted at references to a person as a racialized foodstuff and the word "colored." But to Paula, having a racially mixed bar is not only important, it's also new:

> You see these Black men and Black women mixing with white women and white men. In my day that was not acceptable, whether for straight people or for gay people, to mix the races. Now we're trying to mix it up.

What I took for racism did not seem to perturb Thomas. I can't know whether he forgave Paula or did not consider that there was anything to forgive.

Paula also welcomes transgender people despite misgivings over their being included into some LGBTQ+ acronym—indeed, in the early evening when I was at Easy Street, among the handful of patrons were at least three I took to be transgender or gender nonbinary. Paula does not believe in the "LGBT" acronym, however.

> I'm trying to accommodate everybody—we have quite a few trans people. And I have to let them know, "Listen this is where I stand with trans people: They are not really part of the gay community." They may not be that, but they're still welcome in this community. They are one of the most abused genders or what you'd like to call it.

I was skeptical of her claim to be accepting, but a patron I took for a transgender woman walked over to introduce herself. She handed me a shot of liquor and explained that she'd bought it for Paula who wasn't drinking because of the pain meds she was on, so she was hospitably offering it to me. Again, I found Paula's statement trans-exclusionary, but this was contradicted by her immediate welcome and the affection shown to her by her patron.

Reflecting on her desire to continue the historic legacy of the Easy Street Tavern, Paula stated, "I think it's important we stay open because there's a lot of us out here who need it. Not want it but need it. Being gay is not easy. A lot of the stories, 99 percent are not easy. It's getting easier with the younger generations though." Reflecting on her uneasy relationship to her conservative religious family, Paula concluded, "I didn't tell my people I bought this bar until I closed the sale. I bought the oldest bar in 'Southwest County,' the homo bar. You used to make fun of us for going to the homo bar, but now, come on in!"

Thinking about sharing this story gave me a stomachache. My Lutheran upbringing tells me if I don't have something nice to say, be passive aggressive about it. My social science training teaches me to resist imposing my judgment on places that I've only driven through. But given the lukewarm welcome many gay bars have offered transgender, Black, Indigenous, and people of color, this was exactly the kind of story I'd set out to tell, although I found far fewer of them than I expected. I was committed to sharing this chapter with Paula—I wanted to get her reactions to what she'd said two years earlier and, hopefully, register some changes of heart. When I reached out repeatedly, I got no response.

Paula had died.

I dropped notes of condolences to two of the people I'd met at Easy Street that night, including the transgender show director, but got no reply. The Easy Street Tavern closed in 2019 and remained so, and no new gay bar opened to serve the dozen-county Southwest region. Former employees maintained a tribute page in memory of the bar and Paula, paying for the domain name year upon year.

Paula wasn't the only owner to express things in ways that I found racist and whom I anonymize here to protect them from themselves. After reading their chapter, one owner objected that I made them sound "a bit racist" in the way they discussed people of color, including by saying, "There aren't very many men of color out here, well, some Puerto Ricans, but who knows about them—they're all a little flamboyant." This owner also disparaged rap music in racist ways and demanded I edit their reference to Black people by replacing "Black" with "dark," an edit that made it even more racist!

Such moments put me on the horns of interlocking ethical dilemmas. On the one hand, feminist and queer principles instructed me to collaborate with my interviewees in mutually beneficial ways. Research on LGBTQ+ people, especially projects that find us in our bars, have so often mined us for academic purposes without giving back.

On the other hand, I should not collaborate with forces of exclusion and bigotry, and I shouldn't let my weak stomach for conflict or my respect for their work stand in the way of naming racism and transphobia where I see it. Collaborate without collaboration—competing ethical imperatives each freighted with histories of past mistakes and good intentions. Many of my friends feel I should have named Paula and these other owners and let them cope with the fallout.

And yet, calling out is notoriously unsuccessful at changing hearts and minds, and I didn't have the long-term relationships to engage in "calling in," not with all of the hundreds of people I met for this book, most of whom I met only once for an hour or two.[4] I was mindful as well of the ethical concern to do no harm. One of the bars featured in this book was the object of a social media campaign accusing it of bigotry, on the basis of an anonymous complaint and subsequent dogpile of negative online business reviews by people who were showing solidarity but had never been to the bar. Even as I wanted owners to change, they must be accountable to their local community, not to me, nor to you.[5] By obscuring them, I may prevent that from happening, although it's unlikely that the prejudice they revealed to one stranger is something they are hiding from others. So I corral the most problematic statements into this chapter rather than leaving them scattered throughout the book and ask you to think about Paula and Easy Street Tavern not as exceptional, but as the result of a world in which white and cis people own and run things.

For you who have experienced racism or transphobia at gay bars, or suspected it, I hope seeing it presented so baldly provides a sense of validation. For those who have not considered these forms of safety, I hope your eyes are opened. I myself take small comfort in the fact that, upon seeing their words in draft form, another owner correctly identified their words as racist. I allowed interviewees to change their words because at the end of the day, what someone said in one one-off conversation years ago need not define them in print forever.

Paula, however, never had a chance to be more welcoming, to register a change of heart, or to teach me the Southwest's local ways. I'm old fashioned enough that I won't speak ill of the dead, hence the anonymity, even though Paula spoke ill of others, by my lights. Easy Street was an imperfect place, as are all places, but the need for a gay bar that Paula detected did not mean the rise of a new one to replace the fallen Easy Street Tavern. My gut says that locals either forgave or overlooked Paula's foibles and appreciated what she could offer, but I can't know that. It may be that they gritted their teeth and merely tolerated her, the owner of the only gay bar in the vast region. But Paula's rough ways reflected her region, in ways that aren't easily captured by big-city critiques and that defy easy notions of progress or safety.[6] That's the importance of having more stories to tell—and more storytellers.

Fifteen

Our Gender Is Medicine

Various Bars
INDIAN COUNTRY, OKLAHOMA

Everyone wants to know what was my most memorable gay bar, which is like asking a professor what's their favorite class to teach or a parent about their favorite child. The fact that this book profiles forty-two gives you some indication of my answer. But my spring break in Oklahoma was special for teaching me about the debts we owe to queer Indigenous Americans.

Oklahoma City had come to my attention because it has two lesbian bars and a gayborhood, both of which surprised me. The city's 39th Street Strip was anchored by five independent gay bars and a dated hotel-resort called the Habana Inn that itself contained three gay additional bar-clubs, a gay variety store, and a campily named restaurant, Gushers. Of course I stayed in the resort, a 170-room hotel with exterior hallways ringing two courtyards featuring pools and chaise lounges. There, some men left their doors open while they sprawled suggestively on their visible beds. Some transgender women pulled the vanities up to the door while they applied their makeup, luxuriating in their visibility and in the attention from passersby who slowly cruised the outdoor hallways. The parking lot demonstrated the resort's national draw, with license plates from every state that bordered Oklahoma and from all coasts besides—California, North Carolina, Michigan—and not only from the long-haul truckers+ whose rigs were parked along the side of the huge campus.

But the license plates also illustrated what brought me to Oklahoma: There are many sovereign governments inside one state, governments that issue tribal authority license plates. I saw ones from the Cherokee Nation, the Choctaw, the Muscogee (Creek), the Chickasaw. These citizens—of their tribal nations, and also the United States— are also patrons of the Habana Inn and the 39th Street Enclave, and I could find no information about them, either.

To understand the fast-paced changes in Indian Country, there was no better place to be than Oklahoma. The state has the highest percentage of Native Americans of any in the lower forty-eight, 16 percent.[1] When I visited in 2018, much of the reservation land allocated to the tribes was not recognized by the State of Oklahoma as Indian Country, the legal term for all the stolen lands allocated to tribal authorities.[2] Two years later, however, the U.S. Supreme Court would find that 45 percent of the state was Indian Country, the implications of which it would severely limit a mere two years later.[3]

Indigenous people have a vexed relationship to alcohol because of its role in the settler colonial violence.[4] Federal law long restricted alcohol on reservations that are the land of sovereign nations, and many reservations are dry to avoid the problems that come from community members self-medicating their generational trauma. Thus gay bars are especially charged for the queer Two-Spirit people whose traditional identities are frequently misunderstood by both non-Natives and their own people.[5] Even in Oklahoma, the state with the highest percentage of Indigenous people and the most Indian Country in the continental United States, gay bars don't always serve the people whose land they're on.[6]

And yet, bars have a deep meaning for Indigenous LGBTQ+ people. "Bars have been our churches," described Kelley Blair (Choctaw, Cherokee, and Seminole), one of the three founders of the Central Oklahoma Two-Spirit Society (COTSS). Two-Spirit is a category that encompasses the vast ways that Indigenous communities have described members who identify beyond binaries of gender and sexuality, binaries that were violently imposed during European colonization as one of many tools of dispossession.[7] Not all Two-Spirit people are in the United States; some who may identify as Two-Spirit may themselves be immigrants.[8] Not all LGBTQ+ Indigenous people identify as Two-Spirit, which has spiritual and healing implications, and some settler peoples co-opt the term and Native traditions for their own purposes.[9] But those Indigenous people who do identify as Two-Spirit embody in contemporary times a lineage of people who have existed "since time immemorial, long before the arrival of immigrants from overseas," explained COTSS co-founder Cori Taber (Muscogee and Cherokee).[10]

Describing being Two-Spirit, Cori explained, "We carry a medicine with us that other people are utterly unaware of. And it never leaves our bodies. That's who we *are*. The way that we present gender is medicine." As Kelley described their identity as bisexual *and* Two-Spirit, and their partner as bisexual and gender fluid, they noted that while others might see them as a heterosexual couple, actually, for the two of them, "We're the same." These descriptions were a humbling learning experience for me: I knew Two-Spirit was connected to tradition but hadn't considered the degree to which those traditions were embodied, were holy, or carried such responsibilities.

Kelley is also a counselor and therapist who works especially with gender diverse people, other Indigenous people, and other people of color, including those with alcohol dependence: "My Two-Spiritness, we tend to be natural counselors, that was our role in the tribe as medicine people, so I attribute my abilities to my heritage." They explained that there are many myths about some mythical intrinsic Native susceptibility to alcohol dependence, pseudo-scientific attributions that erase the generational traumas of the enforced removal from sacred lands and lifeways.[11] Kelley justified their description of gay bars as churches, even for Native folks, by adding, "Even our people in recovery, they still go to the bar. They do!" Describing Native LGBTQ+ folks, they explained, "For our community, as much as we want to move away from that, they will gravitate to the bars. And so it's been a conflict for our community, even with our Pride." As at most Prides, alcohol companies are major sponsors and beer and liquor permeate many of the events.

Kelley also sits on the citywide Pride board, helping to organize the annual June festivities. They helped make it possible for the Two-Spirit contingent to open the Pride parade in 2017 with a grand entry, a powwow tradition: "The Two-Spirit community and the LGBT community for Natives will do a dance ahead of time, so we're excited to be able to do that." Such an honor was not straightforward, however:

> We can't have our regalia, which is medicine, around alcohol, so that's the bar scene, so we're going to do it here at the community center. We're still looking for how we can do that traditionally and not impact our communities' traditional ways.

As Kelley noted of regalia in the bar scene, "It depends on the individual. Some'll take their regalia off because they don't want people to touch them with alcohol around, and some people won't wear regalia at all." As Kelley continued, they noted that being in public as Native is difficult and requires warning each other: "Please be mindful that people are going to want to touch you—can I touch your feathers? Touch your hair?" Safe spaces for whom, indeed.

Cori Taber is another COTSS activist, and she described the trajectory of the group's organizing work: "We've seen it shift away from the bars, we're doing work and we have to find ways to do this work in the absence of these other opportunities." Reflecting on this quote years after our interview, Cori clarified:

> Our work is community building, stigma reduction, and suicide prevention as an organization. While we can sometimes connect with people in the bars, there seems to be an ongoing shift online and into other sober spaces.

Cori and Kelley's third co-founder Sage Chanell (Absentee Shawnee) complicated a simple rejection of gay bars by Native peoples, however. "Some don't want to go out to the bars, they think it's sleazy. I get that, but there's so much more than that." Sage described other reasons for Two-Spirit people to be skeptical of bars: "They're scared of exposure, they feel like they're going to have pictures taken. A lot of them aren't out to their families." Cori added that not all in Native communities are as supportive of lesbian, gay, bisexual, transgender, queer, and Two-Spirit (LGBTQ2S) people: "The reason they're afraid of being exposed is the stigma. Many more religious families and communities are less accepting of LGBTQ2S people, choosing to believe this is a choice—and not a good one."

Cori described one advantage of the Oklahoma City (OKC) bars is that they're clustered into a gayborhood, noting dangers surrounding the bars in Tulsa, which are spread out due to old city ordinances that were enforced by discriminatory policing: "I've been pulled over after leaving a bar. They sit there and see if you leave in certain places." Sage concurred, "Tulsa is kind of a scary city. I felt uncomfortable there. Here I feel safe. There's a lot of people I know from wherever if I'm leaving a bar here. There, you're at risk of getting jumped." Indeed, OKC's gay bar district has a vibrant sidewalk scene among the bars and the gay hotel that anchors it with two gay bars of its own, including a country/western one where, amidst the twirling couples and joyful line dancing, a gallant man in boots asked me to dance.

Cori described OKC's bar scene as racially divided and rigidly hierarchical. "This is just like any other LGBT community. The white men have the cultural capital, have the financial capital, so they get to play." Sage concurred, describing her life after winning the title of Miss Two-Spirit International in 2017, something she has written about herself.[12] Sage described her preference for mostly Native audiences over the OKC bar scene:

> If I'm doing high drag, even when I won my title, we try to stay out of the bars, we try to stay away from the club scene. We want to cater to our traditional people. We want to stay out of the big cities. We want our people to feel included."

To me, she recalled how the previous titleholder pushed her to make appearances at the bars, enthusing "I want to see you in your crown!" So Sage did, but to disappointing results. Frowning, she recalled, "I came out in my Native regalia and my crown, and people were like 'oh,'" she shrugged, mimicking their tepid reaction. "If I'm in my slutty stuff or my blingy stuff I will get tipped, I *won*. That night, I didn't get but a little. When I'm dressed like this, that's the support I get?" Sadly, she addressed those queens from the past: "Y'all made me feel like shit." To her previous titleholder, Sage queried incredulously: "This is what you wanted me to do? I don't feel good about it." Now, she says of her sacred regalia: "I don't want to bring that here to the bars." Cori jumped in to explain, "It's a prayerful act to create the garment. You build it and you put it on and then the non-Native American counterparts disrespect it. It hurts." The construction of regalia is passed down within families and the community, and while such garments are the object of much outsider fascination, they are holy and deserve to be discussed with great respect. This is only one of a series of slights she calls "perpetual microaggressions" for being Native in gay bars.

When reflecting on our conversation with the benefit of a few years of hindsight, Cori identified a trend since that time:

> New and different options are surfacing due to a new generation of performers and creators. Drag is happening at venues and events outside bars now, and bars are continuing to expand and revitalize in order to remain relevant.

The outcome, Cori said, is a positive trajectory: "With more options, our community *is* becoming more vibrant and inclusive." Safety is not a given, and it can be achieved.

Cori has traveled widely, drawing favorable comparisons between the Two-Spirit and Native LGBTQ+ folks in Oklahoma City versus Los Angeles: "This community maintains its existence and vibrancy despite the fact that it's a transient city, despite the people who built it are aging, the internet, meth, cellphones, apps, despite all that, the vibrancy exists in the same way that it does in LA." Continuing the comparison between the offerings for LGBTQ+ folks in the two locations, Cori suggested that in one way Oklahoma City may edge out Los Angeles:

> Because we have more desperation, but think on that! In LA, you can be really complacent and go to West Hollywood. Here you only have one choice: OKC. Here there's all these shit towns 450 miles outside where nobody exists except for one crazy bitch queen who will come fucking find us! Those bitches are always being born.

They're also being made. We will find them to the tribe. We will fucking find them and make them. We will build our motherfucking squad from the ground up!

Contrasting this do-it-yourself camaraderie with life in coastal metropolises, Cori observed, "In LA and New York City, drag is fodder for TV. Here people do it for us and us alone, and when we don't get what we want, we *make* what we want!"

Reflecting on the five years since we first spoke, Cori measured the changes that had occurred in the world. "In the past five years, nonbinary and trans people have taken center stage in media." Reflecting on this chapter, she concluded,

> Sage, Kelley, and I all represent different versions of being Two-Spirit. So much variety and diversity existed in our communities historically, and we are revitalizing these traditions with our very existence. Whether it's through ceremony, or drag artistry, or community activism, we are determined to maintain our presence on this land.

That the average gay bar doesn't honor the Native land it's on is not surprising. That gay bars were so hostile in the one-time Indian Territory where 16 percent of the population are Indigenous should not have surprised me, but it did. I met no gay bar owners in the entire country who ever mentioned Indigenous programming, nor have I found any gay bar websites with land acknowledgments, much less any support for returning land. But bars, while they may not always be safe spaces, are also sites for crossing boundaries, for meeting new people and learning about them.

None of the three COTSS co-founders wanted to criticize any bar by name, hence this chapter is the only one not grounded in a particular bar or bars. As Cori concluded, "We are women and men and others who intend to persevere through the strength of our traditions and continue to embrace and encourage others to participate in our cultures." It is a participation I have tried to model by sharing this chapter with Cori, Sage, and Kelley, taking their advice on how best to represent them, and by presenting myself as someone who is learning but who can provide them an opportunity to teach others.[13] It is my hope for Two-Spirit people that you see yourself represented in this book of stories, and that the rest of us will take on the moral obligation of making our spaces safe for you as well.[14]

Sixteen

Conflicts over Safety in the Queer Pub

Wayward Lamb
EUGENE, OREGON

One recent trend over the past seven years is the rise of gay bars that identify as "queer," a refusal of "gay" in the quest to provide safety to all LGBTQ+ people. Most of these bars are in big cities with many other bars, but some are outposts in progressive university towns. But welcoming unruly queerness into the pedestrian world of small businesses reveals community conflict over who gets to exclude whom in the search for safe space, and between owners' obligations to the community and to their own bottom line.

No gay bar owner talked more about safety than Colin Graham of the Wayward Lamb. This surprised me because Eugene, Oregon, is a tolerant, deep-blue bubble in a reliably blue state, a university city that attracts young people from all over the country. Eugene was one of the first cities of the state to recognize LGBTQ+ civil rights and has, a journalist recently wrote, "a loud minority yelling about how LGBTQIA spaces are no longer relevant."[1] Colin explained that the tolerance that some people felt was different from how he experienced safety, however: "Nowhere here did I feel that if I wanted to go express sexual interest to a total stranger that I didn't take my life in my hands or maybe get the shit beat out of me."

When Colin moved to Eugene four years earlier, his thought was "this town needs a friggin' gay bar!" But he corrected me: Wayward Lamb isn't one. "Officially we describe ourselves as a queer pub and event space. That is the phrase that took us a very long time to arrive at." Of early press coverage, he explained, "Anytime 'gay' or 'LGBT' came up, people were up in arms about being left out." Now, "We use the word 'queer' because nobody felt excluded," although he conceded that someone who "is a couple of generations ahead" remembered "when that word wasn't very nice." But regardless of what people call the Lamb, "It's just important that they feel safe more than anything else."

The bar is right in the heart of downtown, with large windows open to the street and no visible symbols of your typical gay bar. The front is the restaurant space with bright, raw wood, while a door leads to a darker, separate event space called The Den, an arrangement the local paper said was "Like a hip, classy mullet: business in the front, party in the back."[2] As Colin laughed, "We're not draped in Pride flags." Such symbols weren't necessary, Colin argued, because smartphones do all the advertising: "Nowadays, you google 'Eugene gay bar.' That's what we do." While most owners agreed that online advertising was the most important source for their business, few others were as stylishly nondescript as the Lamb; the only rainbow I could see was on the custom beer tap handles, including the first-ever one for Pabst Blue Ribbon in the shape of a rainbow unicorn.

Part of being a queer bar is deliberate outreach to the LGBTQ+ community beyond white cis gay men. Wayward Lamb worked closely with the local transgender rights organization Transponder, hosting a monthly "trans, gender diverse happy hour" called We/Us/Ours. Occasional events served LGBTQ+ families and youth, while other slices of the community were served by Taste of Fetish, Noche Latinx, Bear Night, and The Den Male Revue. The Den's stage also regularly featured live music, the Glamazons drag troupe, and Unveiled Queer Burlesque. The HIV Alliance brought HIV testing, safer-sex supplies, and a free needle exchange. Extremely popular were the epic lip-sync battles on Wednesdays. The diverse groups served by these events commingled with sometimes sublime results, such as at the Lamb's clothing-optional underwear parties: "I remember seeing a couple of straight seniors dancing fully dressed, a couple of bears in their jockstraps, straight boobs all over the place, every identity, everybody playing together nice!"

Outreach to the lesbian community has been tricky, however, with some women arguing that they would feel safer at events that "excluded men." Colin drew the line, noting that first of all, such events were illegal according to Eugene's human rights code, and second, "If you're asking us to inspect genitals at the door or we're not coming, what am I supposed to do with trans people?" An early event, tHERsdays that featured the Kings of Eugene drag troupe, was scrapped because transgender people reported feeling excluded. Colin went back to the drawing board:

> We've got another concept—it's about gender. We're going to have a trans DJ, a woman, we're going to have doms, drag kings, and some drag queens that are doing male drag. And we're back to queer.

Here, he explicitly made the link that queer was inherently inclusive, a point contested by older lesbians who sometimes feel erased by the lack of women's programming and whose gender essentialism is often contested by transgender and queer people themselves.[3]

Colin noted that safety was the primary quality that determined the Lamb's success: "Whenever we've had people who've had a bad experience, they've claimed that they ended up feeling unsafe." Door staff is key, he argued, by being "a filter at the door that disallows the un-safety to come in." Laughing, he described bouncers' primary role was "to be anti-douchebag filters." I asked what that looked like, and he explained:

> They change people's attitudes on the way through the door. If they hear a word, they will take someone aside, "Just want to let you know the kind of place we got here. We would love it if you come in but we'd like to insist that that kind of talk is left out here."

But it made me think: "queer" is a word that "wasn't very nice" for older LGBTQ+ people; how to distinguish between a "fag" or "dyke" uttered as a slur or as an affectionate, self-identifying reclamation?

Maintaining inclusion meant welcoming straight people to the queer bar as well, with Colin reporting questions he'd heard: "What do you mean by gay bar? Straight people can't go?" As at other bars, this led some LGBTQ+ people to complain about too many straight people, and Colin mused that safety might be a reason: "Obviously a lot of hetero people may create a sense that you feel less free in what you came to a gay bar to do. Maybe a drunk straight woman got too handsy with a gay." Here Colin engaged in another act of reclamation of the offensive objectification ("a gay"), probably because we had slipped into a kiki during the interview, something I often do myself but have to check in front of students, who can find it offensive.

But as with all other outpost bars, straight inclusion is part of the mission, as Colin explained:

> As corny as this sounds, I want this business to be out there changing hearts and minds and I think we have. For somebody who might have otherwise had an issue with it and to find themselves enjoying themselves and realize it's a gay bar, and to rewire their thoughts about what a gay person is.

In adopting the point of the view of straight people, however, I noticed that Colin had drifted from his own queer pub branding and fallen into calling the Lamb a "gay bar."

Being in a major university town meant that home football game days brought lots of out-of-state fans to the University of Oregon's Autzen Stadium. "The city of the opposite team, if we're a little bit worried about the attention, then we will often hire one of the drag queens to be a visible presence in front," grinning and describing this as subtle. "Subtle?" I asked incredulously. Colin laughed:

> Nobody is going to freak out at the sight of a drag queen, but it sends a message, a tiny little message. It distinguishes one place from another without being intimidating and exclusionary. That's very deliberate on our part. We try to keep it safe.

Being a queer bar isn't just about politics but also business reality. "I can't afford to alienate anyone," Colin conceded, one of the few owners to cite economics as a reason to be integrated with straight people and not just values of inclusivity and nondiscrimination. Indeed, the local paper estimated that the entire county had no more than 18,500 LGBTQ+ residents, although Colin noted the Lamb regularly received patrons from the coast and southern Oregon who drove more than two hours.[4] Straight people are thus essential, he argued, because "If you're going to define yourself as being there for 2 or 7 percent of the population, I don't know how I would get the bills paid."

But being a queer safe space meant making some LGBTQ+ people feel unsafe. Just after the 2016 election, Colin felt compelled to make a social media statement, "reaffirming our being a safe place, but I referred to the election results as being heartbreaking or outrageous." A longtime customer objected, however: "He didn't appreciate my post because he doesn't feel safe coming in my bar because of the way he voted." "Did you take it down?" I asked, and Colin shook his head. "What I wrote was important to far too many other people. But to be honest, if I voted for Trump, I wouldn't feel very safe either."

Being the only public LGBTQ+ place in the county was a "double-edged sword" because people treat the Wayward Lamb "like a community center," Colin said, noting the downside of being a not-quite-for-profit enterprise that often gets treated as if it's a nonprofit. As Colin continued, "People act toward this business like I'm acting on state funds, like I'm an elected official or a 501(c)(3) and I'm not one of those things. I'm not a charity. I'm a for-profit enterprise!" His response to people who demand events that drew from too small a slice of the LGBTQ+ community was: "*You've* got to do it. Rent my space and do it yourself, or you write the checks and I'll do all the work for you." Of the Wayward Lamb's refusal of gayness and embrace of the tenuous safety of queerness, Colin was firm: "I am proof that a queer business can *stay* in business."

Until it couldn't.

The Wayward Lamb suddenly closed in 2018, just another mom-and-mom and pop-and- pop business to fold. A Facebook post by Colin cited "the emotional, physical and mental strain caused by operating a small business."[5] He described the bar's safety as a community enterprise, but one with an unintended byproduct:

> The Wayward Lamb is a safe and inclusive space, not because I declared it to be one, but because a bunch of people gathered there and made it one. All I did was rent a building. The space was more than just a bar, it became a de facto community center that held an inordinate amount of expectations for success.

Indeed, amid the online outpourings of grief and appreciation were public comments that illustrated these ambivalent expectations. One commenter said, "LGBTQ spaces are needed," but argued to "turn it into a nonprofit LGBTQ center because the last thing Eugene needs is another bar."[6] Much angst resulted from the most critical comment: "Finally. This place has been an overpriced, sketchy, uncomfortable boys club since six months after it opened. It's so sad that the only queer-oriented bar in Eugene so clearly put profit over actually supporting the community it tried to drain." Another described the sudden closure as a "cut and run" and decried "no warning to help the community figure out a path forward. Doesn't sound very inclusive or concerned about community," to which another responded matter-of-factly, "This was a bar. Not a queer community center. A for-profit business."

Many commentators praised the feeling of safety the Wayward Lamb had offered, with one bemoaning the loss of "the only real safe space that's ours in town." This prompted a rejoinder: "'Only safe place?' Eugene is an incredibly LGBTQ friendly community. I will say it was one of the only openly gay venues but that is a far different statement than the only safe venue."

A new venue, Spectrum, opened on the site by the end of the year and managed to outlast its predecessor, in part by being more explicitly political than the Lamb. News coverage emphasized new co-owner Helen Shepard's use of they/them pronouns and their performances at the Lamb as part of the Unveiled burlesque troupe. At its opening, Helen described Spectrum as "a place for the queer community to organize," telling another reporter that it would be a place to "plan the revolution."[7]

But much of the language remained the same. The first ad for Spectrum called for support of a new "queer safe space," and their website described it as "not just a gay bar."[8] To a reporter, Helen said the primary impetus for founding Spectrum was because "We need a place where we can go and say I know I'm among like-minded individuals, I know I'm safe, I know this is my culture and my space to feel safe."[9]

I couldn't help but wonder whether Colin's seemingly sudden change of heart mere months after our interview had to do with the impossibility of balancing the inclusivity of queerness with queers' own conflicting definitions of safety—no men, fewer straights, no Republicans. Perhaps Colin's queer pub branding wasn't deep-seated enough, as evidenced by his sometimes-slippage into describing Wayward Lamb as a gay bar. Perhaps, as a recent transplant, it was that his roots in the community weren't deep enough. Perhaps the venue's occasional male stripper revues called the Lamb's queer cred into question. And perhaps a white, cis gay man's ability to offer safety was too steep a climb, either from lack of skills or community forbearance. Even Colin knew that just slapping a queer label on something doesn't make it safe. But if gay bars aren't safe spaces for all LGBTQ+ people, ambivalent community definitions of safety mean queer ones can't be so for everyone, either.

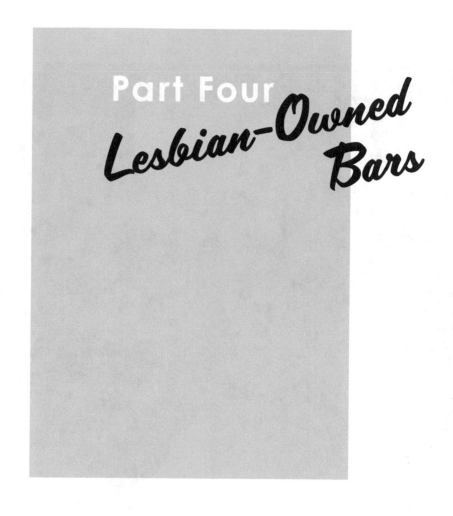

Part Four
Lesbian-Owned Bars

Lesbian bars are scarce, and most exist in cities with gayborhoods such as Walker's Pint of Milwaukee, Wisconsin, where patrons share a moment at the famous bar in the Walker's Point gayborhood. Photo courtesy of Royal Brevväxling. Used with permission.

Seventeen

Lost Womyn's Spaces, Found Lesbian Bars

Wild Side West
SAN FRANCISCO, CALIFORNIA

Lesbian bars are their own special kind of gay bar and have always been rare compared to men's bars.[1] They have been the most common place for cruising, dyke humor, and lesbian camp, the queer cultural forms by which women who love women and the people who love them have resisted life's tangle of misogyny, transphobia, and homophobia.[2] The next chapters detail the surprising diversity of bars owned by or catering to lesbians, from bars that emphatically refuse being a "lesbian bar," to those that describe themselves as "women's bars" or "everybody bars," to those that accept the term. But all of the surviving lesbian bars share an embrace of all LGBTQ+ people and straight people as well; all described themselves as open and welcoming, even to straight men. This poses a challenge both to popular conceptions of lesbian bars as places only for lesbians, but also to the women who desire such spaces today.[3]

The only time I visited Wild Side West was on a date with a guy. I didn't know that Wild Side West was a "mystery" to lesbians, nor that it would struggle to be recognized as a lesbian bar. All I knew was that it was near his house and thus convenient should we want to take things to the next level, which we would. Of course we'd met online—how else was a grad student from the scruffy East Bay to meet a San Francisco professional? Such things were common even before smartphones, another reason to be skeptical that Grindr killed the gay bar.[4] He was a German American techie who was my age but owned a house in Bernal Heights, a stark contrast to my graduate student stipend and uninsulated apartment that was a barely repurposed garage. Bernal Heights is cute, all two-story wooden buildings and small mom-and-pop businesses and happy people walking fluffy dogs, a far cry from my neighborhood where dogs were for home protection, and everyone hustled to pay the Bay Area's skyrocketing rents. The date happened in 2004. I can date it precisely because he showed me a year-old video clip about whistle tips that has since gone on to live in viral infamy.

Dude took me to his neighborhood queer spot: I'm pretty sure he described it as a "welcoming" lesbian bar, the clarification, in retrospect, is telling—others were apparently not welcoming, at least to him. It was a rare sunny day in San Francisco, so the homey interior of Wild Side West was a dark tunnel, but the bartender directed us to the back garden. There the sun shone again on a lush space populated by folk art and junk that, so the legend goes, had been thrown through the windows early in the bar's career but was repurposed as planters. There were other people in the garden, including lesbians, but I only had eyes for the man I was sussing out for future husband material. We only talked long enough to finish one drink before going to his place, where we talked more after sex. He was, that kiss of death: nice. No spark to sustain an interaction beyond orgasm. I never returned to Bernal Heights again; without a car, to get there it took me over an hour, two transfers, and a half-mile walk up one of San Francisco's brutal hills.

A decade after that tepid date, local headlines screamed: "Last Call for City's Last Lesbian Bar." The closure of San Francisco's Lexington Club was bemoaned as a national watershed, leaving a capital of lesbian America without a single lesbian bar. "San Francisco Toasts to the End of an Era," wrote "girl on girl culture" magazine Autostraddle.[5] In the Huffington Post, queer geographer Jack Gieseking diagnosed gentrification for the demise of "the last lesbian bar in San Francisco" in one of many online eulogies.

Yet in the local *SF Weekly*, journalist Anna Ross noted that San Francisco still had, well, *something*, even as she too mourned the sale of "the city's only remaining lesbian bar (assuming you don't count Wild Side West)."[6] In 2022's pandemic times, Wild Side West is still going strong, and folks have long been surprised when I questioned their certainty that San Francisco had no lesbian bar. One of my queer students from San Francisco wrinkled her nose at the bar's Bernal Heights neighborhood as "far." One writer described it as "a lesbian bar in denial."[7] A journalist took pains to describe the bar's "mystery": "Wild Side West doesn't really identify as lesbian. But dykes rule and women come first, so don't you forget it."[8] The "not identifying as lesbian" is somewhat contradicted by the bar's own website, which describes Wild Side West as a "neighborhood institution" founded "by out and proud lesbians"; it is "LGBTQ owned and operated since day one" and "continues to be lesbian-owned," where "every night is a blend of lesbians, locals, eclectic art and neighborhood sports bar."[9] That's an awful lot of lesbians for a place to not be recognized as lesbian!

The widespread mourning of the Lexington despite the thriving Wild Side West reveals much. The first is the widespread concern, since the Lex's closure, about the "death" and "disappearance" of lesbian bars.[10] From a peak of over 200 in the late 1980s, a 2022 list from the Lesbian Bar Project found only 21 in the entire country.[11] By my count, 65 percent of the nation's lesbian bars closed in the twenty years between 1997 and 2017.[12]

The second is the ambiguity about what counts as a lesbian bar. That little study of mine from 2019 enumerated only fifteen lesbian bar listings in the *Damron Guide,* a number that was echoed by the corporate-sponsored crowdfunding campaign, 2020's Lesbian Bar Project.[13] Neither of these counted Wild Side West as a lesbian bar. But who decides what counts as a lesbian bar, anyways? Who mourns the loss of women-forward spaces? What happens when transgender and gender nonbinary people enter "women-only" spaces? And if lesbians own it and patronize it, who cares what identity is imputed to what is otherwise just a small business with a liquor license?

As the lesbians in this section of the book testify, many lesbians never liked women's-only spaces. One described them as humorless and exclusionary. Even among bars described as lesbian bars by patrons and journalists, owners often complicate that simple identifica-tion: Of the fourteen women or gender nonbinary bar owners who I interviewed, one place was described as a lesbian bar, three as wom-en's bars, two as queer bars, and the other eight as "gay" or "every-body bars." But what they shared, although it was left implicit was that these are places not dominated by gay men.

For example, Diva Dee, the owner of the Good Time Lounge in Denison, Texas, reported that when she first bought the region's only gay bar, "A lot of people said, 'You need to turn it into a lesbian bar.' But I don't want a lesbian bar! I want a bar for everybody!" Danny Hart, owner of the Latina-serving Bum Bum Bar in New York City, contrasted her style with a previous owner: "She didn't want men here. She'd kick them out. No! You can't discriminate. This is a bar for women, but everyone is welcome." Jay Blue, one of the co-owners of the racially diverse Q Bar in Greensboro, North Carolina, described her establishment this way: "I would say it's a bar for everyone with a predominantly gay crowd." Jo Strong, who has owned Squiggy's in Binghamton, New York, since 1990, was not inclined to try to make the longtime gay bar into a lesbian bar: "If people ask, I say it is predom-inantly gay because this is where gay people feel the most comfort-able, and it has to be that way." To Deb Barnett of Pueblo, Colorado, the problem with the Pirate's Cove, which she inherited from her les-bian aunt, wasn't the fact that it's a gay bar, but that "it's not a gay bar so much anymore. It's a people's bar. We get a lot of straight couples." Vanna Beldon, owner of the restaurant Flavor and social space Attic in Baltimore, Maryland, described her COVID-closed place as "lesbi-an-owned but not just for women: We're for the whole community." Of her queer karaoke night, she gushed, "You'd be surprised how many [straight] allies love the music: They don't even care with Queeraoke!"

This fact that so many of the women who own LGBTQ+ spaces refuse the label "lesbian" raises many possibilities. One is that les-bian bar owners use other labels while running woman-forward places. Another is that some of the decline in lesbian bars is due to overly strict definitions of what counts as a lesbian bar. Indeed, Wild Side West wasn't counted as one of fifteen of the country's lesbian bars when the Lesbian Bar Project first debuted in 2020, nor during its up-dated list of lesbian bars later in the year. Only in 2021 did Wild Side

West appear as one of the expanded list of twenty-one bars—a 40 percent increase that magically appeared during a pandemic, evidence that overly restrictive definitions about what counts as a lesbian bar had unfairly suppressed their number. But Wild Side West didn't suddenly identify as lesbian for the cash: It was one of three lesbian bars to decline the pandemic relief funds so that contributions could go to bars in greater need.[14] What counts as a lesbian bar is not obvious even to lesbian bar superfans.

There have never been many lesbian bars compared to the number that serve primarily men. The peak of lesbian bars in the United States was around the year 1987, when there were 206 in the country. But in that same year, the *Damron Guide* listed 1,274 bars serving mainly gay men.[15] By 1992, however, lesbian bars collapsed to just thirty-seven: The real decline happened long before the Lexington's closure alarmed journalists. From 2002 onwards, there were never more than thirty-three lesbian bars in the entire country.

But during that same time period, something interesting happened. The numbers of gender-integrated bars serving both women and men skyrocketed, becoming the most common type of gay bar by 1997. Bars serving only gay men went on the decline, too: Gender *segregation* was itself on the decline.

It's unclear from my data what happened. Were these lesbian bars invaded by men, so their gender integration was involuntary? Were men's bars becoming more welcoming to women—not turning them away at the door, not asking them for multiple forms of ID, or not overlooking them at the bar?[16] Was it unified work towards shared goals, for gay marriage and an end to the military ban on openly LGBTQ servicemembers? In my fantasy, the tremendous care work shown by lesbians to gay men during the AIDS crisis spurred mixed socializing, though I have little evidence for this.[17]

Suffice it to say that gay bars were heavily gender segregated until the 1990s when they became increasingly integrated. Further research is also necessary to learn if this gender integration extended to transgender and gender nonbinary people as well.[18] My research assistant Tory Sparks thinks that as lesbian bars closed, "New bars did so with a more fluid idea of sexual orientation, more awareness of transness and bisexuality." Tory reminded me that often women and nonbinary people feel invisible in many gay bars: overlooked by the bartenders, bumped into by men, and made to feel like furniture in the way. To which, they added, "The rise of the 'love is love' politic easily translates into the 'everyone bar.'"

Those few lesbian bars that have existed have long been places to find love, but were also havens from violent attacks on gender-non-conforming butches in the streets.[19] And they were also places where the butch/femme dynamic could blossom, that practice of taking toxic gender expectations and remixing them towards erotic lesbian ends.[20] Women-owned businesses are themselves uncommon, but wage discrimination and homophobia make it especially challenging to run a business that serves a community that makes less money and has more family care responsibilities.[21]

Economics certainly plays a role, but lesbian *culture* does as well; lesbian feminists have long critiqued capitalism, alcohol-based socializing, and spaces that are not welcoming to children.[22] That culture has itself seen shifts—from women identifying as woman-loving dykes to queers disdainful of gender binaries and deliberately inclusive of pansexual and transgender people.[23] Nevertheless, commercial spaces controlled by women, and intended for women, are precarious and precious, and also hard to boundary enforce. But most major cities with gayborhoods managed to have at least one lesbian bar. Until recently, that is.

The loss of lesbian bars represents an important shift away from women's-only spaces as the sole or most-important measure of lesbian community.[24] But even young queer women who support gender-nonbinary people mourn the loss of lesbian bars.[25] Bar owners who embrace a women-first mission have integrated with the support of male patrons, as all the lesbian bar professionals in this section will testify. It is telling that all of the bars recognized as lesbian bars are nestled in gay neighborhoods among other gay bars or are in large cities with several other gay bars. In such company, they don't face pressure to be bars for everyone, as lone outpost bars do.

As the bars in this section of the book also illustrate, many lesbians never wanted a women's-only bar—and designed their establishments to embrace gay men and straight patronage from the start. These institutions seem to have largely avoided the controversies over transgender patronage that have dogged some women's-only spaces. Some owners now describe their bars as "LGBT" or "queer" bars to signal a welcome to transgender patrons, while others have long defined themselves as "everybody bars" to signal their welcome to straights.

Such gender-integrated bars were mourned as "killed" in the "great lesbian bar die off" by the popular history blog *Lost Womyn's Space*. The author, who asked to remain anonymous so as to not be harassed online, documented both the sisterhood such spaces offered but also the sexism, misogyny, and discrimination lesbians often face in gay men's spaces.[26] With meticulous methodology, she mourned women's colleges gone co-ed, the closure of lesbian bars, and the deterioration of women's restaurants, women-only train cars, and other women-only spaces around the world. The blog has been hailed by scholars and informed the groundbreaking 2016 National Park Service documentation of LGBTQ+ America.[27]

Lost Womyn's Space had a strict definition for what counts as a lesbian bar, which the author determined by scrolling through club listings, Facebook pages, consumer review websites, and online photo galleries for evidence. These criteria include the presence of men or "het couples" in photographs, evidence of drag queens, or bars that "downplay [their] female identity," are no longer "specifically identified as lesbian" or are otherwise not "an unapologetic dyke place." The blogger describes bars that identify as queer, LGBT, "gay and lesbian" as "inclusive to the extreme" and "deceptively airy fairy."[28] In criticizing these neologisms, she mourns the fact that "the term 'lesbian bar' has at times been used almost as a dirty word."[29]

The blog also exposes sexism in journalistic accounts, lambasting the author of a 2015 article about London's closed LGBT bars for excluding lesbian bars:

> Even though lesbian bars are rare and getting rarer by the moment, the queers and gay boys still couldn't manage to identify and include the few that existed without being prodded. Very typical as these things go.[30]

Similarly, the blog ridicules the men who leave poor Yelp reviews of the service in places intended for women, dubbing them "the Embittered Boys contingent, who just didn't feel their egos were being coddled in a sufficient fashion."[31]

The blog's author provided a list of implicit justifications for women's-only bars, including charity events and support for lesbian institutions:

> It's hard to imagine that the boys' bars will be putting on a fundraiser for a sister with breast cancer or to raise uniform money for the local dyke softball team. But it's all just a party, ya know? Loss of lesbian community means nothing.[32]

Other reasons why the author was skeptical of establishments "that can't (or won't) identify as 'lesbian' with no qualifications" is that they attract male "voyeurs and predators."[33]

Lost Womyn's Space devoted an extensive post to the Lexington Club's closure in San Francisco, including owner Lila Thirkield's interview with veteran LGBTQ+ journalist and gay bar co-owner Marke B. In it, Thirkield discussed her other bar, Virgil's Sea Room, which she described as "different in that it is an 'everybody bar' but it has a huge queer sense about it, many queer staff members, and some great crossover already."[34] The question of crossover with what or whom was left unanswered: with the ostensibly straight bars nearby, with the old Lexington crowd, or with San Francisco's diverse Ls, Gs, Bs, Ts, and Qs.

If the Lex owner's new bar sounds familiar, it's because that description is awfully close to Wild Side West's, about which one regular reported, "The lesbian owners have always said that it's a neighborhood bar that just 'happens' to get a lot of lesbians—and that's true."[35] Yet another regular described the "sacred" difference between the Lexington Club and Wild Side West (WSW):

> If I'm going to go to a bar with my lesbian friends, I'm going to go to the Lex. If I'm going to go to a bar with almost any other friend, straight women, gay men, whoever, I'd choose a different bar. That's not because the Lex isn't friendly, but because it is (in my mind) a space for lesbian women and F to M trans folks. It's a safe and comfortable place for that community to congregate,

and frankly that's sacred to me. When it comes to WSW, I'd take anyone there without even thinking twice about it. I expect to see straight women and men in there, along with lesbians or trans folks.[36]

This writer, while acknowledging trans men, implicitly excluded transgender lesbians from the space, circumscribing the cissexist boundary policing that likely doomed lesbian bars "only for women." But Wild Side West's queer indeterminate identity and mixed patronage makes it more like the lesbian-owned bars in the rest of the country described in this section of the book than the women-only lesbian bars mourned on *Lost Womyn's Spaces*. And she is right to mourn: In all my travels I found no woman-only lesbian bars anywhere in the country. And even the lesbian-inclusive Virgin's Sea Room, which never made any list of lesbian bars, itself closed in 2021, a casualty of the COVID-19 pandemic.[37]

But even some lesbians who own bars they describe as lesbian bars have unambivalently embraced integration with men, straight people, and gender nonbinary patrons. It would be easy to be cynical about these forms of integration as forced business necessities, watered-down political compromises, unwelcomely criminalized by gender-equality ordinances, or an accidental side effect of straight people's embrace of LGBTQ+ rights. Certainly, GLQ women in straight-integrated spaces face special challenges in finding each other in seas of straight women, a challenge that GBQ men may soon face in gay bars gone straight-integrated.[38] But for gay bars that want to become queer bars, the surviving lesbian bars have lessons on how to stay integral to a community while serving people beyond it. As the lesbians in following chapters testify, owning bars integrated with men, transgender people, and straight women was a deliberate political project, one in which their vision for the world—and for women who love women—is winning.

Eighteen

I Always Hated Lesbian Bars

Sneakers
JAMESTOWN, NEW YORK

Some lesbians don't like lesbian bars, including lesbians who own gay bars—one possible reason for the lack of lesbian bars. Mary Green founded Sneakers in 1986 during the peak of lesbian bars in the United States, and she's outlasted almost all of them.[1] Mary is an athletic short-haired woman in her 60s who wore a polo shirt when we spoke, making her look like the golfer she is. I never asked why the bar has the name that it does. In fact, I never asked about any bar names! Such are the perils of having a gay insider write a book: Bar names for me were obviously what they were, and unremarkable. Sneakers are banned at code leather bars and were long a sign of a collegiate aspirational middle-classness among gay men.[2] They are also comfortable and everyday, just like the bar whose name they share.

When Mary got into the business, hers was the fifth gay bar at the edge of Lake Chautauqua, home of the adult-education movement and convention center known as the Chautauqua Institution that Teddy Roosevelt called "the most American thing in America."[3] Since 2005, Sneakers has been the last gay bar and an outpost bar in a shrinking city of fewer than 30,000 people that has been betting big on a tourism boom from its new National Comedy Museum. The *New York Times* expressed skepticism in a piece "Heard the One About Jamestown?" sniffing that

> the center will have to overcome its proximity to, well, nowhere. The nearest large city is Buffalo, some 75 minutes to the north by car. Cleveland is two hours to the west. Pittsburgh, to the south, is a little farther than that. And New York City? A little more than six hours by car.[4]

The railroad tracks and Chadakoin River separate Sneakers from Jamestown's downtown with its quaint museum honoring hometown girl Lucille Ball, whose statue stands proudly in a village park.

The two times I visited Sneakers on my way from Ohio to see friends in Syracuse, the patronage was about half women, some in couples, with a mix of others including gay men and older working-class straight men. The bar has wood floors and wood lath on the ceiling, giving it the warm feeling of sitting in a gay ship adrift on good vibes. As Mary and I chatted at the end of the bar, one of these men interrupted, pointed at her, and informed me, "This is the sweetest person you'll ever know!" A rainbow awning welcomed visitors into the building that has survived a fire, floods, and not one but two cars crashing into the bar, located as it is on the riverfront corner right across from the Harrison Street Bridge. Inside, a pool table, jukebox, and small stage mark the entertainment options. A sign in the corner near the community bulletin board states "Sneakers is a gay owned & operated establishment," eschewing the word "lesbian" altogether.

When I asked why she and a partner decided to get into the bar business, Mary was emphatic that Sneakers would be a bar with a mixed clientele and not like the existing gay bars in town: "We didn't like the other bars! They were segregated. They were boy bars, you know what I mean? They weren't real thrilled about us lesbians, and we had a lot of straight friends."

Reflecting on her thirty-five-plus years of running a place that is mixed gay-straight by design, she said proudly, "This has always been an okey-dokey place for everyone, so you can bring your friends and family, and it's still like that. It was like that then. It was mixed. It always was and it always will be." Any establishment she was going to own was going to embrace her fun friends, and that was never going to be a bar just for women. As Mary opined, "To have a good time, a bunch of lesbians is usually not it." A lesbian colleague asked me what I thought Mary meant by this statement: What an interview fail—I should have asked for clarification! After all, the lesbians in my life are hilarious, almost always intentionally (just kidding!).

Besides welcoming straight people from the beginning, Sneakers also hosted drag shows by Mary's gay male friends, a rarity in old-school lesbian bars at the time because, as Gayle Rubin recalled of the feminist critique, "You were supposed to think that drag queens were sexist and degrading imitations of women, which I always knew wasn't true."[5] As Mary recalled, "We built—us dyke girls—the stage for the guys to dance on," she explained, detailing all the other work in the bar that they did themselves. Drag in the bar is rarer now, though, because the queens "all got old and fat," and "some moved away and some passed away." This makes Sneakers somewhat of an outlier, not reaping the exploding crop of contemporary drag artists. Instead, the dance floor more often hosts karaoke and live music, including by the men of Fresh Buns, New Meat, a punny name that might not fly in a lesbian space from days of yore.

When I asked Mary if she'd ever considered opening a lesbian bar, she wrinkled her nose and said she'd always hated them: "Why did I hate those kind of bars? Because I had a lot of gay guy friends! A lot of the gay guys are way more fun. They're the funnest to party with, they're the funnest to go out with." Whether this was an act of self-misogyny or an accurate reflection of the lesbian scene in western New York at the time, I didn't interrupt the flow of our conversation. Mary recalled a memorable evening that solidified her dislike of the nearest lesbian bar for its hostility to men and drag:

> We used to go out—my friend Ronnie, he didn't do drag—we would take him to this bar there was in Buffalo, and they wouldn't let men in. There was Chief, the bouncer. Now, we'd go there all the time, we spenta lotta money, we were friendly, but we went there that *one time* and Chief wasn't going to let him in! Well, we said we'll go find some other bar, even some straight bar![6]

Mary recalled the flush early years of the bar and the stark changes that the industry had undergone during her many years in the business: "We figured we were going to keep making that kind of money for decades but that wasn't what happened, but that first year we were rolling in it." Other owners, too, recalled how in "the old days," just hanging out a shingle that said "gay bar" would attract crowds and cash, which allowed owners to hire others to work the bar for them. Mary reminisced how "the first year we weren't here, we had someone we trusted to manage for us, and we traipsed." She recalled summer trips to Provincetown and winter ski excursions in Colorado, and slyly added, "And we snorted a lot of it up our nose back in the 90s."

Sneakers has an older crowd during the day while "the kids" come out at night, and its clientele reflects the region's aging and impoverished population. As one man at the bar interjected, "The economy went to shit ten years ago." Jamestown made its fortunes in the heavy industrial manufacturing of crescent wrenches, washing machines, and lever-pulled voting machines and has suffered the fate of most American manufacturing towns. Today about 30 percent of the population lives below the poverty line. Being a mom-and-mom business in such an economy means it's hard to match current prices with what patrons can afford. Mary recalled that "when we first opened, we were selling twelve-ounce drafts three for a dollar! But a keg has gone from $30 to $80 in thirty years, and that's a lot of money." Of patrons and prices today, she continued, "All the decent booze is $40 so you have to charge $4.50, so they can't really afford it, or then they can only afford one." And further, Mary exclaimed, "A lot of the kids don't drink!" to which two of the men sitting at the bar chimed in. "Me too! I'm diabetic, I got that neuropathy." The other said he was diabetic but still drank: "Hey, you should interview me!" Mary waved him off, "You're not even gay. He's only interested in us. Sit there and enjoy your beer."

For its diversity by sexual orientation, Sneakers is a white crowd in a county that is 94 percent white. There was a year or so when majority African American crowds came, however. She recalled that she had a DJ who began playing rap music, and it attracted Black gay patrons: "I was busy! I was jamming! I was giving it all I had. I was going through bottles of Hennessey like you wouldn't believe."

The crowds weren't worth the troubles they brought, she related, including fights, glass bottles down the pockets of the pool table, and bags-worth of litter in neighboring properties. As Mary complained of the patronage then and the strict rules that link 911 calls to liquor licenses,

> They brought the trouble, they brought the drugs, they brought the cops. If I was going to keep my license I had to get rid of the fights outside. They had nothing to do with what was going on inside, but you're to blame for everything that's happening for the whole block.

Mary told a story about one fight where people were waiting outside her club to ambush someone who was at Sneakers with a friend, and the customer was gravely injured. Nevertheless, because so many 911 calls were placed from near her establishment, she was shut down for over a month and in danger of losing her liquor license. The solution was simple: "I took the rap music out, and they had to go someplace else." The new pace of business suits her: "I make my money seven days a week instead of just on Friday and Saturday. I don't need that trouble."

When I'm in the process of conducting an interview, I'm in the zone—fingers flying to capture the words someone is saying. My brain is doing thirteen things at once: making abbreviations that allow me to reconstruct the conversation in the future, listening to what is being said, while also anticipating how I might guide the conversation across the six main themes that I cover in all the interviews. This means I don't react emotionally to what people are saying in the moment—out of distraction, yes, but also from a scholarly training to just nonjudgmentally let people say their piece, as well as out of an emotionally repressed Protestant background that abhors direct confrontation. All this is to say that when I read this part of the transcript later, I cringed and had more questions than answers: Was it because the new rap-music-loving crowd was younger than her typical patrons that they "brought the trouble"? Was it racist policing that attracted attention to Sneakers when Black people were in attendance? Mary herself had been willing to cater to the new crowd by letting the DJ play music that she herself didn't care for. And Mary was aware that her actions raised the specter of racism, but she was attentive: "It was the drugs and fights that made me have them leave. Not because they were Black."

Mary told me she doesn't even think of retiring from her gay bar because selling the building, which she owns, would mean leaving her home; she lives upstairs. As she mused, "I don't know what I would do. I've thought about it. I would still be sitting in someone else's bar, and it wouldn't be good. And why? I live here, I own it, it's paid for." Working her 60s isn't a chore, though: "I don't consider this a job. It is, but I don't consider it a job, really. So why would I want to be a greeter at Walmart even though they're paying ten bucks an hour?" The only way she could imagine not working there is if she couldn't drink. "If I didn't drink, I wouldn't do it. If they said sometime that I couldn't drink there'd be a FOR SALE sign on the window because I wouldn't put up with him," pointing at the straight patron who'd begged me to interview him.

I reflected on Mary's insistence of a straight-inclusive gay bar since the 1980s, so different from descriptions of big-city gay bars but so common to small-city gay bars. Were they pre-post-gay? Was straight inclusivity invented in a heartland that has long since gone red? Or is there a way in which small-city LGBTQ+ folks are accepted in ways we can't recognize from within our blue bubbles? Other writers have characterized gay bars that welcome straight people as "neoliberal," portraying the consumption of the environment by straight people as coming at the expense of the production of a safe space for LGBTQ+ people.[7] But for Mary, this wasn't a calculated business decision but a social one, of creating a place for her and her friends to hang out and party. There was no ambivalence here. In our 2018 interview, Mary concluded by reflecting on the death of her best friend and partner Marilyn and the economic challenges in Jamestown. Swinging her arm across the sunlit room, she said, "I'm lucky I'm still here. I'm still a gay bar. I still welcome the gay people. Bring your friends! If it wasn't for them and the straight friends and the loyal customers, *pfft!*"

Nineteen

Why Can't We Be Straight Friendly?

Alibis
OKLAHOMA CITY, OKLAHOMA

To visit a city with more than one lesbian bar, I had to visit a metropolis that endured an unspeakable terrorist attack, a city where LGBTQ+ legal activism predates the Stonewall riots, where vast private companies set Supreme Court precedents, a city so metropolitan it has "city" in its name. So I went, of course, to Oklahoma City. You were thinking a different city? Tsk tsk. Well yes, New York City has three lesbian bars that receive much press.

We can guess why New York City might have more than one lesbian bar, but why did Oklahoma City have two as recently as 2022? I can only speculate. Is it because the founder and CEO of Oklahoma's Hobby Lobby, which won the right to deny contraception to its employees in an eponymous Supreme Court case in 2014, funnels so many funds to anti-gay politicians that lesbians must huddle together?[1] Is it because a state politician recently declared homosexuality to be a bigger threat to the American way of life than terrorism or Islam?[2] Possibly, but there are plenty of other red states with Republican politicians spewing homophobic diarrhea, so if public prejudice was the rain that caused lesbian bars to blossom, we'd expect some of them in

Idaho or Arkansas, states with none. I will only note that Oklahoma City is the Horse Show Capital of the World, the home of the Museum of Women Pilots, and you can buy the most charming Oklahomasexual t-shirts at the city's hipster boutiques (do you even have to ask?).

Tiffany McDaniel and Krystal Campbell-McDaniel have owned Alibis in Oklahoma City since 2010, one of two lesbian bars in the metropolitan area of 1.4 million people. Krystal described the decline of lesbian bars as a function of gendered economics and lesbian culture: "I think one of the biggest problems of lesbian bars is the fact that we don't have the expendable income that most of our male counterparts have, that's why we shut down quicker."[3] She also noted cultural challenges for lesbian bars, adding, "I feel that a lot of lesbian bars aren't as open to the straight community. We'll look astray at them as if straight couples are always looking for swinging and push them out. But that's revenue!"

Krystal was one of the three lesbian bar owners (out of fourteen) I interviewed to cite economics as a reason to be mixed, but her partner Tiffany immediately qualified this:

I don't think there's a reason to discriminate because you're straight. That's like you're going down to their level if you kick the straight people out. We want to be allowed so everyone should be allowed.[4]

Krystal then added a case for empathy in welcoming straight people to their lesbian-owned bar: "We don't feel comfortable in some straight bars, we're never outwardly affectionate so we won't go unless there's four to six of us. I would never want someone in my bar to feel like that ever. *Ever!*" Tiffany added, using the metaphor of racial segregation, "Isn't that like having a whites-only bathroom?" As she continued, "That's what makes the world great, the ethnicities and the cultures and being different genders!" The pair thus framed their lesbian bar as a mixed LGBTQ-straight space for primarily political and ethical reasons, despite acknowledging economics.

This diversity extends to viewpoints that would make me uncomfortable. As Krystal elaborated, "I can't understand wanting to be in a room with people who identify like myself and have the same ideas and same dress style." Continuing, she made a case for what cultural conservatives might call viewpoint diversity:

> I want you to sit there and tell me that you're one with nature. I want to hear that! I want to hear that you're kinda racist because you had a bad experience with some group, and I want to talk to you about that. I don't want to be exclusive of that or anything else. I like the diversity of it!

This vision contradictions the visions of safe spaces invoked by the owners of queer bars in which safety is discursive as well as physical, but it does square with the older white feminist conception of "safe space" as one in which differences are bridged for a better future and is also what scientists describe as the first step in actually changing hearts and minds.[5]

This diversity of viewpoints was easily extended to straight men at the bar, some of whom had been patrons since long before the women owned it. Describing the men who were Alibis' regulars, Krystal said they ranged from, "almost homeless to millionaires. The lesbians accept them, almost adopt them, they become family. We call ourselves a big dysfunctional family." This use of "family" was not just a metaphor, Krystal explained: "We have several straight men—if someone needs to be moved or someone's having trouble with a neighbor, the straight men almost act as fathers: They're the first to go fix a tire." This family feeling and mutual aid did not preclude heated discussions, though it brought more fun and the diversity both owners enjoyed.

This familiarity was something neither had felt in one of the lesbian bars in Oklahoma City that has since closed. As Tiffany described it, "It was just an older lesbian bar. If a man walked in, they would look at him funny and he'd leave, and they're no longer in the business. They only picked who they wanted in there: older lesbians." The implication hanging in the air was that this was part of the reason it was no longer in business. Being younger than the old-timers meant the couple didn't feel welcome there, and the feeling was reciprocal, as Tiffany continued: "They still didn't feel comfortable with you in there if you weren't part of that clique, that older generation." Krystal concurred: "It was a different dynamic. *I* didn't feel comfortable in there either." Such generational explanations are commonly used to account for lesbian community decline: that old bar dykes were replaced by young queers. But this generational trope that old lesbians and young lesbians are in conflict goes back to at least the 1950s and is belied by the activism that unites lesbians across generational lines, the positive experiences lesbians have in cross-generational encounters, and that who fits in what generation often varies in different regions of the country.[6] Thus while lesbians and queers often invoke generational explanations, there is reason to be skeptical about sweeping generalizations, even as it is possible that they are valid in some parts of the country.[7]

And yet, Krystal also described a generational difference among lesbians in preferences for women's only spaces and spaces integrated with men, stating, "We still have contact with a lot of the older generation. They're more caught off guard if there's a bunch of men in here, they'll have more of an issue with it." In contrast, she claimed, "The younger crowd, they don't care. Probably from mid-40s on up are the ones who have issues with it, maybe late 40s to early 50s. They don't stay as long when the crowd is more mixed." She understands how the familiarity of her straight male patrons can be off-putting: "Most of the guys who do come in, they joke around. They know where to draw the line . . . mostly. They kid around with us." Describing the difference between herself and older lesbians, "Probably they had to be more protective when they first came out than we do now." In-group kidding is only funny if the other person is actually in the group.

If Tiffany and Krystal value a bar for everybody, that doesn't mean that they don't do things specifically to serve the LGBTQ+ community. This includes an epic Pride weekend that sees their back parking lot, overseen by a lavender wall with an outline of Oklahoma state, transformed into a beach volleyball barbecue by truckloads of sand. But being a community resource is not just in once-a-year programming, but in the hope that they offer to patrons every day. As Krystal passionately explained:

> We've always wanted to be a part of what's important for our community. We're not just serving drinks. We're there for when

someone's thinking of committing suicide. The people we come in contact with, it's important for them to have a place to go when they have a hard time.

She gave an example, "Helping get people sober is important even though we own a bar. We were part of an intervention with one patron because they had a problem, so we helped organize that. It's a community thing, it's not just a bar."

Lesbian bars, then, are not-quite-for-profits, too. Tiffany described how the bar is part of the old-school trend of being home to people as their chosen family: "Even for the transgender and gay patrons, if their parents disown them, now we're their family. We're open on Christmas and Thanksgiving, and that's where they spend their holidays, with their new family." Krystal described how other holidays are important bar celebrations as well: "We do an adult Easter egg hunt for the people who don't have places to go. They come and eat cookout and have fun and play games." I asked if there was a drink minimum or cover for these events. "No, you can buy nothing," Krystal explained:

> And we're still going to have the same events every year for people who don't have family for Christmas or Thanksgiving. The homeless people? Grab yourself a plate! You can't stay in because you don't have an ID but get a plate, please help yourselves.

Cultivating these relationships with straight people has direct benefits, although neither Krystal nor Tiffany framed them instrumentally. When I asked about the friendliness of their interactions with authorities, Tiffany described a familial relationship to a city official: "Our fire marshal, his sister is a lesbian but he comes in here, and on Sundays we have thirty to fifty DEA officers and firemen. They're all on bikes, having popcorn and Bloody Marys and beers." This family relationship led to some brotherly protection after the shootings at Pulse, as she recalled: "After the Orlando thing, we had our big Pride event and didn't allow anyone with backpacks in, but they were checking up on us. It seemed like every thirty minutes a fire truck would drive by just to let us know that he was watching out for us."

As she concluded, "Our fire marshal has been coming in as long as I've been here, so he's very protective and watching out for us: 'Anything you girls need!'" These kinds of close ties to local officials are not unprecedented: Freddie Lutz of the suburban Freddie's Beach Bar (Arlington, Virginia) has a whole wall of honor for Pentagon brass and local police who have regular happy hours in the Barbie-strewn bar. Such connections to local officials might deter some people from coming, especially Black and Indigenous queer people, but for Krystal and Tiffany, law enforcement patronage is what it means to be part of the wider community.[8]

The duo were the *only* owners I interviewed who described feelings of safety as a business concern. Krystal described the advantages of having a close relationship with the straight motorcycle tavern around the corner:

> We have a bunch of bikers who in the evenings will go to a biker bar around the corner. They help us out, if there's trouble they handle it for the bartender. We have a code. If I'm here alone and there's someone who isn't looking right I can just call over there and say "I want sex now" and they would jump and roll up.

Tiffany interjected, "They'd not even say anything, just being here is enough to protect her." Krystal again: "Sometimes you're here alone until the big crowd gets in. It's just a way of being protected. You just never know. I'm never by myself, with them." By this she meant that she could be the only person in her bar, but the motorcycle guys' willingness to "jump and roll up" means she never felt alone, a concern no men bar owners reported.

As Tiffany concluded, there are straight people who don't fit into straight bars, and Alibis serves as an important place for them, a politics of inclusion that is itself pretty queer:[9] "I think there has to be a lesbian and gay space where straight people feel comfortable. Why does it always have to be the other way around?"

It may be that this welcome of straight bars is why the Lesbian Bar Project did not include Alibis on their initial list of the fifteen lesbian bars left in the country. But this inclusion of straight people was common to all of the bar owners I interviewed. I can't know whether owners were telling me what I wanted to hear, were negotiating local antidiscrimination ordinances, were mindful of their local economic circumstances, were being inclusive of bi and pan and trans people in seemingly straight relationships, genuinely liked hanging out in mixed gay-straight environments, or some combination of all of these. But the days of gay bars just for gay people is over, perhaps ushered in by small-city gay bars like Ann Arbor's \aut\ BAR. Passionately, Tiffany exclaimed: "Why can't we be straight friendly? There has to be a slot for everybody!"

Twenty

White Folks, Gay Men, and Straight Black Folks Don't Come

Club Xclusive
HATTIESBURG, MISSISSIPPI

While many lesbian-owned bars have no trouble attracting men, Club Xclusive struggles to attract customers beyond its core patronage of Black women. Shawn Perryon Sr. has owned the venue in Hattiesburg, Mississippi, since 2008, a haven from the forces that shape the local climate: the racism, sexism, classism, and homophobia that can be as smothering as the humidity.[1] For many years it has been the only LGBTQ+ bar in the Mississippi Pine Belt region of 300,000 people, an outpost bar in a city that is approximately equidistant from New Orleans (Louisiana), Mobile (Alabama), and Jackson (Mississippi).

Club Xclusive is also one of the few bars for LGBTQ+ people of color in the entire country, and one of the rare LGBTQ+ bars owned by Black women until the 2019 opening of Herz in Mobile and the 2021 debut of Nobody's Darling in Chicago.[2] When I visited Club Xclusive in 2017, the club was open mainly on Fridays and Saturdays, with Saturday the busiest night. It occupied a low-slung warehouse in an isolated strip mall toward the edge of town, sharing its plaza with a tobacco and liquor store, an antique store, and a rusted-out car. The club serves only beer and wine because Mississippi state law requires liquor license holders to earn 25 percent of their revenue from food receipts, and Xclusive doesn't have a kitchen. I witnessed many patrons drinking liquor in their cars or sipping from flasks in the club, which Shawn tolerates, even though it limits the club's earning potential.

Shawn never intended the bar to be primarily for lesbians: "Everything I do is for the LGBT, but most of the gay men here, for some reason, they feel like I cater only to the girls, the women, but that's not the case. You're judging me because I'm a woman!"[3] The night I was at the club, the crowd was no more than 20 percent men, including Shawn's son: I often met bar owners' birth families in their bars. The fact that Black gay men attend Hattiesburg's straight clubs perplexes Shawn, whose Facebook scrolling shows them partying elsewhere:

> I see on my timeline these gay men. I'm seeing these are not drag queens, these are regular guys. They'd rather go to a straight club because nobody will look at them like they are gay. All the gay men are in the straight clubs.

The lack of men becomes a self-fulfilling prophecy, as Shawn explains: "They can't come in here and meet nobody. They want to go where they can socialize with guys and find them a little friend."

Shawn emphasized the importance of LGBTQ+ spaces even in an era of rising equality, "When gays can go anywhere now and feel like they comfortable." Such comfort was ironic in Mississippi, Shawn described. Referencing a new state law that bucked national trends of gay acceptance, she continued:

> Say a drag queen wants to go to one of the straight clubs in Hattiesburg. They can refuse you coming in there! Nobody's really paying attention to what's going on, is what I'm feeling like, and that's why I work every day!

In 2017 when we spoke, Mississippi had just implemented HB 1523, which authorized discrimination against LGBTQ+ people by anyone with "sincerely held religious beliefs or moral convictions," a law the Supreme Court of the United States later declined to review.[4] In response, many states banned official travel to Mississippi, just as they did to a similar law championed by then-governor Mike Pence in Indiana—homophobic humidity is not just a southern phenomenon. For Shawn, the presence of such laws makes Club Xclusive all the more important: "If we want to go eat somewhere and they refuse us? I don't think it's fair."

Shawn is similarly frustrated with the lack of draw among white LGBTQ+ folks in Hattiesburg: "Living in the South, being a business owner, you don't get the support you deserve. I feel like white people don't even come to my place and I've been here all this time." Indeed, the night I visited, I was the only white person there out of more than 200 partiers, particularly surprising given that Xclusive was, for years, the only gay bar for hours around. The lack of white patrons was especially vexing for Shawn because she has long partnered with the city's LGBTQ+ organization, the Spectrum Center—the first and longest freestanding LGBTQ+ center in the entire state, but one that is largely white.[5] Of white patrons coming to Club Xclusive, "The last two years some did because I was with the Spectrum Center, and we were planning Pride together: they had to come. Because we was everywhere and my place was one of the after parties." This partnership didn't yield the results that she'd hoped for, as she complained: "Now, you know where the location is. The first year, you came, you enjoyed yourself. So, I was looking at it like, maybe some of them would come back." Shaking her head, she continued: "I didn't see them. They didn't come. They didn't drink. And then we got to the second year for Pride; I had to see these same people, and I'm always wondering, 'Why did it take you a whole year to come back to my place of business?'" White people, even those who assert that Black Lives Matter, are usually uncomfortable in Black spaces.[6]

Shawn's wondering ended in 2017 when two white LGBTQ+ community leaders opened a competing LGBTQ+ club in a historic building downtown, far from Club Xclusive's location beside a state highway. This was "a slap in the face" because originally Shawn had approached one of them with the plans for a club that would serve the entire LGBTQ+ community. Instead, this so-called business partner quietly dropped Shawn and "put a white guy in my place, and it kinda crushed me because you didn't tell me. I had to hear about it at Pride." This betrayal undermined Shawn's mission to integrate the LGBTQ+ community: "We would have had the unity with the Black and the whites, but when you made that move you made me feel like that wasn't what you wanted." No one from the other side would speak to me on the record about their reasons why they did not pursue collaboration. Nevertheless, Shawn said magnanimously, "I haven't seen and heard from them since: 'I wish you nothing but the best.'" The new restaurant and club, the Black Sheep's Café and Speakeasy, had an upscale menu and was preferred by the Black middle-class lesbian I chatted with at its bar, but it lasted only about a year before folding. This left Club Xclusive again the only LGBTQ+ bar in the region, albeit not the only public LGBTQ+ space, given the Spectrum Center.

Similarly, straight Black folks don't really attend Club Xclusive, either. Shawn asserted that it wasn't for lack of knowledge:

> Trust and believe—they know that I'm here. They know Club Xclusive. Main thing they say: "That a gay club." That's fine! They're not going to come. Straight people are not going to come."

Here Shawn was the only owner who described straight people as being unwilling to come to her club, perhaps the result of a post-AIDS fracturing of the Black community over issues of LGBT+ acceptance.[7] Hers was also the only Black-owned space that didn't also attract white people, however, a group who have their own prejudices against LGBTQ+ folks. Continuing, Shawn asserted it was probably due to some homophobia, but not one that was all-or-nothing: "Everyone has a gay family member! They'll probably come to support if one of their sisters got a show that night, but after the show they're going to leave."[8] Shawn has reached out to straight bars for partnership deals, but

> They don't want to start with gay stuff because it will mess with the crowd they already get. You know how people can be. Why we gotta be that way? Business is business! I wouldn't feel that way if some straight person wanted to rent my bar!

All this leaves Shawn with a club that she intends for everybody in Hattiesburg but attended almost "Xclusively" by Black queer women.

Echoing other owners, Shawn cited performances and fun as Club Xclusive's primary offerings, not merely being an LGBTQ+ space. "We have entertainment, the biggest party of any gay bar!" She listed lusty lip-sync performances by patrons and striptease dances by Black women, precisely the kind of sexualized entertainment that might turn off more "respectable" middle-class LGBTQ+ people of any race but are especially rare in gay strip clubs that rarely feature performers of color. Step shows are particular draws. Of these coordinated dance routines by groups of friends that are deeply embedded in the Black college experience, she smiled: "The stepping brings out a lot of younger ones, the ones that go to these universities here." Many of these women are members of LGBTQ+ Greek organizations from nearby Southern Mississippi University and William Carey University—college women who undermine any reputation of Xclusive as only for the low-class "ratchet" women disdained by one Black middle-class lesbian at the competing Black Sheep.[9] "They can't even do that stuff there," Shawn explained, because their social scenes are dominated by the straight Black Greek system. "So I have sponsored them. I give them a place to come." Club Xclusive is thus one of those rare gay bars for people of color where special QPOC cultural forms flourish: Here, Black southern lesbian culture has its own building. In the rest of the country, Black lesbians must make do with occasional pop-up parties or house parties.[10]

Patronage at Club Xclusive is anchored by the families of otherwise-unrelated LGBTQ+ people who have banded together, a support structure among Black queer people in the South that in other parts of the country might be termed "houses."[11] These families provide support and care that families of origin may not, in part due to economics and in part due to tension over homosexuality.[12] Shawn is herself the head of the Perryon family, garnering her the honorific "Senior." The Perryons even appeared in the 2014 Showtime documentary L Word Mississippi. These families include both "studs," lesbians with transgressively masculine presentations of baggy t-shirts and baseball caps, and "girls," more feminine-presenting women.[13] As Shawn said, "I'm a stud; the girls are my biggest supporters." Describing one of the families that gathers at Xclusive, she related how "On Sunday, it was their anniversary, and they did a big cookout and I let them open up the place and it was a good time." Again, attendees were almost all cis women except for four feminine men: "They had a good time with the girls, the sissy boys." I should have asked where transgender women can go.

Getting and keeping the club has been a struggle because Shawn didn't come from a background in nightlife and because of the pervasive policing of the Black community. None of the 120-plus white gay bar owners I interviewed reported police troubles. Club Xclusive's first incarnation was in Hattiesburg proper with a business partner. Shaking her head, Shawn described legal troubles perhaps related to the hyper-policing of Black communities: "As soon as we put the money down on the building, she got locked up. I'm stuck with this, and I don't know the first thing about it!" After a year, the team moved the club to the edge of town with a different business partner to avoid the police harassment that came with being in town, but that also didn't go well for personality reasons, with Shawn reporting of her new comrade: "At first it was cool, but she started to get too comfortable, basically didn't want to do anything—for me it seemed like I was working for her!" Now Shawn keeps her business in the family with her sister and her LGBTQ+ family.

Running the club goes pretty smoothly these days. "We don't have too much fighting now, but it was real bad five or six years ago," Shawn said, describing the physical assaults that many owners said were more common between lesbians than gay men. As Shawn detailed, "When you get a bunch of women together and they've been drinking . . ." she trailed off, shaking her head. The main source of drama now is from social media. Shawn pleaded,

> Don't tag me on stuff, don't bring nothing up. I don't need nobody to say nothing about my club. If you want to tell people to come, do it by word of mouth because they don't know how to advertise my business. You can send off the wrong signals. It's not professional.

Continuing, she explained, "because Hattiesburg's *small*. Everybody knows everybody's business and things they have going on, but I'm like, don't bring it to my place of business." The virtual world is not in opposition to queer physical places, but integral to them.[14]

Shawn occasionally experiences a lack of respect by patrons because she's a Black woman:

> Not everybody, mind you, but they don't respect my place of business. I feel like this: I'm Black. They'll go to a white person's place, they're going to go by the rules. I can have the same rules, I can say no smoking, I can say no sitting on the pool tables, just simple things, and they do it anyways.

I witnessed this disrespect myself. On the evening I attended the club, a person on the PA system badgered patrons to stop smoking marijuana in the club, something that irritated Shawn and attracted the attention of the off-duty police officers she hires to provide security. While other gay bar owners recalled instances with one or two disrespectful patrons, only Shawn described such widespread rule breaking. When I asked what Shawn thought might change the relationship with her patrons, she speculated: "If I was a guy they would respect me more, and if I was white, they would respect me more. But because I'm only 5 foot 2 and a half . . ."

Stature doesn't stop her from being the head of her family and a pillar of the Black LGBTQ+ community in the Piney Woods. "First it was just about the partying," Shawn confessed, but running a community institution drew her into doing more for it too: "I started doing other things: hosting Pride, helping with nonprofits." Shawn has collaborated with the city's Spectrum Center to organize a citywide Pride, distributed condoms and STI information to patrons, and organized and sponsored a Black LGBTQ+ Pride event multiple years in a row. Of her Unapologetic Black Gay Pride, Shawn shook her head, "A lot of people think that's being racist, but it's something for the Black LGBT community. The main thing is to raise the basic awareness and to try to bring unity." Thus Hattiesburg has the kind of Black queer Pride celebration that often only occurs in larger cities like Detroit, Oakland, or New York.

Shawn noted how her patrons frequently take up collections for people in need; like other gay bars, Club Xclusive is a charity fundraising powerhouse: "Like when we had a little tornado, like when they had the flood down there in New Orleans, like when we had that shooting at Pulse, we get together and recognize and take up donations to send." The Club frequently hosts benefits for community members who are ill or have died. Shawn recounted a conversation with a long-time patron, "Shawn, I had a friend that I've known forever, and he had cancer and he died." As she explained to me "at gay clubs, we do benefits. We'll get together and put together a benefit show, and we'll donate the door from the shows and give it to the family to help with funeral costs." Club Xclusive, like all successful gay bars, is not just *in* the community, but *of* it as well.

The collapse of her potential partnership with the white LGBTQ+ community leader for a restaurant-club has not put Shawn off her dreams of expanding the building by adding a kitchen and sports bar. She plans to market it on the internet for everyone, not just LGBTQ+ folks: "When you look on Xclusive it says 'gay bar,' but for my sports bar, it won't say gay bar. It's going to be mainly, gays are welcome!" She means this to bring unity, but it's also a business necessity:

> I gotta open up to a variety of people on the business side, people who want to shoot some pool, listen to the jukebox. Because if I open Xclusive everyday like that, who's to say that the LGBT is going to give me the support that I need?

Thus Shawn was one of the very few owners—almost all of them women—who described straight people in economic terms. The sports bar concept would get around one of the difficulties she perceives with the entertainment offered by Club Xclusive. "Straight people will hang with gay people," Shawn affirmed, "but they don't want to see all the shows, and the drag shows, they're not comfortable with that for some reason. But I can still save that for Saturday nights." Such an arrangement would get around the difficulty of serving a community that has so little wealth: "It's really hard to deal with strictly LGBT," she said matter-of-factly.

While these dreams give Shawn purpose, she confessed that running a bar, "It's draining, especially as you get older." Gay bars are often for the young, and many owners talked of the struggles of maintaining a party space in middle age. Shawn made herself a promise to give ten years of her life to the club and then reassess. During COVID the club was shuttered, but occasional pop-up events still bore the Xclusive name. Only later did it dawn on me that the club's name—exclusive—perhaps wasn't communicating Shawn's desire for a crowd that included everyone in the Pine Belt. And the fact that the club shows up online in multiple namings—Exclusive, Club Xclusive, Xclusive Nightclub—may have made it harder to keep it on brand.

The club reopened in 2021, but rebranded as the MvP Lounge, achieving Shawn's dreams of attracting straight people to hip hop performances and nights held by other promoters. Team Xclusive still presented occasional pop-up events in the building, however, and Shawn continued to organize Unapologetic Black Pride, continuing the mission that the head of the Perryon family had communicated to me when we'd spoken years earlier: "I'm trying to bring this unity in the Black LGBT community and raise some awareness and have some parties."

Twenty-One

The Drama of Owning a Queer Bar

Blush & Blu
DENVER, COLORADO

Part of the ambiguity about what counts as a lesbian bar comes from the queer times in which we have been living. The rise of the binary-destabilizing queer identity in the 1990s was often understood as a challenge to women-only spaces, in part for their exclusion of bisexual women and transgender people.[1] It caused a shift within the lesbian community, with scholars describing a "disidentification with the categories 'woman' and 'lesbian'" in favor of "the more inclusive queer."[2] And yet: Queer bars are still sometimes identified by others as lesbian.

Jody Bouffard has worked in—and owned—various lesbian and queer bars in Denver since 1996, selling one off, buying up another, then later consolidating in one location. She and co-owner SJ Paye opened the business that would become Blush & Blu in 2012. It has been publicly hailed as the last lesbian bar in Denver—and Colorado—with the 2021 Lesbian Bar Project describing it as one of the last twenty-one lesbian bars in the country.[3] When I visited in 2018, the website simply read, "All Humans Welcome, Always" and displayed Philadelphia's Pride flag with the Black and Brown stripes added to the rainbow to indicate racial justice.[4]

"Who are my patrons?" asked Jody rhetorically:

> Everybody. All the queers, now. When I first started it was pre-
> dominantly lesbians. Now it's straight, gay, trans, queer, nonbi-
> nary, everybody that doesn't identify in the LGBTQIA-XYZ—type
> *that* in your notes: Ha! That's my customers.

As she told a journalist, for these diverse customers, "A queer bar is
more than just a bar," explaining:

> It's a place where anyone can come and dress however they want.
> They can hold hands with whomever they want. They can sing
> and dance however they want. They can come and just be them-
> selves. These people will always have a place at Blush & Blu.[5]

But even as a queer bar, Blush & Blu still holds a special place for lesbians. As Jody told the Lesbian Bar Project in 2020,

> Women who walk through my doors come from all walks of life
> and different cultural backgrounds, which allows the younger
> generation to have a positive cultural experience. The community
> needs these kinds of bars, for not only the social experience, but
> also to support each other.[6]

To me, Jody particularly cited the support the bar provides for women
who have experienced recent breakups or have been widowed: "I've
seen cancer take a lot of my friends and the older lesbians."

For Jody, this shift from lesbian bar to queer bar has been a delightful change, though some patrons have struggled with gender-neutral
pronouns: "That's confusing to some of the old-timers. It's one thing
if you're going from 'she' to 'he' or from 'he' to 'she.' They can understand that. That's different from going gender neutral or non-gender
conforming, to 'they' and 'them.'" This hasn't been difficult for the
staff, however. She reported:

> The staff at this point has done fabulous, literally asking the cus-
> tomer, "How would you like to be called?" Sometimes you'll get

someone in mid-transition, their credit card is John, and they go by Caroline. The staff has been trained: "What name would you like me to put on your tab?"

Jody was not the only, but was one of the few, owners who brought up trans inclusion as important to business, many of whom stressed the importance of gender-inclusive bathrooms as one important tool.

Jody frames this simple act of respect as integral to the business: "I'm in the customer service business. I'm not serving you accounting, I'm serving you a conversation and a cocktail. It's about the interaction." As she continued, "You can drink at home, and you should be able to feel comfortable while sitting at the bar like you're at home. It's about the customers and making them feel welcome and them meeting one or two new people." Part of this support is provided by the diversity among the bar's staff.

> I may be a lesbian, and it's tagged as a lesbian bar because most of the staff is lesbian, I guess—but I also have trans employees, and queer employees who are nonbinary and don't identify as lesbian at all. So I think that the people I have working for me help foster that village feel.[7]

I observed three employees during the two times I visited the bar, one of them BIPOC, though the crowd at one of the events I witnessed was whiter and more Anglo than I might have expected given that Denver is nearly 30 percent Latinx. Racial diversity only came up in passing during our interview, with Jody asserting a diverse patronage because of her diverse staff.

The only difference among patrons, as far as Jody is concerned, is their drinking patterns.

> Women process alcohol differently than men do, whether gay or straight or whatever. A group of five men doing shots in two hours versus women doing a couple shots in two hours. They're processing that alcohol very differently and reacting very differently. By the end of the day everyone's inhibitions go down and everyone is all WAAAAAHHH! You clean the bar and hope there's no puke.

Being trans inclusive can't override occasional biological explanations, apparently: While research describes women's bodies as processing alcohol more slowly, it is men who are more likely to act out under the influence.[8]

Other changes include Colorado's role as the first state in the country to legalize recreational marijuana. As Jody observed of today's patrons: "They're not drinking like they used to with the pot." In fact, "If someone's eating an edible, they're falling out of their chair with one cocktail when it hits them." Including some, ahem, out of state sociologists, one of whom found himself barely able to walk back to his hotel room after watching *RuPaul's Drag Race* in a gay bar through half-lidded eyes. The legalization also caused a rush on properties, causing a wave of gentrification similar to what has pressed big-city gay bars: "Since legal recreational marijuana, rents have tripled. Literally." Luckily, she owns Blush & Blu outright and has long prized the bar's espresso machine: "They're still drinking coffee, thank God!"

During the nine months before the bar got its liquor license, Jody ran Blush, as it was then known, as a coffee bar. This focus on high-quality nonalcoholic drinks has remained part of the business model, allowing the expanded Blush & Blu to serve a broad clientele. Jody recalled: "On the weekends, I would turn on cartoons for the kids so families could come in; moms would have Bloody Marys, dads would have beers, kids would have hot chocolate."[9] When the next-door space became available, she added Blu as a performance space with stage, doubling the size of Blush & Blu and allowing the upstairs space to feature a pool table and board games, with the old coffee bar now serving liquor as well.

Blush & Blu is in the middle of a one-story commercial strip along East Colfax Avenue, what Jody called "the wickedest street in America," although its connections to sex work and illegal drugs long since have transitioned to funky boutiques and legal marijuana dispensaries. The Colfax Pot Shop anchors the corner of Blush & Blu's side of the street, wedged between Mile High Voodoo Donuts, a tattoo parlor, a dentist's office, and a sushi restaurant. Jody has a relationship with many of these businesses. "I'm covered in tattoos because they opened up the same time I did. I'd start them a tab and sit down in the chair and tip them and before you know it," Jody gestured to two full-sleeve tattoos. Laughing, she continued,

> For New Year's Eve I had the sushi restaurant deliver so people could eat sushi off two beautiful women with koi body paint. I did it because I can. If it pushes the envelope . . . I dropped $500 on raw fish! When can you get sushi for free?

Down the street is Denver's LGBTQ center, known as the Center on Colfax, which came about as a result of a conversation between Jody and one of the staff members: "Let's create a gay district! The center bought their building and has now been there since 2009." The Center has contributed to the fact that about one quarter of Blush & Blu's patrons are transgender. Jody enthused: "We have a huge trans clientele. Ten years ago I had maybe one or two trans customers, now I'd say it was 25 percent of my customers." They contribute to the diversity of Blush & Blu's clientele:

> Thursday nights the Center has a trans support group from 7 to 8. They'll end up coming here for 8 to 9:30, and we have stand-up comedy for straight people from 8 to 9:30—that's two very different demographics, the crowd is very interesting with the regular lesbian and gay clientele.

As the night wears on, she reported, "And then at 10 will come in the hipsters. They drink a ton of PBR and Jameson." These constitute Blush & Blu's "three different demographics that kinda overlap and filter in and filter out. There's no issues, no drama. Everyone knows that SJ and I own the bar. Everyone is welcome." Echoing the tagline on the bar's website, Jody continued,

> All humans are welcome and it's true: If you're an asshole, SJ and I will throw you out. You can have your right to free speech but not if it's making one of our customers feel uncomfortable because you're being an asshole and not making it safe for my customers, which is causing me not to make it safe for you!

Jody's own identity may contribute to her ability to stand up to hostile customers to make the bar comfortable for transgender patrons:

"They know that this is a safe space for them. I've gone toe to toe with guys who want to say inappropriate things. 'Are you going to hit a woman?'" She chalked this up to "the drama that comes with owning a queer bar," before explaining the nuance of the situation: "I present as a woman, but I don't identify as cisgender. I don't like labels; I would label myself as trans." Jody explained, "When I got out here to Colorado at 19, I had every intention of transitioning but that didn't happen because I got a job at a lesbian bar and got more attention with long hair." Responding to absent critics, she conceded with air quotes,

> I'm technically not living an *authentic* life, and I don't have a problem talking about who I am. Someone said, "You're a cisgender lesbian." I replied, "That's how you identify me, that's not how I identify," but whatever. Opinions are like assholes. Everyone has one!

Jody laughed: "It's all great being a bar owner until you have to fix the fucking toilets. I'm not butch enough for that, there's got to be butcher than me!"

Besides straight bands and comedians, the stage also hosts drag shows for both kings and queens. There are many fewer drag kings and even fewer stages that feature them; often it is only lesbian bars that emphasize some sort of parity in performances.[10] One of her queens helped Jody organize one of Blush & Blu's most unique events: "We have a drag queen garage sale! They bring in racks of their old clothes and we have a DJ. I'll sell booths downstairs too. I sold out in two days, and the girls—we're all making money." The drag shunned by old-school lesbian bars isn't just for the regular customers, either: "They'll have me come out in a dress and wig and everyone is taking pictures, politicians are in here." The event's popularity would be evident to anyone by the crowds—and the empty racks and hangers. Chuckling at being the instigator of over twenty years of mayhem in Denver's lesbian and now queer bars, she smiled wickedly: "I'm going to skid in sideways to my grave."

During the COVID-19 pandemic, the bar was shuttered, and Jody reported taking out short-term loans and cashing out a 401(k) to keep the bar afloat, in part because no aid was forthcoming from the city of Denver.[11] The crowdfunding and corporate support of the Lesbian Bar Project granted Jody more than $7,000, which proved lifesaving. It meant the bar was still open to accept the local alternative press award for being the "Best LGBTQ Bar" in Denver in 2021.[12]

Within weeks, however, Jody and the bar were slapped with a lawsuit by three former employees who alleged tip theft, failure to pay minimum wages, and racial discrimination. In the complaint, defendants alleged that Bouffard "weaponized the so-called 'safe space' and the 'family' at Blush & Blu to create a culture of obligation where workers were required to accept mistreatment and brazen underpayment as a 'service' to the bar and broader queer community."[13] Many gay bar staff describe themselves as family. This is nice, but families don't pay each other wages, nor can they fire members they disagree with. Jody responded in the pages of the *Denver Post*, calling the allegations "untrue and shocking," and sending a statement that she "never intentionally belittled anyone in the manner described or otherwise, nor withheld rightfully earned pay."[14] The case is still ongoing.

As I've said before, I like the people I interview, perhaps too much. It broke my heart to read through the allegations in the thirty-nine-page legal complaint. Lesbian bars and queer bars are rare and precious and should be protected. And yet, queer spaces are in the world, and that world includes racism and the power dynamics of the employment relationship.[15] Being a safe space is no protection against discrimination or mistreatment within the LGBTQ+ community. We in the LGBTQ+ community rightfully hold our institutions to high standards, but sometimes those standards are incompatible with the realities of running a small business. But lesbian bars and queer bars are held to a higher standard than men's bars, a standard that says as much about the inclusive politics of the former as it does about the low bar for the latter. And just as observers often report a generational shift between lesbians who identified as bar dykes versus younger ones who identified as queer, it is also true that things that were once acceptable are no longer: This constant evolution, too, is part of the drama of owning a queer bar. As an outsider I hope justice is done that makes everyone whole and leaves no one broken. I want justice and I want LGBTQ+ people to have a space. In other words: I'm queer, and I want it all.

Twenty-Two

Women First, Lesbians Second, But Everyone's Welcome

Walker's Pint
MILWAUKEE, WISCONSIN

Those lesbian bars that have survived have unambivalently managed to welcome everyone, including men, while remaining places that put women first. Bet-z Boenning split with a former business partner over her insistence on excluding men, partnered with the "boy bar" across the street, and welcomed drag queens—all hallmarks of contemporary lesbian bars that break with old-school ones. The memorable St. Patrick's Day confrontation related below illustrates how Bet-z maintains a place that puts women first, lesbians second, and welcomes everyone, including *you*, "as long as you're not douchey."

Bet-z has owned Walker's Pint in Milwaukee, Wisconsin, since 2001.[1] Three-and-a-half blocks from the Milwaukee Beer Museum, it is located in the diverse Walker's Point gayborhood that was in 2018 home to six other LGBTQ+ bars and clubs. (In 2022, it had ten!) The inside of Walker's Pint is the same shade of forest green as the exterior, and the bar itself is adorned with plaques honoring past bartenders and a world-class collection of funny bumper stickers. Every Wednesday night is karaoke, and the bar is packed with events including live music, jukebox bingo, sports watch parties, not to mention a lot of fundraisers.[2] Bars these days, whether straight or gay, have to offer entertainment to bring in patrons.

Bet-z had originally bought the bar with a business partner, but after three years of political differences, Bet-z bought her out: "One of the issues that my business partner and I didn't agree on when we first opened: she would just kick guys out. And I said, 'Absolutely not! We want to be *accepted* by other people!'" In framing this issue around acceptance, Bet-z echoed almost all the other lesbian bar owners I interviewed: acceptance was a moral and political issue, not a forced business compromise. As she continued, Bet-z asserted, "This will always be primarily a women's bar. This is a safe place for lesbians first, women together second, and then everybody after that, but you can't kick out people that are going to support you." In other words, their partnership dissolved over her partner's old-school insistence on women-only spaces and Bet-z's conviction that a space could remain woman focused while welcoming all who support their mission.

This was something she witnessed when the Midwest's premier lesbian bar closed just as she was getting into the business. "When I first opened, Girl Bar was in Chicago still. If you were a dude, you had to go in with a woman otherwise you weren't allowed in. And all of a sudden, I heard it was closing, and then no one could go out." For Bet-z, restrictive bar policies were associated not only with bad politics, but also with business failure.

A memorable evening from years ago illustrates how Bet-z keeps her bar open to all but still maintains a safe space for women:

> It was a Thursday, St. Patrick's Day, and we were packed. Full. Slammed. One guy was extremely rude to one of the customers, really graphic. I didn't see it, but the patron came up and she was so upset. So I went up to him and I said, "This is what I'm hearing, is this what happened? You need to go apologize to her. There's no way you should ever talk to a woman like that." His friends are over by the tapper down there, and they're just laughing that he's getting yelled at by this lesbian, right? So I walked over and said, "You know this is a women's bar, right? You don't have to be here. Please feel free to leave." "You can't make me leave!" and I said,

"What?" and he said, "You can't fucking make me leave, *bitch*!" and I was like, "Hold on one second." I kept my cool. I was really surprised. So I walked up to the music—it was packed, everyone was dancing—I turned the music down and I said, "How's everybody doing?" Everyone's like "YAAAAY!" And I said to the bartenders, "Step back. You're not serving another drink." And everyone was like, WHAAAAAT?" I said, "We have some guys in here who think they're cooler than everyone else and they can disrespect women. So no one gets a drink until these motherfuckers leave," and I just point at 'em. The whole bar just zones in on 'em and their faces got so red and the bartenders are just standing back. It was like two minutes and they were standing there and finally one of my customers gets up—you don't mess with TJ—she goes up to 'em, and says, "Get the FUCK out. I'm thirsty."

Laughing, Bet-z quickly noted that this was a rare instance that happened years ago and that problems with patrons are rare.

Bet-z also struck up a relationship with the gay bar across the street:

Fluid, across the street—that's a boy bar—I started working with them. I said, "Just so you know, my staff and I are going to come support your bar." And we started doing a lot more together. And I think that's important, showing we can work together for things, for charities, and just in general support each other's staff.

The Walker's Pint website provides a link to Fluid, describing it as their "sister bar." What started as a declaration of support, and an encouragement for her staff to buy a drink at the boy bar across the street, turned into joint charity drives under Bet-z's ethic of "We should take care of each other."

Bet-z's politics changed not only her directives to staff, but also the way that she interacted with her own patrons in the bar. "I got to the point where if women were being rude to men, I would say: 'You need to go.' I'm just not dealing with it. Basically, as long as everyone can respect one another and understand the mission here is: women first, but everyone's welcome as long as you're not douchey." In instructing her patrons to be open to men, Bet-z was changing the politics of her community as well as her patronage. She estimates that today, about one quarter of her clientele is gay men, and "It's all ages. All gay, straight, boys, girls, trans, everything!"

This inclusion extends to race. Bartender Lex Stath claims "We're the most integrated bar anywhere." The change was supported by a racially diverse staff. Adding context, Lex continued, "especially for Wisconsin. You know how bad it is, so it's rare for me to go into a place and see the mix of people that come in here." This is especially notable because Milwaukee is one of the most racially segregated cities in the nation.[3] In a subsequent conversation, Bet-z also credited the efforts of their in-house DJ (and official DJ for the Milwaukee Bucks) DJ Shawna for playing musical sets that served their diverse crowd. Bet-z attributes some of her business success to this racial inclusivity: "I think that really helps and helps us to still stay here."

The shift towards gender-integrated nightlife has not been hers alone. Bet-z explained,

> A lot of the neighborhood bars around here have a little bit younger owners, so they kinda get it. They're not afraid to work with us. In the past, the older owners were like, "Ooh, that's a lesbian bar, we're not joining with them."

The culture change toward collaboration with men's bars was not just lesbian bars giving up their gender-segregated environment, but those bars moving toward integration as well—at least "kinda." Bet-z's expansive description of good vibes in the neighborhood apparently also included their immediate neighbor: a straight strip club.

Lesbian camp humor is signaled by the tagline that adorns the bar's logo and t-shirts: "Lock up your daughters."[4] As Bet-z explains, "it's in an AC/DC song, which is awesome," but as a bar motto it came from a friend and former bartender, Sheena. As Bet-z recalled,

> She had just recently gotten broken up with. We were at our favorite bar on the East Side—the Y-Not II at the time—and she was pretty loaded. And someone asked, "What are you going to do?" And Sheena was like "I'm SIIIIIINGGGLLEEE! I'm Single!" She keeps yelling this and then she's shouting, "LOCK UP YOUR

DAUGHTERS, I'M COMIN!" We were like, "Oh my God, that's brilliant, we gotta use that!"

The tagline does conflict with the politics of some of her patrons: "The huge feminists hate it; they'll sometimes cross it off my signs." Others bring their concerns directly to Bet-z: "I have some women who are like, 'Oh, you need to not say lock up your daughters but something different,' and I'm like . . ." Bartender Lex interjected good-naturedly: "Shut the fuck up. Open your own bar!" Bet-z nodded: "It is what it is."

Although Milwaukee is a big city, Bet-z echoed the claims of small-city gay bar owners about the competition not coming from other bars. When my research assistant Tory asked Bet-z whether Walker's Pint sponsored that most lesbian of summer institutions, a softball team, she replied, "No! I couldn't get enough people to show up. They'd always be camping." To get people to come in, lesbian bars must create a welcoming and diverse environment that makes people want to visit when they're not in the woods or on the lake—the other forms of lesbian camp.

The serendipitous possibilities of Bet-z's management philosophy were revealed in one recent, perfect evening:

> My wife brought her boss in here and he's from Ohio. He was here a couple Tuesdays ago, and it was a birthday party, so I brought karaoke in for the birthday person. The boss had never been in a gay bar and he was surprised: "Look at all these people getting along!" And then a 6-foot-5 drag queen walked in and you shoulda seen his eyes: "Whaaaaat?" He thought it was the best thing ever. They came up and talked, and they were hugging, and he told me, "Coming to this was awesome!" His eyes were opened. Hey, we're just like everyone else, man!

Bet-z's ready example of an ideal interaction from just two weeks earlier shows what, for her, is the purpose of her bar: to bring people together to hug away differences. This earned her recognition in 2015 as a "Milwaukee All-Star" from the citywide magazine.[5] And while acceptance has made it so that women can go anywhere, bartender Lex concedes that "It's great for humanity, but not so great for lesbian bars."[6] Bet-z concurred: "I'm working harder today than I was fourteen years ago to get people in here," a common observation from longtime owners.[7] But as Bet-z notes, the rising tide of LGBTQ+ equality has drawn other patrons to her lesbian bar, including her parents' suburban friends: "Acceptance isn't where it needs to be, but it's a lot better than it was. I mean, my parents will come and bring all their friends on party days! They have a blast!"

What counts as a lesbian bar? Mary Green of Sneakers in Jamestown, New York, had explicitly rejected the label for her "gay-owned and operated establishment" because it "welcomes everyone." Yet all the other bar owners I interviewed also welcome everyone, and so walk the line of simultaneously embracing and contesting the label "lesbian bar"—how very ambivalent. Today's lesbian bars all embrace a mission of providing a place for women to socialize and find community, even as they all welcome everyone else—including cisgender straight men. As does San Francisco's Wild Side West, which somehow doesn't quite count as a lesbian bar for women hungering for a women's-only space, or at least one that is more raucous than a chill neighborhood hangout.

I myself have always found a welcome in lesbian bars—a wary one, back in the 1990s, but an open-armed one in the 2010s. Transgender people have always been part of the lesbian community, as has gender nonconformity, and so the shift away from declarations of women's-only spaces has cast a historically accurate welcome towards the whole LGBTQ+ community, increasingly necessary in the current climate where LBQ women can go anywhere.[8] Women finding a welcome in all gay bars—venues that have not always welcomed them, even as women's bars now welcome all—ensures the welcome to the community.[9] The formula for success already being practiced by surviving lesbian bars will soon have to be adopted by gay bars, for which straight people are also increasingly necessary for financial success.

Lesbian bars aren't the only gender-segregated bars that have had to contend with an evolving external world and changes within the LGBTQ+ community. Bars that specifically catered to men have also had to deal with the surge in drag artistry, younger patrons who demand gender inclusion, and clientele who engage with LGBTQ+ community differently than their elders. It is to these cruisy men's bars we now turn.

Part Five
Cruisy Men's Bars

Cruisy men's bars have seen the steepest declines in recent years, buffeted by cultural change within the LGBTQ+ community and technological change from without. But men still gather to partake in "sexy community" at Chicago's Jackhammer, where skin-to-skin intimacy, leather, and kink can bridge social divides. Photo courtesy of Joseph Stevens. Used with permission.

Twenty-Three
Democratizing Sexy Community

Jackhammer
CHICAGO, ILLINOIS

There are gay bars you'd take your dad to and then there are bars where you go to find *daddy*—or to be daddy. This section of the book explores the genre of gay bar I call cruisy men's bars. This includes leather and kink bars, gay strip clubs, and bars for the hairy and husky men called bears.[1] All these bars traditionally served primarily, and often exclusively, cisgender gay men. Like lesbian bars, these gender-segregated bars usually only exist in big cities with at least four gay bars. On the one hand, cruisy men's bars have often denigrated femininity and women in their celebration of macho masculine bonding.[2] But on the other, they celebrate larger and hairier bodies, older men, and the kinks and affectionate eroticism that often get sidelined or belittled in conventional gay bars.[3] While some people find these places sordid, for others that is exactly the appeal. For many men, these are crucial sites of sexual and self-discovery in world that is depressingly devoid of queer sex. At cruisy men's bars, people celebrate the "sex" in homosexuality, creating atmospheres that are intoxicating, anxiety inducing, and just plain *hot*.

Alone amongst themselves in these spaces, gay men have forged what sociologist Jay Orne calls "sexy community," where radical fellowship is possible through the seamless blending of eroticism, sex, and casual but intimate conversation. As Orne writes,

> The hybrid nature of the space—a space for sex connected to a place for talking—infuses both with the sexiness and social togetherness of the other. Even people that you haven't had sex with, and that you never would have sex with, are connected to you through sexy community.[4]

Sexy community unites these otherwise disparate gay subcultures and their bars—whether they be men casually groping and kissing each other among the crowd of a Sunday bear beer bust; men feeling the power of wearing the leather chest harnesses, Muir caps, and engineer boots that are totems of kink culture; or men talking openly about their sexcapades with strippers and go-go dancers.

Cruisy men's bars are the most vulnerable kind of gay bar. There were only about forty of them in the entire country in 2021; 70 percent of them closed between 2002 and 2021, a rate over 60 percent faster than gay bars in general.[5] While the contemporary bar professionals in previous chapters noted that their bars were often meeting sites for LGBTQ+ people who had met online, the men who own cruisy men's bars (and they are almost always men) acknowledge that smartphone hookup apps have short-circuited their bars' historic role in helping men find sex. Chris Daw of C. C. Attle's (Seattle, Washington) succinctly expressed the consensus: "Grindr and Scruff have killed the cruise bar." It used to be that you could only have raunchy flirtation at one of these bars; now you can have it anywhere at any time through a smartphone app, albeit textual and not verbal.

No bar exemplifies the possibilities of, and challenges to, contemporary sexy community better than Jackhammer of Chicago. It is one of the most famous leather and fetish bars in the world, in no small part because the Windy City is host to the International Mister Leather (IML) competition each Memorial Day, one of the most important global events for the leather, fetish, and kink communities. Jackhammer has often hosted IML parties, ranging from Men's Room to the domination jock/gear party called FuKr.

The bar is located four miles north of the gayborhood long known as Boystown, which the local chamber of commerce renamed Northalsted in 2020 to be more gender inclusive.[6] The building is often called the Jackhammer Complex because it includes the multi-level bar and a retail space that sells leather and fetish gear. Jackhammer technically applies only to the main floor of the bar portion of the complex with its pool tables; a 2022 rebrand dubbed other spaces The Rec Room and The Den, while the basement bar has long been known as The Hole, branded as "Chicago's Fetish Headquarters."[7] Street-level retail is provided by LEATHER64TEN, a vendor of a diz-zying array of leather, jockstraps, corsets, and bondage gear for all genders. The store has regular street-level access but also a basement shop that opens directly into The Hole, allowing patrons of the Jack-hammer Complex to purchase fetish gear and supplies like lube, gum, or snacks until 3 am. The Complex is also next door to Touché, the oldest leather bar in Chicago, making the block a one-stop destination for patrons interested in the erotic game of reciprocal eye contact—or more.

The Hole is the type of bar also known as a backroom or dark room bar, where somewhat public sexual activity takes place.[8] I say "somewhat" because while a bar that serves alcohol is technically a public place, backrooms are separate from main spaces, and there is a collective and unspoken norm that what happens in the backroom stays in the backroom—bar staff police nonparticipating gawkers and ban cell phone cameras.[9] Patrons in The Hole are often wearing only jockstraps or underwear, their attire and inhibitions left at the clothes check. I have been to Jackhammer as a civilian, not a researcher, as part of a bar crawl where someone else was driving, and I was med-icating my anxiety with liquor. Still, what was unforgettable was shedding my shirt to descend the clanking metal steps into The Hole. There the air was warmer and more humid, the urgent music more sultry, and the other men's glances more electric—the "menergy" Syl-vester sang about back in 1984.[10]

The most infamous part of The Hole is known as The Alley, a side corridor leading to a side exit where things get hot and heavy. Signs outside announce, "Men Hunting" and "Gentlemen PLEASE watch your wallets. Not all people are honest." I only write about it here because it was so thoroughly described by Jay Orne in their book *Boystown*.[11] Otherwise I would be loath to draw attention to activities that could interfere with a bar's licensing. Liquor licenses include morals clauses; Illinois prohibits "crime or misdemeanor opposed to decency or morality."[12] Such wishy-washy language both facilitates the home rule that permits localities to set their own definitions about what is decent but can also facilitate unequal enforcement against gay bars: gay people in public were long considered immoral just for *existing,* and some of our first civil rights victories were to permit gay people to drink in public. And yet, even the most progressive contemporary interpretations of what is moral and decent are probably stretched to overlook public blow jobs, hand jobs, and fucking.

It's difficult to describe how excitingly sleazy these places are with their funk of sweat, bleach, and poppers. Meeting another man's gaze for more than a beat can prompt him to approach. The places are dark, with facial contours and sultry eyes reflected only in profile by red light or, in the bad old days of indoor smoking, by the sudden flare of an inhaled cigarette. Standing together can facilitate talking, conversation that is accompanied by the unveiled, lusty appreciation of each other's bodies. What starts as looking can become touching, gauging his response for escalation from touching to more: making out, or one of you sliding to your knees in front of an audience. I have lost myself in these spaces—and found myself in the process.

This radical communion led earlier admirers to label gay male cruisers as sexual outlaws with radical political potential.[13] Even today, given the pressure of gay respectability politics, these men engage in acts that are *queer*: political, nonnormative acts that refuse the toxic masculinity and shame that prevents men from showing public affection or sexual attention to one another. Such sexy community also may make it possible for men to transgress racial or class differences, claims made by some writers of color but rejected by others.[14] At the end of the day, these acts of queer sex are potentially scandalous or discrediting to workplaces or families of birth: Queer sex "is the final frontier of distressing difference" for otherwise progressive straight people.[15] Some cruisy bars take advantage of this to prominently screen hardcore gay pornography as a filter for people uncomfortable with sexy community.

Cruisy men's bars shared with lesbian bars a peak of gender-seg-regated gay bars—the 1980s. That was a time when Martin P. Levine wrote that "The fastest proliferating type of establishment in the gay bar business is a place where gay men can declare with gusto that they are not like women," gesturing towards the misogyny and femmephobia that often accompanied those spaces.[16] The rise of gen-der-integrated gay bars that served both men and women in the 1990s accompanied a decline in both lesbian bars and cruisy men's bars, re-placed by bars where men and women socialized together, bars where sexy community was confined to occasional pop-up events.[17] But as Steve Leonard of The Stable (Providence, Rhode Island) said of the straight women who have been such vocal and crucial supporters of gay rights, "We did have a lot of issues with your old-school gay guys that very much want this to be a men's leather bar, yet they're on the front lines fighting for equality!"

And while other bars have been affected by the rising tides of LGBTQ+ acceptance outside the community, cruisy men's bars have been affected by the rise of the gay respectability politics that com-mentators have called "homonormativity," an increasing pressure to be a "good gay" by pushing aside or badmouthing the promiscuous, sexualized forms of community.[18] The rise of asexual activists and others who critique the compulsory sexualization of LGBTQ+ people have also called sexy community into question.[19] This means that cruisy men's bars in recent years have had cultural challenges added to technological ones in their quests to survive and recruit new sexual outlaw bargoers.

Within sexy community itself, patrons increasingly demand changes, including embracing women and transgender kinksters.[20] This can put a strain on spaces and their male guardians who have often repudiated femininity and conflated masculinity with having a penis. Younger LGBTQ+ people increasingly embrace different kinks. To many of the old guard, leather bars are for men wearing leather and Levi's and rubber,[21] and celebrating masculinity and the "serious leisure" of kinks like dominance and submission or public sex.[22] Newer kinks now include puppy play, where people wear styl-ized hoods in the form of dog heads while sometimes role playing at being either puppies or handlers, often but not always with elements of sexual dominance and submission.[23] Newer kinks also include cosplay, where people don elaborate costumes to resemble the fantastic characters of comic books, movies, and video games, especially those inspired by fantasy and science fiction. Such costumes were not welcome in old guard leather spaces, but increasingly, cruisy men's bars are all-purpose fetish and kink spaces that blend older and newer practices. Besides, there is reason to be skeptical of old guard accounts of traditional dark rooms solely as sites of serious pursuits: the management of the notorious Mineshaft in New York City once posted a sign asking patrons not to discuss opera in the darkroom. Such have the various gay worlds always co-existed, however hilariously.[24]

A particular sticking point is nonconsensual touching: older gay men are accustomed to casual ass grabs and cock touches that many people now find abhorrent. To younger LGBTQ+ community members, the casual gropes and chest patting among large hairy men have even been called "bear rape culture."[25] Personally, I find the casual and gentle touches sweet and welcome, if alien to my hug-averse Lutheran upbringing, but I see how they resonate negatively for younger generations. Although I have also often found these touches intrusive, and positively hate casual nipple tweaks, it hadn't occurred to me until middle age that I could refuse them until my students named them as nonconsensual! This realization didn't change my own practices—I was always a look-but-don't-touch kind of person—but it did embolden me to maintain my boundaries. Thus have the spaces of sexy community often assumed a certain relaxation of norms of consent that are currently under dispute by younger kinksters who remind us all that casual touching and public sex can still be consensual.

In many senses, then, cruisy men's bars have faced some of the same challenges that have rocked lesbian bars. This includes a massive generational shift since the early 1990s away from single-sex spaces and towards LGBTQ+ spaces that are open to all genders and orientations, including straight people.[26] It also means the rising tide of drag artistry that has infused spaces that once resisted its charms. Finally, it means historic LGBTQ+ community organizations now find themselves torn between losing their bar, losing their traditions, and losing the young queers on whom they will depend for their futures.

As the subsequent chapters demonstrate, the job of managing a cruisy men's bar is especially challenging because patrons often expect that public sexual activity is permissible. I spoke to the owner of one notorious backroom bar who, straight-faced, claimed that his staff stopped patrons from engaging in sexual activity: He was telling me to ignore my lying eyes. Similarly, the owner of a gay strip club told me that his dancers do not engage in the activities that they clearly were offering to all comers, including me: full nudity in the private rooms and all-body touches.

Jackhammer had long tried to walk the fine line between catering to cisgender male patrons, for whom sexy community meant the exclusion of women, and enforcing their policy of being gender inclusive—the leather, fetish, and kink communities have long included straight and trans people. Women who showed up in gear were declared to be part of the community of The Hole and explicitly permitted in The Alley. More controversial to regulars of The Hole were the straight women gal pals who accompanied their gay male friends down to the backroom bar, and men who were themselves not part of the leather/kink/fetish fraternity. How to create sexy community among nonparticipating voyeurs in a fair way? The Hole solved the problem by requiring all people to either be wearing fetish gear or to take off their shirts before descending the industrial metal stairs—thus the occasional sight of women in bras with shirtless male friends in tow.[27]

The Alley was still a restricted space; staff discouraged women not in gear from gawking at the activities happening within and prevented them from entering. This was allegedly for women's safety; in 2007 a straight woman had called police because a gay man "inappropriately touched" her upstairs at the bar.[28] This policy illustrates that fine line that bars must walk to foster sexy community and also gender inclusivity and consent, especially when attitudes about what acts are permissible vary so dramatically for women and nonbinary people, and for younger versus older patrons.

Jackhammer had been cultivating a reputation for gender inclusivity as early as 2011 when a controversy broke out that challenged that claim. In that year, a bartender misgendered a transgender man and asked him to leave The Alley. After apologizing to the men involved, then-owner Jimmy Keup told the local LGBTQ+ press that this was a learning experience and "a message to the gay community but also to the fetish community that there are other people who are not the same." By 2016 the bar was hosting the monthly TransMale Indulgence, "a transgender man night, along with those who admire them and allies," hosted by Mr. LEATHER64TEN 2016 James Trycha.[29] There were occasional subsequent controversies over misgendering or accusations of transphobia, each of which prompted the bar to announce redoubled efforts towards inclusivity, but also inspired transgender patrons to defend the bar for its past work.[30] Such controversies illustrate that a bar that serves the general public must deal also with their prejudices, making inclusion a process and not a destination.

Jackhammer's inclusive ethos permeated some of the parties they hosted, including for the blockbuster IML weekend. One such annual party, MEN'S ROOM, seemed to indicate its adherence to traditions through its name and its promise of "2 slutty floors of debauchery." But the 2017 invite also clearly stated that "Men's Room welcomes all genders, races, fetishes and weirdnesses. If you experience otherwise, please let one of us know immediately. Spread love, not hate."[31] And while some other leather bars still struggle with how to incorporate drag, Jackhammer had, for more than a decade until COVID-19, hosted the Best Worst Drag Show every Monday night at "ridiculous-o-clock."[32] It was also one of the first leather bars to regularly screen *RuPaul's Drag Race*, itself a showcase for many Windy City queens.

In 2018, it seemed Jackhammer would fall victim to the same forces that have ravaged cruisy men's bars in recent years: their building went into foreclosure, and it looked like an out-of-state investment firm would buy the building and evict the bar. Through the help of a local real estate entrepreneur who took a shine to the business, the sale was stalled until new owners were found who would preserve Jackhammer.[33] 2Bears Tavern Group, helmed by Mark Robertson and Mike Sullivan, agreed to purchase the building and the business, with founding owner Jimmy Keup staying on as general manager. Mike told a local journalist, "Even in a city as open as Chicago there is a need for venues for the community that are safe and comfortable. Jackhammer is just that kind of place."[34] With the deeper pockets of a hospitality group, the duo took advantage of the coronavirus shutdown to do a comprehensive remodel of the complex. Hospitality groups are thus one of the ways to save a gay bar and are proof that new gay bars can open and prosper even amid today's tectonic changes in the LGBTQ+ landscape.

As the bars in these next chapters demonstrate, cruisy men's bars have all had to adapt to remain relevant, with competition from new technologies, changing community attitudes, and changing relationships to the clubs and organizations that sustained these bars through difficult times, including multiple pandemics. Those cruisy men's bars that survive will have to bear the heavy mantle, and conduct the joyful experiments, of remaking sexy community for the entire LGBTQ+ community in communion with the straight.

Twenty-Four

We Were a Bear Bar. The Trans Community Was Extremely Forgiving

Wrangler
DENVER, COLORADO

Bear bars have played an important role in my gay life. The year I gained fifty pounds on a new cocktail of antidepressants was the year I no longer felt cute. Skinny privilege is a thing, and I'd lost it. I had to make my own way into handsome. Luckily my hairy chest, height, white skin, full beard, and "good" fat distribution gave me instant cachet in the bear community.[1] Fat and big-bodied, hairy gay men, who feel so judged in other gay environments, experience a fragile comfort in bear places. The comfort contributes to sexy community where men casually touch each other's bodies, kiss hello on the lips, and tousle stranger's chest hair and beards. This comfort is fragile because the community, for all that it is supposed to be about body acceptance, is still marked by fatphobia, racism, beard envy, and the esteem granted to the coveted muscle bears among us.[2] I'm still surprised, in my late 40s, how much positive attention I get when I am drunkenly convinced to go shirtless in a bear bar or event. It's not like I feel ugly in my everyday life, but my body sees no gym and many carbs, and gay men can be fastidiously gorgeous. But in a bear bar, I'm a star, however unlikely it feels.

Wrangler, the bear bar in Denver, Colorado, provided just such an environment for patrons. But the bar ran into controversy when the doorman denied entry to a man in drag; the state declared that the bar had discriminated against effeminate men and transgender people. Owner Chris Dawkins had to embark on a painful route of community reconciliation and staff retraining to regain the trust of the broader LGBTQ+ community.

The bar staked its claim to Colorado's bear community from its beginning in the late 90s, as Chris recalled: "I wanted to open a bear bar—nobody had ever tried it in Denver." But Chris himself had to be disabused of stereotypes about bears. As he recalled,

> I opened in June of 97 and I had a business partner at the time, and he talked me into buying a $10,000 video projector so we could show Bronco games, and I was like "Gay men don't watch football!"

Except they did: The Broncos went on a winning streak that year, culminating in two back-to-back Super Bowl wins in 1998 and 1999, a statewide fervor that made the Wrangler's huge TV a hot commodity. The sports showings did fit with the branding of the bar as a site for masculine gay men, however. As Chris recalled the bar's longtime branding, before the controversy, "We were a gentlemen's club. We were a boys' bar."

Chris recounted conducting extensive nightlife research in the late 1990s before opening Wrangler, standing outside other gay bars and surveying patrons, even handing them pen and paper so he could enter the results in his computer. As he recalled, "I'm going to get into trouble for saying this. The number one request was a place to go that had no drag queens, where there were just men." As he elaborated what men were reporting to him, "They weren't interested in women, especially not real-real ones, and they didn't like the hair, the attitude, the atmosphere that comes with drag." Old school cruisy men's bars and old school lesbian bars thus had something in common: a misogynist rejection of theatrical femininity and an ignorance of trans women.

Wrangler quickly established a famous event for which it became nationally known: the Sunday beer bust. A beer bust is an event where a person buys a refillable cup that, for one set price, allows for free refills of an inexpensive beer. Most states ban this practice because it's difficult for patrons to keep track of the amount they have drunk: To this I can personally attest, having regularly gotten off my face in San Francisco at The Eagle or Lonestar, where public transportation was my designated driver. I love beer busts because for me, there is something liberatory about being gay in the daylight and home in bed by 10. I had been to Wrangler's beer bust long before this research, skipping out on a 2012 conference to see the local talent and flirt with a visiting ER doctor also drawn to the well-known event. Chris attributed Colorado's permissive beer bust law to the influence of Denver's Great American Beer Festival, an annual event championed by one-time brewer-turned-governor John Hickenlooper.

At the Wrangler's beer bust, staff circulated with pitchers because, as Chris related, "The thing that makes beer bust fun is you get groups of people that are here talking to each other. If you want to get another drink, you don't have to go away . . . until you need to pee!" By the time I spoke to him in 2018, he described a typical bust as "1,000, 1,500 people by 6 pm and they are pounding some beers and shots." Of the event's listing on must-do events in municipal and national gay tour guides, Chris was not exaggerating when he claimed, "beer bust at the Wrangler—that's in the gay bible."[3] The Sundays I went over the years, it was indeed packed and the crowd solicitously friendly to the fresh meat presented by this out-of-towner.

As a bear bar, the beer bust was popular, but that was just one day a week. Weekdays were still slow until Wrangler instituted a new policy in the late 2000s. "We had a gender-matching ID policy," is the way Chris described it to me, meaning that people could not enter the bar if they didn't look just like their government-issued ID. Although the intent was to prevent drag queens from entering, it also potentially affected transgender people, queerdos who had recently dyed their hair, people who had aged, been in an accident, been ill, or gained weight. Specifically, the policy gave door staff a license to scrutinize people for excuses to exclude them, a door strategy at odds with the way other owners described security as their purpose. The LGBTQ+

community response was divided. As Chris recalled, "It was super controversial. I got dragged through the press. It was humiliating. I got death threats. It was relentless for six months." On the other hand? "My sales went through the roof. Beer bust just got bigger, weeknights got bigger." This positive response from the bear community meant the bar didn't back down from the policy.

Back then, Chris justified the policy because Denver's LGBTQ+ scene had lots of different types of bars serving niche audiences:

> It seemed a relevant policy at the time because we had a drag bar and a lesbian bar and a twinkie bar. The community was broken up. There wasn't a hodgepodge bar or an everybody bar. It was a leather, bear, twink, piano, I can't think of all-what else.

In other words, with a fragmented community where seemingly all segments of the community had a space, it seemed fair that Wrangler would be a bar just for cisgender bears. Everyone else could go elsewhere.

This changed when many of the other bars began to close. In 1997 when Chris opened Wrangler, the *Damron Guide* listed twenty-seven gay bars for Denver; by 2002, there were only twenty-two for a city that had added over 200,000 people in that short five-year period. As old niche bars closed, new "hodgepodge" bars opened, and as Chris observed, "Everybody started going into the same pot."

Maintaining the gender-ID matching policy grew to be difficult as its harms became more obvious. "It was wearing on the crew. They didn't support it anymore. Most of them had friends in the community. They were tired of taking shit for this stupid discriminatory policy." Chris recalled to me, "Whether or not that was a mistake, I think it really damaged our image." Ruefully, he said "Yeah, it was good for sales but not everything should always be about money." Recollecting, he continued, "We gave people what they wanted, but that didn't make it right." As he described it, when Wrangler debuted the policy, it was "a little bit wrong, but after a period of time it became so caustic."

Chris polled the staff about whether to abandon the policy: "It was unanimous." Wrangler dropped their gender-ID matching policy. The bar took flak on Facebook, however, from the men who'd appreciated the boys' club atmosphere: "There were a lot of comments. It was an exclusiveness for them, and they appreciated that. Their support was like for a gentlemen's club, but it was time to get with the program." The way Chris described to me what happened made it sound like abandoning the policy was voluntary.

However, as the largest newspaper in the city summarized in 2014,

> Colorado regulators say a well-known Denver gay bar discriminated against a gay man last year by denying him entry while dressed in drag, also finding the bar has a history of discriminating against women and effeminate men.[4]

This stemmed from an incident where Vito Marzano was denied entry to the bar while wearing a wig and makeup.[5] At a picket of the bar, Marzano told journalists, "My understanding is that they (the Wrangler) just don't want drag queens, cross dressers and gender queers in their bar. They only want 'bears' in their bar."[6]

The Civil Rights Division of the Colorado State Department of Regulatory Agencies found that the bar had illegally discriminated "against effeminate men because its dress code bars high heels, wigs, 'appearance-altering makeup' and strong perfume."[7] This last, ironically and surely not intentionally, was actually inclusive of people with chemical sensitivity. But as the AP wire summarized the case for an international audience, "Businesses will have to strike a difficult balance between catering to a niche market as part of a business strategy and making sure they don't break laws against discrimination."[8] This has long been implicit in many gay bars' strategies to market themselves: Lesbian bars often excluded lone men at the door out of protection; gay men's bars often treated women poorly to maintain a men's environment; and bars owned by white people have often discriminated against BIPOC people. With social acceptance of LGBTQ+ people, however, has come the increasing application of antidiscrimination ordinances on LGBTQ+ spaces: Philadelphia found multiple gay bars and their staff had discriminated against people of color in 2017, mandating anti-racism training.[9] Y'all means *all*, and increasingly local governments are willing to intervene in LGBTQ+ places to ensure civil rights for everyone.

Regardless of how Wrangler's gender-matching ID policy had been abandoned, the controversy had taken a toll. I asked Chris what had happened in the four years since the ruling. "The trans community, they were extremely forgiving," but, he sighed, "I think I've seen one drag queen in there, maybe two. They . . . I don't know. There's still a lot of anger there, probably." Chris claimed that there were a lot of women, straight and queer, who came to Wrangler with their gay male bear friends. He also indicated bemusement that Wrangler attracts a lot of straight men for whom gay bars no longer carry stigma: "Nobody cares anymore if the music's good. They come for the DJ, they come for the party." As he laughed, Chris sketched out a sort of post-gay present now that "There are lot more heterosexuals in the gay bars and more gays in the straight bars. Because they're accepted now you used to have to segregate yourself really." I can't say whether any of the men in the crowds I witnessed were straight; I never saw more than a handful of women. And it seems to have escaped everyone that fat queer women are rarely welcomed into LGBTQ+ spaces, except for the occasional size-affirming burlesque event, and thus bear events have the potential to be fat-affirming for *all* genders.[10]

As Chris said of gay men in the old policy days, "That was in a time where maybe a lot of people were one person when they were outside the bar and a different person inside, and they felt comfortable to be themselves." Shaking his head, he said of the changes in those gay men of yesterday, "Now they feel comfortable at a sports bar or Applebee's. That's good that that's gone." Of course, feeling comfortable at a chain restaurant means patrons are no longer mainly spending their dollars in gay bars, which are invariably in the center of cities and far from middle-class LGBTQ+ folks' suburban homes.

Wrangler was so successful that it moved to a larger location despite the controversy. As Chris said of leasing the old location, "I threw all that money away." With the new space, he and his partners own the building. One of the changes in the new place was a shift away from the groping normalized in "sexy community" and towards a more respectable atmosphere: "This isn't one of the bars where everything is painted black with one lightbulb and lots of corners to do whatever you want to do. It's not like that anymore."

Chris described several other changes in hospitality over his thirty-two years in the industry: not just smartphone apps but also *appetizer* apps. "Twenty years ago, you did *not* eat in a gay bar. Ew!" This was my experience as well; for this project I felt I had taken my life into my hands when I ate at the free seafood buffet in gay strip joint Club Bunns to celebrate the owner's birthday. After Wrangler's move to the new building with a full commercial kitchen, Chris said, "We serve a lot of food, which I never would have thought." A gay bar serving food is not a decision that should be taken lightly because it's "much more trouble. There's hardly any profit in it because costs are so high. Your payroll costs are higher because of food." Chris is willing to do it, though:

> I'm glad because it's the only thing in reality that sobers people up, and when there's a beer bust and people are getting rowdy, we'll make two big fresh pizzas and hand them out and the whole crowd just [lowers his arms like a bird gently closing its wings]. When we serve food, everybody calms right the hell down and they go to sleep. They become much less aggressive. Plus why let them go somewhere else?"

As he sees it,

> I've been saying for the past five years that the future is coffee, nonalcoholic options, and good drinks and food. If you're not going to offer those things, you're not going to survive because the days of going out and getting drunk, if they're not gone yet they will be soon.

He added that other apps that had brought positive changes were the rideshares that helped people get home safely after a heavy drinking session: "The only thing that saved us—that was Uber and Lyft, the affordability and the ease: you push a button!"

Wrangler also drifted from its butch-boy image by getting into the fruity drink business, installing frozen cocktail machines. Chris gestured at the pastel cocktails twirling in their plastic tanks:

They're all made with fresh fruits, not nothing artificial. Real cane sugar, fruit juices, and good liquor. And they are strong! They are good for people who want a sweet fruit drink, and they still want to get bombed.

As he noted, "Until a couple of years ago we were the only gay bar that had them." Such drinks didn't necessarily square with the old strategy of being a man's bar for men's men, given that fruity drinks are coded as femme. But it perhaps reflected a newfound recognition of broader tastes within the bear community, including for gender expression.

Chris ended the interview with ambitious plans for the future in the new space, including adding a barbershop, and using the Grubhub app to provide delivery from the kitchen. With enthusiasm, he announced "We're trying to make a little gayborhood over here." As Chris concluded, he described the controversy as

part of our past that I'm not proud to talk about, and yet it's important to talk about the effects both positive and negative. Without it we wouldn't be sitting here, which is good that we survived for thirty-two years. But at what expense?

Apparently the expense was too great.

Two months after I sat to interview Chris, the Wrangler announced it was ending its run. It closed its doors at the end of June's Pride celebrations with one last Sunday beer bust in 2018.[11] Chris gave no interviews to explain why.

It was replaced, less than one year later, by Denver Sweet, a "'bear inspired' LGBTQ friendly bar" that opened south of the capitol off Broadway. It was opened by the Wrangler's two resident DJs, Ken Maglasang and Randy Minten.[12] As Ken told a journalist,

Randy and I wanted to open a bear bar back into the Denver community. The Denver Wrangler was the predominant bear bar for 21 years, and when they closed, it left a big void here in the Denver nightclub scene.

A journalist noted that "In the past, Denver bear bars have been known to be sexist, transphobic, and unpleasant," to which Maglasang responded,

> We really wanted to change that dynamic and set a new precedent for the bear bar. . . . Since we have opened, we have really broken that stigma. We offer a very friendly and welcoming environment. We are the bears you want to party with.[13]

Denver Sweet hosts the weekly "Showbears" singalong for fans of show tunes, the kind of thing an old-school bear bar invested in conventional masculinity might eschew. The bar also features a fancy hat contest with advertising featuring genderqueer icon Billy Porter, and its social media feed highlights slim "chasers," transgender bears, as well as traditional big-boned bears. The bar also proudly trumpets lesbian DJ Sinna-G, dubbed Mama Bear when she spins at the bar. But Denver Sweet still hosts the kinds of masculine-branded events common to bear bars elsewhere: "Come get your beef" Taco Tuesdays, Daddy Wednesdays, the monthly STUDD rooftop leather social. And of course: the Sunday pun on a beer bust, Bears on the Roof Bearbust, supporting local charities, part of gay bars' marquee role in community fundraising.

Personally, I'm glad that bear bars are surviving. I may not *need* them, but damn, I find them good fun and ego boosting. But I'm also glad that they are becoming places where I can go with non-cis-bear friends. My slim ex Jesse was literally pushed aside by strange men wanting to rub my belly on multiple occasions in multiple bars. Twink and genderqueer friends often express trepidation about facing hostility in a "man's man" environment. We must have places for fat hairy men that don't treat others as poorly as we sometimes get treated elsewhere.

Twenty-Five

Rebranding The Eagle
for the Next Generations

The Baltimore Eagle
BALTIMORE, MARYLAND

Leather bars are iconic kinds of leather bars, and there is no more iconic name for a leather bar than "The Eagle." The Eagle is a name shared over the years by hundreds of gay bars on four continents, all modeled off the original Eagle's Nest that opened in New York City in 1970. As Maryland's Baltimore Eagle website described them in 2021, the various Eagles "began opening all over the world not as part of a brand, but as a movement." These aren't franchises or brands or centralized in any way, but independent bars that share an aesthetic: leather and kink and masculinity and earnest sleaze. The bars also cater to a wider variety of ages and body types than the average gay bar, making them attractive to folks beyond the leather and kink communities.[1] And as one of those sleazy gay men, I've always preferred them to a twink bar any day, even back when I was a twink.

When an eagerly anticipated new Eagle opened in Baltimore at the beginning of 2017, it rose from the ashes of two other bars: the first Baltimore Eagle, which had closed at that address in 2012, and The Hippo, a legendary Baltimore club whose liquor license was acquired by The Eagle's new owners when it was gentrified out of existence and replaced by a CVS Pharmacy.[2] As The Baltimore Eagle co-owner Robert Gasser told a journalist in 2017, "With gay bars shutting their doors here and across the country, people told us we were crazy to reopen one."[3] The bar's struggles illuminate the challenges facing cruisy men's bars and the creative ways that entrepreneurs have responded to a changing LGBTQ+ community while still sticking to tradition.

Co-owner and general manager Chuck King described the $1.7 million renovation: "It can't just be a small, dark leather bar. It's just not profitable."[4] He outlined the bar's multi-revenue-stream business plan:

> We did a lot of research. We looked at the bars that were closing, at their business models, what they offered. We decided to take the risk to diversify the business because you can't just have a leather bar.

What resulted, Chuck summarized:

> In a nutshell, we say it's a 10,000-square-foot adult entertainment complex that offers food, beer, spirits, retail, nightlife, and entertainment for the LGBT community, or a friend or supporter. Our whole motto is "be you."

Straight allies were thus part of the mix from the jump, part of a gender shift even among sexy men's bars towards serving everyone.

The multiple revenue streams reflected both innovation and tradition. Like leather bars of yore, the complex featured a dark downstairs bar called Code, named for the dress codes of traditional leather bars that required fetish gear to enter and prohibited sneakers, cologne, and makeup in order to cultivate an atmosphere of macho fantasy through the refusal of bourgeois trappings. But unlike the Eagles of old that sometimes looked askance at women or newer fetishes, the new Eagle advertised on its website that Code's "Dark corners and low light make the perfect place to cruise porn-stached daddies, leather clad studs, pups and the fetish men and women of the region." Keeping up with the times means this Code bar also prohibited cell phones, facilitating sexy community by allowing what happened in the Code to stay in the Code and not end up on social media. Code also welcomed newer fetishes, organizing large events for human pups and their handlers as well as furries, those fans of full-body stylized animal fur suits.[5]

And just as the historic original leather bar Febe's of San Francisco had a fetish store on site, so too did Baltimore's Eagle. This expansive one was bright white and airy, selling colored handkerchiefs, leather harnesses, and other kinky accouterments in a sleek setting. But this shop and the downstairs Code bar were only small parts of the complex, the majority of which was designed to serve people beyond the leather and kink communities.

Upon entering the building, and to reach Code, patrons passed through Tavern, the gastropub sports bar that was unique in three ways when compared to Eagles of the past. First were the broad bright windows opening onto the street, providing unprecedented views to and from the sidewalk. Second was a full menu of food, a rarity in leather bars specifically, and gay bars in general. Third was the all-gender bathrooms with multiple stalls with—and I cannot express my pleasant surprise enough—DOORS THAT CLOSED AND LOCKED. These are rare in gay bars, especially in the sleazy bars of yesterday, because, ahem, multiple people often pile into the stalls to have sex, and one way to prevent this is to remove the doors leaving anyone doing their business open to view. Locking doors are essential, however, to making a formerly cis men's space welcoming to women and gender-nonconforming people, much less neighborhood straight folks. While Tavern provided a welcome to all through pub food, it also embraced the past through its glass cases of leather and kink memorabilia from current and historic motorcycle clubs, leather organizations, and leather bars.

By day, Tavern exemplified the new gay bar: openly welcoming straight folks and all LGBTQ+ people, but by night, the vast windows could be closed off by thick curtains so that, Chuck explained, "Guys can dance in jockstraps on the bar." All these options, and the deliberately inclusive language, led one surprised patron to describe The Baltimore Eagle as simultaneously inclusive *and* cruisy:

Unlike any other leather bar I've ever heard of—part leather bar, part nightclub, part rooftop bar, part sports bar/tavern, part leather shop, part backroom bar . . . something for everyone. And very trans friendly.[6]

The liquor license that The Eagle acquired from the defunct Hippo permitted off-license bottle sales even on Sundays, meaning one corner of the building functioned as an independent liquor store serving the neighborhood on days when others were closed. The Eagle employed a smartphone app for liquor delivery that further extended the reach of this additional revenue stream. As Chuck explained, "It really helps because now we're serving customers who never would have seen and heard about us, getting exposed to our name alone is a good thing."

The new Baltimore Eagle added a dance floor, branded the Eagle's Nest—a large, air-conditioned space with a stage and red walls and velvet curtains that evoked the Moulin Rouge.[7] This permitted the space to be, variously, a full-room dance floor, a venue for weddings and celebrations, and a site for community meetings, fetish demonstrations, and drag brunches. The 2018 drag brunch I attended in the Nest was a delightful mix of sixty patrons, straight and gay, white and POC, some in leather. Only the gay couples, but none of the straight, were sharing kisses or holding hands, meaning queer romance could blossom despite the mixed crowd. The show featured their rotating cast of drag queen comedy and lip-syncs, a boylesque strip by Tommy Gunn who raised more than $200 for charity, and a Shake Your Tail Feathers contest that provoked audience members to waggle their butts to cheers from the room. When the four queens went out onto the second-floor patio to smoke and relax after the show, Tommy opened the door and shouted, "Ladies, I've called the burn ward because y'all's pussies was on fire!"

The bar's embrace of drag put it at odds with some old-timers and required justification and separation. As a journalist reported, "Some in the leather community were uncomfortable with the idea of drag queens in The Eagle," but co-owner John Gasser was nonplussed: "Leather's just another form of drag."[8] Chuck King explained that the loss of The Hippo meant that "The drag community didn't have the home like they had at The Hippo," but that it wasn't as simple as just opening The

Eagle to drag: "We had to convince them to come over here and try it out because we were just a leather bar, and we had to overcome that." Part of making the upstairs a welcoming space for drag was to treat it as reverently as the downstairs Code, by installing a full-on dressing room for performers with a rare private bathroom. As Chuck explained, "We made a place upstairs that is equal to the space downstairs."

To reassure the leather crowd of the Code bar, Chuck added, "We had to make sure there was a separation. If you have drag in the leather bar, that would ruin it. That is a sacred space." But, as another Eagle manager and Black drag king, Chris Jay, told a journalist, "To deny that leather people don't also enjoy drag is kind of like a generalization that's not necessarily true all the time." Jay continued:

> To say that the drag community is not also part of the leather community is not always true. To not address that intersection, I feel like you really miss out on the ability to service the community in a full-bodied way.[9]

There was even an "intersection" to be made in the performances themselves. Of one of the regular shows, Chuck said, "We decided to make it more a leathery drag show and do some burlesque and fetish demonstrations."

When asked what about the business side was hard for customers to understand, Chuck first gave the most common answer: the resentment over cover charges. But his second issue was one unique to cruisy men's bars: "They often don't understand that they can't just full on have sex in our establishment." When I raised my eyebrows, he added, "as much as we would love to let them!" As he explained, "If we see it we have to stop it. They get mad at us but they're breaking the law. Go out of our sight!" I asked if this was a difficult rule to enforce, and Chuck was noncommittal: "People understand most things, but once there's alcohol involved it's like talking to a wall sometimes." I wondered about his answer, just as I looked askance at the owner of a different city's Eagle who said that his staff stop men from having sexual contact on the premises. All I can tell you is: That bar owner is extremely, regularly, routinely—*famously*— unsuccessful.

While pundits think of social media as a drain on gay bars, bar owners use it to promote and advertise and, in the case of The Eagle, to emphasize their inclusivity. The partners' business plan embraced social media, holding weekly marketing meetings and hiring a company to execute their marketing plan. Chuck explained the expertise was necessary, although "It's not cheap, and it's a constant attention to detail. If you let it go for a week, you're so backed up." This helped address what he said was the largest business challenge: "making sure that we have enough business, making sure that we welcome gay, lesbians, bisexual, transgender, everybody."

As he said of the LGBTQ+ community, echoing other bar professionals about the change in patrons over recent years, "We're a very fickle crowd. We demand more entertainment, more excitement. If we're not constantly changing and evolving and having new ideas and new events, you start to lose the crowd." He continued, citing inclusivity as a business necessity: "there's all these little things that you have to pay attention to, and if you don't, you're going to lose a segment of your business."

Chuck dismissed claims that smartphone apps have closed gay bars and that every bar was a gay bar, citing Baltimore's tourist areas that attract suburban day-trippers:

> That's bullshit! I don't feel comfortable going to other straight bars. I can go to Fells Point or Downtown, but I still wouldn't feel comfortable, my husband and I having a romantic evening and making out. You get a lot of dirty looks, and you'll be lucky if they don't throw a punch.

Passionately he explained, "We need our space, our safe space, our sacred space. Maybe in 50 years, maybe it will change." The loss of LGBTQ+ social spaces, he maintained, represented a backwards step: "If gay bars go away the gay culture will go a little bit underground. That would be a step in the wrong direction for us." And yet, cruisy men's bars have been ravaged since smartphone apps came out, meaning some steps in that direction have already occurred.[10]

A community confrontation illustrated the challenges of trying to serve the entire LGBTQ+ community. Controversy erupted in 2017 when the Baltimore Eagle signed onto a neighborhood petition to curtail the operating hours of a gas station across the street that was alleged to attract noisy and violent patrons, drug dealing, and dangerous drivers.[11] Queer community activists noted, however, that the gas station was the only late-night refuge for Black transgender sex workers in the gentrifying neighborhood. In leaked communications, one of the Eagle's business associates subsequently slurred the women as "tr███y prostitutes," dismissing their concerns for their sex work as much as their gender.[12]

This conflict was an education for Chuck. The four partners of Baltimore Eagle disavowed the statement by one of the people they did business with but were considered guilty by association. As Chuck recalled to me, "I had never heard that term 'cisgender.'" This ignorance showed in some of his comments to journalists, which did little to quell the uproar.[13] In the meantime, several event organizers canceled their 2017 events at The Eagle.

The Director of the Baltimore Transgender Alliance, Ava Pipitone, told a local paper that the bar's owners are "literally coming in like ambassadors of white settler colonialism to displace the neighborhood," linking the petition to histories of Native American removal and genocide.[14] A sex worker activist from Baltimore's Sex Worker Outreach Project (SWOP) invoked the spirit of the early LGBTQ+ rights movement, which was led by transgender women of color, saying it's "appalling and an embarrassment to our ancestors and to our elders who came before us and made it so places like the Eagle could exist."[15] At an open mic community meeting, a member stood up and, in Chuck's recollection, announced "I've got a problem with The Eagle. They're white cisgender assholes and transphobic and we have to boycott."

Chuck was at that open mic meeting, unbeknownst to its organizers. To hear the vitriol leveled against him by strangers was upsetting: "After she got out everything, I had to say, 'may I speak,' and the moderator said, 'sure.'" Chuck steeled his nerves, stood up, and said "My name is Charles, and I am the general manager. And I appreciate what you've said and it hurts, but I have to tell you that you're wrong and explain our side of the story." Mouths dropped open in surprise to learn that representatives of The Eagle were in the room. Chuck recollected:

Things calmed down a little bit. The people were appreciative that we cared to show up and from that, some leather men and women, we formed a committee for meetings and reaching out to the trans and the Black community, meeting with them one on one and in groups.

Out of these meetings emerged a series of community conversations hosted at The Eagle and co-sponsored by a local racial justice organization and regional leather and kink organizations. A prominent announcement on The Eagle's website described them: "A two part series of classes and conversations organizing white people in the LGBTQIA+ and Leather/Fetish/Kink communities on the topics of racial justice, white privilege, and mobilizing against white supremacy and racism within our community." The announcement carefully noted the limited accessibility of Eagle's Nest due to its stairs, and also asked attendees not to drink alcohol during the event.

As Chuck concluded, "I don't regret any of it because I learned a lot when I met with some of the individuals. I couldn't empathize with them before, and now I can say I sympathize." As he added of learning about the lives of sex workers and transgender women, "There's a lot of battles I'd never considered, and we learned a lot and we're grateful for the experience. And people got to know who we are and that we're not who we were claimed to be."

He changed the programming and advertising at The Eagle. It began offering events specifically for people of color, and new advertising prominently featured Black and gender nonbinary leatherfolk. Chuck concluded, "I lost days of sleep over that situation," but now, "it's healed, not a hundred percent. There's a scar." All these community conversations and actions of accountability were necessary, he said, "to rebrand The Eagle for the next generations." As we ended the interview, Chuck said offhandedly: "We might lose our asses, but it's going to be a lot of fun trying. There's always bankruptcy if we have to go that route."[16]

That comment proved to be a premonition.

Navigating the community conflict didn't prepare Chuck or his partners to weather conflicts with their lender and the father–son team who owned both the building and "The Baltimore Eagle" trademark—ironic given that the general Eagle "brand" has never been claimed or owned by anyone. Things reached a head when Chuck King and his partners publicly closed The Eagle in July of 2018, paying employees with liquor from stock and returning the leather and kink memorabilia to the organizations that had loaned them. This led to messy public squabbles between the building owners and Chuck and his partners, all of which was avidly covered in the local press.[17] Bars that don't own their buildings—or their names—are vulnerable.

But Chuck King never renounced the bar business to any of the journalists who flocked to cover the controversy, telling one, "The last thing I want to do is caution anybody, especially an LGBT individual who wants to open up an LGBT establishment, to not do it." As he explained, "Because even though we went through hell the last year and a half, it was still the most enjoyable job of my life."[18]

The Baltimore Eagle continues under new ownership and management, and there is a happy story for Chuck, as well. After closing the Baltimore Eagle, he and his husband Greg King moved to the gayborhood of Wilton Manors, Florida, adjacent to Fort Lauderdale. There, they fell in with a new group of investors determined to launch a new Eagle in a neighborhood that some might think was already saturated with gay bars. Chuck became the new general manager of Eagle Wilton Manors, bringing his Baltimore expertise and management philosophy to the team. Within six months of opening, COVID-19 hit, closing the fledgling business. But in 2020 it emerged from the lockdowns stronger than ever, he reported. Upon reading this chapter in 2022, Chuck conceded, "It's still kinda hard visiting the past when we put so much passion into that place, but I firmly believe we wouldn't be where we are at today if we didn't go through that experience." Chuck's husband, Greg King, concluded:

> The business not only survived but thrived, reaffirming for us, that even in a time of wider acceptance for LGBT people, even in a market filled with LGBT bars, those that adapt to the needs of the twenty-first century-LGBT market will find success.

Twenty-Six

Leathermen at Drag Bingo

Leather Stallion Saloon
CLEVELAND, OHIO

To visit the country's oldest continually operating leather bar, I only have to drive forty minutes from my small-town Ohio home. Cleveland's oldest gay bar may even be the longest-running leather bar in the entire world.[1] Since 1970, the Leather Stallion Saloon has occupied a single-family house in a light industrial area a mile east of Cleveland Public Square in the central business district, with summertime entry through the side alley and into the spacious, covered courtyard in the back.[2] The bar was often the only source of life on the street until a swanky Black nightclub opened in 2018, drawing crowds with performances by Megan Thee Stallion and Gucci Mane, but also some violence that unnerved longtime neighborhood tenants.[3] The bar is thus in an enlivening neighborhood even as its clientele has expanded because of the closure of other gay bars in Cleveland—by my count, more than half between 2008 and 2016.[4] But then, the rust belt city had itself been shrinking: by 22 percent between 2000 and 2020.

It was to the Leather Stallion Saloon that I went with friends on the Sunday of the Pulse mass shooting, to be in solidarity with our people. But at the door was a voluntary fundraising cover charge. For my $3 donation I got a free—wait for it—water gun. So on the day of what was, at that point, the worst mass shooting in U.S. history, I found myself holding a bright yellow miniature machine gun (which now lives at the bottom of a drawer in a biohazard specimen bag offered by Amy, my archaeologist friend). But in watching the playful water squirting among the somewhat subdued crowd, I was reminded that my particular brand of queer politics was not shared by all gay men, just as my understanding of the bar as a leather bar was not shared with all locals.

The Leather Stallion Saloon was the first bar I visited when I moved to Ohio in 2008 from Oakland, California, where my favorite bar events had been the Sunday beer busts at The Eagle or the Lone Star. Reading online reviews that the Stallion's Sunday day drinking was the best gay event in town, I donned the black leather biker pants I'd bought in Berlin during my German fieldwork, my black calf-high engineer boots, and the leather cuff I'd bought at San Francisco's Folsom Street Fair and drove into Cleveland for the first time. Upon arrival, my usual clinical anxiety was heightened by the realization that everyone else was in shorts and flip-flops, and I was the only person wearing any leather. I quickly learned that unless one of the local leather or kink clubs was holding an event, the bar wasn't that cruisy or leathery at all. But when they were, you could experience all the signs, sounds, and touches of a cruisy men's bar, such as the raffle ticket gimmick where for a certain dollar amount, you get as many tickets as will fit up your inseam, with the seller generously rounding your crotch to give you value, and friction, for money.

Michael Dominguez has managed the Leather Stallion Saloon since the new owner, Ken Myers, took over in 2014, but he'd been drinking there since the late 1980s: "This has always been one of my favorite bars." He was thus in a position to comment both on the long-term and recent changes in the bar. As Michael recalled, "It used to be that people were in their leather on Saturday and Sunday. In the 90s people became a little bit more lax in regard to that." At the same time, leather and kink organizations moved away from the Leather Stallion towards a competitor, A Man's World (which had been, I didn't tell Michael, my favorite gay bar in Cleveland). Only the Uni-corns Motorcycle Club stayed loyal to the Stallion, a group that had been founded by the founder of the bar itself, Al Brightman. But when Man's World closed in 2013, Michael and the new owner began a concerted and successful effort to woo groups back into the fold: "We were trying to accommodate them here, to get them to come back and do their events here." He then rattled off a list of organizations that had recently held events in the bar, including the Rangers ("Northeast Ohio's Leather/Levi/Uniform Club"), The Sisters of Perpetual Indulgence ("The Rock'N'Roll Sisters"), the Arktos Bears Social Club, and ONYX, "an organization that supports ethnic and racial diversity in the gay leather community."[5]

That so many organizations call the Leather Stallion Saloon home justifies Michael's description of the bar as "*the* leather bar, *the* bear bar for the City of Cleveland." The owner of Vibe, a gay bar across town, acknowledged as much when he told a reporter that despite rising LGBTQ+ equality, "Where else are the leather boys going to go? Certainly not to the Olive Garden."[6] Michael explained that Leather Stallion Saloon has "always served the leather community and the leather community has always served the gay community—raising funds, especially with AIDS." Gay bars are charity fundraising powerhouses, and it's not just drag queens who are the catalysts. The leather, kink, and BDSM communities have long thrown themselves into fundraising, with the Leather Stallion playing host to events of the Cleveland Leather Awareness Weekend (CLAW) that has, over the years, raised over $1 million for AIDS, LGBTQ+, and other local charities.

HIV/AIDS had other effects. The bar didn't allow drag queens or women in its early days, but former owner Brian Molnar told a reporter that he "changed the door policy to allow women when I bought it," adding that "the rise of AIDS changed the scene a lot. The emphasis was less on cruising and more on being inclusive."[7] "You would have drag queens and bikers working together," he explained, because "everyone was seeing their closest friends wither away and die from AIDS, and it brought people together."[8]

Such an attitude didn't seem to have penetrated from owner to all of the patrons. Ken, the new owner, had to occasionally take to Facebook to proclaim the Stallion an inclusive establishment. For example, in 2020, Ken wrote,

When I first took over in 2014, a small group of patrons were very vocal about not allowing women or members of the trans community into the bar. They were politely but firmly told they would need to find a new bar.[9]

The post, prompted by the Black Lives Matter uprising that summer, also affirmed the Leather Stallion's goal of "rejecting hate, racism, or discrimination." Drag queen Anhedonia Delight, however, replied publicly to the post:

> Unfortunately many of your patrons are definitely undercover racists/bigots and I personally have seen it because POC friends of mine have felt unsafe/treated disrespectfully for no apparent reason by some of your clientele. . . . Trust me, I'm not just a drag queen, I have my Masters as a social worker.

These are experiences my friends of color have had there, as well, though not perhaps any more so than in other Cleveland gay bars: ownership can set the tone, but patrons do as they will until specifically asked to leave.

Under the previous ownership, I witnessed their fortieth anniversary party in 2010 with my friend Eric. The good: the owner gave touching and generous gifts to longtime patrons, including Browns season tickets to a Black couple who had fallen in love at the bar thirty-nine years earlier. The bad: it was the most offensive drag show I have ever seen. One white queen in blackface mocked Michelle Obama by implying that she had a penis. Another dehumanized Muslim women—at a time when the United States was bombing the Middle East—by wearing a burqa and simulating sex with stuffed animals. A third also did blackface for a drunken Donna Summer number that almost included falling off the makeshift stage. Eric and I looked from each other, in disbelief, toward the Black men in the audience to gauge their unperturbed reactions, and then back to the bigoted trainwreck on stage. This is just one of many reminders that my assessment of what constitutes anti-Black racism need not necessarily be shared by others.

That was the only drag I'd seen under that previous ownership (and thank goodness). When I commented to Michael, in 2018, that there was almost always a fundraiser or a drag show or both when I'd been to the bar, he said, "Yeah. Normally we don't have drag shows, but a lot of the groups bring them in." He paused, indicating that the integration of drag with leather still wasn't seamless. "I have to walk a line. You try to please everyone, and you can't do it. The old guard doesn't want to see women and drag queens, but it's part of what we are." Besides, he added, "There's a cross-connection between the drag and leather. They work hand in hand." He went on to describe an event the day before that illustrated this: "It was an impromptu event to raise money for one of the drag queens who has supported the leather community. She has a leather title, Miss Cleveland Leather."

Regarding events, Michael said, "I try to keep my calendar full. I'm willing to work with anybody." The calendar is indeed always full with patio barbecues in the summer and potlucks the rest of the year, sports night on Thursdays and a complimentary nachos bar on Fridays. The Stallion is one of those old-school gay bars that is open year-round and offers food on holidays like Christmas and Thanksgiving for folks who prefer their chosen families to their birth ones, whether due to geography or prejudice. "We do have some guidelines, though," Michael cautioned: no Jello shots, long forbidden in Ohio, and groups have to pay for their own DJs, rules that reduce the costs associated with entertainment. And being a cruisy men's bar in Cleveland, he added, meant that "You have to watch it with the strippers. Here in Ohio, there's guidelines for strippers with regards to the law: stay away six feet, you're really not supposed to tip them by touching them." True to his advice, the only stripping I've ever seen in the bar is by overenthusiastic patrons, including one who stripped off his pants to reveal an ass-less singlet (you know who you are!).

Michael describes the patrons as "mostly men over 40," but notes a recent change towards young mixed groups of all genders coming in since the closure of Bounce, Cleveland's largest dance club and gay bar, in 2017.[10] Michael explained:

> The kickball league, there's a lot of young people in that. Bounce closed last year and was supposed to host their draft day so they asked if they could do that here. They'd been doing bar crawls here already.

Indeed, the league's bar crawls were famous, or infamous, for suddenly swamping bars with young, fresh faces. I asked if there was any difference between younger patrons and the old guard, and his answer surprised me: "When you're using credit cards with millennials, they want to just buy one drink and just pay for it even though they're going to be back. It slows down my efficiency to get to someone else." Michael was not the only owner who talked about the difficulties of negotiating patron preferences and credit card technology to efficiently open and close tabs. But all agree: The simple days of all-cash transactions are long gone.

Young patrons were also vocally supportive of transgender friends and colleagues. With pride, Michael noted that "Our softball team is having a fundraiser for a team member who is transitioning. Whatever he needs, they want to help." He noted that the GDI Outlaws—a new leather, kink, and BDSM club that had recently sprung up and had held events at the bar—was explicitly inclusive of all genders under a progressive mission of "consent, intersectionality, and bodily autonomy." In 2022, the bar also organized an explicitly all-gender bear event, a cosmopolitanism still rare elsewhere.

When asked if Grindr and other apps had changed the bar business, Michael said he believed so, noting that it's long been a reality that "People meet online. It's kind of impersonal, but some people like that." The website for the Unicorn Motorcycle Club was sharper, flatly stating that "Social networking and increased public acceptance have resulted in a decline in the traditional gay-oriented bar and organizations as they existed 45 years ago."[11] Indeed, the fact that cruisy men's bars are closing 70 percent faster than rates for gay bars in general is evidence that recent changes have hit them harder—leaving only about forty left in the entire country in 2021.[12] The Unicorn's site went on to praise the Leather Stallion Saloon's current owner despite the many changes he had instituted, however, stating that "Ken has shown great foresight to incorporate changes in the operation of our bar, which are working to spur new interest while holding on to the ideals for a leather bar."[13] I may not find the bar that leathery, compared to those in other cities, but for the local leathermen, Ken and Michael have managed to accommodate newcomers while hewing to tradition.

It was smartphones that caused the biggest change in the bar business, claimed Michael, echoing other bar professionals, and scholars, in his critique of patrons' increasing shyness: "Why are you sitting on your phone, go talk to somebody!"[14] Michael sadly noted, "I have this one patron, he looks at his porn there at the bar," which is one way to keep the bar a cruisy space, I suppose, albeit a privatized one: "sexy" without the "community." I asked if there were any upsides to smartphones for bars, and he paused, before saying proudly, "If you do a Google search for gay bars in Cleveland, we're the first to pop up." Mostly it's downsides, however:

> My problem with regards to stuff online is Yelp wanting money, "We can help you make your business bigger and better." We're a small bar! We don't have that kind of money to be putting out $100 a month. . . . I get shitloads of robo calls saying "Your business is in danger of being taken off our listings, so pay for something." We pay for our website and that's it.

"Well," he corrected himself, we do "pay to support community sports teams," a mission that many gay bars of all kinds have adopted as part of a not-quite-for-profit responsibility to offer non-alcohol-related socializing opportunities. Michael enumerated: "We sponsor the rowing; we have two pool teams in the fall; our softball team, the Mustangs." I asked if these teams had events at the bar, and he nodded: "Our softball team has an event once each month during the summer, and they don't charge at the door like most."

I asked about the local economy, meaning northeast Ohio, which has struggled since the 1970s, but Michael took it to mean the neighborhood. "I think we're pretty much on the upswing. They're starting to develop this area, though that's not a good thing for us in regards to parking." Indeed, street parking was never an issue when visiting the bar, even after the new nightclub opened across the street: Now I might have to park *two* blocks away, instead of one. The biggest complaint, he averred, was costs. "With regards to customers, some of them don't understand why your pricing is a little higher than other bars, but you're downtown!"

Another new challenge for the bar, according to Michael, is security. "The area is a lot different from what it was. The homeless, we can't do anything about it. The shelter is two blocks from us. It's a county-owned building." I asked whether it was complaints from customers, and Michael nodded: "There are break-ins in cars." Unhoused and visibly poor people are not safe in gay bars, and some of the discomfort white folks feel in the neighborhood may be due to the presence of Black people on the street. There are always some Black men in the Leather Stallion Saloon—Cleveland is a Black-majority city—but rarely very many unless the Black leather organization Onyx is hosting an event. Michael added that the shelter also was home to many sex offenders, as indicated by the legal notifications: "There's not a week that doesn't go by that we don't get a letter." The bar responded by adding security guards and boosting camera surveillance, including installing a video screen making the feeds visible to patrons. The only downside to this, Michael said, echoing other owners, was its drain on the internet signal. Michael was matter of fact: "With regard to what happened in Orlando, I think any bar needs to watch their security." He contrasted the Leather Stallion's open door with another gay bar in the city that requires patrons to be buzzed into the bar: "I would hate for it to have to be something that happens here, but . . ." and here he trailed off before saying quietly, "Anyone could walk in here, just like at a mall." Here he made his fingers into guns and mimed shooting all over the place. "That's my concern. There's so many crazy people."

I asked Michael why people go out rather than staying in. Laughing, he said "*I* don't want to be alone." With seriousness, he said. "They want to meet other people. The unique thing about this U-shaped bar, it's a very neighborhood-type thing and they talk to one another." My personal experience supports Michael's next assertion: "If a new person comes in they'll say, 'hi.' On our Facebook page we've gotten so many nice reviews from people who feel welcome here." As he said, with a laugh, "They're more welcoming here. A lot of them are older. They want to get to know people. And they have no agenda. Or maybe they do want to have sex with you!" And to this, as well, I can attest, as do younger friends who have sometimes experienced the older regulars' come-ons as pestering, a difference in generations of what constitutes consent in a men's space.

It was upon these regulars, and the summer Sunday sessions, that the bar largely depended. As Michael explained,

> Most of our regulars are in here four to six times a week. They might not be making as much money anymore because they're retired, but they'll keep coming around as long as the bar's open and until they're . . .

and here he motioned under the ground. Indeed, many bars talked about the loyalty of regulars as being key to their businesses. When I asked if the changes had affected the old guard, Michael answered in the affirmative, noting that Leather Stallion Saloon was reaching new patrons while retaining the old. With obvious delight, he exclaimed of the old guard, "They're very supportive, and now they come to some of the events. They come to the drag bingo! I didn't think some of them would come to that, but they did!" But in a shrinking city like Cleveland, with a shrinking gay bar scene, where else are they to go?

Twenty-Seven

Queering the Gay Strip Club

The Stag PDX
PORTLAND, OREGON

When The Stag PDX opened in 2015, it cheekily billed itself as "Portland's premier male strip club," a not-so-subtle dig at the thirty-year Silverado, the country's oldest all-nude male strip club (in)famous in Portland. Often known by its airport identifier PDX, Portland is famous for its fifty-plus all-nude strip clubs, the product of a 1987 Oregon state Supreme Court decision that granted First Amendment protections to nude performances, making it home to the only legal all-nude revues west of the Rockies.[1] It's impossible to know how many gay strip clubs there are in the country: Many states prohibit full frontal nudity, others have a six-foot rule to separate dancers and viewers, while still others mandate tipping from hand to hand only. Portland permits full nudity and only prohibits patrons from touching dancers—but not the reverse. This is all part of life in this fast-growing Pacific Northwest city that is also thirty minutes from my childhood hometown of Camas, a beacon of cosmopolitanism to this small-town boy whose public high school graduating class was 140 people (Go Papermakers!).

Strip clubs are one kind of gay bar that cultivates "sexy community" through interactions between its dancers and patrons, for whom cash tips are a gateway to an erotic experience fraught with friction of both the metaphoric and the physical varieties.[2] These dancers, like the go-go dancers who populate less risqué establishments, sinuously collect and transmit erotic energy from within the club.[3] Gay strip clubs have struggled to adapt to changes among queer men who focus on consent and gender inclusivity, making The Stag PDX's repeated resurrection a case study in queering the gay strip club.

There is something about having a muscled young man who is way out of your league look deeply into your eyes, take your hand with its outstretched bill, and guide it down his oiled torso to his substantial crotch barely restrained by insubstantial underwear. You know it's all for the cash tip. And you don't care. And when he comes around after his set, touches you on the leg in front of your friends, and leans forward and whispers into your ear, so close that his lips graze your lobe, "Do you want to see more?" you do, you really do. So when he takes you by a sweaty hand and guides you to the back, you go, because $20 seems a small price to pay to be admired by someone so into you. You're not supposed to touch, but every dancer I've succumbed to has taken my hands and placed them on their body while straddling me with full friction. Sexy community can be had one on one.

The Stag moved to distinguish itself from its delightfully sleazy forebear through luxurious decor: tufted leather seating, raw wood, hunting lodge accessories, taxidermied antlers, filament bulbs suspended from nautical rope, and dark paisley wall treatments.[4] The stage area boasted a pole and exercise equipment where dancers alternated between feats of strength and elegant moves; in the back were velvet-curtained booths for private dances. Stag also offered a large selection of local microbrews and high-end cocktails, stressing an upscale experience.[5] The bar was by far the best-looking gay bar I'd ever been in, and it quickly became my favorite place to visit when I was home seeing my parents, a place to meet James to share concern about our mutual friend, who was long ill but had been a stalwart gay bar companion for us both (RIP Dan).

The bar also differentiated itself from its local competition by inviting straight women into the space. The competing Silverado was famous at one point for its "No bachelorette parties" sign and for briefly trying to impose a higher cover charge for women, with staff telling a local paper that for every complaint they got about the cover, they received "the same amount of complaints that we get from male customers who don't like groups of screaming and giggling women."[6] Silverado also had a famous sign reading "If You're Here, You're Queer," which the same official said was intended to "Let straight men know right off the bat that they aren't welcome."[7] Old-school gay strip clubs thus shared with old-school lesbian bars a preference for a single-sex, no-straight-people environment.

Meanwhile, The Stag managed to walk that fine line between making itself straight inclusive without alienating its primary GBQ male clientele. It merely asked bachelorette parties to eschew the "flashing penis crowns" that distract the dancers.[8] It welcomed straight men, with bar manager Kam telling me, "They can come in with their girlfriends because if they don't feel comfortable, they can go play video poker or play at the pool table." Indeed, I had seen several man–woman couples in the club, including a few where the woman bought a lap dance for her man, a strangely satisfying queer sight. As a journalist reported approvingly,

> While the patrons are 90 percent male, not a single one side-eyed me, a woman, as I sat alone at the bar. By the time I left, someone had bought me a no-strings-attached drink and I had at least two new best friends. All in all, Stag might be my new favorite place in Portland.[9]

On a couple nights I've been at The Stag, women have been as much as one third of the patronage, and their presence has been unremarkable.

By the time I began this project, the bar's ownership had turned over for the first time (it has new ownership since 2021, the third team, so this chapter is not about the club's current ownership team—let's be clear about that). Michael had, in 2017, bought his first nightclub, claiming LGBTQ+ nightlife was on the upswing: "Anyone could open a gay bar in Portland."[10]

We were sitting in the basement office while a steady stream of employees trailed in to use the lockers and clock in. A drag queen sailed into the crowded space to shimmy into a dress while Michael editorialized, "Bitch, you gonna fit in that thing?" Drag queens were the emcees in the club, and their fellow artists often popped by to say hello, so it wasn't uncommon to see three or four queens at the edge of the stage. The Stag's weekly drag brunch—oddly, long the only drag brunch in town—was billed as "a monthly gospel brunch featuring Black queens." The brunch was also cited by a local paper as a comfortable place for LGBTQ+ people who don't drink alcohol to enjoy a gay time.[11]

When I asked about the biggest challenges to business, Michael didn't hesitate. "Weather," an ominous answer in famously rainy Portland. Personnel management was also a challenge, reported Michael. "It's fun, but it's a lot of headaches, a lot of babysitting. You've got these dancers, they all say that they're straight and then two weeks later," he flopped his wrist dramatically, implying that heteros became flexible in the context of The Stag. "It's funny," he laughed. "We always joke: the straight guys come and dance, but twenty dollars is twenty dollars," citing the then-cost of a one-song private dance. "A lot of the workers too, they're straight. Some of them have been strippers, and they end up sleeping with each other. It just never ends, the bullshit." Certainly, one of the femme gay dancers who chatted with me complained that the gay male dancers received fewer tips from the gay male patrons, who always gravitate to the straight guys who "couldn't give a shit" about them, adding ruefully, "Where's the solidarity?"

I asked how Michael dealt with the bullshit, and he was conciliatory: "We have a good, close-knit family-oriented group around here." At this moment the operations manager Nicole walked into the office, a petite tattooed woman with shoulder-length hair. Michael greeted her by honking her breasts and, without missing a beat, described a sort of post-gay, post-MeToo paradise:

Everyone's very welcoming and comfortable. I grab her tits all the time! More than that! But like, whatever, I grab my straight friends' dicks, nobody gives a shit anymore. Everyone in Portland is very comfortable, with, with, with . . .

". . . this environment," Nicole finished his sentence for him with a smile.

To me, this was textbook sexual harassment, making it hypocritical that an owner would be so concerned with his employees sleeping together. Such seeming violations of consent also didn't bode well for the management of a strip club where boundaries were already blurry but also were legally regulated.[12] Certainly this was not the kind of close-knit family I was familiar with, but queer families are different from the straight family of my birth. And yet, when one family member is your employer, and the #MeToo movement is in full swing, maybe keep your mitts off the mammaries, especially in front of strangers. Being a safe space is no guarantee against mistreatment or misunderstandings between queer employers and their employees. Nicole wryly explained, "I'm more of a bro to some of these people."

When I asked how he would describe the bar, Nicole edged in: "We have always catered towards men, the gay gentlemen. We have a motto . . . ," and here Michael interjected, waggling a finger at the staff: "Be nice to the women, be nicer to the men!" Nicole explained, "If we catch a dancer who is paying too much attention to the women, the other gay gentlemen here are watching, so we tell him, 'Don't forget to pay attention to them too.'" Michael laughed, "Most of the boys know who spends money, but they don't listen to fucking rules!"

I asked how it was possible to have a bar that celebrates men in a radically queer city like Portland, Oregon, and Michael gestured expansively, "We have something for everyone," claiming that his patronage was "everybody!" And here he wasn't exaggerating. Unlike strip clubs where there was only one slot for a dancer of color,[13] The Stag's lineup regularly featured many dancers of color who attracted a similarly racially diverse patronage, although the same disclaimers apply: Dancers of color are praised for conforming to white fantasies in terms of body shape and dancing style.[14] Though the average evening's cast featured only toned muscle boys, the bar did host the occasional Werk Your Body: A Body Positive Bear/Cub Event, which billed itself as "all your favorite big boys and curvy bodied beauties."[15] The Stag also hosted the monthly DOE, a night celebrating lesbian dancers and patrons that was, surprisingly for a city with over fifty strip clubs of women dancers, the only lesbian strip-club night in the city. During 2019, DOE even featured a special event featuring only women of color.[16]

The club also regularly booked transgender and nonbinary dancers including the charming Nikki, who urged me to log onto Insta where her online bio read: "PDX Glitterbeast. stripper, singer, gogo, drag, MC, nonbinary, femme."[17] The Stag was long the only strip club in the country, straight or gay, that regularly hosted nights celebrating transmasc and transfemme performers. Their party Trance was billed as "trans girls strip at Stag,"[18] while T-Bone was billed as "the only all trans male revue in the country." Michael was justifiably proud of these events, but they contradicted his earlier assertation that "We don't have female strippers."

When I asked about carding people at the door, Michael described two issues. He cited the nearby shelter for unhoused people by name as he explained, "We have a lot of people who tried to use a Transitions Project ID," but "the police do not allow that as a correct form of ID. Legally I can't serve you so you have to move on." When I asked if there were other issues with identification at the door, Michael's answer surprised me. "A lot of people from Canada with their Canadian ID don't bring their passport with them so we have a form, a statement of age form," so that "If something went down, I could say, 'They promised me they were this age.'" When I asked if such a form could be used by a homeless person without a state ID, he shook his head and changed the subject. Canadians who can travel the 300 miles from the border can be trusted; poor people from around the block cannot.

I asked if there were ever issues with gender presentation and ID, and Michael again shook his head: "It's a sensitive subject for a lot of people but most trans folks are used to it," referring to the door person's confusion between a person's presentation and the picture or gendered name on their ID. The Stag was familiar with it, however, because "We have a couple of trans dancers, one of whose preferred name is not his legal name, but we say 'You match the picture, so you're obviously this person.'"

As Michael explained, their inclusive policy attracted employees along with positive press. As he recalled, "one girl came in here from Trance and said, you're the only bar in the city that lets us dance. She came to me and said, 'I have a dick and I would like to dance.'" As he shrugged, "that's the only requirement," explaining that this wasn't discriminatory, recalling a transgender male porn star: "Viktor Belmont got naked and called out, 'Do you want to see my dick?'" Belmont had praised the club to a local journalist, noting,

> Cis-male gay bars aren't always the most welcoming spaces, [but] Portland has a really great culture around sex work and strip clubs, and people really value performers. I never thought I'd dance at a trans masc space, and to have the opportunity is incredible.[19]

I tried to change the subject by asking what patrons don't understand about the business, but Michael continued with a transphobic slur, "I don't want to sleep with a tr██y but be who you want to be. You can be purple and look like fucking Barney but you be you." Viktor Belmont still on his mind, Michael explained, "and he was just so into educating people. I didn't know what 'cisgender' means until two days ago." Nicole explained wryly, "These are old gay guys." As Michael concluded, "You should be able to celebrate all types of masculinity whether your original birth is male or female. It's what I am proud of for this club." The policy was not uncontroversial: One online commentor complained, "If you want to rebrand as an 'all-inclusive LGBTQ strip club,' gay men can and will simply go elsewhere," not an idle threat when Silverado was mere blocks away.[20]

T-Bone also attracted some criticism in the local press for excluding nonbinary bodies and featuring only dancers with "passing privilege," that is, transgender men who could be taken for cisgender. This charge was vigorously contested in the local press by the events producer, herself transgender: "I was never not going to hire someone because of passing privilege."[21] She described the allegations as "disgusting. The intent of the events was to create a space for trans people to strip, shake their ass, make some money and have everyone have a good time."[22] As reporter Elise Herron editorialized in conclusion, "Stag should both be pushed to respond to concerns about inclusion of nonbinary dancers and lauded for starting conversations about trans visibility in queer and sex worker spaces."[23] Yet before COVID-19, few other strip clubs in the country, gay or straight, had been as inclusive.

Michael's claim of having something for everyone extended to music. In addition to the monthly gospel brunch, the bar featured Black and Latinx music.[24] As a local reporter opined, it

> could be due to the management change, but lately Stag has been celebrating bodies that stray away from the classic Magic Mike image. Drag queen MCs host different music themed nights—like trap, Latin, and pop—as well as a weekly amateur night and a drag brunch.[25]

The night of the interview, a toned, nearly naked man padded into the office wearing only sneakers and barely-there undies. Michael introduced him: "This is one of our fabulously straight, pain-in-the-ass bartenders," he said, as he casually groped the bartender's crotch. "This is the one who's gonna be a dad," Michael explained to the man's shocked response, "Jesus, Michael!" His boss laughed, saying, "All the daddies come to him. He's the Jew. I'm going to buy you a menorah. I was someplace last night where they said "no hat" and I said "hey, what about a yarmulke?" The bartender retorted, "I work more than everyone else here," to which Michael replied, "I'm just giving you shit, you Jew!" I was sitting there, with my laptop out, my fingers clacking furiously over the keys, with my eyes wide and my mouth agape that he would use such anti-Semitic language in front of a stranger who was recording things—and he had explicitly given consent to be quoted by name!

Just then a woman in lingerie came into the office. Michael gleefully introduced her, "Now it's your baby mom!" Michael turned to me, "He's the one who ate her out and is like, 'I lost my underwear, I lost my heart!" The pair glared at him while the woman approached the bartender and said, "Come here, you've got glitter on your face!" Incredulous, he replied, "I've been here for five fucking minutes!" While she used her fingernail to scrape the glitter from her beau's face, Michael observed her low-cut dress critically, remarking, "Your areola is coming out," before turning to me: "She's six weeks, not very far along." With concern, the woman turned to me, "Please don't put in that I'm pregnant. I haven't told my mom yet." I told her I wouldn't, but then she asked when the book would be out. "Not for three years," I guessed optimistically. "Oh, in that case, you can. I'll have told my mom by then." Three years, ha. The kid's in school now.

Manager and bartender Kam told me he was straight and had

helped the previous owners launch the bar and stayed on after the ownership change. I asked what kind of bar it was, and he equivocated, citing himself as contributing to a kind of post-gay reality: "If you want everyone to be equal, I'm helping that . . . everyone is here, so that's why I say that this is an everybody bar." I looked at him skeptically, recalling the queer stream of glittered go-go boys and drag queens who had sailed in and out of the cramped office. Kam clarified: "But it's important to be a gay bar, because it's their safe zone. They're comfortable here. They're not going to be shamed here." Post-gay and safe space for gays were not incompatible, apparently.

After the interview, I was ambivalent. The Stag was the most innovative strip club in the country, gay or straight, for any gender. And yet, the ribald, gropy chaos in the back wasn't what you would normally think of as the "family-oriented" atmosphere Michael described. The retorts flew so fast and furious that I couldn't keep track of the zingers—from my notes I can't tell you who said, "This bitch has given more rides than Greyhound," nor to whom.

Michael's casual treatment of his staff looked like all kinds of harassment and discrimination to me. It belied a casual understanding of consent and bodily autonomy which didn't bode well for the owner of a strip club, much less one that was trying to be queerly inclusive of everyone. So it was with little surprise that I learned that The Stag had closed its doors toward the end of 2020, citing the COVID-19 pandemic—bringing to a close Michael's complicated, messy, glorious run of the queer strip club. I was never able to get in touch with him, so I don't know how he felt about the bar's closure or how he was quoted in this chapter. You can bet I double-checked to ensure I had his signed informed consent from the night of our interview, and with optimism that he would be embarrassed at his words, I don't use his last name.

But luckily for me, like a baby-oiled phoenix, new owners stepped forward to reopen The Stag in late 2021. As with so many other clubs, I couldn't do a follow-up interview: Jesse has long since grown tired of me turning our shared travels into my personal work. For the new owners and staff of Stag PDX, may their family prosper in queer, inclusive—and consensual—ways.

Part Six

How to Save a Gay Bar

Twenty-Eight

Crowdfunding While Black

Alibi Lounge
NEW YORK, NEW YORK

Most plans to save a gay bar come to naught. By the time a gay bar's troubles become public, it is usually too late. Owners are often too ill, too broke, too jaded, or just too plain *worn out* to go on despite a sudden surge of community support. Increasing attention to the fragility of gay bars has stimulated concern for how to save them—this section collects some strategies. What they share is long lead times: most successful strategies can't create change on a dime.

But crowdfunding does. Crowdfunding campaigns to save gay bars proliferated in the COVID-19 pandemic, and a couple blockbuster campaigns garnered international media attention.[1] Most crowdfunding campaigns don't meet their goals, however. The story of one of the most successful gay bar crowdfunding campaigns illustrates the pluck, the

---

Image on opposite page: Sisters of Perpetual Indulgence and supporters gather in front of San Francisco's Stud, which lost its building in 2020 but continues as a worker-owned collective. The Stud Collective has been instrumental in landmarking and preserving other LGBTQ+ spaces while searching for a new home for their storied bar to come out of exile. Photo courtesy of Gooch. Used with permission.

luck, and the intersecting interests necessary to create the rare, perfect storm: the upswell of donations that propels a crowdfunding campaign far beyond its original goals and actually saves a gay bar.

Alexi Minko opened Alibi Lounge in the historically Black neighborhood of Harlem in 2016. When we met in 2020, he was sleek and tall, his sparkling eyes and dark skin offset by a crisp white button-down shirt and suit jacket. As the signature cocktail on the bar's list proclaims, "Elegance is an Attitude." Alexi waved me off the sidewalk and down four or so steps into the partial-basement bar, the only natural light coming from the all-glass door. The bar was only as wide as the narrow building, and I was welcomed into the space by a red carpet that extended the length of a room framed by mirrored walls, palms, and potted orchids. He popped a bottle of Veuve Clicquot champagne and held out a glass; it felt rude to say no, although the delicate-stemmed glass was perched precariously at my elbow as I crouched over my laptop in the tufted leather and chrome bar seat, furiously transcribing our conversation.

What had surprised Alexi, upon moving to Harlem in 2015, was the lack of rainbow flags anywhere. As he told a journalist, "I walked about 20, 30, blocks, and I didn't see anything that represented the LGBT image whatsoever!"[2] He set out to open a club that would cater to Black LGBTQ+ people in the neighborhood, telling another journalist, "For us here in Harlem, being a people of color's village, in the sense that we're a community, having a space that is *for us, by us,* is truly important."[3] Thus his plans for Alibi's echoed what makes gay bars for people of color so special, even as they remain among the most fragile and rare type of gay bar.

His planning applications to the city didn't mention that it was a gay bar, however. Alexi's elegant and expressive comportment literally gave him away, which meant that when he stood on the street gathering signatures to support his business application, almost everyone assumed it was going to be a gay bar. One woman even told him, as he recalled, "In the 90s you would have got shot in the head!" Planning approval was forthcoming, the landlord consented to a bar, and upon opening the first gay bar in Harlem in many years, "We were the only ones that had gay flags flying"—until they were set on fire during Pride week in 2019, an act of arson that attracted national media attention and earned the perpetrator an indictment on hate crime charges.[4]

Although trained as a lawyer from a family of lawyers, Alexi had previous nightlife experience. He was co-founder of a successful nightclub in Libreville, Gabon, his hometown. He also became a partner in a bar in Paris. But most of all, he recalled fond childhood memories of being raised in a bar in Central Africa:

> Because my mom was a single mother, she hired a nanny-slash-bartender. Every summer we would spend our time with the nanny, in Africa when the bars open at 10 am, and my siblings and I would be doing our homework and coloring while the nanny was behind the bar.

But even being an African immigrant gay bar owner hasn't necessarily meant that Alibi Lounge has served other African immigrants. As Alexi mused,

> The other day I started playing African music, not pop music, real African music like my parents used to, and it hit me. I'm an African dude that has a gay lounge, and I've never had an African gay night. What the fuck am I doing?!

Pondering whether the closet was too great a barrier to immigrants entering Alibi, he wondered if "I could come up with a way for people to know that it's a safe haven. Maybe on Mondays, it's slow, we put a curtain at the door and have a private event." And, now that Alibi has survived homophobic attacks and a brutal pandemic, maybe it can embrace the immigrants who are rarely acknowledged as part of the LGBTQ+ community and are often actively excluded from it.[5]

March of 2020 was a brutal month for Alexi Minko, and not just because of COVID-19. On March 11, six people entered Alibi Lounge and viciously assaulted him and a patron with furniture, sending both of them to the hospital with serious injuries and leaving the bar smashed up. Five days later, the New York's governor closed all bars and restaurants. Reeling from a smashed-up body and an indefinite closure order, Alexi drafted a Notice of Surrender to the landlord to close Alibi Lounge for good.

But a protégé who was crowdfunding to support his restaurant was relentless in urging Alexi to launch a campaign of his own. Alexi gave in, but only "to get him off my back. There was this sense of why would I ask for money? I went into business, not to ask for money. That's for nonprofits." He also confessed to two other barriers: "I really felt it was in bad taste to be asking for money, and then there was that thing of feeling like I was admitting failure." Grimacing, he recalled "Ahhhh it was very hard to put myself out there." As he noted, "No business owners want to receive money by sitting at home. I don't know anyone! We love that grind!"

The crowdfund had a push from Malik Saaka, a local activist who helped promote the campaign. As Alexi recalled, "Within a day it became this beautiful circus" because of the "story about the resilience of what we were trying to do: save the only Black-owned LGBTQ establishment in Manhattan." Funds started trickling in, and then it became a flood. Local news coverage and online promotion made the campaign go viral: The campaign eventually netted $184,000! And while he was grateful for the outpouring of generosity, Alexi couldn't help but wish that the funds had come the normal way, in better times: "One of the very first donations was $1,000. What on earth! Why couldn't you have come and spent it at the bar?"

The success of the campaign through the long year of 2020 was bolstered by consistent media attention and allowed Alexi to weather other troubles than the COVID-19 shutdowns. Alibi Lounge was burglarized in July, with the front door battered down.[6] Later in the year, the campaign helped drum up an additional $12,000 to renew the bar's lease.[7]

Alexi is still befuddled about why his GoFundMe was so successful. He credits some of his success to the vulnerability and authenticity he displayed in his campaign writeup: "I had told that story the right way, which was the truth, the naked truth." But he also attributes it to positive thought, the universe rewarding him for being a person with good intentions, and, laughing, "voodoo."

I was moved by the campaign too, as part of my personal project of redistributing my unneeded government stimulus checks to gay bars in need. Alexi wrote heartfelt emails, in which he was vulnerable and charming and hopeful. Even in faraway Ohio, I felt I had a stake in preserving one of the country's few Black-owned gay bars. Alexi told me that he hoped that the success of the Alibi Lounge GoFundMe would raise the profile of other gay bars' crowdfunding. "I think one of the positive effects was that the experience of Alibi Lounge really helped shed that big light over bars that have also done a GoFundMe and that they were also deserving." He noted that one campaign was so inspired that they plagiarized his campaign's language word for word—"the Alexi method," Minko laughed lightly.

But Alexi's win overshadows the defeat that made the three-year-old Alibi Lounge the oldest Black-owned gay bar in New York in the first place. Club Langston was the long-running Brooklyn Black gay bar that fell into trouble in 2019 through a combination of back taxes, code violation fines, and rising rent.[8] Its GoFundMe plea for $73,000 attracted little attention until co-owner Calvin Clark mounted a poignant, dramatic demonstration in front of the bar that attracted regional media coverage.[9] For ten days he stood on a platform in front of the sign-festooned bar, fasting, with conspicuous white tape over his mouth, remaining in place for the entire last twenty-four hours.

It wasn't enough.

Langston's only raised $16,000, and the storied club closed for good two weeks later, dramatizing the vulnerability of gay bars that serve people of color, which close at rates 68 percent greater than do others.[10] It also illustrates how crowdfunding by Black folks is less likely to be successful than by whites, largely due to Black folks networks' having less cash to begin with and also because white folks are less likely to donate to Black campaigns.[11] But it also illustrates how the Black Lives Matter uprisings of 2020 may have shifted things, at least temporarily.

So why was Alibi Lounge's campaign so successful? I can only speculate that Alexi benefited from three intersecting, rising tides. The #BLM uprisings of 2020 brought a national focus on Black-owned businesses that sent well-meaning white people suddenly reaching for the wallets. The second was the national attention paid to the crisis of closing gay bars, bolstered by four slick corporate campaigns to save them and media coverage at the local and national levels. These included the Lesbian Bar Project with actor, activist, and club owner Lea DeLaria as its face. Grindr partnered with GayCities to create the LGBTQ Nightlife Relief Fund. Queer to Stay was an initiative by broadcaster Showtime and establishment LGBTQ+ lobby group HRC, which actually contributed to Alexi's Alibi Lounge, making it one of nine establishments in the whole country to receive funds in 2020. Absolut Vodka leveraged the eyeballs and time of viewers to prompt an additional $25,000 in donations to their $175,000 Out & Open program, providing business consulting services to gay bars and restaurants, a project for which I consulted.[12]

Finally, with the city's pump already primed with the tears of Langston's closure, and with national attention on Black-owned and LGBTQ+ serving spaces, Alibi Lounge benefited from diverse sources for its many, many small donations from around the world. Alibi is also located in New York City, the largest city in the United States, a hub of media and a city with which tens of millions of tourists have an emotional relationship. It's a city large enough to sustain another Black-owned gay bar in the neighborhood, even. Husbands Charles Hughes and Ricky Solomon's opened Lambda Lounge six blocks away in 2021, in part to drive sales of their boutique vodka, also named Lambda.[13]

Alibi's wasn't the only crowdfunding campaign to break six figures, but it was the most successful one by a sole owner. All of the others were also in big-four, wealthy cities with established gayborhoods. The historic Stonewall Inn in New York City raised more than $300,000, Akbar in Los Angeles earned over $230,000, The Eagle Los Angeles garnered over $150,000, and San Francisco's Twin Peaks earned over $110,000. But these were by far the exceptions that proved the rule: most gay bar fundraisers didn't meet their goals, and many didn't even earn $5,000.

Of the thirty-eight gay bar crowdfunding campaigns still public in 2022, the median amount earned was under $24,000—enough to limp along for a couple of months for Blackstones in Portland, Maine, but not nearly enough to get San Francisco's The Stud a new home. The Lesbian Bar Project, by far the highest profile and most lucrative corporate-crowdfund venture, only disbursed between $9,000 and $17,000 for the bars that opted into the pool's two rounds of funding.[14] Milwaukee's This Is It!, the city's oldest, raised over $12,000 . . . but of a $25,000 ask; it was subsequently saved when Ru girl All Star Trixie Mattel stepped in.[15] Trans-owned Temptation Bar in small-town Cookeville, Tennessee, only raised $4,168 of an $8,000 ask.

I'm ambivalent about crowdfunding as a solution for saving gay bars. On the one hand, mutual aid and community fundraising have a long and deep history in gay bars. Garlow's in small-town Gun Barrel City, Texas, raises more for charity every year than what the average family of four makes in its rural county. Long before websites like GoFundMe and Kickstarter, LGBTQ+ people organized community benefits to fund community members' cancer treatments, top surgeries, storm-damaged homes, AIDS hospice care, and burial expenses. I still see these flyers in gay bars, though increasingly with a QR code for an online crowdfunding campaign rather than an old-fashioned bucket of bills at a drag show benefit. And many gay bars, like Troupe429 in Norwalk, Connecticut, were themselves the product of crowdfunding campaigns that gauged community interest in a new space and provided it much-needed startup funds.

On the other hand, crowdfunding reveals social failures. Most campaigns don't reach their goals.[16] They reveal the discriminatory forces that leave LGBTQ+ patrons poorer than straight ones, and LGBTQ+ owners undercapitalized and more vulnerable than straight bar owners to rising rents, declining populations, or shifting economic tides. Crowdfunding is a distinctly neoliberal solution to a structural problem, literally commercializing peoples' pain to pry private dollars from individual pockets.[17] If LGBTQ+ spaces are so important, why isn't there government or foundation support for them? Alibi Lounge is an exception to the general rule that the most successful campaigns are those by white cisgender folks: campaigns by Black, Indigenous, and people of color succeed at much lower rates.[18] That Alexi needed crowdfunds to persist through so many challenges is also a reminder of the barriers to opening a gay bar, and of keeping one open.

The COVID-inspired proliferation of gay bar crowdfunding means the practice is likely to persist into the future. Successful campaigns will be those that are able to reach beyond the pink dollar and tap directly into straight people's pockets: Allies can show their support beyond merely attending our spaces. Such campaigns will also be planned long enough before the owner is at the end of their rope. But there must be other ways to save bars—ones that don't depend on charity, because charity begins at home, and queer folks often don't have enough money to save our spaces on our own.

Twenty-Nine

Nonprofit Ownership Means We Celebrate Pride Every Week

The Park Dance Club
ROANOKE, VIRGINIA

One of the largest dance clubs in Virginia is also the only gay bar in the country that is owned by a nonprofit entity. Freed from the profit motive, the club serves its multiracial clientele—and accommodates their hunting knives—with a community board and a policy of not banning problem patrons. This unique ownership structure means that profits benefit the community, and, instead of throwing a one-day annual event to commemorate the Stonewall riots, The Park Dance Club stands as a monument to LGBTQ+ pride every week.

The Park Dance Club in Roanoke, Virginia, has been a venerable show bar since 1978. It serves vast parts of both Virginias on either side of the Blue Ridge Mountains as the only gay outpost for more than a hundred miles in any direction.[1] As a journalist rhapsodized, "People have traveled to this spot, sometimes driving for hours from the surrounding rural communities and Appalachian towns. Here, they found family."[2] The Park Dance Club is also the only physical LGBTQ+ bar or club in its city of about 100,000 people.[3]

The bar is in an inconspicuous building on a light industrial hillside overlooking the railyards that birthed Roanoke, low-slung brick and metal machine shops that gave way to a CrossFit gym, doggie day care, and artisanal taco restaurant. Show director Enya Salad easily rattled off a list of the bar's drag triumphs: "We've had five Miss Gay Americas in this bar, two Miss U.S.-of-A-at-Larges, and other national pageant winners out of this bar. We're huge, and we've always brought big-name entertainers." Along with a steady stream of Ru girls, the club also plays host to many of these statewide and national pageants including, in 2021, Mr. and Ms. Gay Virginia United States at Large and Miss and Mr. Gay United States at Large.

When the bar closed suddenly in 2013, it sent shockwaves through the community. A temporary owner stepped into the breach, but when she was unable to keep the bar, the community came up with a unique business model with potential for other cities: the regional LGBT Pride nonprofit assumed ownership of the for-profit club.[4]

Jason Gilmore was the president of Roanoke Pride, Inc., when we spoke in 2017, which made him the *de facto* executive in charge of the club. He explained how Elizabeth Bowers, who had rescued the club from its first closure in 2013, made a charitable donation of the business and its building to Roanoke Pride, Inc., giving the nonprofit a new, for-profit LLC subsidiary. It is, to my knowledge, the only for-profit bar owned by a nonprofit in the United States: while other gay bars are treated as community owned, in this case, it's true. All the profits from the club go to Roanoke Pride, which uses them to organize quarterly events, the annual one-day Pride festival, and to fund its Prism Foundation, which provides scholarships and makes charitable donations to address poverty and homelessness.

Jason conceded to community ambivalence about the situation: "Pride owning the bar is not without controversy. Some don't understand the nonprofit owning the bar." Others wonder about the propriety of the nonprofit's involvement in the nightlife industry or in selling alcohol, although such models exist in Europe: Finland's largest gay club, DTM ("Don't Tell Mama"), was long owned by the national LGBTQ+ civil rights organization, SETA. But as Jason confessed, "When for-profit entities are involved, they're always the villain for some in the community." Pride's elected board of directors functions as the governing body of The Park, and they hired a general manager to oversee day-to-day operations, Michael Smith, who had worked for the bar before its ownership transition. It also means The Park serves as a formal meeting space for Pride and Prism, providing a home to organizations that had, until then, operated out of post office boxes.

Jason himself had no previous experience in the nightlife industry other than a long association with The Park Dance Club: "I had always partied here with friends, so it was always a home for me." Pride's acquisition of the club meant he was a nonprofit president who was also a for-profit club executive:

> It's been a learning process. While I have a business degree and marketing degree, a BBA—I've always done business stuff—but I'd never had anything to do with running a club and a bar and a restaurant. It's a very different beast.

One of the learning curves was the variability in the industry. "Just because there's a trend over a quarter doesn't mean it will hold the next. It's a fickle business," Jason explained. The new ownership structure did not prevent The Park Dance Club from gaining its first liquor license, adding spirits to its beer and wine offerings for the first time in its long history. It also revamped its restaurant, which is required by Virginia's liquor laws in order to serve spirits. Having full food service also made possible the club's popular drag brunches, which allow people from a wider array of abilities and life circumstances to enjoy drag: a sweet photo on the internet shows a drag queen interacting with a patron in a wheelchair as the sun streams in. Jason noted with pride, "So far we haven't run any deficit. Some months we've had less income than others." He concluded that local factors drive success or failure. "You've got to keep reinventing the wheel and find what works and what doesn't." What worked, at least as the COVID pandemic waned in 2021, were biweekly electronic dance music (EDM) Thursdays, open stage Sundays for new performers, a community-building talent night featuring amateur performers, and "Just Dance" Saturdays, which packed them in on the two nights I attended.

Straight allies are key to The Park's business plan, especially in a region of just over 300,000 people. As Jason explained, "With the changing overall of our world and the more inclusiveness, a lot of our LGBT brothers and sisters go to mainstream establishments downtown." He noted that "If you're trying to run a business that breaks even, it's hard where we've evolved to with our culture, without our allies." The plan, then, is to slightly rebrand the club from its past as a "gay" club: "I've been trying to brand us as Roanoke's hottest dance club, so that's spawned off of the LGBT love of dance music." He stated that this had been a success, with "On any given Saturday night it's 40 percent allies, sometimes more than that, and they come because it's fun and safe and it's inclusive and a lot of them have friends in our community." Jason opined that gay-only bars will still exist in big cities, but "I think midsize cities are the ones that have the hardest time because you only have so many people to draw from, so it becomes more and more difficult to stay viable." LGBTQ+ acceptance, then, means new clientele—allies who might also be drawn in by the Park's featured location on the Virginia tourism website, whose longtime slogan "Virginia is for lovers" now applies to everyone.

Community ownership brings responsibility to everyone in the community, with music as one indication. Jason directs the DJs to serve everyone: "If I notice a trend and I'm listening in a rut of the same type, I tell them, 'Get out of the rut! Get a mix!' We have to have a very diverse crowd. Without mixing it up, you're catering to a specific group." He noted that the bar specifically requests that DJs play country music blocks and hip hop blocks, two genres that are often excluded from the playlists in gay bars that are heavy on pop and house music. This seemed to succeed, with Enya Salad contrasting The Park's integrated crowd and the segregation in gay bars in all nearby cities, where "You have Black night and you have white night." The night I attended, the crowd indeed appeared to be almost a third people of color in a county that is 90 percent white. This was part of a long trend, reported Cass Adair:

> Roanoke's LGBTQ bars were probably less segregated than their straight counterparts, you might even think of these spaces as hinting at this as a brand-new kind of Southern culture, one that was more tolerant, racially integrated, and probably a lot more fun.[5]

Another sign of community responsibility? Polls on The Park Dance Club website ask what *RuPaul Drag Race* performers to bring to the bar, to the regional Pride celebration, and what hours and days are best for the club to host performances.

Community ownership also shapes Jason's management style with problem patrons, saying that he does not subscribe to the common practice of banning people. Jason explained,

> I tell all of my security: Defuse them. Get both of the parties separate to talk, ask them, "Did you come here to have a good time?" Taking that into account, they'll think about it, they'll knock off the drama, and they'll go their separate ways.

Describing his impulse to ban two patrons recently, he concluded:

> That's a Band-Aid. So I made the two of them talk. Whatever your resolution, if it's to be friends, if it's to speak to each other, if it's to ignore, I don't care, but come together to resolve this because this place is big enough for the both of you.

He described this strategy as an act of community accountability and financial acuity: "If you're looking at this as a community and a business, it's smart for both." Jason was the only owner who described this strategy of not banning patrons, and he was one of the few owners to be so open about the need to retain every patron for economic reasons.

The Park has been challenged by its successes. "Our numbers are up greatly, that has been a challenge. Our numbers have been the highest that they've been in ten years." Jason said that another challenge to "maintaining a certain level of excellence" has been "consistency, both with the people you're getting in the building and what you're providing them." The last challenge he cited was security.

Bar security has special resonance in Roanoke beyond the happenstance that our interview took place on the one-year anniversary of the 2016 Pulse nightclub massacre. Roanoke faced its own gay bar shooting in 2000 when a man entered a previous gay bar, The Backstreet, to "waste some fa██ots," shooting six people and killing another. The subsequent march and mass coming-out was described by the local paper as Roanoke's own Stonewall.[6] Such a shooting was extreme but not unprecedented: A patron of The Park Dance Club recalled passing cars shooting BBs at patrons lining up outside in the 1980s.[7] Jason explained that The Park is the only bar in the region to wand patrons with a handheld metal detector, telling me that they regularly discover knives that the doorman holds so patrons can retrieve them at the end of the night. When I expressed surprise that The Park took the trouble and liability to store people's private property, Jason thought I was expressing surprise that people had knives at all: "Oh, we have a lot of people into hunting here, and a lot of people that come here just carry a pocketknife every day." With pride, Jason noted that The Park has the best safety record in town.

Both Jason and Enya noted the favorable impression The Park Dance Club, and its nonprofit mission, had made on visiting Ru girls, with several making donations to the Prism Foundation. As Jason said modestly, "We're just very hospitable. We make sure they get here on time, at the airport, we get them food, they go out. We're just being southern." Just being southern—and Appalachian—perhaps. The Park Dance Club is also a world leader in innovative business strategies that merge community organizations, nightlife spaces, and charity, although challenges remain in keeping the Roanoke Pride board democratically elected and in compliance with the thicket of intersecting regulations. But unlike privately owned gay clubs, the Roanoke Pride website lists by name all of its constituents: the four members of the board of directors, the five programming staff, and the ten members of the Pride events committee. The website similarly recruits volunteers and paid staff members, an openness few other clubs offer. As Jason concluded, however, the unique ownership structure means that, "With Pride Inc. owning the bar, we celebrate Pride every week."

Thirty

Part of an Otherwise-Straight Hospitality Group

Chumley's
STATE COLLEGE, PENNSYLVANIA

Another gay bar with an innovative ownership structure is Chumley's of State College, Pennsylvania. Want to save a gay bar? Band together with other businesses, even straight ones. State College is a university town smack dab in the middle of the state, a welcome halfway point on my drive from Philadelphia towards Pittsburgh. Penn State University dominates the regional economy of 158,000 people located in the hilly terrain of central Pennsylvania's Happy Valley, and it similarly drives the patronage of Centre County's only gay bar. Longtime manager Ellen Braun explained the appeal of Chumley's:

> We're in the middle of a conservative area of the state and it's a liberal town, but liberals feel a little bit besieged so this is the cool place if you're older and don't like a loud place with a line to get in, where you can have a conversation.

Gay people aren't the only ones who need gay bars.

Uniquely, Chumley's bar was long part of a hospitality conglomerate, the Hotel State College & Company, for whom the gay bar was only one part of its business holdings. While plenty of other gay bars are part of holding companies of multiple gay bars, the Company owned four other bars, ostensibly straight ones, a restaurant, and a hotel. I know of no other gay bar owned by as large a conglomerate that doesn't have gay ownership or other gay businesses. And if there are any, they surely aren't as long-lived as Chumley's, founded in 1984.

Chumley's functions as an outpost bar, but there is another located fifty minutes away. Few outposts are as centrally located as Chumley's, however, in the heart of downtown amidst other bars that serve the university crowd and directly across the street from Penn State's Old Main building—it couldn't be any closer to campus. As Ellen described Chumley's relative to other small-city gay bars of its era, "It's a little unusual because it's right on the main street instead of in a back alley or in a sketchy section of town."[1] Contemporary gay bars, even outposts, are usually in the center of town, however. Chumley's is such a fixture that the collegiate apparel merchants in town long sold replicas of the bar's old sign, a rainbow-backed logo of a Picasso-esque smiling face in profile.

Ellen noted the advantages of being part of a hospitality group, including controlling costs and increased offerings. As bartender Justin Griffin explained, the group ownership model is an ideal response to the changes in the market with the rise of LGBTQ+ equality sending LGBTQ+ patrons everywhere:

> Chumley's is a good model for that because you don't have a captive audience now, so reducing overhead allows you to keep a community space. We have lower overhead because we're part of a bigger business. We serve a full menu from the restaurant upstairs. They have a full kitchen, and we just get our food from there.

Gay bars, these days, serve good food, and to this I can attest: I had a tasty hot sandwich before getting back on the road, driving back to Ohio from Philadelphia.

Ellen shaped Chumley's role in the hospitality group by playing on some preconceptions about gay bars. As she explained, "I've tried to pick the stereotypes that work in a more neutral way. So, everyone I know says all the gay bars have the best drinks. We used to just serve shots and beer, so now we serve the best cocktails." This attracts straight patrons for whom cocktail quality, regardless of whether they are served in an LGBTQ+ space, is attractive.

For many patrons, Chumley's is just one little bar, and they don't understand that it doesn't set its own rules, nor that happenings in the city's only gay bar can easily have wider effects on a larger company. Of being a stickler for liquor rules, Ellen cautioned that she was responsible to the wider pool of employees: "If we get in trouble, these whole 300 employees could be out of work, so we run a tight ship because we're part of a bigger business. That, people don't always think about." This coordination runs to all levels of business decision making. "We do our pricing with the other businesses, we choose our entertainment too—we don't imitate them, but we have to collaborate with them and keep in mind we're representing a bigger business." Being part of a conglomerate brings responsibilities, then, as well as reduced risks and increased offerings.

Occasionally, management makes decisions that ruffle feathers. Ellen recalled the arbitrary replacement of the bar's frosted windows looking in from the street. As she explained, it was done with the justification that "Gay people don't need to be in the closet anymore." This prompted a range of reactions that broke along generational lines. Ellen reported that "Older people are like, 'People are looking at us,' and the younger people don't seem to care or notice." On reading this chapter four years after our initial interview, Ellen added "We wanted the bar to be approachable and welcoming for people who might see the frosted window as hiding something. It's a great bar, and we wanted people to be able to see that." She also added that it wasn't just generational lines—that folks from cultures where being LGBTQ+ is not as accepted were also shy about the openness to the street.

Ellen and Justin described a dip in patronage that occurred in the late 2000s that they survived by being part of a business group. Justin described it as the result of Grindr and LGBTQ+ equality: "It happened coterminously, with online dating and broad-based social acceptance. Out of nowhere, and it happened overnight!" Shaking her head, Ellen recalled, "It wasn't easy." Justin agreed: "It was definitely a crossover period that was difficult to manage." Ellen explained that transitional time to a journalist:

> Bars in cities, gay or straight, are seeing much more mixed crowds, so gay bars are competing at a different level now. We had to make some serious decisions about how to stay relevant and viable, and still committed to cultivating diversity. . . . That mission has done a lot to make us an all-around better bar. The challenge has been healthy for us and makes our jobs all the more interesting and fun.[2]

Of that transition time, Ellen told me, "If the owners had wanted to get rid of us then they could have, when our sales weren't so good." Now, she notes, their sales are better than some of their sister businesses, which they now buoy in turn. As Ellen parsed the community tightrope they walk, "Now we focus on keeping a reputation that keeps us as being a gay bar but doesn't define us *as* a gay bar." Spaces may be post-gay, but that doesn't mean they don't extend a particular welcome to LGBTQ+ people.[3] And yet: Chumley's still describes itself as a gay bar. Talk about ambivalence.

To reinvent the bar in that difficult period, Ellen launched a program of live entertainment, one of many strategies to save a gay bar. "Not just drag," Ellen explained, "but live music that you couldn't find at other businesses. Maybe gay friendly, but not only gay people or gay themed." Later, Ellen clarified, "We didn't want to pigeonhole us into too narrow a concept of what a gay bar is." There was some concern at the time from longtime patrons that management was trying to turn it into a straight bar. As Ellen perceived the newfound patrons, however, "Honestly I think the proportion of gay people is still the same—it's taken me a while to even sort that out." Bartender Justin interjected,

> Some of the older guys who've been there for a long time would bitch, "Oh, all these straight kids." Justin laughed and said, "No, that kid's gay, that guy's gay, that guy's in a poly relationship with three people." That's the nice thing about being open: Customers don't dictate who the other customers should be.

The move has been a success; the local TV station cited Chumley's as "One of the best places to catch live music in Centre County."[4]

The shift attracted a broader range of LGBTQ+ people than had previously patronized Chumley's, too. As Ellen mused,

> It used to be mostly men and mostly of a certain age, and even when younger ones were coming in, it was mostly young guys and mostly twinks rather than bears, and now it really is, like, a very amorphous mix, its many, many, things. More women come in now, and definitely more nonbinary and trans people as well.

Of the hippie, nature-loving Radical Faeries, bears, and lesbians who now attend, Ellen took away the lesson that, "I didn't realize I was neglecting other groups by not promoting things differently."[5] Adding entertainment, and varying the genres of performance, ended up serving the broader LGBTQ+ community, making Chumley's more inclusive in turn.

Ellen and Justin described two cautionary tales that motivated their approach to attract the broadest possible patronage. One was the fate of Gay Night at their sister business in the hospitality group, the nightclub then known as Indigo. When a competing nightclub opened across town and also tried to offer a gay night, Ellen recalled, "It divided the crowd. They got shut down within a year but by then, Indigo had lost half their crowd . . . it just never took off again. It lost the niche." She noted that a similar thing happened in nearby Altoona, Pennsylvania:

> There was an old, established gay bar. A new gay bar opened, divided the crowd, and then one got shut down and then the other was wounded; that remaining bar faced a struggle to survive. A sad evolution.

For Ellen, these were a lesson about keeping their niche while constantly attracting straight allies: "It made me really conscious we had to tread carefully here to keep a good balance."

Chumley's is careful not to divide its crowd, then, and to actively promote inclusivity of all. As Justin says, the bar's gay reputation deters some straight people who do not enter—not out of homophobia but because they are conscientious about not disrupting a precious LGBTQ+ resource: "Straight friends, they felt they were usurping someone else's space." As Justin encouraged them, "But this is putting your money where your mouth is!" To women who proposed a night just for lesbians, Ellen responded, "You can promote a ladies' night at Chumley's but not at the exclusion of anyone else." Justin recalled a conversation with one patron, recalling that he told her, "Who's not going to come in on a ladies' night: a lot of people! But if Sylvia wants to advertise, 'Come on, ladies!' we'll promote it as your night but everyone else is welcome." Similarly, they book Spanish-singing musicians, but it is not billed as a Latinx night. Added Ellen, "I feel firmly we need to not cater to niches at any specific time." For a while the bar was closed on Sundays, Ellen recalled, "And that would be a night where we could have people hire the place and have your night and it could be a private party. We're allowed to do that. We could even have a queer redneck night!" Community accountability means being open to all LGBTQ+ people, and straight allies, all the time.

Ellen rehearsed for me what she would say if the worst would happen:

> I have been waiting for the shoe to drop with my boss, what if he says, "Okay, it's time. You're busy but we want to not call it a gay bar." How would I argue my point? My argument would be: it's the perfect filter. The reason its busy is because it keeps the idiots out and encourages people who want to live in a town with a gay bar. It's cool. People want that.

You don't need a coast to be cosmopolitan if your little city has a gay bar. Resolutely, she continued, "I live in dread of that day because I'll fight for that."

In early 2020 the shoe dropped.

The Hotel State College & Company was sold to a new hospitality conglomerate, the Philadelphia-based Pat Croce & Company, founded by a former owner of the Philadelphia 76ers and whose main holdings were in Florida. Updating me, Ellen wrote, "We didn't know these guys and had no idea where their priorities lay. We were very aware that we could be on the chopping block." CEO Jeff Sorg of the new company told me about his conversations with Ellen about the decline of gay bars as they were taking over:

> This is good, so the argument goes, you don't need gay bars any-more because they're not needed. But there's the important voice of, "But there's still an important community that needs Chumley's, that has a specific history in this space and this town." It's not lost on me that where we are right now in America today, gay bars are again very important.

Ellen was won over, describing the new hospitality group as "far more worldly, ambitious and creative than our previous owners, who were pretty reluctant owners of a gay bar." As evidence, she cited their ease in discussing LGBTQ+ issues, their sponsorship of State College's first gay Pride in 2021, and the extensive investments Pat Croce & Company made in the space. If we didn't need gay bars yesterday, we might need them today or tomorrow.

Jeff and his colleagues took advantage of the 2020 shutdown to ren-ovate and enlarge Chumley's, doubling its frontage and adding outdoor seating that enhanced its street visibility in the center of town. Jeff talked about Chumley's as a brand, but not in a way I was used to, in the way that "branding yourself" can often seem shallow or mercenary. Rather, Jeff's use of the word "brand" could be easily swapped with "community":

> I came to know the Chumley's brand and love the team and just how important a gay bar is in State College as a contra cultural touchstone. I got to see how many locals and good friends viewed Chumley's as this great cocktail bar, and a refuge.

The investments in the space, and the refresh of the logo, have been great for business. Ellen crowed: "Last year, even with COVID restric-tions, we had our busiest day ever for Pride, and our monthly sales have doubled and even tripled." Continuing, she described, "We're getting even more of a mix of sexual and gender diversity than ever, have a very substantial international presence—grad students, pro-fessors—and are seen as the most cosmopolitan choice for food and drink in the area."

No doubt Chumley's has stayed gay because of the work of Ellen, who identifies as straight, a reminder that straight people have always been pillars of the LGBTQ+ community.[6] If some bars have become post-gay, maybe Pat Croce & Company has become post-straight. But Chumley's hasn't stayed gay in an old-fashioned way. Chumley's successes might be a useful model for other erstwhile-straight hospitality conglomerates to add a "cool" bar that "keeps the idiots out." As Ellen concluded, Chumley's has managed to remain a gay bar while being open to all, because "Society's changing and people are more flexible in their identities, and we are too."

Thirty-One

The Benefits of Employee Ownership

Caven Enterprises' JR's, Sue Ellen's,
TMC, S4, and Rose Room
DALLAS, TEXAS

Texas' largest dance club has something in common with the country's oldest lesbian bar: they are both part of the same employee-owned corporation. In fact, those employees also own the country's most well-appointed drag theater, a neighborhood bar and grill, and a former leather bar that now slings sex in the form of shirtless go-go dancers. These five bars and clubs, and the city block they all share, have brought extraordinary stability to Dallas's gay neighborhood and extraordinary benefits to their employee-owners. They have also brought an ambitious, risky land deal that has provoked community ambivalence about gayborhood change. Want to save a gayborhood? Want to save a gay bar or five? Sell them to their employees.

When you visit Oak Lawn, Dallas's gayborhood, you cannot miss the city block at the intersection of Throckmorton and Cedar Springs Road. It is certified as "*the* crossroads" for queer Dallas by the Texas Historical Commission, which honors the intersection as the center of LGBTQ+ community: When queer heritage gets recognized, its often where the bars are. Tory and Blanche and I stayed in a rented apartment just off the main drag, happy to park the car and have three nights in one place instead of driving hours to a new motel every night. This allowed us to experience one of the most pedestrian-friendly neighborhoods in car-centric Dallas, and its pretty-gay sidewalks. There were queers everywhere, mainly men, and some daytime grocery shoppers wore the booty shorts and lace mesh tops normally seen in nightlife.

Four rainbow crosswalks frame the heart of one of the largest gayborhoods in the country, albeit one that receives less attention than its coastal sisters. Oak Lawn congealed around a cluster of gay bars and nightclubs in the 1970s, five of which today share the same corporate owner, Caven Enterprises, the rump remnant of Frank Caven's sprawling gay bar empire that over time spanned multiple states and over sixty bars.[1] From a portfolio that mainly served white men, over the years the company grew to embrace the broader LGBTQ+ community, including ditching the notorious name for its flagship club, the Old Plantation (now S4), bowing to employee pressure in the 1980s to open a bar for lesbians, and hiring a person of color to serve as CEO in 2022.[2]

"Party at the block," says Caven's website, whose five LGBTQ+ nightlife spaces are all superlatives in their own way, securing fully half the spots on *USA Today's* top-ten list of gay bars in Dallas, out of the fifteen that existed at the time.[3] Founded in 1978, TMC, formerly the leather bar named Throckmorton Mining Company, is Dallas's oldest gay bar. Now, the bar cultivates sexy community through its pole-dancing go-go dancers whose skimpy undies leave lithe muscular bodies on full display. Before COVID-19, TMC cleaned up in the local gay press awards, winning "Friendliest Staff," "Best Gay Bar," "Best Theme Night" for its Trashy Tuesdays, as well as "Best Club DJ" for DJ Mateo.[4]

Sue Ellen's is the oldest lesbian bar in the country and probably also the largest, a cavernous two-story space that opened in 1989. It is next door to—as any fan of the 1980s soap opera *Dallas* could guess—JR's Bar & Grill. Like other contemporary lesbian bars, the bar welcomes gay men, transgender folks, and straight people, with co-manager Ginda Bayliss describing Sue Ellen's as "an everything bar. The days of bars being gay or lesbian—you can only be here, you can only be there—*pfft*! It's just everybody now." On the day we visited, Ginda deferred to a gay man reading his iPad at the bar when asked why we needed lesbian bars today: "Hey, what do you think? You're an honorary lesbian!" The man laughed and earnestly explained, "You still have to have a lesbian bar because of all the functions that we have. The girls have their own [charity] benefits, softball teams, functions . . . there still needs to be a place." Yet Ginda marveled at the reaction visiting lesbians had to Sue Ellen's: "People come in from out of town and they see a proper lesbian bar and they are amazed!" It may have a "big boy crowd" and welcome straight people, but for out-of-towners, at least, Sue Ellen's is a "proper lesbian bar."[5] The bar handily wins the *Dallas Voice*'s "Best Place for Lesbians" year on year.

Neighboring JR's is one of the city's longest-running gay bars, slinging drag and drafts since 1980. The second-story balcony allowed Tory and I to observe the bustle of the gayborhood while I had actual liquor rather than the soda or occasional Miller Lite that were my typical "working" drinks: Interviewing requires sharp wits, but hospitality sometimes means accepting what is offered, and low-alcohol bottles mean precision on alcohol consumption. JR's logo looked so familiar to me because I used to live near the JR's in Washington, DC, and had been to the one in Denver as well, surviving testaments to Frank Caven's onetime gay bar empire. Like those JR's, the original one is a pillar in the community and award winning as well: it pulled down the pre-coronavirus award "Best Bartender" for Usloy Reyna, who was hailed as going "from homeless to honoree" since leaving Houston as a climate refugee from Hurricane Harvey.[6]

S4 or Station 4 marks the fourth renovation of the club that was once the Old Plantation. Now it is Texas's largest dance club—24,000 square feet of laser lights, smoke machines, confetti cannons, and heaving bodies. Of Station 4, wrote one commentator, "Friends visiting from LA or New York and looking to dance will feel at home."[7] The club is 18 and up, allowing a broader swath of the community access to an LGBTQ+ space; we were carefully carded before being granted the ubiquitous plastic wristbands that accumulated at the bottom of the folders holding my research notes. For us over-21s, there were a dizzying seventeen drink stations scattered throughout the two-story club. Some were even insulated from the "bone-chilling sound system" so

Tory and I could actually have a conversation, and I could hear the constant ringing in my ears. But calm is not why people come: S4 advertises DJs of global renown and celebrity sightings, marking it as a gay nightclub rather than just a gay bar.

Inside S4 is the separately branded Rose Room, the country's largest purpose-built drag cabaret theater and probably the best equipped between Las Vegas and New York City. The Rose Room features a stage with a giant LCD screen, banks of professional lighting, and smoke and wind machines. The stage's catwalk extends into cabaret seating that is backed by theater seats, making it a sleek experience for drag aficionados. Its drag queens regularly win "best in the city" from the readers of the *Dallas Voice*, the spot is ranked first on top-ten gay venues in Dallas, and its show director, Cassie Nova, was one of the grand marshals in the 2022 Pride parade. Tory and I saw RPDR alumna Kennedy Davenport buck and kick and furiously whip her hair to a packed, screaming crowd of 300 who sent dollar bills twirling onto the catwalk.

While many in the community know that the bars are all owned by the same company, less known is the fact that it is employee owned. In 2006, Caven Enterprises converted to an employee stock ownership plan (ESOP), in which vested employees accumulate stock in the company. Caven offers its employee-owners retirement accounts, health insurance, and paid vacation time—benefits almost unheard of in the nightlife industry. As determined by federal regulations, employees vest in steps starting at the end of one year of employment, becoming fully vested after five years. When employees leave the company, their shares are bought back by the ESOP, leaving them with a chunk of change to serve as additional retirement funds. This means that the most innovative structure for gay bar ownership is in conservative Texas and not some coastal gayborhood.

Sue Ellen's founder and co-manager Kathy Jack came to work for Caven in 1986 to manage the Old Plantation, but at her instigation Frank Caven opened a lesbian bar, his first. Here she is, over thirty-five years later, still stewarding the club she helped found, in part because of the benefits. Kathy praised the ESOP as "Once you're fully vested, it's a great thing," though she noted that new employees often faced some of the less-desirable jobs such as barbacking at the ear-splitting

S4. In addition, Caven offers a 401(k) retirement account with a 4 percent match—again, rare in nightlife. Kathy explained about the ESOP:

> It's a built-in retirement, and we don't pay anything into it. When you leave you get a little bit of money, and if for any reason they sold the business and the property, we would all get a little dividend, so it makes it a whole lot better.

Caven spokesperson Chris Bengston, also part of the company for over thirty-five years, described the ESOP as an important part of the company's public relations. One of her most important jobs is regularly appearing before city agencies to maintain the clubs' after-hours licenses that allow dancing until 4 am when alcohol service closes at 2 am. As she reported, "you have to show that you are a good neighbor, that you are not being detrimental to the neighborhood." Being an ESOP is part of their justification for their licenses: "We give them this wonderful booklet, and what we give back in donations, and one of the things that we talk about is that we are an ESOP and how seriously the employees take the company—for it to do the right things."

Both Kathy and Chris said being part of an ESOP motivated workers. Chris argued of the ESOP: "It might in some ways bring you a better quality of employee, because we all work together to make sure that there isn't waste. You want to be frugal because that's your bottom line." Kathy laughed and explained:

> We take pride in napkins! I find people doing it all the time—I do it—I find a bunch of napkins on the bar and I just put them back, because, you know, you cut down on waste. Save money! Save my money!

As Chris said of the ESOP, "it brings us longevity. The people in our company, especially in upper management, have been here twenty years plus."

The ESOP also helped the bar and its owner-employees weather the COVID-19 pandemic. Because the bars' workers are salaried employees instead of contract workers like in many places, and because the group has a central office with professional office staff, they were able to successfully apply for federal support from the Paycheck Protection Program to the tune of over $850,000. Sue Ellen's weathered COVID-19 so successfully that it even declined funding from the Lesbian Bar Project so that other, more vulnerable lesbian bars would be able to receive support from the corporate-and-crowdfunded kitty. And Caven employees took many of their entertaining skills to the internet to entertain patrons during the COVID-19 public closure orders. Station 4 and JR's streamed JR's Monday night weekly drag show, Cassie Nova's FreakShow, on Twitch. S4 also shared streams of DJ sets including from Gay Latino Dallas, El Concentido, and women artists DJ Genesiis and DJ Deanne. And the clubs were able to be cautious about reopening, requiring masks and temperature checks because, as Chris said with seriousness, "If something happens, you're affecting 150 employees."

The ESOP also meant that in 2021 Caven Enterprises could make a Texas-sized land deal that would benefit its employees even as it called into question the relationship between the company and the gayborhood that had grown around it. Under the terms of a May deal, Caven Enterprises agreed to sell its buildings and land, including two large parking lots, to PegasusAblon, which in turn promised to maintain the clubs' existing buildings while constructing two high-rise residential buildings behind them.[8] As the breaking news explained, "As a condition of the sale to PegasusAblon, the bars must remain to become an integral part of the new development."[9] The plan is that Caven will lease its buildings from PegasusAblon and continue to run its venues that will now be backed by hundreds of residential units, looming over the bustling clubs. In the past, Caven's bars had been spectators to the gradual gentrification of the neighborhood, but now they had stepped directly into the business of redevelopment.

The reasons given for the deal were twofold. One was to preserve the bars and clubs in light of frequent buyout offers for the land, some of the most valuable in the city: Gay bars often make their neighborhoods so hip they can no longer afford to stay in them.[10] The second was to increase revenues and cut costs. As Caven Enterprises board member Ed Oakley explained, "We have three and a half acres, 150,000 square feet of land; the buildings take up about a third of that. And so we're paying property taxes on parking spaces that are much needed but they don't generate anything."[11] A journalist summarized internal talks: "Bringing in Ablon was seen as a way to develop the land without kicking out the businesses."[12]

Developer Mike Ablon promised to preserve and augment the neighborhood, telling a journalist, "I was not going to be the person who tore down the gayborhood."[13] Under the agreement, he explained, "I must keep what's there, and I must keep the buildings, and I must keep the culture, and I must keep the people, and I must keep the venues."[14] Promised amenities in the new development included retail for restaurants or a coffee shop, a park-and-ride dropoff area suited for the contemporary reality of rideshares, as well as a pocket park with waterfall. As Ablon observed of "the crossroads" adjacent to the Caven block, "You can't stand in the middle of the street to wait for each other, so I'm going to build an urban room, a gathering spot, an urban collection point."[15]

An anonymous group calling itself the Gayborhood Neighbors Association called the development plan divisive and a betrayal of the relationship between the bars and the neighborhood. Of the Caven bars, the group railed that "Their decisions consistently represent their profit interests as businesses and not the interests of the larger Oak Lawn residents or LGBTQ+ community."[16] They noted the deal called into question the definition of Oak Lawn itself: "We need to ask ourselves: Is the gayborhood the buildings and bars? Or is the gayborhood the high concentration of LGBTQ+ homeowners, residents and allies who live and play here?"[17] The editorial attracted lively online comments both pro and con, while a website affiliated with *RuPaul's Drag Race* alumna Alyssa Edwards, a resident of nearby Mesquite, Texas, endorsed the proposal and directed fans to a petition in favor of the proposal, selling celebratory "We saved the gayborhood" t-shirts after the rezoning necessary to secure the plan was approved.[18]

For the employee-owners of Caven Enterprises, the deal meant a windfall that benefited all of them, not just a single owner. But the deal was based on a promise from the developer to maintain the buildings as is and to offer them on long-term leases to the clubs. Only time will tell whether the developer keeps his promises, whether some future sale of the property means that a future owner has different plans for the bars, or whether the current employee-owners decide to sell the geese that have laid their golden eggs for decades. But the deal illustrates the many benefits of employee ownership for gay bars, including a surprising one: the ability to sell their buildings and still save themselves.

Thirty-Two

#SaveTheGayBars from Another Pandemic

Troupe429
NORWALK, CONNECTICUT

The COVID-19 pandemic posed an existential threat to gay bars' survival.[1] Coronavirus also sparked some of the most creative Hail Marys to save gay bars.[2] This chapter is about the bar that I'd argue was *the* most creative. The actions of Troupe429 in Norwalk, Connecticut are both a testament to a gay bar's survival in the face of yet *another* pandemic, on top of racism and HIV/AIDS, but also may provide inspiration for gay bar owners facing the stiff headwinds for LGBTQ+ establishments. If you can save a gay bar through coronavirus's heartbreaking losses, maybe others can save theirs in the new normal-to-come.

Coronavirus was not as devastating to gay bars as I had feared, although they suffered great losses. By my count, nearly 16 percent of gay bars closed between 2019 and the spring of 2021, after one year of the COVID-19 pandemic.[3] This was surprising. On the one hand, that two-year drop exceeds the 14 percent drop in the number of gay bar listings during the worst five years of the AIDS pandemic. On the other hand, though, 15 percent of gay bars evaporated in the previous two-year period, 2017–2019. All of which is to say: The decline in gay bars was basically *constant* despite COVID and surprisingly didn't accelerate.

Troupe429's slick and sassy website trumpets its multiple awards as "Best Gay Bar in New England." Don't call it a gay bar, though: It's a bar and performance space that welcomes all identities (and yet, in some cheekily ambivalent symbolism, the numbers in the bar's name spell G-A-Y on a touchtone phone). The bar is a classic contemporary small-city bar. It is smack dab in the middle of slowly revitalizing downtown Norwalk, a city that is 69 percent white: diverse for Connecticut. Troupe429 is in a renovated brick nineteenth-century building that backs onto the Norwalk River with large plate-glass windows that look out onto the important Wall Street. It's almost exactly an hour's drive from the nearest gay bar in New York City, Harlem's Alibi Lounge. I stopped at all of them on my tour from Philly through all of New England with my Georgia-born friend Ezra in tow; we had only the day before seen a black bear (the non-human kind) and a dinosaur-sized "snappy-tailed cooter" (his memorable name for a snapping turtle) on the road near the Middletown Cabaret of Middletown, New York.

Troupe429 had its origins in the trauma of the Pulse nightclub massacre. Husbands Casey Fitzpatrick and Nicholas Ruiz had been throwing pop-up parties in New York City under the Troupe429 brand in the late 2010s and were concerned by the closures of gay bars in Connecticut, Casey's home state. But the sudden attack on a gay club moved them to action. "We decided to open after the Orlando Pulse terrorist attack," Casey remembered, recalling the intense need "to do *something*. We felt the best way to do something was to open another space for queer people. It was scary, but it was exciting, and we just didn't look back." They found the perfect space in Norwalk, Casey quit his day job, and the bar opened in November of 2017.

The bar had cultivated many strengths heading into the pandemic, both in its interior design and in its programming. Their space maximized the number of people who were welcome in the space by making it wheelchair and cane accessible and installing a fully accessible bathroom alongside gender-neutral ones. They also introduced activities for people not into drinking or dancing, including a high-end coffeemaker, a nonalcoholic cocktail on tap, a vintage Wizard of

Oz pinball machine, a dart board, and a feminist bookshelf highlighting women authors. These not-quite-for-profit touches meant the bar served as much as a community center as a for-profit business.

Another strength was their support from—and for—diverse constituencies. Casey attributed the diversity to the patrons themselves:

> The community here has made this bar the most diverse bar that I've ever been into. I didn't make that, the community made that. [That said,] you have to set up specific programming to make it open to gender nonbinary or trans folks.

This programming also included the monthly Siren party (the largest women's night in the state of Connecticut), weekly drag shows hosted by Robin Fierce and Sienna Rose, open variety show nights for queer people of color, and monthly burlesque hosted by Professor M, "the Black kingpin of swagger with the voice to make you stagger." The events quickly made the bar a mainstay in southern Connecticut: Governor Ned Lamont actually campaigned there in the week before his 2018 reelection.

Casey and Nicholas also curated a comprehensive social media strategy covering multiple platforms with frequent posts that solicited multiple forms of engagement. The platforms on which they blasted content ranged from the usual suspects (email, Instagram, Snapchat, and Facebook) to the less common (Twitter and YouTube) to the totally unexpected: LinkedIn and branded GIFs on Giphy. These advertised all of the bar's quickly established annual traditions that marched across the calendar, from Summer Camp to Scaryoke to Drinksgiving to Britmas (a tribute to Christmas and Britney Spears, actually a biannual event, with Britmas in July). They followed a more somber June tradition: painting the street-facing windows with the names of all the victims of the Pulse shooting, over half of whom shared Nicholas's Puerto Rican heritage. These regular events, and the engaging posts promoting them, built up more than 10,000 Instagram followers and tens of thousands of YouTube views, for example. These virtual investments paid dividends when physical places were closed due to COVID-19, dividends both for the bar and for alleviating the isolation of its patrons.

On March 15, 2020, the governor of Ohio was the first to issue closure orders for public places, quickly followed by the governors of more than half of the country's states.[4] Shuttered bars, clubs, and restaurants decimated the nightlife industry. This left LGBTQ+ people without a place to gather in public, deepening the isolation, and threw tens of thousands of LGBTQ+ workers into unemployment.[5] As the co-owner of Chicago's SoFo Tap, Meeting House, and Jackhammer, Mark Robertson told *The Daily Beast*, "The vast majority of bars don't operate with margins to be able to sustain themselves for two weeks, four weeks or eight weeks without cash flow."[6] An indefinite closure was thus as devastating as it was confusing: government rules shifted by the week, accompanied by rumors and inaccurate reportage. It may be hard for people in the future to remember how scary it was for all of us in those weeks of March and April, long before vaccines were available, as supermarket shelves went empty and death tolls mounted. But it was even scarier for organizations that depended for their existence on the very human need for close human contact, so lifesaving psychologically but now physically dangerous.

While all businesses waited for government stimulus funds—approved by Congress in March but still undistributed months later—the nightlife industry faced additional challenges.[7] Support for small businesses like gay bars was largely channeled through the Paycheck Protection Program. But the people who provide the sparkle to queer nightlife—the DJs, drag artists, and go-go dancers—are gig workers and therefore aren't on the payroll. There was nothing to protect them. True, there was federal support for expanded unemployment benefits. But these were difficult to access for even the most well-organized gig workers and completely inaccessible to those whose nightlife work is off the books and not in something like a declared LLC.[8]

On March 16, after Connecticut Governor Lamont ordered all bars and restaurants shuttered, Nicholas and Casey sprang into action. While many gay bars deployed creative strategies to bring in income and provide support for their communities, no gay bar did as much as Troupe429, nor did them so quickly or so *fabulously*.

For example, many bar owners around the country threw themselves into politics, lobbying for relief. Nightclub owners launched the National Independent Venue Association under the leadership of lesbian Dayna Frank. San Francisco bar and nightclub operators lobbied the city government for a Music and Entertainment Venue Recovery Fund.[9] Drag artists pushed for New York City to officially recognize the art form through the mayor's Office of Nightlife.[10]

But few sprang into political action as quickly as did Casey, who on March 17 launched a Change.org petition calling on the Connecticut governor to permit bars and restaurants to sell alcohol through carry-out or delivery as New York had done. As he wrote,

> Bar owners with fully stocked inventory will now have that inventory sit for many weeks or months with no revenue. They should have the right to sell this inventory to pay their rent, mortgage, utilities, and ongoing bills.[11]

The petition quickly attracted more than 9,000 signatures. Two days later, the state did relax restrictions, but it was only a partial success: pickup was allowed only with the purchase of food prepared on the premises.

Where many bars published their staff's Venmos and Cash Apps so that patrons could show some financial appreciation while they were out of work, Troupe429 went further. Before March had rolled out like a lamb in quarantine, the bar had released trading cards for their staff. Each "Troupetender" card featured a cute headshot, a QR code linked to the employee's online cash account, and a recipe for a cocktail. The seven cards also solicited patrons to post pictures of themselves sipping the cocktails on social media, engaging patrons and allowing them to "see" each other, if only on Instagram. Also before March was over, Troupe429 introduced a SoundCloud account, posting a series of "house party mixtapes" by DJ Code Villain, DJ Linkx, and DJ OMG Yaaas Kween, Nicholas's own alter ego.

Many bars began selling merchandise to bring in badly needed income during the shutdown. The Stud in San Francisco rolled out a special edition t-shirt as a fundraiser, for example. To Troupe429's existing merch, however, Nicholas added a Save the Gay Bars line of hats, mugs, and of course, a cloth face mask (wearing mine around my small town prompted many funny conversations and coming-outs, including at the post office).

Some bars moved their community programming online. New

York City's Marie's Crisis began broadcasting show tune sing-alongs on Facebook. Chicago's Sidetrack rushed to produce new episodes of its YouTube drag talk show, *IMHO Show*. In greater Los Angeles, Latinx nightclubs Club Cobra and Club Chico began broadcasting go-go dancers and drag queens on OnlyFans.[12] These shows, however, represented a mere fraction of the bars' regular weekly schedules, and virtual tip jars didn't bring in the same cash as the regular live shows. Still, it was something for both workers and community members, and for LGBTQ+ people with disabilities, online offerings were often more accessible than the physical places had ever been.

But when the Troupe429 "bar and performance space" began posting online shows, it did so with a frequency and an intensity unrivaled by bars outside major cities. Its quarantine drag shows featured wind and smoke machines, costume changes, and DJ interludes. Anita Manager's Sip & Simmer drag queen cooking show released an episode devoted to Troupe429 with a recipe that paid tribute to Girl Scout cookies, while song stylist Professor M crooned for a cabaret fundraiser for bar staff. The bar released a short documentary film about local drag queen Robin Fierce directed by Troupe429 bartender Kamikaze Jones. The bar also brought its high-quality production skills to a nearly three-hour Pride celebration on YouTube that featured drag performances by queens and a king, hula hoop burlesque, cabaret, spoken word, and live singing by two celebrity actors: Tony-nominated Robin De Jesús and Kate Nash of Netflix's *GLOW*.

When the governor delayed opening bars and restaurants in the summer of 2020, Nicholas and Casey brainstormed for a way to bring in revenue. Since retail establishments were allowed to be open, and the bar had always championed music, they partnered with record-collector friend Joe Masher to convert the dance floor into a vinyl record store.[13] Their press release trumpeted that the "LGBTQ bar is reopened and reimagined as a pop-up record & refreshment experience: Visitors can browse thousands of records under the most disco balls in the state." This allowed the bar to participate in national Record Store Day with a food truck and the come-on that Troupe429 Records had the "largest vinyl collection of Madonna in the state of Connecticut."[14] The last Saturdays in late summer were declared

Record Store Gay[15] until the store was retired once bars were again permitted to open, and the dance floor was again needed.

In January of 2021, Connecticut was one of the only states on the Eastern Seaboard to allow for seated, socially distanced shows. Nicholas and Casey again sprang into action, building a cabaret stage and launching a weekly show that provided much-needed entertainment to locals and much-needed income to performers who had been out of work for almost a year. As Casey explained,

> I drove to New York City and picked up each performer in my car, armed with masks and hand sanitizer, and brought them to Troupe429. They each performed two sold-out shows, and then I drove them home in the same night.

As special as the performances were for the community, this alone time with artists of both local and international fame was special for Casey.

> Getting to chat for hours with these performers about their lives during the pandemic and then being able to offer them a paid in-person gig where they could connect with an audience and make money to pay their bills, it was truly an honor.

He recalled that legendary drag grand dame Lady Bunny, "had not performed live in over a year, which she had never experienced in her entire professional career." Each performer signed a pink Legend's Wall in the drag dressing room. Casey described it as a monument to that time:

> The wall is a testament to what we all achieved. When I step back and look at all the names, it gives me chills remembering that moment in time. Each and every one of those performers helped save our gay bar.

The full impact of coronavirus on gay bars may not become clear for years. Members of the LGBTQ+ community were disproportionately affected by the disease: losing jobs, suffering from isolation, caring for ill loved ones.[16] Many died. This left holes in the community that will continue long into the future: missing DJ sets, absent drag performances, and empty seats at the end of many, many bars.

This includes the empty seat for Casey's own father.

As Casey and Nicholas worked to save their ailing business, Casey's father fell ill with the coronavirus. They cared for him in between running the weekly cabaret shows and other events. As Casey told me,

> I would work during the day and then care for my dad at night. It was almost closing time at the bar when I found out he was taken to the hospital. I had one hour with him before he was moved to the COVID-19 wing, where he passed.

Pausing, he recalled, "It was so painful," before adding, "He was always a champion of me and Troupe429, so I know he's looking after all of us right now."

I had no idea about Casey's private struggles when I chose his and Nicholas's bar for this chapter: It was their creative resilience, and not their loss, that inspired me. It was the success of their innovations that meant the duo saved Troupe429 without relying on the common tactic of crowdfunding. This was despite the fact that Troupe429 was itself launched with a successful $15,000 crowdfunding campaign on Kickstarter from over 200 backers.

Regarding the relatively stable rate of gay bar decline both before and during COVID-19, I suspect that the most vulnerable establishments had closed before the public closure orders. I also suspect that gay bars, more than straight bars, had reserves of community goodwill upon which to draw during their troubles, and so fewer of them closed than I would have expected. And it's also possible that gay bar owners were just more creative on average in mobilizing their communities to rally around them while they were challenged. Us queers, we do have flair.

Further challenges for gay bars will pop up in the future. Troupe429's ability to marshal virtual resources to create real-world community may provide a model for people in the future to save their gay bars. But some of our habits may have changed durably due to the new era of cascading coronavirus pandemics. I'm not the only queer person to tell journalists that my bargoing has been curtailed over concerns for me and my loved ones' chronic health conditions.[17]

Casey recalled needing gay bars in his youth even before he was old enough to attend them: "Triangles Café, in Danbury, had a rainbow flag at the end of the road. As soon as I got my driver's license, I would just drive past it and know that someday that space would be for me." Now he and Nicholas make sure that Troupe429 is that space for the people of their region. As one online reviewer declared, "This is the future of gay bars."[18] And with Nicholas and Casey's sparkling creativity, and in the memory of those we've lost, let that future continue.

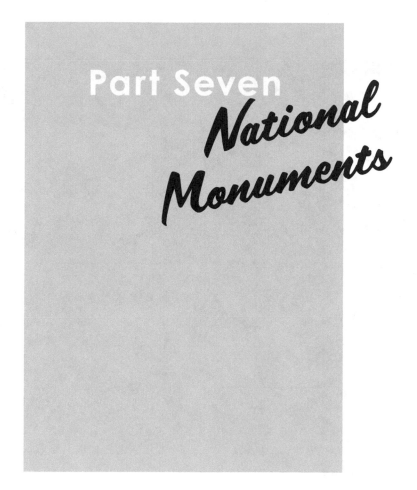

Part Seven
National Monuments

Often ignored by our nation, gay bars are our national monuments. The Stonewall Inn in Greenwich Village is a living archive to the LGBTQ+ rights movement but is also an operating small business. It still is a focal point for protests and memorials, such as this one for the victims of the Pulse nightclub massacre, here commemorated with flowers, votive candles, and a Puerto Rican flag. Photo courtesy of Monika Graff, licensed by Getty images.

Thirty-Three
National Archive

The Stonewall Inn
NEW YORK, NEW YORK

"WHAT IS PAST IS PROLOGUE" is engraved in the limestone of the National Archives in the nation's capital, directly under the statue depicting Future. When he laid the building's cornerstone, President Herbert Hoover described it as a "temple of our history."[1] The building holds records, yes, but it also holds people. Archivists beaver away in the recesses while, out front, tourists solemnly file past sturdy glass reliquaries containing the documents of the U.S.'s political DNA.

A gay bar, too, is a kind of living archive, "a system of learning, storing, and transmitting knowledge."[2] It contains within it a sideways local history that you can't always find in mainstream newspapers whose serious stories don't include our playful romps and queer gossip—the tea we love to spill.[3] Gay bars contain ways of being in the world that do not always thrive outside their walls, ways informed by traumas that might seem as ancient as the old-timer on the next barstool.[4] But that classical Greek temple of the National Archives? It dates to 1935. What feels familiar because it seems ancient may not be so old at all.

For the global LGBTQ+ movement, there is no living archive more venerated than New York City's Stonewall Inn.[5] Co-owner Stacy Lentz updated Hoover's description of a "temple of our history" by telling me in 2018 that "Stonewall is not just a bar. This is a church. No, this is the megachurch." A place of worship can be an archive, a living one of devotional practice and venerated stories. Proud to be part of the team that brought the bar under lesbian and gay ownership, Stacy declared, "Stonewall is globally known as the birthplace of LGBT rights. Here you can walk into a place of history." Indeed, the 1969 assault that prompted an uprising is commemorated on the walls in vintage documents, including one reading, "This is a raided premises—Police Dept. City of New York."

But ask any academic and they'll express ambivalence about the centrality of Stonewall. How the Stonewall uprisings became the story we tell about LGBTQ+ liberation is a story of its own, one that highlights the perfect imperfections of any archive as queer as a gay bar.

In 1934 when the National Archives was built, The Stonewall Inn moved to 51-53 Christopher Street, where it still stands; in 1930 it had opened around the corner as a speakeasy.[6] It would be more than thirty-six years before it became one gay bar among many in Greenwich Village, a post–WWII era during which a previously uncommon institution spread across the country: the gay bar by and for gay people, and increasingly owned by them. What is familiar may not be so old at all—The Stonewall Inn didn't become gay until 1967.[7]

It is conventional to date LGBTQ+ history into "before" and "after" Stonewall, despite the fact that there had been many previous LGBTQ+ protests and political actions, earlier calls for "gay power." What was different about Stonewall was that gay activists around the country were prepared to memorialize it. It was not the first riot, but it was the first to be called "the first," and that act of naming mattered, as did subsequent, stridently public commemorations.[8]

Scholars have detailed several pre-Stonewall police raids in cities across the United States that prompted activist responses—and local political gains—but they either faded from local memory or did not inspire activists in other cities.[9] For example, San Franciscans mobilized in response to police raids on gay bars in the early 1960s, which came to a head during a raid on a New Year's Eve ball in 1965 that fomented a scandal that brought down the police commissioner.[10] It attracted wide media attention and heterosexual support, and galvanized local activists, but was subsequently forgotten. In 1966, again in San Francisco, queer people rioted at Compton's Cafeteria, smashing all the windows of a police car, setting fires, and picketing the restaurant for its collusion with police. The city's gay establishment did not participate, however, and distanced themselves from the transgender and street youths who had organized the protests whom the assimilationists deemed too "violent."[11]

Los Angeles bar raids also prompted resistance. The 1967 police assault on the Black Cat bar, for instance, led to a demonstration 400-people strong that was featured on the evening news. That demonstration played a role in the founding of what still is the leading national gay magazine, *The Advocate*.[12] While the Black Cat demonstration garnered support from heterosexual activists for Chicano and Black civil rights, no further coordination occurred, and the event was not commemorated. When police again descended on the LA nightclub The Patch, patrons struck back immediately, marching to city hall to lay flowers and singing the Black civil rights anthem, "We Shall Overcome." But its anniversary passed without remembrance. Los Angeles activists did organize a one-year vigil on the anniversary of the night the LA police beat a gay man to death in front of the Dover Hotel, but this 120-person-strong rally and march to the police station did not inspire activists in other cities.[13]

Activists were busy before Stonewall on the East Coast, too. In Washington, DC, LGBTQ+ veterans chose the Pentagon as their place to picket, making it onto national television with signs reading, "Homosexual citizens want to serve their country too."[14] Subsequent demonstrations targeted the White House and the offices of federal agencies. New York City's Mattachine Society secured legal gains in 1966 when it organized a "sip-in" at the bar Julius' to secure the legal right of homosexuals to gather in public in New York State. None of these actions inspired commemoration, locally or in other cities, leading scholars to ask: Why not?

There was an annual demonstration for gay civil rights before Stonewall, however, and it provides the best example of how gay politics grew and changed before the 1969 rebellion. Beginning in 1965,

Philadelphia gay and lesbian activists began an annual picket of Independence Hall on the Fourth of July to protest state treatment of homosexuals. Soberly dressed men and women with carefully worded signs walked solemnly in front of this iconic building where the Declaration of Independence and U.S. Constitution were debated and signed.[15] These "Annual Reminders" were the result of coordination by activists in New York, Washington, and Philadelphia, evidence of burgeoning regional cooperation by gay rights activists in the 1960s.

Gay politics had become more radical in the late 1960s, owing to the influence of the Black Power movement, second wave feminism, and the protests against the Vietnam War.[16] Radical organizations advocating "gay power" had already sprung up in the 1960s, including in New York City's Greenwich Village, where The Stonewall Inn was located.[17] These new activists stereotyped the actions of their "homophile" forebears as conservative, objecting to the way they downplayed sex and fought for inclusion into mainstream institutions. The new "gay liberationists" thus archived the homophile's contributions out of the consciousness of a struggle that was now credited solely to Stonewall.[18] All archives collect some traces of the past and forget others.[19]

There were unique characteristics of Stonewall, of course. In his detailed history of the bar and those nights, historian David Carter lists many: It was the only bar raid that prompted multiple nights of riots; it was the only raid that occurred in a neighborhood populated by lots of other LGBTQ+ people who might participate; and the bar was located in a transportation hub surrounded by many public telephones that were used to alert participants and media.[20]

What was different about Stonewall was that organizers decided to memorialize it, and to make it a national, annual event. At a meeting in November of 1969, regional activists broke with the somber image of the Philadelphia Annual Reminder and vowed to secure a celebratory parade permit on the anniversary of the raid on The Stonewall Inn, calling it Christopher Street Liberation Day—early namings stressed the public street over the private bar.[21] East Coast organizers reached out to groups in Chicago and Los Angeles who readily agreed to remember something that happened elsewhere, in part because it was one of the few acts of LGBTQ+ resistance to get widespread media coverage.

But this media coverage was itself the product of previous ties between the homophile LGBTQ+ activists and journalists.[22] Interestingly, San Francisco's gay and lesbian establishment declined to participate because they had already made inroads with heterosexual elites. As one explained, "I did not think a riot should be memorialized."[23] Only a small "gay-in" occurred, which was itself raided by police. Meanwhile, large, coordinated marches in Los Angeles, New York, and Chicago in 1970 were the first gay Pride parades and sparked an idea that spread—to more than 116 cities in the United States and 30 countries around the world, including to tiny towns without gay bars at all, like Independence, Kansas.[24]

Thus it was a national act of commemoration that represented a truly new political phenomenon, not the riot itself. As sociologists have claimed, "Without the existence of homophile organizations elsewhere, many of them founded only in the late 1960s, a national event would have been unthinkable."[25] Stonewall was an "achievement of gay liberation," and not its cause.[26]

This achievement led to another act of national commemoration in 2016, forty-seven years after the uprising: The Stonewall National Monument was created as the first property in the National Park Service to recognize LGBTQ+ people. Despite scholars' insistence that the Stonewall rebellion was an outcome of a preexisting movement, President Obama reified its mythic place as the birthplace of a moment, not a child of an existing one: "The riots became protests. The protests became a movement. The movement ultimately became an integral part of America."[27]

This celebratory commemoration was accompanied, however, by a tragic one. Two weeks earlier, a shooter murdered forty-nine revelers at Pulse nightclub. At the Stonewall National Monument inauguration ceremony, Interior Secretary Sally Jewell said, "The tragic events in Orlando are a sad and stark reminder that the struggle for civil rights and equality continues."[28] The official photographs provided by the Department of the Interior to mark the monument's designation included one of the impromptu Pulse memorial altars laid in front of The Stonewall Inn mere days earlier. Thus it was that two gay bars became national monuments in June 2016: one by blood on June 12 and the other by presidential proclamation on June 24.

The Stonewall National Monument is a particularly queer site in the national pantheon. The only site dedicated to LGBTQ+ people, it is also the system's smallest: The federal government owns only the 0.12-acre Christopher Park where protestors, partiers, and pilgrims have gathered since 1969.[29] Only the Stonewall's façade and building footprint are protected; the bar as a building and business is privately owned—a fitting monument to a people who have always relied on privately owned places to gather in public and who have never been fully claimed by their nation.

Stonewall is also the only national monument to an operating bar and nightclub. You can certainly get a nice cocktail at Yosemite's Ahwahnee Hotel or at the Grand Canyon's Bright Angel Lodge steakhouse, and there are regular theatrical productions at the Chamizal National Memorial and Ford's Theatre. But in all the National Park Service, there is only one place where you can see drag shows, DJs, and "sexxxy dancers."[30] Thus Stonewall's legacy is also secured through the joy we make in it next weekend: All archives, even as they contain the past, also point to the future.[31]

These events are necessary to keep Stonewall a popular fixture for today's LGBTQ+ community, explained co-owner Kurt Kelley. "The days of just going and sitting in a bar are over. This younger generation wants to be entertained." Citing LGBTQ+ social acceptance, he continued, "I have a lot of friends who don't even like going to gay bars, they go to the straight bar. Luckily, we have the Stonewall, so this is always going to be a gay bar." Being an iconic shrine does not pay the bills; most tourists take selfies on the sidewalk without setting foot inside. But they're still at the monument, sort of: The publicly owned sidewalks and streets are part of it.[32] An archive can mark the passage of the private to the public, just as the monument's private bar gives way to its monumentalized public streets.[33]

The duo tag teams the bar's operations. As co-owner Stacy Lentz admitted, "I don't have the first clue about running a bar, for me it's all about the activism and using it as a place to help the community." While Kurt speed-counted one-dollar bills for the till, he explained, "All my life I was a bartender, so I've always been in the nightlife."

When they acquired the bar in 2006, their vision was a historic renovation that would transform it into a site worthy of pilgrimage—no more dowdy "old men's bar" with pockmarked drywall. This is how I remember the bar when I made my first visit in the 1990s with Gus— or was it Carlos? Back then, I couldn't take the one gay and lesbian history course offered by an adjunct professor out of fear that the title would out me to my parents, back when transcripts were still sent to college students' home addresses. Instead, I read my friends' textbooks, teaching myself the history of my people, and this included an exciting trip to New York City to be confronted with the disappointingly frumpy Stonewall Inn.

Today, however, baroque light fixtures and daylight through windows illuminate rich wood-paneled walls framed with vintage newspaper clippings that one might find in any archive: "Village raid stirs melee," and "Homo nest raided: Queen bees are stinging mad." And yet, this is not a historic restoration. Contemporaries[34] recall a dark, cheap, filthy "hellhole" with blackened walls and windows, what a camp diva might call a dump.[35] A queer archive need not be historically accurate; it is permitted fictional origins if it tells a story that serves the present.[36]

Kurt met with a marketing expert who dismissed their dream of lesbians, gay men, bisexuals, transgender folks, and queers socializing together: "It'll never happen. They don't mix." Defiantly, Kurt recalled his answer: "Watch me!" "Today," he pronounced with satisfaction, "It's totally mixed. You know, you're getting sports teams, Stacy with her lesbians, I started bear parties and the leather parties, and before long everyone knew about it." Now, they describe their patrons as between 21 and 80, rattling off regulars who are "lesbians, gay men, bears, leathermen, transgender folks, drag queens, and straight allies." These last were important to embrace. As Stacy noted,

> We also get a lot of straight friends who want to support their LGBT friends, to be allies. A lot of mixed crowds. The acceptance has played a role—it's why we've marketed that "acceptance started here."

Archives do mark beginnings, after all.[37]

Would this acceptance have led my straight Lutheran parents to take my siblings and me to Stonewall if I were a child today? After all, a working bar isn't like any of the other national sites we journeyed to in the massive silver Ford Econoline my mom called the Queen Mary. We had adventures: a failing alternator at 10,000 feet in Rocky Mountain National Park, getting lost in East Saint Louis on our way to the Gateway Arch, and nearly running out of gas on the dirt road from remote Chaco Canyon. Do today's parents see Stonewall as part of the national story?

Owning the LGBTQ+ megachurch, and keeping it accepting of the entire community, brings its challenges. As Stacy said, "We're held to a much higher standard in terms of service and door people so that gets really tricky. They expect us to have not as many slip-ups." The bar received national press when a door person from their contracted security agency denied entrance to a blind person because of their service dog.[38] Kurt grumbled about "a gang-up social media culture" but nodded as Stacy waxed passionate: "It's Stonewall! It has to represent them. You can't make mistakes." The bar has invested in additional training to provide the younger crowd with the service—and the inclusion—they expect.

Despite this change, Stacy worries the Stonewall may be an archive of community ways that are fading: She equated community with the legacy and future survival of gay bars:

> I feel kinda sad for the younger generation. They've all this access and privilege, and they don't understand "community." They don't have community like we did. There is a rich history of gay bars as gathering places, and that's where I fear that young people are missing out. It's important to have face-to-face spaces and places rather than just being online.

An archive is also a place of dreams, maybe especially queer ones.[39]

Stacy noted ruefully, "Be careful what you wish for. We were always persecuted; once it stopped, we stopped being community." As she described the LGBTQ+ amalgamation, "We're splintering and dividing more than we ever did, whereas years ago we all stood together and that's how we got the rights that we did."

This is one way to tell the story, but the archives don't support its claims. Accounts of the Stonewall before the riots sometimes depict a patronage of young white men; lesbians hardly frequented the bar, although the African American Stormé DeLarverie was at the rebellion at some point.[40] Sylvia Rivera, sometimes heralded as the transgender Latinx leader of the riots,[41] was marginalized and persecuted by the white gay and lesbian leaders of the movement.[42] And Stacy's description of recent "splintering" contradicts Kurt's triumph over today's united socializing among the Ls, Gs, Bs, Ts, and Qs. Must a monument only be to unity?

After all, contradictions abound in the most complete archive of Stonewall texts, Marc Stein's modestly named *The Stonewall Riots: A Documentary History*.[43] Did the uprising occur over two nights? Four? Six? Were the "queens" at the raid mostly effeminate gay men, drag queens, or transgender women?[44] Who threw the first brick? Contemporaneous accounts emphasize pennies being thrown at the cops; the only firsthand account mentioning a thrown brick was speculated.[45] Marsha P. Johnson, the Black transgender woman frequently described as having thrown the first brick,[46] said she wasn't even there when the riot started, and the precise roles of Black butch Stormé DeLarverie and Latinx Sylvia Rivera are similarly unclear.[47] What complicates the picture is that the crowd that gathered outside during those many nights of unrest included homeless youths, neighborhood denizens, and rubberneckers who likely never set foot inside the bar but who were crucial to the rebellion.[48] As Stein states flatly, "What exactly happened during the Stonewall Riots? This is an impossible question to answer."[49] This, from the event's most thorough archivist, but also a historian attentive to the nuances and contradictions in the archives (plural).

Stacy reflected on owning this national monument to our LGBTQ+ past: "Teaching history is important for this reason: If you don't know your past, you can't change your future." The past is prologue. If a straight national archive is a place where an individual can be alone with the past,[50] the queer archive, the Stonewall, is a place where people can be together with the future.

After all, the Stonewall is a lively repository of togetherness both dramatic and formal (drag! karaoke! sexxxy dancers!), and the everyday and informal (sassing a bartender, a flirtatious pas de deux of glances, an idle scrolling of a cell phone in public). It may be "the megachurch" for history-minded devotees, but for locals it's just another place to go out, see a show, grab a drink, people watch—actions that will never be owned by the nation. Much of our LGBTQ+ heritage is privately owned anyways: Many gay bars are literally museums of ephemera! They contain the signs of defunct gay bars, handsewn banners, trophies for past victories, and rare photographs in the museum-quality holdings in Menjo's of Detroit, Gabriel's Downtown of Mobile, or The Raven of Anchorage. Menjo's even preserves the disco ball under which a teenaged Madonna Ciccone danced longer ago than she'd like to remember.

Now that countries increasingly preserve intangible cultural heritage, however, perhaps we should go further and demand public protection for limp wrists, butch swagger, tongue pops, queer haircuts, and bisexual lighting. After all, without these, Stonewall's archive won't be complete. These are our most important registers: the everyday LGBTQ+ ways of building a queer future yet to come.[51]

Thirty-Four

National Memorial

Pulse
ORLANDO, FLORIDA

Before President Obama could declare The Stonewall Inn the first LGBTQ+ national monument in June 2016, another national memorial was created through spilled blood and shattered bodies.[1] A gunman entered Orlando, Florida's Pulse nightclub and killed forty-nine, wounded fifty-three, and sent hundreds fleeing for their lives. When he designated Pulse a national memorial in 2021, President Biden said he was "enshrining in law what has been true since that terrible day five years ago: Pulse nightclub is hallowed ground."[2] But this sacred monument refuses to recognize the rage we feel in the wake of the attack, rage that is necessary to create change.[3]

"#Pulse, the new #stonewall," declared tweets within hours of the attack, part of a flood of comparisons that equated the two bars. "Like the Stonewall Inn, Pulse now serves as a brick-and-mortar monument to queer resilience," wrote one journalist.[4] Another speculated that, "The Stonewall Inn could've easily been The Pulse."[5] In New York City, the largest vigil for the victims took place in front of The Stonewall Inn itself, as signs and hashtags proliferated, including in Arabic and

Spanish, declaring solidarity with the victims of Pulse through the phrase "We are Orlando."[6]

But that phrase took on different inflections whether it was coming from right-wing politicians, straight white suburbanites, or queer Muslims. And these radically different inflections foreshadowed the questions raised by the planned Pulse Memorial and Museum: What are they a monument to? Who and what gets mourned, and in what ways? Who is the "we" in "We are Orlando?"

Broad identification with the horror was facilitated by its scale and in the way it unfolded in real time over social media, leaving an excruciating electronic snail trail of the trauma. You can still read the horrifying Pulse Facebook post from 2:09 am: "Everyone get out of pulse and keep running,"[7] or the 5:53 am tweet from the Orlando Police: "The shooter inside the club is dead."[8] The virtual world links the physical world, but also the present with the past, uniting viewers, including me, into a morbid kinship across time and space.

When I woke on that sunny Sunday morning, like many queers I understood viscerally that these were my people and that it could have been me, and not in an abstract, "wrong place, wrong time" kind of way. I thought about getting patted down for weapons at Tracks in DC, drinking at London's Admiral Duncan months before it was nail bombed, and getting punched in the face by a stranger while walking home from the White Horse in Oakland, California. Gay bars have never represented safety to me.[9]

That Sunday morning, I reached out to my family—not my parents, but my gay one—and Marcelo Vinces and Marco Wilkinson readily agreed to go out to the Leather Stallion Saloon, the bar for a blue-sky Sunday in Cleveland.[10] Upon entry I was shocked to be provided a gun. Well, a small sunny yellow replica of an assault rifle that squirts water. It was for a preorganized, unrelated fundraiser. That nobody thought, "Hey, let's not give away guns on this particular day" was a reminder to me that not every queer was moved by the tragedy in the same way.

On the patio we were approached by a newscaster who asked us for comments. Marco declined. Marcelo blasted the NRA and gun lobbyists for creating a nation with more gun shops than Starbucks, eloquent in his fury. I said something bland about protecting and defending our LGBTQ+ spaces. I made the broadcast. There was no place for Marcelo or his Latino rage. This was a preview of the public limits on queer mourning, on who is the acceptable "we" of the tragic Orlando.

The horror became a screen on which people projected their pre-existing political projects to understand why it happened. For the police officer father of one of the murdered dancers, Pulse was evidence that an armed reveler could have stopped the assault.[11] For anti-gay politicians, Pulse was evidence of immorality: Kenneth Lewis, a Florida assistant state attorney, took to Facebook to urge, "All Orlando nightclubs should be permanently closed. With or without random gunmen they are zoos; utter cesspools of debauchery."[12] For gun control campaigners, this was another reason for federal gun restrictions.[13] Meanwhile LGBTQ+ Muslims found themselves erased and victimized by talk of jihad and terrorism.[14] But for the vast majority of Americans, the meaning of the assault was hate against gay people. "We will not let hate win" was one of Pulse co-owner Barbara Poma's most frequently quoted lines, later to be inscribed in the museum she proposed to memorialize the lives lost.

Homophobic hate and terrorism crowded out other possible meanings and became the dominant framings of the killings. President Obama proclaimed of Pulse that "this was an act of terrorism but it was also an act of hate," an equation repeated by many federal agencies.[15] This focus on homophobic terrorism obscured the specificity of who was in that gay bar that night, of who was dancing on Saturday.

It was Latin Night at Pulse every Saturday, and over 90 percent of the victims were Latinx, as reported by Steven Thrasher of *The Guardian*.[16] As an election year, 2016 was divisive—characterized by increasingly anti-immigrant, xenophobic, and anti-Latinx sentiments, yet no major news outlets asked whether Latin Night was targeted. Instead, everyone presumed Pulse was chosen because it was a gay space.

Similarly, few outlets asked why there were so many Latinx people in Orlando who needed Latin Night in the first place. That is, in English language reportage. Before noon on the day of the attack, however, Spanish-language Univision had provided context unmatched by any English-language outlet before or after:

Pulse celebrated its traditional "latin night" [*sic*] in a city where 24% of its 2.4 million inhabitants is Hispanic. . . . Orlando's Hispanic population has increased sharply in recent years, especially amid the wave of Puerto Ricans who have left the island because of the acute economic crisis.[17]

I translated it easily; major English-language outlets couldn't, or didn't. Few journalists followed Steven Thrasher to cover Orlando's Hispanic Federation press conference that called for bilingual support services for poor migrants and recognition of the attack as being on Latinx people.[18] Instead, abstract talk of gay people, who are usually implicitly read as white, crowded out the specific LGBTQ+ people of color who were killed.[19]

As "We are Orlando" spread outwards, Latinx writers issued increasingly insistent reminders that this was not just a gay tragedy and that the well-meaning "we" was erasing the specificity of who was killed. Juana María Rodríguez called for Pulse to be affirmed as a place of "queer latinidad."[20] Novelist Justin Torres wrote "In Praise of Latin Night at the Queer Club" for the *Washington Post*, in which he intoned: "You have known violence. You have known violence. You are queer and you are brown and you have known violence."[21] For Mathew Rodriguez, it was an assault on "my people, *mi gente, mi familia*,"[22] even as Juana María Rodríguez acknowledged queers' "complicated emotions associated with *familia*."[23] Writers linked the killings to other violence against queer Latinx people, ranging from Christian homophobia, to Puerto Rican debt colonialism that had driven so many young people from the island, to American gun violence that disproportionately affects people of color, and to the more than a hundred pending legislative actions targeting Latinx immigrants in the United States. Homophobia was only one of many violences that inspired queer rage at that time.

"We" are Orlando, went the ubiquitous phrase, but some of us got to choose to be so in an act of voluntary solidarity; others bear its weight every day, Salvador Vidal-Ortiz reminded.[24] As much as I felt in my bones that it could have been me that night at the gay club, this stiff-hipped, early-to-bed whitey-McWhite goof probably would not have been at Latin Night.

Enmeshed with explanations of homophobia was the assumption of terrorism. If the homophobia of the crime was overdetermined by the fact that Pulse was a gay bar, terrorism was overdetermined because the shooter was a Muslim Afghan American who swore allegiance to ISIS in 911 calls to law enforcement. But given that similar acts of mass violence by white men are rarely labeled acts of terror,[25] many of these accounts of terrorism implicitly drew upon an equation that Muslim equaled anti-gay.[26] This was contested in many statements by Muslim organizations and Muslim LGBTQ+ people who called for caution in applying the terrorism label and pleaded for some recognition of Islamophobia in responses to the shooting.[27] Instead, investigators of the killer were frequently described as "trying to determine whether terrorism, homophobia or both pushed him over the edge."[28] Because the shooter was himself killed by law enforcement, no one could ask him. Instead, the FBI used anti-terror legislation to prosecute his wife for aiding and abetting the attack.

But this trial, which didn't conclude until 2018, uncovered uncomfortable answers to the question: Why did Pulse happen? No evidence was found that the attacker was secretly gay and committed the attack out of internalized homophobia, one early and frequent speculation. There was no record of an international plot, just "self-radicalization" from websites. His cell phone records showed he had never been to Pulse before, nor were any records discovered of any visits to LGBTQ+ websites either. And the botched FBI interrogation with the shooter's widow raised the specter of anti-Muslim prejudice in the law enforcement response—she was acquitted on all counts.[29]

The trial also revealed that there was no evidence that the assailant knew Pulse was a gay club. Cell phone records did show him casing an open-air mall that night, and then googling "Orlando nightclubs."[30] He next went to straight nightclub Eve where he lingered, before proceeding to Pulse. Analysts concluded that visible armed security presence at these other locations led the assailant to seek a softer target. This led a journalist to ask: "How could the Pulse attack be a hate crime against gay people if the perpetrator chose it randomly?"[31] Indeed, the FBI refused to classify the Pulse shooting as a hate crime, to many gays' fury, while queer scholars cautioned against the racism and xenophobia that impact which crimes get increased punishment and why white victims are so often the ones granted special protection from hate.[32]

The trial's revelations led some journalists to revisit the attacker's own stated reasons for attacking the club: as an act of revenge for U.S. assaults in Syria and Afghanistan.[33] Of U.S. military actions in the Middle East, the murderer said, "The airstrikes need to stop," adding, "They're killing my people."[34] As one writer concluded, "The Pulse shooting proves that initial narratives about mass shooters' motivations are often wrong—and those narratives can be far more powerful than the truth."[35] There is more evidence that the Pulse shooting was an act of rage against U.S. foreign policy than against gay people, but our inability to hear such rage prevented us from hearing the assailant's own stated reasons for his murderous actions.[36]

"Outlove Hate" became the tagline of the foundation set up to memorialize Pulse, and rage has no place in the plans. Barbara Poma, co-owner of the club, created the OnePULSE Foundation, which launched a multimillion-dollar fundraising campaign for a memorial and museum. These were the subjects of a high-profile design competition for the memorial and museum that attracted many of the biggest names in global architecture.

2021's winning plans call for a park-like memorial on the site of the nightclub and a museum some blocks away. In the plans for the proposed memorial, the nightclub itself is present as a dark structure set apart from a park by a moat-like reflecting pool. This pool, traced with forty-nine rainbow lines representing each of the "angels" killed that night, is bisected by a moat that allows visitors to walk a bent path through the footprint of the club whose inside is never visible. Instead, high walls present a claustrophobic geometry of looming façades that guide the walker to the other side, having passed across the invisible impressions of erased walls that once framed beverage service stations, bathrooms, and a dance floor.

There is no evidence of the Latinidad that queer Latinx writers pleaded for, the spirit of solidarity that recognizes a diverse and contradictory Latinx community. None of the winning design's texts or symbolism evoke the Spanish language, Puerto Rico, or migration. Rainbows and hearts proliferate, but trendy prismatic ones that contribute to the abstract pro-LGBTQ+ message, not the fiery Sagrado Corazón of Catholicism or the Philadelphia Pride flag with its Black and Brown stripes. This is a gay memorial, not a Brown one.

The museum, some blocks away, is proposed to be a lofty land-mark that resembles a cross between a power plant cooling tower and an upside-down white clothes basket. The plans for its contents have been kept deliberately vague, with only a statement that initial exhibits will not mention the attacker in any way—his rage will not be on display, and so his abhorrent reasoning and the U.S. foreign policy that inspired it obscured. Instead, the motto "Outlove Hate" is displayed on signs under carvings that express the museum's values: unity, hope, acceptance, and love. There is no room for anger, nor is there any Spanish language in the current plans. For the time being, and at least from the outside, this is a gay museum, not a Brown one.

There are probably good reasons to treat the club building as an abstract shape to be traversed rather than preserving the floor plan, the bullet-sprayed walls, or the rear wall that was destroyed by police in an attempt to free hostages. But I wonder if a rebuilt nightclub might have been a better memorial, a living one to missing dancers rather than a monument to angels.[37] Early on, Barbara Poma had suggested that Pulse would be opened elsewhere at some point.[38] And two weeks after the shooting, the club hosted Latin Night for Pulse, a street party with music and dancing and a drag show by Pulse's Latin Divas.[39] There, in response to a question about what should happen to the club, patron Mark Aistrake replied, "You wouldn't want them to rebuild something else," to which another patron, Natalie Gonzales, replied that they should keep the club: "And if they did I would be there. It would be hard. But then I would end up just having a blast. I would be there."[40]

It might be tacky to have a rebuilt Pulse serving two-for-ones during happy hour and with drunk 20-somethings bumming cigarettes outside. It might feel like dancing on graves. I can imagine family members saying it would be disrespectful. But just as their queer children cannot always rely on them, we can't rely on straight family members to know what their queer children would have desired. After all, one family wouldn't even claim their gay son's body.[41] Sandy Hook Elementary was rebuilt on the site of that horrific mass shooting, but only after demolishing the building. And Pulse Memorial Dance Club would join the many other gay bars hallowed by death: I know of at least four gay bars whose grounds have been blessed by the cremains of former revelers, none with more than Mary's of Houston,[42] and many, many gay bars display the photos of those who have passed. In this way almost any gay bar, like the modest Garlow's in Gun Barrel City (Texas), can be a living memorial.

After all, the original Pulse was itself such a memorial from the very beginning. Co-founder Barbara Poma dedicated the club to her brother John, who died from HIV/AIDS in 1991. The club was founded "in an effort to keep her brother's spirit alive," with the website explaining in 2016 that the co-founders "coined the name Pulse for John's heartbeat—as a club that is John's inspiration, where he is kept alive in the eyes of his friends and family."[43]

A gay club could have been the memorial, then.

Such a view is shared by Zachary Blair, one of Poma's most incendiary critics. Blair proposed, among other things, that Pulse be reopened as a club and be turned over to its workers to be an egalitarian model for other LGBTQ+ businesses, allowing patrons to dance in memory of the lost.[44] His writing crackles with rage, blaming the deaths on the Pomas for running an unlicensed nightclub whose out-of-code renovations had never been permitted by the city.[45]

Blair also faults Poma for the fact that the memorial and museum will be privately owned, paying her a six-figure salary. The city of Orlando offered more than $2 million for the property, more than its appraised value. Poma declined to sell, citing a desire to stay involved and her family's attachment to the club. Although the club has been closed, the memorials outside are owned by her family. Like The Stonewall Inn, then, the second national monument to LGBTQ+ people is in private hands.

This is by design. The federal declaration of Pulse as a national memorial is only three sentences long. One establishes the memorial, a second prohibits it from becoming part of the National Park Service, and the third bars any federal funds from being spent on it. There is no mention of Latinx or LGBTQ+ people. The designation has the same value as the federal declaration that November 14 is National Pickle Day: It's a symbolic gesture towards a constituency that can use it for marketing. And maybe that's something to get angry about, too. It figures that a complex intersectional memorial would be both outside the care of the nation and beyond its imagination.

Rage has a long history in queer activism: mourning for the lost, yes, but also militancy to give meaning to their lives by changing the world in their names.[46] *United in Anger* is the title of the ACT-UP documentary about the heroic HIV/AIDS activist group. As Puerto Rican artist-scholar Larry La Fountain-Stokes argued, "Anger, fury, and rage are also useful—and at times absolutely necessary—emotions that we must tap into to address the profound violence we suffer."[47] LGBTQ+ people experience many violences in our vast diversity; there are many more than just homophobia.[48]

I don't know whether a club-as-memorial would have any more room for rage than the proposed memorial and museum, but sometimes we do dance furiously. A queer monument to Pulse should have room for Larry's and Marcelo's rage. And it should honor the Latinidad of most of the victims so that this erasure isn't the source of its own rage. Just because it's a national memorial doesn't mean it has to fail us in as many ways as the nation has.

I did not visit the site. I couldn't bear to become a pilgrim to a site whose very existence seems destined to be a disappointment. I didn't need to go there to feel vulnerable, and I have other ways of honoring those affected. In truth, I had already traveled so much for this project, and Jesse was rightfully concerned about the amount of time this project had taken from our time together. If I go to the site in the future, it will be out of professional obligation to see whether the museum exceeded its original plans.

Barbara Poma's justification for the museum and memorial is that "It's not to just honor my brother anymore. It is to honor all the families affected."[49] And in his remarks upon signing the legislation authorizing the National Pulse Memorial and Museum, President Biden did not mention LGBTQ+ or Puerto Rican people at all, only describing the lost dancers as "family members, parents, friends, veterans, students, young, Black, Asian, Latino—all fellow Americans."[50] They were those things. But family is complicated and vast for queer people, and most of the victims were young, LGBTQ+, and Latinx. We're angry about it, and we want to mourn *them*. In making it a memorial for *everybody*, Pulse risks being a memorial of *nobody*.

Thirty-Five

Municipal Landmark in Exile

The Stud

SAN FRANCISCO, CALIFORNIA

Gay bars are increasingly recognized as city monuments, part of a trend toward making LGBTQ+ history visible and recognizing queer contributions to public life.[1] Perhaps no bar has been as involved in various municipal landmarking strategies as The Stud in San Francisco, California. Part of this has to do with its unique ownership structure: as the only worker-owned cooperative gay bar, its collective of about eighteen people means a lot of fingers in a lot of pies. And what pies they are: The members are deep in the city's politics, journalism, drag scene, kink communities, nightlife service staff, and community organizing.[2] These ties mean that Stud Collective members were involved in some of the country's most innovative historic preservation maneuvers. But municipal landmarking couldn't protect The Stud from losing its building, making this a story of historic preservation and historic loss.

The Stud has long been an integral but quirky outlier in its gay neighborhood, SoMa (South of Market Street). San Francisco used to have three gay neighborhoods, but the dissolution of Polk Gulch in the early 2000s means that SoMa is the oldest, despite the Castro being more famous.[3] SoMa coalesced around the leather bar Tool Box, which opened in 1961. At the Tool Box, masculine homosexual men cruised each other in Levi's or leather jackets, bucking perceptions of gay men as effeminate and fusing this masculinity with a culture of communion through kink and radical sex, or "sexy community."[4] Heterosexual viewers in the nation got a peep inside when huge pictures of the Tool Box were plastered in the first national feature on homosexuality, *Life* magazine's famous 1964 exposé "Homosexuality in America."[5] The bar closed in 1971 and was partially demolished, leaving a famous mural of leathermen cruising open to the air and for all to see.[6] The urban development of the block continued apace over the decades; today a Whole Foods stands on the spot.

In 1966, two leather bars opened in SoMa one mile away from the Tool Box on Folsom Street, making that road a byword for leather and kink. These two bars, Febe's and The Stud, became the twin seeds from which grew an entire gay neighborhood devoted to masculinity and sex. By the mid-1970s, Folsom Street became the "Miracle Mile," a full-fledged gayborhood catering to leatherfolk and cruising gay men, featuring a gay bar district, leather shops, sex clubs, and bathhouses.[7] The Stud started as a place where Hell's Angels hung out, but by 1970 had become the black sheep of the SoMa bars, attracting dancing hippies with its psychedelic mural and hosting eclectic live music shows and far-out performances on its tiny stage. It was also just too far north to be included in the blocked-off streets for the Folsom Street Fair, the open-air leather and kink festival that started in 1984 and still takes place today, growing into California's third-largest street fair—but probably the only one with a clothes check.

When The Stud moved three blocks within SoMa in 1987, the gayborhood and the bar were both reeling from two cataclysms. The first was urban redevelopment. City-sponsored slum clearance for the multi-block convention center had wiped out vast city blocks of SoMa's single- resident occupancy hotels and low-income apartments that had housed many of the single gay men who moved there.[8] This pressure, reflecting SoMa's proximity to the central business district and the civic center, meant that The Stud experienced the urban redevelopment pressures thirty years earlier than they were identified by later scholars of gentrification in gayborhoods.[9]

The second catastrophe was the AIDS pandemic. Like many bars, The Stud held fundraisers for ailing patrons, participated in HIV-prevention work, and, heroically, maintained the health benefits of struggling employees. Unlike other gayborhoods, however, SoMa's businesses weren't replaced with new gay owners as they were in the Castro, where the activism pursued by small business owner Harvey Milk and others long outlived his 1978 assassination. This meant the AIDS crisis caused a shift in SoMa away from the gay scene and towards general music halls and restaurants catering to a predominantly heterosexual crowd. This displacement accounts for the erroneous but "persistent belief, often expressed within both the gay community and the nongay press, that the leather population has been hit harder by AIDS than other groups of gay men."[10] In other words, it was the replacement of gay people and businesses with straight ones that restructured SoMa into a live music scene, one birthed by The Stud itself.[11]

Part of the bar's broad draw that kept it vital through both crises was the eclecticism of its bill, booking performers like Etta James (who performed regularly between 1976 and 1984), blues artist Elvin Bishop, women's bands Sweet Chariot and Pegasus, and of course, the iconic Sylvester and his backup singers, Two Tons O'Fun, who later became the Weather Girls.[12]

During this time, The Stud maintained a reputation as the most diverse bar in SoMa. Some of this diversity was racial, with many noting how it was a favorite haunt of Black genderqueer artist Sylvester and his crew.[13] The diversity was also subcultural: While other SoMa bars catered to butch kinksters, at The Stud, hippies rubbed elbows with other nonconformists ranging from goths to new wavers to punks. The Stud was also praised as a place of gender diversity. Stud cofounder George Matson told community historian Mark Freeman, "A lot of women also came and said it was the first gay men's bar that they felt comfortable in."[14] Skeptics might note, however, that the bar didn't employ a woman bartender until the 1990s—which was itself much earlier than other SoMa bars, some of which, it might be noted, still haven't.[15]

It was the community devastation by AIDS that led San Francisco nightlife personality and drag artist extraordinaire Heklina to start her famous show "Tr█████yshack" at The Stud in 1996, a name she retired only in 2014 under pressure to drop the transphobic slur.[16] "Everyone has a Stud story," co-owner Nate Allbee told me, and, Dear Reader, I'm no exception. By the time I first visited The Stud in 1999, it had for three years been a raucous hub of these weekly artsy-punk drag shows. It was the first time I saw drag as performance art rather than gender illusion. Once there, I saw a drag queen dressed as murdered child beauty queen JonBenét Ramsey in a baby doll outfit do a strip-tease to "Good Ship Lollypop," coyly revealing hand-shaped bruises before dramatically unfurling a sash reading "DADDY DID IT." I saw two drag queens dressed as cows squat and excrete chocolate pudding that they rubbed on each other's faces, spattering the front row of the crowd. I saw a drag queen with a frog puppet on her arm earnestly reenacting Debbie Harry's appearance on *The Muppet Show* complete with the duet with Kermit of "The Rainbow Connection."[17]

And it was at The Stud I went to parties including "Sugar," featuring deep house music, and "Reform Skool," whose edgier aesthetic of schoolboys gone bad was complemented by go-go dancers, one of whom was especially memorable. He'd given me his number months before but stood me up on a date that took me an hour and a half to get to on public transportation. The night he pulled me behind the dressing room curtain with a sweaty hand, I knew this was my one shot and I took it, literally. I was on duty that night for a federally funded research project about risk taking in bars. Here, I had taken the risk because he was out of my league, had previously shown interest, and had stood me up: a perfect cocktail of rejection, pheromones, and opportunism. Naively, I confessed all in my field notes and was quietly but firmly fired.

Shiny tall condo buildings popped up in SoMa in the 2000s to loom over the alleys that had once been cruisy sex sites. These new residents brought classic gentrification pressures, making noise complaints against the bars and clubs that had made the neighborhood so vital in the first place.[18] As a massive new condo building rose next door to The Stud in 2015, the building's longtime owner sold to new ones who hiked the rent from $3,800 to $9,500 per month.[19] Like so many other gay bars in coastal cities marred by gentrification, The Stud was in danger of being pushed out of the neighborhood it had helped make vibrant in the first place.[20] Instead of closing, however, patrons and fans banded together to create a new powerhouse organization that would innovate in gay bars and the ways they are recognized by their municipalities.

The first innovation was collective ownership, launching a groundbreaking experiment: Could a nightclub be run by a cooperative? Eighteen nightlife professionals—including bartenders, DJs, drag artists, journalists, door security, and politicos—came together to buy The Stud in 2017, making it the first LGBTQ+ nightclub to be owned and operated by a collective (but not the first to be collectively owned: The Park Dance Club in Roanoke is owned by a community-run nonprofit).[21]

Group ownership isn't a piece of cake, with Stud Collective member Nate Allbee explaining that they had few models for how to organize themselves: what kind of collective ownership would they implement? What voting rules to solve disagreements? Who could talk at meetings, and when? Egalitarianism was a concern for the diverse group, as he recalled, "With Roberts Rules, we really had to train ourselves to speak. Society rewards people who speak up and get their opinions across and that comes with a lot of racial and gendered dynamics."

After experimenting with different organizational forms, the group elected Rachel Ryan as the president and full-time manager of The Stud, vesting her with the power to make day-to-day decisions. As Allbee explained,

> We switched to a manager model where there are three elected members of the cooperative who are running the bar and making all the decisions and the rest meets once a month . . . It's worked fantastically. I'd urge any other group that's starting a cooperative nightclub to follow that model as well.

Being a collective means that the bar is owned by people who do the jobs at The Stud, by people who know the business inside and out, but it also includes owners who are people of influence in city politics.

Nate isn't the only politico in the group, which also includes Democratic Party chair Honey Mahogany. She was the only Black transgender woman to hold such a rank in the country and is also an alumna of

RuPaul's Drag Race, the first and one of the only San Francisco queens to make the show. Honey talked about the relationship between her work and her ownership, saying, "Our battle to save The Stud really showed me how politically engaged, how important that is, what a difference that can make."[22]

The second difference members of Stud Collective made was two new ways that gay bars could be municipally landmarked. The first was the creation of the country's first Legacy Business Program, which recognized the small businesses that are critical institutions for "maintaining a city's cultural identity."[23] This is, to my knowledge, the first U.S. recognition that for-profit enterprises serve not-quite-for-profit purposes. Amidst San Francisco's runaway gentrification and the pressures of corporate chains on mom and pops, the designation granted small financial benefits to business owners and gave landlords financial incentives for offering ten-year leases. The program was a project of Supervisor David Campos, whose legislative aide was none other than future Stud Collective member Nate Allbee. The Stud was among the first businesses added upon the registry's launch in 2016 and was the second gay bar to be added, behind the bear bar Lone Star Saloon.

The third trend in municipal landmarking that was spearheaded by Stud Collective members is LGBTQ+ gayborhood preservation.[24] In May 2018, the San Francisco Board of Supervisors approved the Leather and LGBTQ District, "the world's only municipally-recognized cultural district celebrating kink and fetish culture."[25] It was part of a new movement for historic cultural districts in the city that included the Latinx Calle 24 District, the SoMa Pilipinas District, and the world's first Transgender District—also promoted by Nate Allbee in David Campos's office and co-founded by Honey Mahogany. These were not merely symbolic designations—each district receives funds from community impact fees paid by real estate developers and an important role in neighborhood planning decisions.

For example, in 2020 the Board of the Leather and LGBTQ Cultural District presented a petition to the San Francisco planning commission requesting that a large new residential project have increased soundproofing for walls and windows so that the existing nightlife scene would not attract complaints from new residents.[26] The president of the Leather District cited protecting The Stud as a reason for the demands on new developers, including by asking them to rehouse displaced bars and clubs in newly constructed buildings.[27]

As activist Brenden Shucart enthused,

> Though many revered figures in the Kink Community have been instrumental in bringing the Leather District into the world, there is one person whose contributions deserve special recognition: Stud Collective President Rachel Ryan.[28]

As Ryan told a journalist, "when we formed The Stud Collective two years ago, we set out to save one bar that was near and dear to our hearts; but at the same time my hope was that we could inspire other folks to join this movement to help save other institutions."[29] And when the leather and kink communities gathered for the ribbon cutting of the new Leather and LGBTQ Cultural District, they did so not in front of one of the leather bars, but at The Stud. As Ryan noted at the event, "We have been threatened by attempts to 'clean up urban blight' and by rising rents and evictions, but we have fought to keep our bars and businesses open."[30]

The Stud's designation as a Legacy Business and an integral part to the Leather and LGBTQ Cultural District did not protect it from COVID-19 shutdowns, however. At the beginning of the coronavirus pandemic, the announcement from San Francisco's oldest gay bar resonated across the country: The Stud was closing! Marke B.—journalist, DJ, and co-owner—mourned:

> I am weeping for that beautiful, scrappy space—its gold and red velvet-and-sequined curtains parting for kooky drag shows, its graffiti-laden bathroom stalls, its very naughty green room, its dance floor packed with gorgeous creatures from all walks.[31]

Within weeks, the building's owners painted over its façade, reducing to the plainest of beige what had been a multicolored queer and trans mural, an indignity compounded by its perpetration in June, Pride month.

But was The Stud's closure a foregone conclusion? Its building had been sold out from underneath the business three years earlier before

Stud Collective took ownership. This meant the bar was vulnerable heading into 2020, one of the 16 percent that closed in that pandemic's first year.[32]

Unlike those bars, however, The Stud's owners vowed to find a new "forever home" and to remain a going concern: a bar without walls, a community seeking a center. Such a plan might seem to be a pipe dream—The Stud Bar Stabilization Fund's crowdfunding only garnered $23,000 from a half-million-dollar ask, a reminder that blockbuster GoFundMes are the exception, not the rule. And while Stud Collective owners cite the bar's rich history as a reason for saving it, plenty of other shuttered gay bars have their own rich and untold histories.

But if any bar can survive in exile, it's The Stud. The bar has already survived so much in its gay neighborhood, bringing a diversity that some gayborhoods struggle to retain and changing city law not once but twice. If gay bars are monuments in San Francisco, it's in no small part due to the scrappy band that has vowed to take The Stud into a new building for another half century.

Losing their building didn't stop The Stud Collective from continuing to act from exile. During the pandemic, the Collective engaged in political lobbying for direct municipal support of nightlife. They were cited as the source of key lobbying for San Francisco's Music and Entertainment Venue Recovery Fund, which provided municipal funds to businesses crushed by the COVID-19 pandemic. Special attention went to Supervisor Matt Haney's legislative aide and Stud Collective member Honey Mahogany.[33] This fund, initially $1.5 million but subsequently doubled, provided direct support from city budgets to nightlife venues, some recognition that small businesses provide much of the *life* to city life.

Stud Collective also maintained its programming. If anyone felt the bar's claim to be in existence was tenuous after its building was literally whitewashed, active online programming kept the bar alive. To its *Stud Stories Podcast* series on queer history, The Stud added weekly drag transmissions on the online platform Twitch. These weekly broadcasts of some of the co-owners and other beloved regulars from The Stud's stage made it as accessible to people with disabilities as it did to former Studgoers, like myself, who live far away.[34]

Perhaps only a gay bar as famous and storied as The Stud has a chance to survive in exile. Other closed bars have reopened under new owners, although it's debatable whether the spirit of a place can be maintained by new owners and new staff. Hershee Bar in Norfolk, Virginia, then the oldest lesbian bar in the world, was demolished by the city in 2018.[35] It announced return plans in 2021 that may yet come to fruition.[36] Atlanta's Eagle closed in 2020 due to COVID-19 and planned redevelopment in its building. In exile, the building was designated as the first LGBTQ+ landmark in the Deep South, but the bar plans to reopen.[37]

But as gay bars increasingly turn towards municipal recognition and historical landmarking to preserve sites that increasingly cater to non-LGBTQ+ people, virtual offerings and occasional pop-up parties that recapture the spirit of lost bars may be a trend for the future. The Stud's location will receive one of fifty bronze plaques on the "leather history cruise," endorsed by the civic Land Use and Transportation Committee,[38] a plaque that will be but a dim "afterglow" of the club's past glories.[39] Whether other gay bars continue their virtual transmissions after COVID as a way to increase their service to their communities, and whether The Stud can maintain its offerings in a post-COVID-19 world, remains to be seen. But it is already a monument in more ways than one. And as a journalist wrote wistfully, but hopefully: "The Stud is dead, but long live The Stud."[40]

Thirty-Six

AIDS Altars in Plain Sight

The Raven
ANCHORAGE, ALASKA

You can't write about gay bars without writing about AIDS. The topic is difficult for me: It is important, it is something that preoccupies me, and it is something I prefer not to think about. This was the penultimate chapter I wrote and is the penultimate presented here. This is not for lack of the topic's importance. No other force than HIV/AIDS has shaped my gay life more, even as, through sheer luck, I have remained seronegative. My formative gay years of the early 1990s were filled with the mass death and disappearances of my elders; only a couple of my peers were taken from me. But AIDS has driven my fears, at times my self-loathing, and always lurks in the background of my current happinesses.

More than 14 percent of gay bars closed between 1987 and 1992 during the depths of the AIDS pandemic.[1] For epidemiologists, the remaining gay bars were low-hanging fruit where well-meaning straight researchers could find a "high risk population" that was "hard to reach."[2] But gay bars were much more than vectors of a virus. They were tender places of caring and support.[3] They were among the first places where gay men organized in defense of their own health in the face of utter social neglect.[4] They're the places where seroconversion was first disclosed to friends, mouth to ear in the thumping din. Their patios are sites of memorials and repositories of scattered ashes, hallowing their grounds.

And they're the places you scooped up free condoms from fishbowls to cope with HIV/AIDS, *the* pandemic.

In my eyes, those buckets of condoms in gay bars are little AIDS altars in plain sight. An altar is a site of sacrifice and prayer. An AIDS altar recalls the pandemic's victims but also offers small latex intercessions for the living. The ever-refilling bucket of condoms in a gay bar recall the late artist Félix González-Torres's candy spill sculptures in which visitors are invited to take a piece from an installation that slowly shrinks. One, *Untitled (Revenge)*, features colorful blue candies in a large square on the ground, as large as a grave. Many of his works memorialize lovers and friends lost to HIV/AIDS, the shrinking piles of candy mirroring wasting bodies in whose loss the visitor is complicit. Taking a condom from a gay bar's bucket is a prayer, making you complicit in a future intercession for another, a poignant act of solidarity with the lost and the living simultaneously.

The buckets of condoms in gay bars are so ubiquitous as to pass below consciousness, as unremarkable as rainbow neon beer signs or the stacks of flyers and newspapers near the door. Many of these condom containers still have signs nearby that encourage patrons to take some to protect themselves, sometimes accompanied by statistics about current rates of sexually transmitted infections. The little-known story of those signs, and the scientific evidence for their usefulness, is the story of a student at the University of Alaska and the then-three gay bars of Anchorage.

Tammi Jo Honnen didn't know that her 1990 undergraduate psychology thesis would go on to be cited by public health professionals for the next thirty-plus years. Upon my invitation to an interview about her long-ago project, she reported, "My husband put it in there on the internet and saw it was described as, 'Have a martini and condom' and that wasn't it at all!" She had designed a simple experiment for the senior research seminar taught by the late Professor Chris Kleinke in 1989. She wondered if signs could increase the amount of condoms taken by customers, recalling that

That was the heyday, at least in Alaska, of the AIDS epidemic, so I just thought, "What can we do to encourage using condoms?" I think Alaska was way behind the East Coast, because my brother lived in New York City.

Tammi Jo approached fifteen bars to see if they would post signs above fishbowls of free condoms. All three of Anchorage's gay bars signed on. She doesn't today recall their names, but the 1987 *Damron* lists them as The Raven, The Jade Room, and The Village. She had no hesitation in approaching the gay bars: "My brother was gay, my sister was gay, I had a lot of gay friends. I didn't feel awkward going into the bars. I just told them what I was doing, and what I hoped it would do, and they were on board." None of the twelve "straight bars," as she described them, would participate, however.[5] As she recalled of the late 1980s, "It was a pretty closeted place, Anchorage, Alaska—it was all about 'See my rig and gun.' Your rig was your big truck, and your gun rack was there in the back." Tammi Jo continued, "They just said, 'No, we don't want any part of that,' probably because I told them my goal was to affect the AIDS epidemic."

The signs, which went on to be footnotes in the global fight against HIV/AIDS, read: "In the State of Alaska 38 people have died from AIDS. Many more have tested positive. Condoms can reduce the spread of AIDS."[6]

When the signs were present, patrons took 47 percent more condoms than when they were absent. As the research paper summarized the signs' effects, "Because free condoms and educational pamphlets were available prior to the study, it would appear the signs functioned in a prompting capacity rather than simply educational."[7] The other finding that is cited: All three bars volunteered to keep the signs after the experiment ended. For the owners of The Raven, The Jade Room, and The Village, participating in community health promotion was its own reward, a reflection of gay bars' not-quite-for-profit missions.

It may be difficult to remember, but the idea of businesses promoting condoms to gay men was controversial in 1989. When the owner of a gay bar in Ann Arbor, Michigan, refused AIDS activism on the premises as "depressing," a gay couple opened a competing gay bar that put it out of business. Two marketing professionals described the condom industry's neglect of gay men during the AIDS crisis as criminal: "Failure to aggressively promote a known preventive such as condoms to gays constitutes negligent homicide."[8]

But 1989 also saw yet another iconic public health intervention arise in gay bars, this time in the Biloxi, Mississippi, bar called Joey's On the Beach. The Popular Opinion Leader intervention still trains community members to teach safer-sex skills in informal conversational settings like bars; the Centers for Disease Control and Prevention today describe it as one of the most important tools in the public health arsenal against HIV.[9] Researchers back then approached extroverted bargoers in Joey's and trained them to initiate conversations with strangers about safer sex. To test whether these popular opinion leaders were successful, they also studied bars in which the intervention was not deployed: the lone gay bars in Monroe, Louisiana (probably Corky's Lounge) and Hattiesburg, Mississippi (likely Le Bistro). Returning to Biloxi one year later, the researchers found there was a 30 percent reduction in men reporting unsafe sex and a 35 percent increase in condom usage, results so successful that the intervention was immediately deployed to Corky's and Le Bistro as well.

The intersection of public health and gay bars was not always so positive. One of the first federally funded surveys of gay male sexual behavior, in 1983, recruited participants in part by standing outside bathhouses and gay bars.[10] This study found that gay bargoers had more sexual partners and riskier sexual practices than gay professionals or gay couples, but it didn't control for class differences or ask about open relationships. The study became an oft-cited justification for the scrutiny of gay bars that associated them solely with risks and not as havens from prejudice or isolation.[11] This justified the creepy medicalization of our party places.[12] Sometimes all kinds of scrutiny collided: One night in 2000 when a co-worker and I were in San Francisco's The Stud for a federally funded research project, fully one fifth of the bargoers were there to survey each other: about bargoing risks, about safer-sex practices, about which liquor they preferred. Of course we all interviewed each other: We had our quotas to fill.

The malign intersections of gay bars and public health were not always perpetrated by community outsiders. In 1996, a national panic ensued when computer disks containing the names of more than 4,000

AIDS patients in Pinellas County, Florida, were mailed to the county health department, the *Tampa Bay Tribune*, and the *St. Petersburg Times*. A health department employee was accused of taking the disks to a Treasure Island, Florida, gay bar, Bedrox, on his personal laptop, and broadcasting test results to all present.[13] Though he initially said he'd taken the data home for work, he later confessed that he'd used it to screen potential dates, a service he also offered to friends. The data privacy catastrophe was "the largest security breach of its kind in the nation" although not strictly illegal: At the time, Florida was the only state in the nation that did not explicitly bar health department employees from taking information out of their offices.[14]

As public health improved in both ethics and methods, researchers have continued to revisit Tammi Jo's research topic. In 2010, San Diego researchers found that gay bars were the businesses most likely to participate in condom distribution.[15] In 2009, a New York City team found that 80 percent of patrons who saw condoms took them and that 73 percent of those who took them reported using them.[16] But my perception that fishbowls of condoms are ubiquitous in gay bars? Not so much. Researchers found only 40 percent of New York City gay bars had them in 2009,[17] three years *before* pre-exposure prophylaxis (PrEP) was approved by the FDA. People increasingly opt for pharmaceutical, and not barrier, protection; the link between condoms and gay bars has faded during my gay lifetime.[18]

Of the three Anchorage gay bars that played a role in this footnote in AIDS history, only The Raven has survived. It is one of only two gay bars in the largest state in the union, in a city that contains more than half of its population. For a city of less than 300,000 people, Anchorage feels spread out, simultaneously larger and emptier than many other cities of its size. This is fitting for a state that is uncritically obsessed with its frontier status and for a city whose municipal boundaries encompass so much wilderness that it's larger than the whole state of Rhode Island. When I visited with my parents in April, it snowed almost every day, so we found warmth at The Raven's horseshoe bar at happy hour where regulars gather on weekdays to watch the local five o'clock news, providing sharp running commentary and restaurant recommendations to visitors

The Raven's logo is still a Native American form line image of a raven, perhaps apt given that 10 percent of Anchorage is Indigenous. Anchorage attracts peoples from all over the region and the tropical Pacific as well. The logo adorns a tall billboard framed by the Chugach Mountains in the distance, making it easy to find the free-standing green building in a light industrial district eight blocks east of Anchorage's modest downtown. Described by a lower forty-eight journalist as "ridiculously laid-back," the bar features a mascot, Winston the Penguin, who migrates around the bar in changing costumes and accessories.[19] The bar's own move to a new location in 2000 gave it the title of Northernmost Gay Bar in the United States—albeit not by much, as Alaska's other gay bar, Mad Myrna's, is only one block south.[20]

Founding owner Larry Kaiser passed in 2018, but The Raven continued on under longtime local bartenders Roger Sagraves and Scott Stroud; Scott had worked there since 2000, while Roger had been staff at the Mad Myrna's around the corner.[21] Patrons colluded in their romance, carrying love notes scrawled on scratch paper and bar napkins between the two when they worked competing shifts. The pair were determined that the bar survive Larry's passing. As Scott said, "We thought we could do it and so we did," with Roger noting, "This place is gay history! They made the AIDS quilt here for Alaska!" He's not kidding: The bar's crammed display cases and upstairs storage are an archive of Anchorage LGBTQ+ history, with wall decorations including signs from fallen Anchorage gay bars, including a beautiful stained-glass window from The Village, featuring its anchor logo and the words "Lounge – Disco."

The Raven has survived the other pandemic, COVID-19, too, instituting table service, requiring all visitors sign a guest log, and moving activities outdoors to the spacious patio when possible. "We followed the rules," Roger said, noting, "and that gentleman over at the bar was one of many who said 'This is the only place I will come because you guys are following the rules.'" When a patron called the bar to say that he had tested positive for coronavirus, Scott and Roger could get no advice from public health authorities, so they acted decisively on their own: They shut the bar and together called everyone in their visitor logs to alert them. As Scott said, "It's our community! These are our friends! They needed to know." This is the kind of community care that was promoted since the early days of HIV/AIDS, perhaps giving gay bars an edge over straight ones. The near-ubiquitous description of coronavirus as "the" pandemic revealed so dramatically the gap between straight people, enduring their first pandemic, and the rest of us, for whom this is merely another.

The Raven still offers free condoms in a dispenser on the wall, courtesy of the Alaskan AIDS Assistance Association (Four A's). The clear plastic of the appliance makes its contents of blue Crown condoms openly visible. The irregular pentagon of the dispenser resembles the shape of home plate or an upside-down house; the tip or chimney features a perfect circle through which the corners of condom wrappers poke, easily and discreetly plucked one by one, with gravity moving another inexorably into its place. The pile is reassuringly *there*, but immeasurably diminished, a modest supply of hope and a silent reminder of loss.

Four A's has offered STI testing at the bar, part of gay bars' not-quite-for-profit missions. A proudly displayed certificate in a dusty case from Four A's lauds founding owner Larry Kaiser for his "tireless efforts" against the pandemic.[22] Signs for condom use around the bar from the Alaska Native Tribal Health Consortium, descendants of Tammi Jo's research, urge "Wrap it up Alaska," reminders that communities of color are always affected more by pandemics.[23] Lube used to feature in a summer patio fundraiser, with scantily clad wrestlers wallowing in inflatable kiddie pools sloshing with it.[24] They no longer occur, Roger explained, because "The insurance company doesn't like that!" And The Raven is tagged on Instagram with condom packs, a cheeky one featuring a walrus that reads "Keep your *oosik* covered" (a Native Alaskan word for a mammal's penis bone).[25]

Condoms mean less today than they did in my gay youth—in the post-PrEP revolution that I have experienced as the most significant event in my gay lifetime. The second, for this asthmatic, was the ban on indoor smoking that occurred at the turn of the millennium (sorry, same-sex marriage). Now, for their safe-sex strategy, many gay men prefer the pills, rigorous medical monitoring, and occasional STIs instead of religious condom use. My attachment to free bar condoms says as much about my age and fear of the side effects of medication as it does about Tammi Jo's undergraduate thesis. There were many years—and many, many tricks—for which I only used free condoms from bars to have sex. Free condoms were in my luggage, my jackets, and soggy at the bottom of my washing machine from unemptied pants pockets. While the gay-bar-related public health campaigns of San Francisco (STOP AIDS) and New York City (Gay Men's Health Crisis) are justly famous, the northernmost gay bar in the United States also played, and continues to play, its own important part in HIV/AIDS prevention that is, to me, sacred work.

Tammi Jo didn't know, when she started her research, that her brother had HIV. By the time she graduated in 1989, he had died. "My brother was the kind of person who didn't want to know bad things until he had to, so he never got tested even though his partner was positive," she remembered. In a way, the continued survival of The Raven is a monument to Tammi's loss, to Larry Kaiser's life's work, and to the loss and living of so many others. She recalled, "We lost an entire generation of mostly young men. I haven't read that article since the day it got published. I just wanted to get my grade, you know?" Describing how Professor Kleinke mailed her a copy back when it was published: "It tickled me at the time, but gosh that was a long time ago." And to the people describing COVID-19 as "the" pandemic, AIDS probably seems like a long time ago, too. But it's not to those of us who are still living it.

Thirty-Seven

A Post-Gay, Not-Gay, Very Gay, Un-Bar

Dacha
WASHINGTON, DC

Dacha in Washington, DC, is definitely *not* a gay bar. It is a ten-minute drive from both the U.S. Capitol and the White House, monuments that define the nation even as they have long been fraught places for LGBTQ+ people.[1] Dacha is a beer garden and café at the auspicious intersection of Q Street where it hits 7th, one of the main commercial corridors in the Shaw neighborhood, which is home to both the "Black Harvard" (Howard University) and to some of the city's most pitched battles about gentrification and the displacement of Black by white people.[2] Summer tourists to our nation's capital can stop into Dacha and rub elbows with locals over a beer or a *radler*, the German mix of beer and either soda pop or fruit juice. If any gay bar can be a monument, or an archive, or a site of pilgrimage, what can a "not-gay, un-bar" offer the LGBTQ+ patron in a world where many of us increasingly choose to spend our time in non-gay venues? If this book is a revolving disco-ball mosaic of the country's gay bars, I had to return to DC—not because it is the seat of the nation, but because it contains the monuments of my baby gay origin story and a model of what gay bars may be evolving into.

Dacha co-owner and co-founder Dmitri "Dima" Chekaldin sighed and wrinkled his nose when I asked him about winning "best straight bar" four years in a row from the region's LGBTQ+ newspaper while simultaneously being recognized as a gay bar in reviews on Yelp and in local news coverage.[3] "A beer garden is not a bar. A beer garden is a community space," he began, disputing Dacha's listing as a bar at all. Indeed, the physical bar is covered by blue tent pavilions, and the ground under the picnic tables is gravel and garden paving stones, a reflection of the site's recent past as a vacant lot. This beer garden, Dima specified, "is an open space, not a bar, it's not a restaurant, it's *more* than that."

He then disputed Dacha's identification as gay: "By definition you *can't* have a beer garden as a gay beer garden. You can have a beer garden that belongs to a community and a community is everyone: straight, gay, disabled, Black, white, Hispanic, a mix of people." Noting my skeptical look, Dima was firm: "If you were to call a beer garden a gay place, you would literally discriminate and why would you want to do that?" Here he echoed other bar owners—and many erstwhile cosmopolitan straight people—for whom excluding straight people in gay bars is tantamount to racial segregation.[4]

Dima was also articulating the logic described by sociologists as *post-gay*, the belief that the United States is, or is on the verge, of becoming a "society wherein sexual orientation will cease to be central (or possibly, even relevant) to a person's social position, life experiences, and conception of self."[5] Cementing his implicitly post-gay declaration, Dima shrugged: "It never even crossed my mind, 'Oh, it's a gay bar.'" Patiently, but with a smile, he explained:

> We are a German beer garden owned by Russian people. All we want to have here is *gemütlichkeit* [warm feelings of good cheer]. That's it. We want to have a good time with our friends, our family, our kids, our dogs, our lovers, mothers, fathers, etc.

Indeed, I'd met Dima's mother and partner the day before, at his condo, where Jesse and I had watched the annual Pride parade from his building's rooftop deck—a sunny rainbow-soaked afternoon that was decidedly *not* post-gay.

So a beer garden cannot be gay. And yet: This beer garden was overseen by a giant mural of a stylized, sultry Elizabeth Taylor, the AIDS activist diva who lives on in classic movie showings and drag impersonations. The beer mats at service points were rainbow. The tank tops worn by staff were pink and featured the campy mural. Dacha held weekly Cause Tuesdays, fundraisers that have featured the local HIV/AIDS clinic, the LGBT Victory Fund, Gays Against Guns, and Helping Individual Prostitutes Survive. The beer garden's Monday Meetups have also featured LGBTQ+ Ivy League alumni. Taken as a whole, Dacha's events reflected a wider diversity of LGBTQ+ experiences than most *gay* bars. True, on the particular day I visited it was Pride weekend, but the blue tents over the physical bar were festooned with far more rainbow windsocks and Pride flags than were two nearby actual-gay bars. Gay bars may celebrate Pride every day, I suppose, but they might make *some* effort. And it might be easier to be the rainbow-strewn, post-gay bar in the gentrifying Shaw—Washington DC's "Best Gayborhood"—an award the neighborhood won once it was no longer only queer Black people who lived there.[6]

Dacha is a post-gay space, then, a beer garden whose gay friendliness is matched by its friendliness to everyone in the community and their little dogs too: Bowls of water explicitly invite furry friends to sit in the shade under tables. But the crowd: Is it post-gay? Dacha's voluminous and overwhelmingly positive press coverage never hesitates to note how many LGBTQ+ people go there. The crowd on the sunny June Sunday when Dima and I talked was, in my professional estimation, 70 percent LGBTQ+. This included a toned twink in a midriff-baring Nancy Pelosi cut-off, three lesbians with killer asymmetrical haircuts, a Black man wearing a rainbow t-shirt celebrating the Navy, and a mixed-race group of femmes who were of indeterminate sexuality until one of them, chilled by the mist blowing from fans, literally wrapped themself in a rainbow flag. True, this was the day after the Pride parade, but Dima admitted that it was like this all year round on this particular day of the week: "It just so happens on Sundays we're more gay again, just by definition, because gays don't have as much obligations and so Sundays they can party a little bit more." Some LGBTQ+ people may be post-gay, but they can be even *more* postgay on Sundays, an excess that starts to seem, well, a little bit gay.[7]

Post-gay people may not *need* gay bars, but they still *enjoy* them, at least occasionally.

And Dima and his co-owner Ilya Alter are both gay, too. This I knew about Dima without having to ask: We were briefly sweethearts as students at George Washington University just two neighborhoods over. I awkwardly relinquished my virginity to him in Mitchell Hall, a personal monument only two miles away, back when I was myself still ambivalent about being gay. I asked Dima if there was still a place in the world for a space just for LGBTQ+ people, and without hesitation he replied,

> Yes. As a gay man, I will tell you unequivocally, "Yes," and I will explain why. In society, people have different interests, and you should be able to have a very particular interest that is prevalent in a certain assembly space like a bar: a bear bar, a lesbian bar.

After all, he noted, "Straight people have particular interests and gathering spots too," naming heterosexual strip clubs and private clubs as examples. "Especially with certain niches of the gay world which we have—and we have plenty—we have absolutely the right to exist and flourish and have fun!" So Dacha's post-gay world has room for gay bars, especially ones that serve the niches of LGBTQ+ subcultures—just not in beer gardens.

Dima reflected on changes that occurred since he'd been my first kiss in 1994. "We've walked a long AIDS walk, a long road from the days when you and I were in college, where things were seemingly open under Clinton, but they were not." Those were indeed heady times that included my first visit to a lesbian bar, The Hung Jury. Challenged upon entry because the women had all gone on ahead and the club didn't admit men alone, the bouncer asked how could she possibly know that I was gay? Witheringly, I observed: "I'm wearing *a vest*." Mollified, she let me in, where I danced with my women friends before Bill Clinton's second inaugural. Amidst some "firsts" in his LGBTQ+ political appointees, there were the disastrous tides that swelled into Don't Ask, Don't Tell and the Defense of Marriage Act. But Dima contrasted then with now:

> We have marriage equality, we have lots of freedoms, so there's no more need, in my opinion, to dedicate all the bars to be gay or

straight. There does not need to be a separation in the vast majority of cases.

So the vast majority of the United States—and its bars—can be post-gay, even if there's still room for some gay ones. Dima's statement also suggests that straight bars must learn to be "post-straight," however, a post-gay twist that pundits have not yet explored.[8]

Our conversation had occasionally been interrupted by discreet questions from Dacha's staff, but now a matter required Dima's undivided attention, so he hugged me goodbye. I ruminated on how our conversation exposed the limitations of the post-gay concept about which scholars are so ambivalent.[9] Post-gay living often happens in pretty gay contexts, and often only the most privileged can partake: the people who want to marry, cisgender folks whose rights are secured, those whose queerness passes under straight radars, white folks who move through life with less friction, and those who have the money and leisure to party every Sunday. The world is not post-gay for most LGBTQ+ people, and politically radical queer people do not even welcome such a world.[10]

Against fears that the post-gay future isn't very gay, however, Dacha provides hope that queer culture can flourish in environments that aren't specifically LGBTQ+. Maybe it doesn't matter if a place is a gay place seven days a week if the Ls, Gs, Bs, Ts, and Qs take over on Sundays, or after 2 am in the all-night diner, or in one section of the public beach. Pop-up drag shows are flourishing across the country in bars and clubs that never used to host them, a creep of LGBTQ+ culture into previously straight venues.[11] Maybe camp restaurants like Dacha and San Diego's insideOUT will spring up everywhere, employing unabashedly LGBTQ+ staff and creating public space for LGBTQ+ patrons, our unique cultural forms, and the allies who love us.

This already seems to be happening. Todd Howard ran Charlottesville, Virginia's sleek Escafé as a restaurant during the day whose only overt gesture towards LGBTQ+ people was the "lettuce, gouda, bacon, and tomato sandwich"—the L.G.B.T.! But on weekend evenings, Todd's staff pushed the tables to create an LGBTQ+ dance club that he described as a "mission" as much as a business.[12] The bar, like

Chumley's in State College, Pennsylvania, thus served as a place for cosmopolitan straight people and queer people alike.

Fox Market and Bar opened as a "queer bar" in rural East Montpelier, Vermont (population: 2,600), albeit one that serves "gaggles" of children who delight in its board games and shelves of graphic novels and straight teachers who hang out after picking up wine and cheese in its deli.[13] That an avowed queer bar can serve all people, including the kids of straight families and grocery shoppers, gestures to how LGBTQ+ culture can thrive even in small towns in supposedly post-gay times. After all, Ann Arbor's /aut/ BAR and State College's Chumley's were *straight* friendly before queer friendly was a thing.

Dacha is not alone: There are other queer post-gay places that refuse to be called bars. I talked to co-owner Jon McRae of "Sister Louisa's Church (It's a Glory Hole)" in Athens, Georgia, a branch of founder Grant Henry's Atlanta bar known as "Sister Louisa's Church of the Living Room & Ping Pong Emporium . . . Come On In Precious!" The bar is crammed with campy religious art, including one painting of Jesus overlaid with cartoon letters, "I want to be inside of you" and another that says "Jesus ♥ the gay!" There is a stuffed alligator eating a puppet of queer icon Pee Wee Herman. A sign advertises Hot Doug's Sausage Superstore. But when my friend Amy asked Jon if it was a gay bar, he was quick to deny it. "We'd never call ourselves that," he emphasized, adding "A bar with lots of gays? Absolutely." When I asked Jon what kind of bar it was, he didn't skip a beat: "It's an art gallery that serves alcohol." A passerby butted in: "Do you sell the art?" "No!" Jon exclaimed. "We just sell alcohol!" LGBTQ+ culture thrives in the South, even in boozy boutiques that are not gay and seem pretty bar-like, for all that they too are un-bars.

And it thrives in San Francisco, where Chris Milstead ran Driftwood on the site of a string of cruisy men's bars that included The Ramrod, My Place, Chaps, and Kok.[14] Fans of leather and kinky sex decried the bar's refusal of the label "gay" or "queer" and its shift from a dark dive into natural wood and vinyl records. They seemed to be validated by Chris's words to me, that "I didn't want to have any label, 'Is it a gay bar, a straight bar?' It's an everyone bar." And yet, as Chris observed, the cruisy spirit of the location caused exhibitionism in mixed company that sounds pretty queer:

Gay and straight, that back area has the sex area, the couches back there. It doesn't matter who you are, that space has that energy, and it's not going away no matter who you are. Look at those straight people making out in the back, gay people, any people, they're not shy to do that. And that's why I kinda like an everybody bar.

Fears that LGBTQ+ people are inhibited in post-gay spaces may not be borne out.

These examples put me in mind of Hamburger Mary's Bar & Grille, the closest thing to a franchised gay bar that has ever existed. Each "open air bar and grille for open-minded people" brims with camp and kookiness and serves as a diner during the day and a nightclub in the evening. Hamburger Mary's has nearly twenty locations around the United States, but somehow it manages to fly under the national radar.[15] While some observers mistakenly call it a chain, each is independently owned and managed so that you can get regional tacos in Houston or cheese curds in Milwaukee. True, some Mary's are in gayborhoods like San Francisco's Castro in California and Wilton Manors in Florida. But others are in Toledo (Ohio), Ontario (California), Grand Rapids (Michigan), and Kansas City (Missouri)—home stage to *RuPaul* finalist Mo Heart, proof that a heartland franchise can nurture superstar drag talent.[16] Ru girls, and famous drag queens like Lady Bunny, often tour the country by hopping from one Hamburger Mary's to another, cementing their role as key nodes in the queer connective tissue that drag queens weave across the country.

Hamburger Mary's exemplifies many of the recent trends in successful gay bars. They explicitly welcome straight people. Food is a focus, not an afterthought. Community events and fundraising are integral. And drag artistry and patron entertainment is core to the business model. For the twenty-odd Hamburger Mary's establishments, that calendar includes a busy "Mary"-go-round of Mary-oke, Hambingo Mary's, Dining with the Divas, and weekend drag brunches.

In some ways, Hamburger Mary's flirts with the post-gay. There are few rainbows or trans Pride flags in evidence at many locations, and the language on the websites doesn't mention anything LGBTQ+. As Mary's owner Douglas Hanchett Jr. in Ypsilanti, Michigan, explained to the press, "This is a safe place for everybody. Everybody is welcome."[17] My research assistant and co-author Tory observed that mainly straight folks go, and some gays, but—no queers. The franchise application similarly mentions nothing LGBTQ+, gesturing instead to its corporate virtues of "individuality and nonconformity."[18] This raises the question: How is the nonconformist from gritty rust belt Ypsilanti different from the nonconformist in slick gayborhood West Hollywood? When a quirky one-off bar is replaced by a chain, does it feel like Walmart crushed a mom-and-mom and pop-and-pop business?

But, Hamburger Mary's menus are *ridiculously* campy. The flatbread pizzas are named for the iconic Golden Girls.[19] Children are welcome to lunches and brunches, but the menu still includes single entendres to "tater ta-ta's," "guacamole B.J.," and the "mother clucker." Burgers invoke gay divas ranging from Tina Turner, Buffy the Vampire Slayer, and Barbra Streisand, while cocktails namedrop Sarah Jessica Parker, Daenerys Targaryen, and *Will & Grace's* Karen Walker. The references aren't exactly clever and teeter on the brink of being basic. But they are very, very, *very* gay (queer? not so much). But the locations are embraced by their LGBTQ+ patrons and communities. "Rarely does the queer community mourn the loss of a franchise restaurant," one Chicago writer observed of the gayborhood Andersonville location's closure, but "Hamburger Mary's is an exception."[20]

And serving children is a plus for these communities. One doctor explained how their parent-clients often "cited Mary's as a place for their children to first be out or the first place they didn't have to worry about which bathroom they chose to use."[21] And, Dr. Caramiello continued, Hamburger Mary's plays a "role as an introduction to the LGBTQ+ community to the straight, baby-ally community." Allies have to start somewhere, and maybe it starts with a drag queen and a burger. Explained Milwaukee Mary's owner Gary Olson, "We're educating people."[22] These family-friendly venues may not facilitate the sexy community sought by men in their cruisy bars, nor the woman-forward environment of lesbian bars, but these are gay spaces doing gay things in often-straight places. Newbies are always going to need LGBTQ+ places, and restaurants and cafés can fill that need, alongside gay bars.

I thought back to my conversation with Dima, who measured Dacha's post-gay present against our shared gay past: "Now it doesn't have to be strictly gay or straight as when you and I were teenagers." And such a view from pre-COVID DC is echoed by the dreams of 1980s Appalachia. Michael Trivette, owner of New Beginnings in Johnson City, Tennessee, told me of straight people in his club: "It's one of the blessings of our equality," adding "It's what I always wanted; it's the rest of the country that caught up." Post-gay may be new for intellectuals in big cities on the coasts, but its long been the reality for many in the American interior.

The story I have been able to tell about gay bars has been so steeped in that gay past, my own queer story—there is no view from nowhere. This is why I chose in this book to tell the stories of so many bars; drive-by barhopping madness was my method, putting unanticipated strains on my mental health, my finances, my relationship, and my car's transmission. Little Blanche was scarred, too: Leaving her alone in cheap motel rooms with brawling neighbors gave her a fear of being left alone, and after she chewed up two rooms—chew up one, shame on you; chew up two? shame on me!—she has now endured half a life of being crated in strange places.

The conversations I had with gay bar owners and managers can't necessarily tell us about how LGBTQ+ patrons feel about the straight people in their midst: The patron of one Tennessee bar disparaged the straight swingers who "invaded" his gay bar once a month, although his account criticized their fatness and oldness as much as their straightness. The longtime show directors I interviewed can't tell us about how new drag queens feel about the television show that introduced them to the art form. Nor can they tell us whether making monuments of gay bars actually changes the social landscape of neighborhood or city. Someone else will have to interview the straight people who are increasingly and earnestly adopting queer culture, their success at which seems to validate David Halperin's quip that "Homosexuality is wasted on gay people."[23] Others will have to tell about the individual city-based club nights that serve parts of the LGBTQ+ community who don't have bars of their own, or the guerrilla strategies by which LGBTQ+ people have always just gone ahead and taken the places we want or need, whether that be a straight bar or an IHOP or the clothes aisle at the Walmart for an impromptu catwalk.[24] These are important stories to tell, too.

My long road trips and six years of interviewing allowed me to celebrate the vast diversity of gay bars and our LGBTQ+ community, to give shine to parts of the country that don't have a gay press or a nationally read newspaper to publicize their goings-on. If you take any lessons from this mirrored mosaic of American LGBTQ+ places, I hope that I've disrupted regional stereotypes and sketched for you the vast diversity of gay bars. I've tried to draw connections—among rural roadhouse outposts to each other, and between them and massive, big-city gayborhood dance clubs. All of them are bound together by our shared queer culture and our messy, ambivalent desires.[25] For reasons both shallow or deep, I wanted to visit states I'd never been to like Arkansas and Alaska, and to revisit cities that are near and dear to my little queer heart. I wanted to find gay bars owned by all sorts of different people, in all sorts of locations. It took 10,000 miles on my car to find those stories, and so many of them didn't fit into this book, as excessively queer as it is. When it comes to gay bars, there are so many stories to tell: from different locales, from different bodies, for different ends.[26] As Danny Chang of Honolulu's Wang Chung declared, gay bars are both "dying" and "evolving," and there is no reason to believe that those processes will look the same everywhere in our vast, diverse country.

More importantly, there are stories to be *made*. Gay bars are most successful, and the night that much more fun, when we go to them not to be entertained, but to be *entertaining*. So go out alone with a joke or a quip on your lip and share it with your seatmate at the bar. As The Stud's Nate Allbee encourages, "If you find your community, you can actually be the star."[27] Ask the bartender how long they've been working there and how business has been. Chat to the drag artists about how they learned their craft. Suggest changes to the owner to make their bar—your bar, *our* bar—more inclusive. Be an open-minded ear to the stranger next to you. Help us be the storytellers we need to be to sustain ourselves in this sometimes gay-friendly, but still overwhelmingly straight, world. In the words of the feminist philosopher Kylie Minogue, your disco needs you! And what we need is more storytellers. Including, and especially, you.

Acknowledgments

Heartfelt thanks to all the people who sat down with me to tell their stories, with my sincere apologies if your words did not make it into the book. If there are any smart things in this thing, they came about because of others: through their stories in their own words, through conversations with friends, through writing for imagined audiences, through my reactions to things others have written, to the support of friends and colleagues and family and strangers. A special thanks to the journalists who have covered nightlife over the years; I couldn't have done it without you. All the accountants, barbacks, bartenders, burlesque performers, cleaners, dancers, DJs, drag artists, door people, emcees, loyal regulars, managers, nightlife photographers, owners, promoters, and show directors have my admiration and my thanks for maintaining our LGBTQ+ spaces throughout many difficult times.

More than half of the project was funded by Oberlin College through support from the Dean of the College of Arts and Sciences, faculty research support, multiple grants-in-aid, and undergraduate research assistant grants, with thanks to Angela Szunyogh, Pam Snyder, Lizzie Edgar, and colleagues of the Research and Development Committee of the General Faculty. The rest was self-funded, including by an advance on the book and consulting work for Absolut.

Tory Sparks was my "right-hand them": the lead undergraduate researcher of the first team; my assistant on the first road trip; an interviewer on their own in Nebraska, Illinois, Iowa, and Wisconsin; and later co-author, including of Chapter 11. They also provided expert, detailed, tough-love feedback on the final draft. Jack Spector-Bishop was a skillful assistant who also conducted interviews on his own in California and Nevada. Wren Fiocco, Carter Rasnic Olson, Mikaela Howard, Charlie Sherman, Yael Benvenuto Ladin, and Pearl Puzak all contributed skills, eyes, and heart to the project as undergraduate research assistants.

Friends, colleagues, and strangers were generous with feedback on chapters (and sometimes with their gay bar companionship): Chris Barcelos, KJ Cerankowski, Cati Connell, Jan Cooper, John D'Emilio, Eric Estes, Al Evangelista, Theo Greene, Jesse Keating, Chong-suk Han, Lucas Hilderbrand, Katie Horowitz, Libni López, Ghassan Moussawi, Anthony Ocampo, Patrick O'Connor, C. J. Pascoe, Gretchen Purser, Sarah Quinn, and Marc Stein. I have to especially thank my Indigenous, Black, person of color, immigrant, transgender, lesbian, disabled, and nonbinary readers for giving their time and expertise to someone who doesn't share their experiences: Your insights taught me a lot and have, I hope, allowed more readers to see themselves in this book. None of these readers could stop me from making mistakes, but you can't even *imagine* what a mess things would have been if so many people hadn't been so magnanimous.

Certain masochistic readers, friends, and sometime-gay-bar companions lavished attention on full early drafts, including Phillip Fucella, Libby Murphy, Lisa Ross, and Lisa Stampnitzky; their feedback buoyed me. Jack Gieseking provided extravagant and wise commentary on a late draft.

I also benefited from conversations with Ann Cooper Albright, anonymous reviewers, Bernadette Barton, Michael Brown, Japonica Brown-Saracino, Jenny Fraser, Connor Gilroy, Larry Knopp, Sookyoung Lee, Martin Manalansan, Nisarg Mehta, the whole ¿Qué Tal? writing café crew, Christie Parris, Danielle Skeehan, and Jason Spicer. Melissa Petro was the first to support my public writing. Anne Trubek encouraged my trade aspirations and was an early supporter. Kris Clarke set me up and put me up in Fresno. I especially thank Amy

Margaris for letting me be her work wife and for always—over fifteen years—lending an ear and a troubleshooting brain.

Ezra Baker was a welcome co-pilot on the New England leg. I had many other memorable gay bar companions on my travels, among them Kazim Ali, James Barbat, Kaisa Hammonds, Jason Haugen, Jack Johnson, Tim Jones, A.K., Larry La Fountain-Stokes, Isaac Martin, Garrett Mattson, Ken Mattson, LaDene Mattson, Jimmy McGuire, Paul Nicastro, Dan Ocampo, Andrew Pau, Armando Rosario, Amy Stone, Marcelo Vinces, Rebecca Whelan, and Marco Wilkinson.

I thank my agent Brenna English-Loeb and my editor Marcela Maxfield, the whole team at Stanford University Press, and the fairy godmother of an anonymous reader who went above and beyond.

And I thank you for reading. Go out there to be entertaining and to make some stories of your own—and then tell them!

Reader's Guide

A guide for book groups, classrooms, and motivated readers of *Who Needs Gay Bars?*

SETTING UP A GROUP

This book brings the gay bar to life beyond its usual club or tavern setting. Here are some considerations for setting up a reading group:

- ▶ How often will you meet? Where will you meet?

- ▶ Do any members have accessibility needs that must be met so they can fully participate?

- ▶ Will food and/or beverages be served at your group? How will this be done respectfully to those who do not drink alcohol or those who have allergies or restrictions? How will drinkers get home safely?

- ▶ Will any members of the LGBTQ+ community be present? If not, why not? How will all members be made to feel comfortable without being asked to speak for their identity or communities?

- ▶ How could a commitment to an aesthetic bring the book to life for the group? Will sequins, (p)leather, fringe, mesh, and hats be encouraged?

Proposed beverages

H_2O

Mismatched fancy glass as available (champagne flute, carnival glass goblet, etc.)

Still or sparkling water as desired

Cucumber slice (or not)

A Not-so-Dark and Stormy

Highball glass or 8-ounce 1980s fast food commemorative cup

1.5 ounces Ritual nonalcoholic rum alternative

3 ounces Vernors ginger ale or your local brand

Sprig of mint

Press

Iittala Ultima Thule On the rocks highball glass or similar

1.5 ounces Jim Beam or other bourbon

1.5 ounces tap water (essential)

1.5 ounces 7-Up

No garnish

GUIDING QUESTIONS

1. Have you ever been to an LGBTQ+ bar? If so, what was your first time like? If not, what do you imagine them to be like?

2. What was your experience reading *Who Needs Gay Bars?* What surprised you? Did any particular phrase or event stick with you?

3. Did your opinions regarding LGBTQ+ bars change after reading *Who Needs Gay Bars?* Why/how so?

4. In *Who Needs Gay Bars?*, author Greggor Mattson features over 40 individual bars and their owners. Which most captivated you, and why?

5. Which kinds of gay bars and lesbian bars were new to you?

6. For whom are bars safe spaces, and under what conditions?

7. The author mainly interviewed gay bar owners and managers. What can they tell us? What can they likely *not* tell us?

8. The LGTBQ+ community largely depends upon privately-owned spaces to socialize and meet each other. Where do your communities meet, and how are those spaces similar to, or different from, bars and nightclubs?

9. Did any of the statements in the book rub you the wrong way? Why?

10. What are the ways in which the LGBTQ+ community is diverse within itself? What are the difficulties in recognizing and honoring that diversity?

11. Did reading this book inspire you to change your habits in going out? If so, in what ways? If not, why not?

12. How do you feel about gay bars closing? Why?

13. Should gay bars receive support from the public? If so, what form should this support take?

14. What are the downsides of idealizing gay bars? What are the downsides of dismissing them altogether?

$\mathcal{M}$ATTSON'S READING LIST OF LGBTQ+ PLACES IN THE U.S.

Men in Place, Miriam Abelson

Feels Right, Kemi Adeyemi

Real, Queer America, Samantha Allen

Moby Dyke, Krista Burton

Cruising, Alex Espinoza

Queering the Midwest, Claire Forstie

Together, Somehow, Luis Manuel Garcia-Mispireta

There Goes the Gayborhood, Amin Ghaziani

A Queer New York, Jack Gieseking

The Bars are Ours, Lucas Hilderbrand

Ingredients for Revolution, Alex Ketchum

Ishtyle, Kareem Khubchandani

Brown and Gay in LA, Anthony Christian Ocampo

When Brooklyn Was Queer, Hugh Ryan

How Place Makes Us, Japonica Brown-Saracino

Still Straight, Tony Silva

Queer Carnival, Amy Stone

Notes

Preface

1. This preface was adapted from Greggor Mattson, "Before It Was Hingetown," in *Cleveland Neighborhood Guidebook*. eds. staff of *Belt Magazine* (Cleveland: Belt Publishing, 2016), 53–56. Used with permission.

2. Katie Horowitz, *Drag, Interperformance, and the Trouble with Queerness* (London and New York: Routledge, 2019); Ken Schneck, "We Say Goodbye to Bounce Nightclub Hinge Lounge," *Cleveland Magazine* (January 5, 2018), https://clevelandmagazine.com/in-the-cle/articles/we-say-goodbye-to-bounce-nightclub-hinge-lounge

3. D. X. Ferris, "Out Behind The Shed," *Cleveland Scene* (August 13, 2008), https://www.clevescene.com/cleveland/out-behind-the-shed/Content?oid=1520648

4. http://mbaxamerica.com/stern-week-1-championing-responsible-redevelopment-in-cleveland/ (accessed 2016).

5. Sheehan Hannan, "Two of Arts," *Cleveland Magazine* (November 1, 2015), https://clevelandmagazine.com/in-the-cle/the-read/articles/two-of-arts; Lee Chilcote, "How One Couple Turned a 'Toxic Corner' of Cleveland into a Development Hotbed," *Vanity Fair* (September 22, 2015), https://www.vanityfair.com/culture/2015/09/hingetown-neighborhood-cleveland

6. Hannan, "Two of Arts"; Chilcote, "How One Couple Turned a 'Toxic Corner' of Cleveland into a Development Hotbed"; Michael K. McIntyre, "Cleveland's Hingetown Neighborhood Earns Praise in New Vanity Fair Issue," *Cleveland Plain Dealer* (September 15, 2015), https://www.cleveland.com/tipoff/2015/09/clevelands_hingetown_neighborh.html

7. P. E. Moskowitz, "Can One Young Guy Lift Cleveland Out of Misery? (No, Not LeBron James)," *Talking Points Memo* (March 24, 2015), https://talkingpointsmemo.com/theslice/can-graham-veysey-make-cleveland-not-suck; Ferris, "Out Behind The Shed."

8. Hingetown, *Meet the Neighbors: Dean Rufus House of Fun* (Cleveland, 2015), https://www.youtube.com/watch?v=ewKoyh8Yma8

9. Ferris, "Out Behind The Shed."

10. Ferris, "Out Behind The Shed."

11. Moskowitz, "Can One Young Guy Lift Cleveland Out of Misery?"

12. Momentous, "Rebirth in the Rust Belt: A Forgotten Corner of Cleveland Bounces Back," *Insider* (blog) (April 2, 2020), https://momentousrealty.com/rebirth-in-the-rust-belt-a-forgotten-corner-of-cleveland-bounces-back-22/

13. Michelle Jarboe, "Graham Veysey Blurs Neighborhood Lines with Hingetown Projects: 2015 People to Watch," *Cleveland Plain Dealer* (December 30, 2014), https://www.cleveland.com/business/2014/12/graham_veysey_blurs _neighborho.html

14. Jarboe, "Graham Veysey Blurs Neighborhood Lines."

15. Brandon Andrew Robinson, *Coming Out to the Streets: LGBTQ Youth Experiencing Homelessness* (Oakland: University of California Press, 2020), 99.

16. Samantha Allen, "The Gay Bar Is Dying. Long Live the Queer Café," *The Daily Beast* (February 17, 2018), https://www.thedailybeast.com/the-gay -bar-is-dying-long-live-the-queer-cafe; "Do Gay People Still Need Gay Bars?" *BBC News* (April 1, 2014), https://www.bbc.com/news/magazine-26817128; André-Naquian Wheeler, "The Gay Bar Is Dead: How the Queer Space Killed It," *i-D.Vice* (August 2, 2019), https://i-d.vice.com/en_us/article/vb98a3/gay-bar-is -dead-queer-space-mood-ring-myles-loftin; June Thomas, "The Gay Bar: Is It Dying?" *Slate* (June 26, 2011), http://www.slate.com/articles/life/the_gay_bar /2011/06/the_gay_bar_6.html; Samuel Clowes Huneke, "The Death of the Gay Bar," *Boston Review* (February 17, 2021), http://bostonreview.net/gender-sexu ality/samuel-clowes-huneke-death-gay-bar

17. Bryce J. Renninger, "Grindr Killed the Gay Bar, and Other Attempts to Blame Social Technologies for Urban Development: A Democratic Approach to Popular Technologies and Queer Sociality," *Journal of Homosexuality* 66, no. 12 (October 15, 2019): 1736–1755; Scott E. Branton and Cristin A. Compton, "There's No Such Thing as a Gay Bar: Co-Sexuality and the Neoliberal Branding of Queer Spaces," *Management Communication Quarterly* (November 16, 2020), https://doi.org/10.1177/0893318920972113; Greggor Mattson, "Bar Districts as Subcultural Amenities," *City, Culture and Society* 6, no. 1 (2015): 1–8; Lori L. Reid, Carolyn J. Aman Karlan, and Michael D. Bonham-Crecilius, "Inclusion and Intrusion: Gender and Sexuality in Gay, Lesbian, and Straight Bars," in *Together Alone: Personal Relationships in Public Places*, eds. Calvin Morrill, David A. Snow, and Cindy H. White (Berkeley: University of California Press, 2005), 134–158; Petra L. Doan and Harrison Higgins, "The Demise of Queer Space? Resurgent Gentrification and the Assimilation of LGBT Neighborhoods," *Journal of Planning Education and Research* 31, no. 1 (March 1, 2011): 6–25; Allie Pape, "Gay Bar Deathwatch," *Eater SF* (February 13, 2013), https://sf.eater.com/2013/2/13/6480369/gay-bar-death watch; Huneke, "The Death of the Gay Bar"; Thomas, "The Gay Bar."

18. Greggor Mattson, "Are Gay Bars Closing? Using Business Listings to

Infer Rates of Gay Bar Closure in the United States, 1977–2019," *Socius* 5 (January 1, 2019), https://doi.org/10.1177/2378023119894832

19. Schneck, "We Say Goodbye to Bounce Nightclub Hinge Lounge."

20. Michael Musto, "RIP Gay Bars," *Village Voice* (January 14, 2010), https://www.villagevoice.com/2010/01/14/rip-gay-bars/

21. Greggor Mattson, "Urban Ethnography's 'Saloon Problem,' and Its Lesson for Public Sociology," *City & Community* 6, no. 2 (2007): 75–94.

22. Kate Sosin, "The Damron Address Book, a Green Book for Gays, Kept a Generation of Men in the Know," *Los Angeles Magazine* (June 25, 2019), https://www.lamag.com/culturefiles/damron-address-book/; Martin Meeker, *Contacts Desired* (Berkeley: University of California Press, 2006); Lucas Hilderbrand, "A Suitcase Full of Vaseline, or Travels in the 1970s Gay World," *Journal of the History of Sexuality* 22, no. 3 (September 2013): 373–402; Larry Knopp and Michael Brown, "Travel Guides, Urban Spatial Imaginaries and LGBTQ+ Activism: The Case of Damron Guides," *Urban Studies* 58, no. 7 (2021): 1380–1396.

23. OL Team, "Out Leadership Releases the Annual State LGBTQ+ Business Climate Index for 2022," *OutLeadership* (June 2, 2022), https://outleadership.com/insights/state-lgbtq-business-climate-index/

24. Jaime Hartless, "'They're Gay Bars, but They're Men Bars': Gendering Questionably Queer Spaces in a Southeastern US University Town," *Gender, Place & Culture* 25, no. 12 (December 2, 2018): 1781–1800.

25. Jack Halberstam, *In a Queer Time and Place: Transgender Bodies, Subcultural Lives* (New York: New York University Press, 2005); Scott Herring, *Another Country: Queer Anti-Urbanism* (New York: NYU Press, 2010); Karen Tongson, *Relocations: Queer Suburban Imaginaries* (New York: New York University Press, 2011).

26. Amy L. Stone, "The Geography of Research on LGBTQ Life: Why Sociologists Should Study the South, Rural Queers, and Ordinary Cities," *Sociology Compass* 12, no. 11 (2018): e12638.

27. Clare Forstie, "Theory Making from the Middle: Researching LGBTQ Communities in Small Cities," *City & Community* 19, no. 1 (2020): 153–168; Greggor Mattson, "Small-City Gay Bars, Big-City Urbanism," *City & Community* 19, no. 1 (2020): 76–97.

28. Greggor Mattson and Tory Sparks, "'We Have a Gay Bar Here.' You Don't Need a Coast to Be Cosmopolitan," in *Red State Blues: Stories from Midwestern Life on the Left,* ed. Martha Bayne (Cleveland: Belt Publishing, 2018), 109–114.

29. Daniel Marshall, Kevin P. Murphy, and Zeb Tortorici, "Queering Archives: Historical Unravelings," *Radical History Review* 14, no. 120 (2014): 1–11; see also Danielle C. Skeehan, "Archive," *Early American Studies* 16, no. 4 (2018): 584–590.

30. Lee Chilcote, "Got to Get Down to Hingetown: Introducing Ohio City's Next Hot Block," *FreshWater* (July 25, 2013), https://www.freshwatercleveland.com/features/hingetownohiocity072513.aspx

31. Chilcote. "Got to Get Down to Hingetown"; Moskowitz, "Can One Young Guy Lift Cleveland Out of Misery?"

Chapter 1

1. Neil J. Smelser, "The Rational and the Ambivalent in the Social Sciences," *American Sociological Review* 63, no. 1 (February 1, 1998): 1–16.

2. Justin Luke and John Blair, "Op-Ed: Gay Nightlife Is Dead—Long Live Gay Nightlife," *Advocate* (April 16, 2014), http://www.advocate.com/commentary/ 2014/04/16/op-ed-gay-nightlife-dead-%E2%80%94-long-live-gay-nightlife

3. Ian Kumamoto, "Gay Bars Have Been Closing En Masse. Maybe That's a Good Thing.," *Mic* (June 15, 2022), https://www.mic.com/identity/gay-bars -closing-queer-people-of-color

4. Clare Forstie, "After Closing Time: Ambivalence in Remembering a Small-City Lesbian Bar," in *Queer Nightlife*, eds. Kemi Adeyemi, Kareem Khubchandani, and Ramón H. Rivera-Servera (Ann Arbor: University of Michigan Press, 2021), 132.

5. "What Is Love," words and music by Dee Dee Halligan and Junior Torello, 2004, Hanseatic Musikverlag GMBH & Co. KG (GEMA). All rights administered by Warner-Tamerlane Publishing Corp. All rights reserved. Used by permission of ALFRED MUSIC.

6. I was not alone in learning about my people from tabloid television: Joshua Gamson, *Freaks Talk Back: Tabloid Talk Shows and Sexual Nonconformity* (Chicago: University of Chicago Press, 1998).

7. Matthew Singer, "In The City: The Story of Portland's Original All-Ages Gay Nightclub," *Willamette Week* (August 26, 2014), https://www.wweek.com/ portland/article-22975-in-the-city.html

8. Robin Will, "Portland's Legendary Youth Clubs: 1977–1998: Mildred's Palace, Metropolis, The City, Rage," *GLAPN* (August 19, 2018), https://www .glapn.org/6058CityNightclub.html

9. Marjorie Skinner, "Last Night in the City," *Portland Mercury* (August 27, 2014), https://www.portlandmercury.com/portland/last-night-in-the-city/ Content?oid=13398621

10. Japonica Brown-Saracino, "The Afterlife of Identity Politics: Gentrification, Critical Nostalgia, and the Commemoration of Lost Dyke Bars," *American Journal of Sociology* 126, no. 5 (March 1, 2021): 1017–1066; Juana María Rodríguez, "Public Notice from the Fucked Peepo: Xandra Ibarra's 'The Hookup/Displacement/Barhopping/Drama Tour,'" in *Queer Nightlife,* 211–221.

11. Gary David Comstock, *Violence Against Lesbians and Gay Men* (New York: Columbia University Press, 1991), 5; Leila J. Rupp and Susan K. Freeman, *Understanding and Teaching U.S. Lesbian, Gay, Bisexual, and Transgender History* (Madison: University of Wisconsin Press, 2014), 218.

12. Jason Whitesel, *Fat Gay Men* (New York: New York University Press, 2014); Caleb Luna, "Jockstraps and Crop Tops," in *Queer Nightlife,* 31–41; Brian Heyburn, "Gay Bars: A Sanctuary for All?" in *Our Happy Hours: LGBT Voices*

from the Gay Bars, eds. S. Renée Bess and Lee Lynch (Sardinia, Ohio: Flashpoint, 2017), 118–120; Kevin Gotkin, "Crip Club Vibes," *Catalyst: Feminism, Theory, Technoscience* 5, no. 1 (2019): 1–7.

13. Jesus Cisneros and Christian Bracho, "Undocuqueer Stress: How Safe Are 'Safe' Spaces, and for Whom?" *Journal of Homosexuality* 67, no. 11 (2020): 1491–1511.

14. Katy Steinmetz, "The Transgender Tipping Point," *Time* (June 9, 2014), http://time.com/135480/transgender-tipping-point/; Clare Forstie, "'Bittersweet' Emotions, Identities, and Sexualities: Insights from a Lesbian Community Space," in *Selves, Symbols and Sexualities: An Interactionist Anthology,* eds. Thomas S. Weinberg and Staci Newmahr (Thousand Oaks, CA: Sage, 2014), 183–200.

15. Kristen Hogan, *The Feminist Bookstore Movement: Lesbian Antiracism and Feminist Accountability* (Durham: Duke University Press, 2016).

16. Theodore Greene, "The Whiteness of Queer Urban Placemaking," in *The Gayborhood: From Sexual Liberation to Cosmopolitan Spectacle,* eds. Christopher T. Conner and Daniel Okamura (Lanham, MD: Rowman & Littlefield, 2021), 143–158; Ryan Stillwagon and Amin Ghaziani, "Queer Pop-Ups: A Cultural Innovation in Urban Life," *City & Community* 18, no. 3 (September 1, 2019): 874–895; Kemi Adeyemi, "The Practice of Slowness: Black Queer Women and the Right to the City," *GLQ: A Journal of Lesbian and Gay Studies* 25, no. 4 (October 1, 2019): 545–567; Rochella Thorpe, "'A House Where Queers Go': African-American Lesbian Nightlife in Detroit, 1940–1975," in *Inventing Lesbian Cultures in America,* ed. Ellen Lewin (Boston: Beacon, 1996), 40–61.

17. F. Scott Fitzgerald, *The Crack-Up* (New York: New Direction, 1956), 69. On ambivalence in queer thought, see also Heather Love, *Feeling Backward: Loss and the Politics of Queer History* (Cambridge, MA: Harvard University Press, 2007).

18. Greggor Mattson and Tory Sparks, "'We Have a Gay Bar Here.' You Don't Need a Coast to Be Cosmopolitan," in *Red State Blues,* 109–114.

19. Amin Ghaziani, "Post-Gay Collective Identity Construction," *Social Problems* 58, no. 1 (February 1, 2011): 99–125.

20. *Ohio Magazine* (January 2014).

21. When I came out, we were boycotting both Budweiser and Coors, and for whatever reason I've stayed loyal to the perfunctory taste of my gay youth.

22. For an extended meditation on this very question, see Jeremy Atherton Lin, *Gay Bar: Why We Went Out* (New York: Little, Brown, 2021).

23. Maria Luisa Maniscalco, "Serendipity in the Work of Robert K. Merton," in *Robert K Merton & Contemporary Sociology,* eds. Carlo Mongardini and Simonetta Tabboni (Abingdon: Transaction, 1998), 278.

24. Lin, *Gay Bar,* 13.

25. "Queer Heroes NW 2020: The City Nightclub," *GLAPN,* http://www.glapn.org/672020CityNightclub.html

26. Connor Reed and Thom Hilton, Portland's Wildest LGBTQ Bars That

Are Ready for Pride," *Eater Portland, OR* (June 1, 2022), https://pdx.eater.com/maps/portlands-best-queer-bars-lgbtq

Chapter 2

1. Lauren Slagter, "Future of Ann Arbor's LGBTQ-Friendly Courtyard Uncertain as Bookstore Closes," *Michigan Live* (November 11, 2018), https://www.mlive.com/news/ann-arbor/2018/11/common_language_braun_court.html

2. Greggor Mattson, "Are Gay Bars Closing? Using Business Listings to Infer Rates of Gay Bar Closure in the United States, 1977–2019," *Socius* 5 (January 1, 2019), https://doi.org/10.1177/2378023119894832

3. Billi Gordon, "Jim Toy: Advocate Extraordinaire, Persona Grata," *Huff-Post* (March 7, 2016), https://www.huffpost.com/entry/jim-toy-advocate-extraord_b_9343334

4. Jason A. Michael, "Ann Arbor's Aut Bar Announces Closure," *Pride Source* (June 9, 2020), https://pridesource.com/article/ann-arbors-aut-bar-announces-closure/

Chapter 3

1. Greggor Mattson, "Small-City Gay Bars, Big-City Urbanism," *City & Community* 19, no. 1 (2020): 76–97; Amin Ghaziani, "Cultural Archipelagos: New Directions in the Study of Sexuality and Space," *City & Community* 18, no. 1 (March 1, 2019): 4–22;Theodore Greene, "Queer Cultural Archipelagos Are New to Us," *City & Community* 18, no. 1 (2019): 23–29; Jen Jack Gieseking, *A Queer New York: Geographies of Lesbians, Dykes, and Queers* (New York: New York University Press, 2020).

2. Emma Mishel, "Discrimination Against Queer Women in the US Workforce: A Résumé Audit Study," *Socius* 2 (2016), https://journals.sagepub.com/doi/10.1177/2378023115621316; Emma Mishel, "Contextual Prejudice: How Occupational Context and Stereotypes Shape Bias Against Gay and Lesbian Employees," *Social Currents* 7, no. 4 (2020): 371–391.

3. Mattson, "Small-City Gay Bars, Big-City Urbanism."

4. When slurs are used as reclaimed words by LGBTQ+ people to describe themselves, I have left them in the text as is. When someone is referring to someone of a different identity than their own, I have redacted it.

5. On metronormativity, see Jack Halberstam, *In a Queer Time and Place: Transgender Bodies, Subcultural Lives* (New York: New York University Press, 2005). On the vibrancy of rural queerness, see Mary L. Gray, *Out in the Country: Youth, Media, and Queer Visibility in Rural America*, vol. 2 (New York: New York University Press, 2009); Scott Herring, *Another Country: Queer Anti-Urbanism* (New York: New York University Press, 2010); Miriam J. Abelson, *Men in Place: Trans Masculinity, Race, and Sexuality in America* (Minneapolis: University of Minnesota Press, 2019).

6. Emily Kazyak, "Disrupting Cultural Selves: Constructing Gay and Lesbian Identities in Rural Locales," *Qualitative Sociology* 34, no. 4 (2011): 561–581; Scott E. Branton, "Negotiating Organizational Identity: The Communica-

tive Resilience of Small-Town Gay Bars," *International Review of Qualitative Research*, (November 5, 2020), https://doi.org/10.1177/1940844720968186

7. Mattson, "Small-City Gay Bars, Big-City Urbanism."

8. Greggor Mattson, "Bar Districts as Subcultural Amenities," *City, Culture and Society* 6, no. 1 (2015): 1–8.

Chapter 4

1. Some people wanted the history chapter to come first, but this book isn't about the past but the present and future. God bless the historians who allow the sociologists to live un-chronologically!

2. Whether they were owned by gay people, however, was quite another matter. Straight people have always owned gay places and continue to. See, for example Will Fellows and Helen P. Branson, *Gay Bar: The Fabulous, True Story of a Daring Woman and Her Boys in the 1950s* (Madison: University of Wisconsin Press, 2010).

3. All information about the Garden of Allah is from the excellent community history: Don Paulson and Roger Simpson, *An Evening at the Garden of Allah: A Gay Cabaret in Seattle* (New York: Columbia University Press, 1996).

4. Ray Oldenburg, *The Great Good Place: Cafés, Coffee Shops, Bookstores, Bars, Hair Salons, and Other Hangouts at the Heart of a Community* (New York: Marlowe, 1989). More recently, historians have argued that a public sphere was also forming in domestic spaces. See Stephen Vider, *The Queerness of Home: Gender, Sexuality, and the Politics of Domesticity After World War II* (Chicago: University of Chicago Press, 2022).

5. Go read his forthcoming book on gay bars from Duke University Press, the introduction to which I was generously allowed to read.

6. Dennis Altman, *The Homosexualization of America, the Americanization of the Homosexual*, vol. 1 (New York: St. Martin's, 1982); John D'Emilio, "Capitalism and Gay Identity," in *Powers of Desire: The Politics of Sexuality*, eds. Ann Snitow, Christine Stansell, and Sharon Thompson (New York: Monthly Review, 1983), 100–113; Amy Gluckman and Betsy Reed, *Homo Economics: Capitalism, Community, and Lesbian and Gay Life* (New York and London: Routledge, 1997).

7. Richard F. Freitas, "'The Land at Our Feet': Preserving Pioneer Square's Queer Landscape," master's thesis, University of Washington, 2017, 9.

8. Eric Cervini, *The Deviant's War: The Homosexual vs. the United States of America* (New York: Picador, 2021); Anna Lvovsky, *Vice Patrol: Cops, Courts, and the Struggle over Urban Gay Life Before Stonewall* (Chicago and London: University of Chicago Press, 2021).

9. Gary L. Atkins, *Gay Seattle: Stories of Exile and Belonging* (Seattle: University of Washington Press, 2003).

10. Paulson and Simpson, *An Evening at the Garden of Allah*, 29.

11. George Chauncey, *Gay New York: Gender, Urban Culture, and the Making of the Gay Male World, 1890–1940* (New York: Basic, 1994), 228; Chad Heap, *Slumming: Sexual and Racial Encounters in American Nightlife* (Chicago: University of Chicago Press, 2010); Nan Alamilla Boyd, *Wide-Open Town: A His-*

tory of Queer San Francisco to 1965 (Berkeley and Los Angeles: University of California Press, 2005).

12. Esther Newton, *Mother Camp: Female Impersonators in America* (New York: Prentice Hall, 1972); Heap, *Slumming.*

13. Lvovsky, *Vice Patrol.*

14. Chauncey, *Gay New York,* 348; Nancy Achilles, "The Development of the Homosexual Bar as an Institution," in *Sexual Deviance,* eds. John Gagnon and Bill Simon (New York: Harper and Row, 1967), 228–244.

15. Allan Bérubé, *Coming Out Under Fire: The History of Gay Men and Women in World War Two* (New York: Free Press, 1992), 124, 271; Thomas Jacob Noel, "Gay Bars and the Emergence of the Denver Homosexual Community," *Social Science Journal* 15, no. 2 (1978): 59–74.

16. Boyd, *Wide-Open Town,* 125; Bérubé, *Coming Out Under Fire,* 271.

17. Edward W. Said, *Orientalism* (London: Routledge & Kegan Paul, 1978).

18. Paulson and Simpson, *An Evening at the Garden of Allah,* 121, 135.

19. Paulson and Simpson, *An Evening at the Garden of Allah,* xiii, 15; David L. Eng, *The Feeling of Kinship: Queer Liberalism and the Racialization of Intimacy* (Durham: Duke University Press, 2010); Christina B. Hanhardt, "Safe Space Out of Place," *QED: A Journal in GLBTQ Worldmaking* 3, no. 3 (2016): 121–125.

20. Paulson and Simpson, *An Evening at the Garden of Allah,* 67, 70.

21. Paulson and Simpson, *An Evening at the Garden of Allah,* 34.

22. Paulson and Simpson, *An Evening at the Garden of Allah,* 50, 63; Elizabeth Lapovsky Kennedy and Madeline D. Davis, *Boots of Leather, Slippers of Gold: The History of a Lesbian Community* (New York and London: Routledge, 1993); Nikki Lane, "All the Lesbians Are White, All the Villages Are Gay, but Some of Us Are Brave: Intersectionality, Belonging, and Black Queer Women's Scene Space in Washington DC," in *Lesbian Geographies: Gender, Power, and Place,* eds. Kath Browne and Eduarda Ferreira (London and New York: Routledge, 2016), 235–258.

23. Frank Perez and Jeffrey Palmquist, *In Exile: The History and Lore Surrounding New Orleans Gay Culture and Its Oldest Bar* (Hurlford, Scotland: LL-Publications, 2012), 40.

24. Aaron Lee Bachhofer II, "The Emergence and Evolution of the Gay and Bisexual Male Subculture in Oklahoma City, Oklahoma, 1889–2005," PhD dissertation (unpublished), Oklahoma State University-Stillwater, 2006.

25. Daneel Buring, *Lesbian and Gay Memphis: Building Communities Behind the Magnolia Curtain* (New York: Routledge, 1997), 38.

26. David Carter, *Stonewall: The Riots That Sparked the Gay Revolution* (New York: Macmillan, 2004), 70.

27. Lvovsky, *Vice Patrol,* 148.

28. Donald Webster [Sagarin, Cory Edward], *The Homosexual in America* (New York: Greenberg, 1951), 120.

29. Sidney Abbott and Barbara Love, *Sappho Was a Right-on Woman: A Liberated View of Lesbianism* (New York: Stein and Day, 1972). Quoted in Josh

Sides, *Erotic City: Sexual Revolutions & the Making of Modern San Francisco* (New York: Oxford University Press, 2009), 40.

30. Keith L. Moore, "Queen City of the Plains? Denver's Gay History 1940–1975," master's thesis, University of Colorado-Denver, 2014, 81.

31. John D'Emilio, *Sexual Politics, Sexual Communities* (Chicago: University of Chicago Press, 1998 [orig. 1983]), 32.

32. Allan Bérubé, *My Desire for History: Essays in Gay, Community, and Labor History* (Chapel Hill: University of North Carolina Press, 2011), 71.

33. D'Emilio, *Sexual Politics, Sexual Communities*, 33.

34. David K. Johnson, *The Lavender Scare: The Cold War Persecution of Gays and Lesbians in the Federal Government* (Chicago: University of Chicago Press, 2004); Cervini, *The Deviant's War*.

35. See, for example, Noel, "Gay Bars and the Emergence of the Denver Homosexual Community"; D'Emilio, *Sexual Politics, Sexual Communities*; Lvovsky, *Vice Patrol*.

36. Joseph Harry, "Urbanization and Gay Life," *Journal of Social Research* 10 (1974): 238–247.

37. Martin P. Levine, ed., *Gay Men: The Sociology of Male Homosexuality* (New York: HarperCollins, 1979), 148.

38. Elizabeth A. Armstrong and Suzanna M. Crage, "Movements and Memory: The Making of the Stonewall Myth," *American Sociological Review* 71, no. 5 (October 1, 2006): 724–751.

39. Katherine McFarland Bruce, *Pride Parades: How a Parade Changed the World* (New York: New York University Press, 2016).

40. Atkins, *Gay Seattle*.

41. Kevin McKenna and Michael Aguirre, "A Brief History of LGBTQ Activism in Seattle," *Seattle Civil Rights & Labor History Project* (Seattle: University of Washington Center for the Study of the Pacific Northwest, 2016), https://depts.washington.edu/civilr/lgbtq_history.htm; Julian Barr, "Pioneer Square and the Making of Queer Seattle," *GIS Public History Project* (2018), https://www.arcgis.com/apps/MapSeries/index.html?appid=594c28fb10b84bbda054 5a2846fb4d1b; Atkins, *Gay Seattle*, 109.

42. Northwest Lesbian & Gay History Museum Project, "1960s: Queen City Comes Out: Exploring Seattle's Lesbian and Gay History," *outhistory: It's About Time!*, https://outhistory.org/exhibits/show/queen-city-comes-out/pio neer-square/1960s

43. Barr, "Pioneer Square and the Making of Queer Seattle."

44. Marcia M. Gallo, *Different Daughters: A History of the Daughters of Bilitis and the Rise of the Lesbian Rights Movement* (Emeryville, CA: Seal, 2007).

45. Felice Newman, "Why I'm Not Dancing," in *Lavender Culture*, eds. Karla Jay and Allen Young (New York: Jove, 1978), 144.

46. Marc Stein, *City of Sisterly and Brotherly Loves: Lesbian and Gay Philadelphia, 1945–1972* (Chicago: University of Chicago Press, 2000); Tommi Avicolli Mecca, "It's All About Class," in *That's Revolting! Queer Strategies for Resisting*

Assimilation, ed. Mattilda Bernstein Sycamore (Brooklyn: Soft Skull, 2008), 29–38.

47. Christopher Agee, "Gayola: Police Professionalization and the Politics of San Francisco's Gay Bars, 1950–1968," *Journal of the History of Sexuality* 15, no. 3 (2006): 462–489.

48. Boyd, *Wide-Open Town*; Agee, "Gayola"; Fellows and Branson, *Gay Bar.*

49. The California date is well known. I thank Lucas Hilderbrand for pointing out the lateness of Virginia's legal case. See Patricia Cain, *Rainbow Rights: The Role of Lawyers and Courts in the Lesbian and Gay Civil Rights Movement* (Boulder: Routledge, 2000); Lvovsky, *Vice Patrol.*

50. Phillip Fucella points out that this was similar to arguments for gay literature and pornography: it was freedom to own, not freedom to make, that carried the day.

51. Boyd, *Wide-Open Town*, 62.

52. Mattilda Bernstein Sycamore, "There's More to Life Than Platinum: Challenging the Tyranny of Sweatshop-Produced Rainbow Flags and Participatory Patriarchy," in *That's Revolting!* (Berkeley: Soft Skull, 2008), 4; Priyank Jindal, "Sites of Resistance or Sites of Racism?" in *That's Revolting!* (Berkeley: Soft Skull, 2008), 39.

53. Erin O'Brien and Bob Perkoski, *Rust Belt Burlesque: The Softer Side of a Heavy Metal Town* (Athens, Ohio: Swallow, 2019).

54. Paulson and Simpson, *An Evening at the Garden of Allah*, 164.

55. Paulson and Simpson, *An Evening at the Garden of Allah*, 85, 98.

56. Paulson and Simpson, *An Evening at the Garden of Allah*, 166.

57. Paulson and Simpson, *An Evening at the Garden of Allah*, 108.

58. Paulson and Simpson, *An Evening at the Garden of Allah*, 144.

59. Paulson and Simpson, *An Evening at the Garden of Allah*, 167.

60. José Esteban Muñoz, *Cruising Utopia: The Then and There of Queer Futurity* (New York: New York University Press, 2009).

Chapter 5

1. The lesbian bar Sisters in Portland, Maine, had closed in 2005. See Clare Forstie, "After Closing Time: Ambivalence in Remembering a Small-City Lesbian Bar," in *Queer Nightlife,* eds. Kemi Adeyemi, Kareem Khubchandani, and Ramón H. Rivera-Servera (Ann Arbor: University of Michigan Press, 2021), 130–142.

2. Japonica Brown-Saracino, *How Places Make Us: Novel LBQ Identities in Four Small Cities* (Chicago: University of Chicago Press, 2017).

3. Ray Routhier, "Styxx, Portland's Biggest Gay Nightclub, Is Closing After 35 Years," *Portland Press Herald* (December 4, 2016), https://www.pressherald .com/2016/12/04/with-the-closure-of-styxx-portlands-only-gay-nightclub -some-worry-about-the-loss-of-a-cultural-center/

4. I don't name the individual out of their preference to center the flag and not their own identity: https://www.theriverofpride.com/the-river-of-prides -history/

5. Eva Reign, "This Pride Flag Redesign Represents LGBTQ+ Diversity—And

It's Going Viral," *Them* (June 11, 2018), https://www.them.us/story/pride-flag -redesign; Ben Deane, "The Philly Pride Flag, Explained," *Philadelphia Inquirer* (June 12, 2021), https://www.inquirer.com/philly-tips/philadelphia-pride-flag -20210612.html

6. Twilight Guard, "A Dying Breed," *Twilight Guard* (November), http:// www.thetwilightguard.org/tg_news.html

7. Hannah Cain, "Cusack, Ralph," *Querying the Past: LGBTQ Maine Oral History Project Collection* 43 (November 21, 2018), https://digitalcommons.usm .maine.edu/querying_ohproject/43

8. Kevin graciously allowed me to quote them by name.

9. Quote used with permission.

10. Will Fellows and Helen P. Branson, *Gay Bar: The Fabulous, True Story of a Daring Woman and Her Boys in the 1950s* (Madison: University of Wisconsin Press, 2010).

11. Jane Ward, *Respectably Queer: Diversity Culture in LGBT Activist Organizations* (Nashville: Vanderbilt University Press, 2008).

12. Elizabeth Clemente, "Blackstones at a Crossroads," *Portland Phoenix* (January 13, 2021), http://portlandphoenix.me/blackstones-at-a-crossroads/

13. Theodore Greene, "Gay Neighborhoods and the Rights of the Vicarious Citizen," *City & Community* 13, no. 2 (June 1, 2014): 99–118.

14. "River of Pride Flag at Pride Portland! 2019," *Pride Portland* (May 8, 2019), https://prideportland.org/press-releases/river-of-pride-flag-2019

15. Lauren Fox, "Let There Be Light: Once-Shattered and Shuttered Portland Gay Bar Opens Up to the World," *Boston Globe* (August 11, 2019), https:// www.bostonglobe.com/metro/2019/08/11/once-shattered-portland-gay-bar -has-found-new-light/R3jzuMTLMR0nZMvTs0qWeL/story.html; Brandon Voss, "Gay Bar Gets New Windows—28 Years After Vandals Smashed Them," *Logo TV News* (July 20, 2019), http://www.newnownext.com/portland-maine -gay-bar-blackstones-new-windows-vandals-broken/07/2019/; Troy R. Bennett, "28 Years After Vandals Smashed Its Glass, Portland's Last Gay Bar Has Windows Once Again," *Bangor Daily News* (July 18, 2019), http://bangordaily news.com/2019/07/18/news/28-years-after-vandals-smashed-its-glass-port lands-last-gay-bar-has-windows-once-again/

Chapter 6

1. Tim Hollis, *Florida's Miracle Strip: From Redneck Riviera to Emerald Coast* (Jackson: University Press of Mississippi, 2010); Harvey H. Jackson III, *The Rise and Decline of the Redneck Riviera: An Insider's History of the Florida-Alabama Coast* (Athens and London: University of Georgia Press, 2013); Jerry T. Watkins, *Queering the Redneck Riviera: Sexuality and the Rise of Florida Tourism* (Gainesville: University Press of Florida, 2018).

2. Greggor Mattson, "Small-City Gay Bars, Big-City Urbanism," *City & Community* 19, no. 1 (2020): 76–97; Clare Forstie, "Theory Making from the Middle: Researching LGBTQ Communities in Small Cities," *City & Community* 19, no. 1 (2020): 153–168.

3. Amin Ghaziani, "'Gay Enclaves Face Prospect of Being Passé: How Assimilation Affects the Spatial Expressions of Sexuality in the United States," *International Journal of Urban and Regional Research* 39, no. 4 (July 1, 2015): 756–771; Jason Orne, *Boystown: Sex and Community in Chicago* (Chicago: University of Chicago Press, 2017); Tyler Baldor, "No Girls Allowed?: Fluctuating Boundaries Between Gay Men and Straight Women in Gay Public Space," *Ethnography* 20, no. 4 (December 1, 2019): 419–442.

4. Jason Orne, "Gayborhood Change: The Intertwined Sexual and Racial Character of Assimilation in Chicago's Boystown," in *Home and Community for Queer Men of Color: The Intersection of Race and Sexuality*, eds. Jesús Gregorio Smith and C. Winter Han (Lanham, MD: Rowman & Littlefield, 2020), 85–106; Baldor, "No Girls Allowed?"

5. B. Joseph Pine II and James H. Gilmore, *The Experience Economy: Work Is Theater & Every Business a Stage* (Boston: Harvard Business School Press, 1999).

6. Shaka McGlotten, *Virtual Intimacies: Media, Affect, and Queer Sociality* (Albany: SUNY Press, 2013).

7. Tyler Baldor, "Acquainted Strangers: Thwarted Interaction in Digitally Mediated Urban Gay Bars," *Social Problems* 69, no. 1 (2022): 58–73.

8. Ryan Stillwagon and Amin Ghaziani, "Queer Pop-Ups: A Cultural Innovation in Urban Life," *City & Community* 18, no. 3 (September 1, 2019): 874–895.

9. Owner Kelly Sanders came up with the name with the help of "a lot of wine." See Shaun Treat, "A Farewell to Mable Peabody's Beauty Parlor and Chainsaw Repair," *We Denton Do It* (September 6, 2017), https://wedentondoit.com/blog/2017/9/6/a-farewell-to-mable-peabodys-beauty-parlor-and-chainsaw-repair

Chapter 7

1. José Esteban Muñoz, *Cruising Utopia: The Then and There of Queer Futurity* (New York: New York University Press, 2009).

2. Girl, you were so memorable, but I forgot to ask the spelling of your name.

3. Esther Newton, *Mother Camp: Female Impersonators in America* (New York: Prentice Hall, 1972), 3.

4. Lawrence La Fountain-Stokes, *Translocas: The Politics of Puerto Rican Drag and Trans Performance* (Ann Arbor: University of Michigan Press, 2021).

5. I prefer this living, fleshy, biological metaphor to describe how people animate these places. Others prefer the metaphors of archipelagos or constellations. See Amin Ghaziani, "Cultural Archipelagos: New Directions in the Study of Sexuality and Space," *City & Community* 18, no. 1 (March 1, 2019): 4–22; Jen Jack Gieseking, "Mapping Lesbian and Queer Lines of Desire: Constellations of Queer Urban Space," *Environment and Planning D: Society and Space* 38, no. 5 (2020): 941–960.

6. See, for example, Niall Brennan and David Gudelunas, eds., RuPaul's Drag Race *and the Shifting Visibility of Drag Culture: The Boundaries of Reality*

TV (London: Palgrave Macmillan, 2017); Cameron Crookston, *The Cultural Impact of RuPaul's Drag Race: Why Are We All Gagging?* (Bristol, UK: Intellect, 2020); Mark McCormack and Liam Wignall, "Drag Performers' Perspectives on the Mainstreaming of British Drag: Towards a Sociology of Contemporary Drag," *Sociology* (May 6, 2021), https://doi.org/10.1177/00380385211008387

7. Newton, *Mother Camp*, 5.

8. Troy R. Bennett, "No Longer Underground, Maine's Drag Queen Scene Is Mainstream and 'Finally Cool,'" *Bangor Daily News* (January 26, 2020), https://bangordailynews.com/2020/01/26/news/no-longer-underground -maines-drag-queen-scene-is-mainstream-and-finally-cool/

9. Patrick Saunders, "My Sister's Room Moving to Bigger Midtown Space," *Project Q Atlanta* (December 10, 2018), https://www.projectq.us/my-sisters -room-moving-to-bigger-midtown-space/

10. Katie Horowitz, *Drag, Interperformance, and the Trouble with Queerness* (London and New York: Routledge, 2019).

11. Piet Levy, "Drag Superstar Trixie Mattel Now Co-Owner of This Is It!, Oldest LGBTQ+ Bar in Wisconsin," *Milwaukee Journal Sentinel* (February 2, 2021), https://www.jsonline.com/story/entertainment/2021/02/02/drag-super star-trixie-mattel-now-co-owner-it-oldest-lgbtq-bar-wisconsin/4290883001/

12. Newton, *Mother Camp*; Leila J. Rupp and Verta Taylor, *Drag Queens at the 801 Cabaret* (Chicago: University of Chicago Press, 2003).

13. Lori Hall-Araujo, "Ambivalence and the 'American Dream' on *RuPaul's Drag Race*," *Film, Fashion & Consumption* 5, no. 2 (December 1, 2016): 233–241; John Mercer and Charlie Sarson, "Fifteen Seconds of Fame: *RuPaul's Drag Race*, Camp and 'Memeability,'" *Celebrity Studies* 11, no. 4 (October 1, 2020): 479–492; Zeena Feldman and Jamie Hakim, "From *Paris Is Burning* to #dragrace: Social Media and the Celebrification of Drag Culture," *Celebrity Studies* 11, no. 4 (October 1, 2020): 386–401; Crookston, *The Cultural Impact of RuPaul's Drag Race*; Dieter Brusselaers, "'Pick up a Book and Go Read': Art and Legitimacy in *RuPaul's Drag Race*," in RuPaul's Drag Race *and the Shifting Visibility of Drag Culture*, 45–59.

14. Horowitz, *Drag*; Jaime Hartless, "Questionably Queer: Understanding Straight Presence in the Post-Gay Bar," *Journal of Homosexuality* 66, no. 8 (July 3, 2019): 1035–1057.

15. I refer here only to the United States version of RPDR; the other national versions are more inclusive: Julia Yudelman, "The 'RuPaulitics' of Subjectification in *RuPaul's Drag Race*," in RuPaul's Drag Race *and the Shifting Visibility of Drag Culture*, 15–28; Brennan and Gudelunas, RuPaul's Drag Race *and the Shifting Visibility of Drag Culture*; Jonathan Ward, "Serving 'Reality' Television 'Realness': Reading *RuPaul's Drag Race* and Its Construction of Reality," *Comparative American Studies: An International Journal* 17, no. 1 (January 2, 2020): 23–40.

16. Jack Halberstam, *In a Queer Time and Place: Transgender Bodies, Subcultural Lives* (New York: New York University Press, 2005); Horowitz, *Drag*.

17. See Cory G. Collins, "Drag Race to the Bottom? Updated Notes on the

Aesthetic and Political Economy of *RuPaul's Drag Race*," *TSQ: Transgender Studies Quarterly* 4, no. 1 (February 1, 2017): 128–134.

18. This is not to imply that Cleveland queens are not worth $6,000 apiece, because they are!

19. Nishant Upadhyay, "'Can You Get More American Than Native American?': Drag and Settler Colonialism in *RuPaul's Drag Race*," *Cultural Studies* 33, no. 3 (May 4, 2019): 480–501; Ami Pomerantz, "Big-Girls Don't Cry: Portrayals of the Fat Body in *RuPaul's Drag Race*," in RuPaul's Drag Race *and the Shifting Visibility of Drag Culture*, 103–120; Sabrina Strings and Long T. Bui, "'She Is Not Acting, She Is,'" *Feminist Media Studies* 14, no. 5 (2014): 822–836; Matthew Goldmark, "National Drag: The Language of Inclusion in *RuPaul's Drag Race*," *GLQ: A Journal of Lesbian and Gay Studies* 21, no. 4 (October 1, 2015): 501–520. See also C. Winter Han, *Geisha of a Different Kind: Race and Sexuality in Gaysian America* (New York: New York University Press, 2015); La Fountain-Stokes, *Translocas*.

20. Feldman and Hakim, "From *Paris Is Burning* to #dragrace."

21. Hall-Araujo, "Ambivalence and the 'American Dream' on *RuPaul's Drag Race*"; Mercer and Sarson, "Fifteen Seconds of Fame"; Feldman and Hakim, "From *Paris Is Burning* to #dragrace"; Crookston, *The Cultural Impact of RuPaul's Drag Race*; Brusselaers, "'Pick up a Book and Go Read.'"

Chapter 8

1. Another way to describe what I am calling racial camp is *disidentification*. I leave it to others to tease out their interrelationship(s). See José Esteban Muñoz, *Disidentifications: Queers of Color and the Performance of Politics* (Minneapolis: University of Minnesota Press, 1999).

2. Susan Gubar, "Racial Camp in *The Producers* and *Bamboozled*," *Film Quarterly* 60, no. 2 (December 1, 2006): 26–37; Anna Pochmara and Justyna Wierzchowska, "Notes on the Uses of Black Camp," *Open Cultural Studies* 1, no. 1 (December 20, 2017): 696–700.

3. Gubar, "Racial Camp in *The Producers* and *Bamboozled*," 26.

4. Greggor Mattson, "Gay Bars and the Impact of the Coronavirus Pandemic in the United States," *SocArXiv* (June 16, 2021), https://doi.org/10.31235/osf.io/4uw6j

5. Martin F. Manalansan, *Global Divas: Filipino Gay Men in the Diaspora* (Durham: Duke University Press, 2003); Chong-suk Han, "Asian Girls Are Prettier: Gendered Presentations as Stigma Management Among Gay Asian Men," *Symbolic Interaction* 32, no. 2 (May 1, 2009): 106–122; C. Winter Han, *Geisha of a Different Kind: Race and Sexuality in Gaysian America* (New York: New York University Press, 2015).

6. David L. Eng, *The Feeling of Kinship: Queer Liberalism and the Racialization of Intimacy* (Durham: Duke University Press, 2010); Han, *Geisha of a Different Kind*, 97; Derek Ruez, "'I Never Felt Targeted as an Asian . . . Until I Went to a Gay Pub': Sexual Racism and the Aesthetic Geographies of the Bad Encounter," *Environment and Planning A: Economy and Space* 49, no. 4 (April 1,

2017): 893–910; C. Winter Han, *Racial Erotics: Gay Men of Color, Sexual Racism, and the Politics of Desire* (Seattle: University of Washington Press, 2021). Tan Hoang Nguyen might call this "the pleasures of subjection." Tan Hoang Nguyen, *A View from the Bottom: Asian American Masculinity and Sexual Representation* (Durham: Duke University Press, 2014), 27.

7. Kanalu G. Terry Young, *Rethinking the Native Hawaiian Past* (New York and London: Routledge, 1998), 52–53; Stephanie Nohelani Teves, "A Critical Reading of Aloha and Visual Sovereignty in Ke Kulana He Māhū," *International Journal of Critical Indigenous Studies* 7, no. 1 (January 1, 2014): 1–17; Jamaica Heolimeleikalani Osorio, *Remembering Our Intimacies: Moʻolelo, Aloha ʻĀina, and Ea* (Minneapolis: University of Minnesota Press, 2021).

8. I thank Chong-suk Han for this insight.

9. Han, *Geisha of a Different Kind*, 65.

10. Han, *Geisha of a Different Kind*; Karen Shimakawa, *National Abjection: The Asian American Body Onstage* (Durham: Duke University Press, 2002); Chong-suk Han and Kyung-Hee Choi, "Very Few People Say 'No Whites': Gay Men of Color and the Racial Politics of Desire," *Sociological Spectrum* 38, no. 3 (May 4, 2018): 145–161.

11. Sonali Patel, "'Brown Girls Can't Be Gay': Racism Experienced by Queer South Asian Women in the Toronto LGBTQ Community," *Journal of Lesbian Studies* 23, no. 3 (July 3, 2019): 410–423; Allan Bérubé, "How Gay Stays White and What Kind of White It Stays," in *The Making and Unmaking of Whiteness*, eds. B. B. Rasmussen et al. (Durham: Duke University Press, 2001), 234–265; Chong-suk Han, "They Don't Want to Cruise Your Type: Gay Men of Color and the Racial Politics of Exclusion," *Social Identities* 13, no. 1 (2007): 51–67.

12. Franklin Odo, *No Sword to Bury: Japanese Americans in Hawaii* (Philadelphia: Temple University Press, 2004), 200; Jonathan Y. Okamura, "Why There Are No Asian Americans in Hawaiʻi: The Continuing Significance of Local Identity," in *Asian American Family Life and Community*, ed. Franklin Ng (New York and London: Routledge, 2013), 251–268; Jim Carlton, "Hawaii's Governor Embodies Japanese-Americans' Rise in Island State," *Wall Street Journal* (December 5, 2016), https://www.wsj.com/articles/hawaiis-governor -embodies-japanese-americans-rise-in-island-state-1480933802

13. Han, *Geisha of a Different Kind*; Khoa Phan Howard, "The Creepy White Guy and the Helpless Asian: How Sexual Racism Persists in a Gay Interracial Friendship Group," *Social Problems* (September 8, 2021), https://doi.org/10.10 93/socpro/spab052

14. Hawaii: Life in a Plantation Society," *Library of Congress*, https://www .loc.gov/classroom-materials/immigration/japanese/hawaii-life-in-a-planta tion-society/

15. "Mr. Sun Cho Lee" by Keola and Kapono Beamer, from their 1975 album *Hawaii's Keola & Kapono Beamer* on Tantalus Records, now Starscape Music. Used with permission. Pidgin is also known as Hawaiian Creole English.

16. Stephanie Nohelani Teves, *Defiant Indigeneity: The Politics of Hawaiian Performance* (Chapel Hill: University of North Carolina Press, 2018).

17. Gubar, "Racial Camp in *The Producers* and *Bamboozled*," 26.

18. E. Patrick Johnson, "'Quare' Studies, or (Almost) Everything I Know About Queer Studies I Learned from My Grandmother," *Text and Performance Quarterly* 21, no. 1 (2001): 3.

19. Teves, *Defiant Indigeneity*.

20. Nguyen, *A View from the Bottom*; Chong-suk Han, Kristopher Proctor, and Kyung-Hee Choi, "I Know a Lot of Gay Asian Men Who Are Actually Tops: Managing and Negotiating Gay Racial Stigma," *Sexuality & Culture* 18, no. 2 (June 1, 2014): 219–234.

21. Manalansan, *Global Divas*; Greggor Mattson, "Style and the Value of Gay Nightlife: Homonormative Placemaking in San Francisco," *Urban Studies* (2015), https://doi.org/10.1177/0042098014555630

22. Andrea Castillo, "A Lifeline for LGBTQ Latinos on the Brink of Closure," *Los Angeles Times* (February 15, 2021), https://www.latimes.com/california/story/2021-02-15/a-lifeline-for-lgbtq-latinos-on-the-brink-of-closure; Julie Compton, "Black-Owned Gay Bars Are Dwindling. Can They Survive Covid?," *NBC News* (September 27, 2020), https://www.nbcnews.com/feature/nbc-out/black-owned-gay-bars-are-dwindling-can-they-survive-covid-n1241100; Maia McDonald, "Chicago Has One of the Country's Longest-Running Black-Owned Gay Bars—And It's on the South Side," *Block Club Chicago* (June 30, 2021), https://blockclubchicago.org/2021/06/30/jeffrey-pub-south-shore-chicago-has-one-of-the-countrys-longest-running-black-owned-gay-bars-and-its-right-in-south-shore/

23. See, for example, Darius Bost, "At the Club: Locating Early Black Gay AIDS Activism in Washington, D.C.," *Occasion* 12 (June 2018): 201; Jesus Cisneros and Christian Bracho, "Undocuqueer Stress: How Safe Are 'Safe' Spaces, and for Whom?" *Journal of Homosexuality* 67, no. 11 (2020): 1491–1511.

24. Theodore Greene, "Aberrations of 'Home': Gay Neighborhoods and the Experiences of Community Among GBQ Men of Color," in *The Handbook of Research on Black Males: Quantitative, Qualitative, and Multidisciplinary*, eds. Theodore S. Ransaw, C. P. Gause, and Richard Majors (East Lansing: Michigan State University Press, 2019), 189–209.

25. Elijah Anderson, *Black in White Space: The Enduring Impact of Color in Everyday Life* (Chicago: University of Chicago Press, 2022); Rasha Kardosh et al., "Minority Salience and the Overestimation of Individuals from Minority Groups in Perception and Memory," *Proceedings of the National Academy of Sciences* 119, no. 12 (2022): e2116884119.

26. Reuben A. Buford May, "Velvet Rope Racism, Racial Paranoia, and Cultural Scripts: Alleged Dress Code Discrimination in Urban Nightlife, 2000–2014," *City & Community* 17, no. 1 (2018): 44–64.

27. See, for example, Kemi Adeyemi, "The Practice of Slowness: Black Queer Women and the Right to the City," *GLQ: A Journal of Lesbian and Gay Studies* 25, no. 4 (October 1, 2019): 545–567; Richard T. Rodríguez, "Beyond

Boystown: Latinidad on the Outskirts of Queer Chicago Nightlife," *Latino Studies* 18, no. 2 (June 2020): 277–285; Kareem Khubchandani, *Ishtyle: Accenting Gay Indian Nightlife* (Ann Arbor: University of Michigan Press, 2020).

28. Theodore Greene, "Queer Cultural Archipelagos Are New to Us," *City & Community* 18, no. 1 (2019): 23–29; Theodore Greene, "The Whiteness of Queer Urban Placemaking," in *The Gayborhood: From Sexual Liberation to Cosmopolitan Spectacle*, eds. Christopher T. Conner and Daniel Okamura (Lanham, MD: Rowman & Littlefield, 2021), 143–158; madison moore, *Fabulous: The Rise of the Beautiful Eccentric* (New Haven: Yale University Press, 2018).

29. Ramón H. Rivera-Servera, *Performing Queer Latinidad: Dance, Sexuality, Politics* (Ann Arbor: University of Michigan Press, 2012), 143; see also Marcus Anthony Hunter, "The Nightly Round: Space, Social Capital, and Urban Black Nightlife," *City & Community* 9, no. 2 (April 13, 2010): 165–186.

30. Mia Tuan, *Forever Foreigners or Honorary Whites? The Asian Ethnic Experience Today* (New Brunswick and London: Rutgers University Press, 1998); Rosalind Chou and Joe R. Feagin, *Myth of the Model Minority: Asian Americans Facing Racism* (London and New York: Routledge, 2010); Muñoz, *Disidentifications*, 200.

31. Theodore Greene, "'You're Dancing on My Seat': Queer Subcultures and the Production of Place in Contemporary Gay Bars," *Subcultures: Studies in Symbolic Interaction* (2022): 137–166; see also Adeyemi, "The Practice of Slowness"; Rodríguez, "Beyond Boystown."

32. moore, *Fabulous*.

Chapter 9

1. Fiona Buckland, *Impossible Dance: Club Culture and Queer World-Making* (Middletown, CT: Wesleyan University Press, 2002); Juana María Rodríguez, *Queer Latinidad: Identity Practices, Discursive Spaces* (New York: New York University Press, 2003); Ramón H. Rivera-Servera, *Performing Queer Latinidad: Dance, Sexuality, Politics* (Ann Arbor: University of Michigan Press, 2012); Jafari S. Allen, *There's a Disco Ball Between Us: A Theory of Black Gay Life* (Durham: Duke University Press, 2022).

2. Amy L. Stone, "The Geography of Research on LGBTQ Life: Why Sociologists Should Study the South, Rural Queers, and Ordinary Cities," *Sociology Compass* 12, no. 11 (2018): e12638.

3. "Promoter On Focus," *Adelante* (November 2, 2009), https://adelante magazine.com/chicocobra-club-promoters/; "Welcome to the Insta-Hood!: Marty Sokol," *Ladycultblog* (blog) (June 23, 2018), https://ladycultblog.com/2018/06/23/welcome-to-the-insta-hood-marty-sokol/

4. Hugo Cervantes, "East LA's Club SCUM Hosts the Spanish-Language Queer Punk Party of Your Dreams," *Remezcla* (July 2, 2019), https://remezcla.com/features/music/la-club-scum-latin-queer-punk-party/ See also Daniel Jack Lyons, Daniel Hernandez, and Eve Lyons, "The Nightlife Outlaws of East Los Angeles," *New York Times* (October 19, 2019), https://www.nytimes.com/2019/10/19/style/the-nightlife-outlaws-of-east-los-angeles.html

5. Phillip Zonkel, "Club Cobra North Hollywood Gay Latino Bar to Re-Open This Week," *Q Voice News* (June 14, 2021), https://qvoicenews.com/2021/06/13/club-cobra-north-hollywood-gay-latino-bar-to-re-open-this-week/

6. "Top Latin Dance Spots in L.A. for a Muy Caliente Evening," *Discover Los Angeles* (October 24, 2019), https://www.discoverlosangeles.com/things-to-do/top-latin-dance-spots-in-la-for-a-muy-caliente-evening; See also Rivera-Servera, *Performing Queer Latinidad*; Richard T. Rodríguez, "Beyond Boystown: Latinidad on the Outskirts of Queer Chicago Nightlife," *Latino Studies* 18, no. 2 (June 2020): 277–285.

7. Chong-suk Han and Kyung-Hee Choi, "Very Few People Say 'No Whites': Gay Men of Color and the Racial Politics of Desire," *Sociological Spectrum* 38, no. 3 (May 4, 2018): 145–161; Chong-suk Han et al., "West Hollywood Is Not That Big on Anything But White People: Constructing 'Gay Men of Color,'" *The Sociological Quarterly* 58, no. 4 (2017): 721–737; Benjamin Forest, "West Hollywood as Symbol: The Significance of Place in the Construction of a Gay Identity," *Environment and Planning D: Society and Space* 13, no. 2 (1995): 133–157.

8. Nico Lang, "North Hollywood's Beloved Queer Latino Bar Celebrated Trans Joy—And Gave People Jobs," *Them* (December 18, 2020), https://www.them.us/story/club-cobra-north-hollywood-queer-spaces-closure-covid-19

9. Daniel Hernandez, "A Gay L.A. Nightclub Is Live-Streaming a Drag and Go-Go Show. How It Supports Performers," *Los Angeles Times* (March 22, 2020), https://www.latimes.com/entertainment-arts/story/2020-03-19/gay-nightlife-club-cobra-stream-performances-relief-fund

10. Zonkel, "Club Cobra North Hollywood Gay Latino Bar to Re-Open This Week."

11. Roman Navarrette, "Queery: Erick Velasco and Jose Resendez," *Los Angeles Blade* (August 27, 2020), https://www.losangelesblade.com/2020/08/26/queery-erick-velasco-and-jose-resendez/

12. Hernandez, "A Gay L.A. Nightclub Is Live-Streaming a Drag and Go-Go Show."

13. Lang, "North Hollywood's Beloved Queer Latino Bar Celebrated Trans Joy."

14. Zonkel, "Club Cobra North Hollywood Gay Latino Bar to Re-Open This Week."

15. Theodore Greene, "Queer Cultural Archipelagos Are New to Us," *City & Community* 18, no. 1 (2019): 23–29; Theodore Greene, "The Whiteness of Queer Urban Placemaking," in *The Gayborhood: From Sexual Liberation to Cosmopolitan Spectacle*, eds. Christopher T. Conner and Daniel Okamura (Lanham, MD: Rowman & Littlefield, 2021), 143–158.

Chapter 10

1. Amin Ghaziani, "Measuring Urban Sexual Cultures," *Theory and Society* 43 (2014): 371–393; Amin Ghaziani, *There Goes the Gayborhood?* (Princeton: Princeton University Press, 2015); Greggor Mattson, "Style and the Value of

Gay Nightlife: Homonormative Placemaking in San Francisco," *Urban Studies* (2015), https://doi.org/10.1177/0042098014555630

2. Laurie Delk, "New Exhibit at the San Diego History Center Sparkles and Shines," *Baltimore Sun* (June 17, 2019), https://www.baltimoresun.com/legen dary-drag-queens-of-san-diego-history-center-story.html; see also Clare Sears, *Arresting Dress: Cross-Dressing, Law, and Fascination in Nineteenth-Century San Francisco* (Durham: Duke University Press, 2014).

3. Ghaziani, *There Goes the Gayborhood?*; Wayne Brekhus, *Peacocks, Chameleons, Centaurs: Gay Suburbia and the Grammar of Social Identity* (Chicago: University of Chicago Press, 2003); Theodore Greene, "Gay Neighborhoods and the Rights of the Vicarious Citizen," *City & Community* 13, no. 2 (2014): 99–118.

4. Héctor Carrillo, *Pathways of Desire: The Sexual Migration of Mexican Gay Men* (Chicago: University of Chicago Press, 2018); Jason Orne, "Gayborhood Change," in *Home and Community for Queer Men of Color: The Intersection of Race and Sexuality*, eds. Jesús Gregorio Smith and C. Winter Han (Lanham, MD: Rowman & Littlefield, 2020), 85–106.

5. Carrillo, *Pathways of Desire*, 145.

6. Carrillo, *Pathways of Desire*, 135; Theodore Greene, "The Whiteness of Queer Urban Placemaking," in *The Gayborhood: From Sexual Liberation to Cosmopolitan Spectacle*, eds. Christopher T. Conner and Daniel Okamura (Lanham, MD: Rowman & Littlefield, 2021), 143–158; Jen Jack Gieseking, *A Queer New York: Geographies of Lesbians, Dykes, and Queers* (New York: New York University Press, 2020).

7. It closed in 2022 to provide more space for the booming Barrel & Board.

8. "MO's Is Celebrating 30 Years: A Legacy of Fun, Community & Love," https://urbanmos.com/

9. Nikki Lane, "All the Lesbians Are White, All the Villages Are Gay, but Some of Us Are Brave: Intersectionality, Belonging, and Black Queer Women's Scene Space in Washington DC," in *Lesbian Geographies: Gender, Power, and Place*, eds. Kath Browne and Eduarda Ferreira (London and New York: Routledge, 2016), 235–258; Kemi Adeyemi, "The Practice of Slowness: Black Queer Women and the Right to the City," *GLQ: A Journal of Lesbian and Gay Studies* 25, no. 4 (October 1, 2019): 545–567; Richard T. Rodríguez, "Beyond Boystown: Latinidad on the Outskirts of Queer Chicago Nightlife," *Latino Studies* 18, no. 2 (June 2020): 277–285, https://doi.org/10.1057/s41276-020-00247 -7; Kareem Khubchandani, *Ishtyle: Accenting Gay Indian Nightlife* (Ann Arbor: University of Michigan Press, 2020); Greene, "The Whiteness of Queer Urban Placemaking."

10. Theodore Greene, "'You're Dancing on My Seat': Queer Subcultures and the Production of Place in Contemporary Gay Bars," *Subcultures: Studies in Symbolic Interaction* (2022): 137–166.

11. Carrillo, *Pathways of Desire*, 134.

12. Christina B. Hanhardt, *Safe Space: Gay Neighborhood History and the Politics of Violence* (Durham: Duke University Press, 2013); Allan Bérubé,

"How Gay Stays White and What Kind of White It Stays," in *The Making and Unmaking of Whiteness,* eds. B. B. Rasmussen et al. (Durham: Duke University Press, 2001), 234–265; Theodore Greene, "Aberrations of 'Home': Gay Neighborhoods and the Experiences of Community Among GBQ Men of Color," in *The Handbook of Research on Black Males: Quantitative, Qualitative, and Multidisciplinary,* eds. Theodore S. Ransaw, C. P. Gause, and Richard Majors (East Lansing: Michigan State University Press, 2019), 189–209.

13. Jason Orne, *Boystown: Sex and Community in Chicago* (Chicago: University of Chicago Press, 2017); Ghaziani, *There Goes the Gayborhood?*; Greggor Mattson, "Bar Districts as Subcultural Amenities," *City, Culture and Society* 6, no. 1 (2015): 1–8; Ghaziani, "Measuring Urban Sexual Cultures."

14. "Paris A. San Agustin Quion," *San Diego Pride,* https://sdpride.org/paris-quion/

15. Albert H. Fulcher, ed., "Legendary: San Diego Drag Queens Honored at the San Diego History Center," *LGBTQ San Diego County News* (blog) (July 5, 2019), https://lgbtqsd.news/legendary/

16. San Diego LGBT News Staff, "Local Drag and Trans Activists to Be Honored on Friday Evening," *San Diego Gay and Lesbian News* (June 30, 2021).

17. Tim Bergling, *Reeling in the Years: Gay Men's Perspectives on Age and Ageism* (New York: Psychology Press, 2004); Imani Woody, "Aging Out: A Qualitative Exploration of Ageism and Heterosexism Among Aging African American Lesbians and Gay Men," *Journal of Homosexuality* 61, no. 1 (2014): 145–165; Paul Simpson, *Middle-Aged Gay Men, Ageing and Ageism: Over the Rainbow?* (Houndmills, Basingstoke, Hampshire: Palgrave Macmillan, 2015).

18. Mary L. Gray, *Out in the Country: Youth, Media, and Queer Visibility in Rural America,* vol. 2 (New York: New York University Press, 2009); Clare Forstie, "Theory Making from the Middle: Researching LGBTQ Communities in Small Cities," *City & Community* 19, no. 1 (2020): 153–168.

Chapter 11

1. Dereka Rushbrook, "Cities, Queer Space, and the Cosmopolitan Tourist," *GLQ: A Journal of Lesbian and Gay Studies* 8, no. 1 (2002): 183–206; Amin Ghaziani, *There Goes the Gayborhood?* (Princeton: Princeton University Press, 2015); Scott E. Branton, "Negotiating Organizational Identity: The Communicative Resilience of Small-Town Gay Bars," *International Review of Qualitative Research* (November 5, 2020), https://doi.org/10.1177/1940844720968186

2. Parts of this article adapted from Greggor Mattson and Tory Sparks, "'We Have a Gay Bar Here.' You Don't Need a Coast to Be Cosmopolitan," in *Red State Blues: Stories from Midwestern Life on the Left,* ed. Martha Bayne (Cleveland: Belt Publishing, 2018), 109–114. Used with permission. See also Greggor Mattson, "Small-City Gay Bars, Big-City Urbanism," *City & Community* 19, no. 1 (2020): 76–97.

3. Alison Gowans, "Resistance and Joy: Iowa City Pride Marks 50 Years

While Remembering History of Protest," *The Gazette* (June 28, 2020), https://www.thegazette.com/life/resistance-and-joy-iowa-city-pride-marks-50-years-while-remembering-history-of-protest/

4. "The Eden Girls," *Haus of Eden* (2018), https://officialhausofeden.wixsite.com/home

5. "Green with Envy. . . . Hazy Buchanan," *Drag Adventures* (blog) (February 28, 2018), https://dragadventures.wordpress.com/2018/02/28/hazy-buchanan/

6. Christine Hawes, "For I.C. Kings, Drag King Performances Are About More Than Theatrics," *Iowa City Press-Citizen* (June 8, 2018), https://www.press-citizen.com/story/life/2018/06/08/iowa-city-lgbtq-ic-kings-drag-troupe-studio-13/683013002/

7. Mary Helen Kennerly, "Nine Disability Friendly Businesses in Iowa City to Visit This Holiday Season," *Little Village* (blog) (November 7, 2018), https://littlevillagemag.com/nine-disability-friendly-businesses-in-iowa-city-to-visit-this-holiday-season/

8. Robyn Burns, "Queerness as/and Political Attunement: A Brief Response to Anderson & Knee (2020) *Queer Isolation or Queering Isolation?*" *Leisure Sciences* 43, no. 1–2 (March 1, 2021): 125–130; but see Gavin Brown, "Homonormativity: A Metropolitan Concept That Denigrates 'Ordinary' Gay Lives," *Journal of Homosexuality* 59, no. 7 (2012): 1065–1072.

9. Douglas Crimp, "Mario Montez, For Shame," in *Regarding Sedgwick: Essays on Queer Culture and Critical Theory,* eds. Stephen M. Barber and David L. Clark (London and New York: Routledge, 2002), 64; but see also Hiram Pérez, "You Can Have My Brown Body and Eat It, Too!" *Social Text* 23, no. 3–4 84–85 (September 21, 2005): 171–191.

10. Christine Hawes, "Sash Bash Offers Kink Education in Iowa City March 6–8," *The Real Mainstream* (blog), (March 5, 2020), https://therealmainstream.com/sash-bash-offers-kink-education-in-iowa-city-march-6-8/

11. Paul Brennan, "'Basix Is Staying Here': Beloved Cedar Rapids LGBTQ Bar Gets a New Owner," *Little Village* (January 24, 2022), https://littlevillagemag.com/basix-is-staying-here-beloved-cedar-rapids-lgbtq-bar-gets-a-new-owner/

12. CR Pride (June 3, 2022), https://www.facebook.com/CedarRapidsPride/posts/2715254615273657

Chapter 12

1. See, for example, the analysis by Christina B. Hanhardt, "Safe Space Out of Place," *QED: A Journal in GLBTQ Worldmaking* 3, no. 3 (2016): 121–125.

2. Hannah Quinlan and Rosie Hastings, *The UK Gay Bar Directory* (London: Arcadia Missa, 2017), i.

3. Portions of this chapter adapted from Greggor Mattson, "Post-Orlando Truth for You: Gay Bars Aren't 'Safe Spaces,'" *The Daily Beast* (June 18, 2016), https://www.thedailybeast.com/articles/2016/06/18/post-orlando-truth-for-you-gay-bars-aren-t-safe-spaces Copyrighted 2017. The Daily Beast Company

LLC. Used with permission. To which I would add: I had to pay *them* $625 to regain the rights to what I wrote, for which they originally paid *me* $500, I think!

4. Vanessa R. Panfil, "Gayborhoods as Criminogenic Space," in *The Gayborhood: From Sexual Liberation to Cosmopolitan Spectacle*, eds. Christopher T. Conner and Daniel Okamura (Lanham, MD: Rowman & Littlefield, 2021), 67–83.

5. James H. Sanders, Karen Hutzel, and Jennifer M. Miller, "White Folk in Black Spaces," *Journal of Cultural Research in Art Education* 27 (2009): 132; Elijah Anderson, *Black in White Space: The Enduring Impact of Color in Everyday Life* (Chicago: University of Chicago Press, 2022).

6. Jim Farber, "How 'Gay' Should a Gay Bar Be?" *New York Times* (June 24, 2017), https://www.nytimes.com/2017/06/24/fashion/how-gay-should-a-gay -bar-be.html

7. Matt Lavietes, "James Bond Walks into a Gay Bar. But Should He?" *NBC News* (October 15, 2021), https://www.nbcnews.com/nbc-out/out-life-and -style/james-bond-walks-gay-bar-rcna3115

8. It was me. In Lavietes.

9. Dawne Moon, "Insult and Inclusion: The Term Fag Hag and Gay Male 'Community,'" *Social Forces* 74, no. 2 (1995): 487–510; Tyler Baldor, "No Girls Allowed? Fluctuating Boundaries Between Gay Men and Straight Women in Gay Public Space," *Ethnography* 20, no. 4 (December 1, 2019): 419–442.

10. See, for example, Christen McCurdy, "Lady Liquor: Straight Women, Gay Bars and Safe Spaces," *Bitch Media* (December 6, 2012), https://www. bitchmedia.org/post/lady-liquor-straight-women-gay-bars-and-safe-spaces -LGBT-discrimination; Jeremy Helligar, "5 Simple Rules for Straight Women in Gay Bars," *HuffPost* (March 20, 2014), https://www.huffpost.com/entry/5 -simple-rules-for-straight-women-in-gay-bars_b_4986849; Miz Cracker, "Beware the Bachelorette! A Report from the Straight Lady Invasion of Gay Bars," *Slate* (blog) (August 13, 2015), https://slate.com/human-interest/2015/ 08/should-straight-women-go-to-gay-bars-a-drag-queen-reports-on-the-lady -invasion.html; Laura Bell, "A Guide for Straight Women at Gay Bars, by a Queer Woman," *Vice* (blog) (May 15, 2018), https://www.vice.com/en/article/ vbqmn3/a-guide-for-straight-women-at-gay-bars-by-a-queer-woman See also Corey W. Johnson and Diane M. Samdahl, "'The Night They *Took* Over': Misogyny in a Country-Western Gay Bar," *Leisure Sciences* 27, no. 4 (July 1, 2005): 331–348.

11. Rose Dommu, "Dear Gay Men, Stop Telling Women They Can't Be in Gay Bars," *Out* (July 30, 2017), https://www.out.com/2017/7/30/dear-gay-men -stop-telling-women-they-cant-be-gay-bars; Chelsea Christene, "The Problem with Trying to Keep Women out of Gay Bars," *Ravishly* (May 10, 2019), https://ravishly.com/problem-trying-keep-women-out-gay-bars

12. Tatiana Matejskova, "Straights in a Gay Bar: Negotiating Boundaries Through Time-Spaces," in *Geographies of Sexualities: Theories, Practices, and Politics,* eds. Kath Browne, Jason Lim, and Gavin Brown (London: Routledge, 2007), 137–150; Baldor, "No Girls Allowed?"

13. Jaime Hartless, "Questionably Queer: Understanding Straight Presence in the Post-Gay Bar," *Journal of Homosexuality* 66, no. 8 (July 3, 2019): 1035–1057.

14. Mark Casey, "De-Dyking Queer Space(s): Heterosexual Female Visibility in Gay and Lesbian Spaces," *Sexualities* 7, no. 4 (November 1, 2004): 446–461; Jaime Hartless, "'They're Gay Bars, but They're Men Bars': Gendering Questionably Queer Spaces in a Southeastern US University Town," *Gender, Place & Culture* 25, no. 12 (December 2, 2018): 1781–1800.

15. Chloë Curran, "Get Out of My Gay Bar, Straight Girl," *Jezebel* (January 12, 2013), https://jezebel.com/get-out-of-my-gay-bar-straight-girl-5975192

16. Justin Torres, "In Praise of Latin Night at the Queer Club," *Washington Post* (June 13, 2016), https://www.washingtonpost.com/opinions/in-praise-of-latin-night-at-the-queer-club/2016/06/13/e841867e-317b-11e6-95c0-2a6873031302_story.html

17. Dan Savage, "What We Find in Gay Bars and Queer Clubs," *The Stranger* (June 15, 2016), https://www.thestranger.com/features/2016/06/15/24215049/sanctuary-what-we-find-in-gay-bars-and-queer-clubs

18. Jason Whitesel, *Fat Gay Men: Girth, Mirth, and the Politics of Stigma* (New York: New York University Press, 2014); Kevin Gotkin, "Crip Club Vibes," *Catalyst: Feminism, Theory, Technoscience* 5, no. 1 (2019): 1–7; Caleb Luna, "Jockstraps and Crop Tops," in *Queer Nightlife*, eds. Kemi Adeyemi, Kareem Khubchandani, and Ramón H. Rivera-Servera (Ann Arbor: University of Michigan Press, 2021), 31–41.

19. C. Winter Han, *Racial Erotics: Gay Men of Color, Sexual Racism, and the Politics of Desire* (Seattle: University of Washington Press, 2021); Marcus Anthony Hunter, "The Nightly Round: Space, Social Capital, and Urban Black Nightlife," *City & Community* 9, no. 2 (April 13, 2010): 201; Brandon Andrew Robinson, "'Personal Preference' as the New Racism: Gay Desire and Racial Cleansing in Cyberspace," *Sociology of Race and Ethnicity* 1, no. 2 (2015): 317–330.

20. Kristina B. Wolff and Carrie L. Cokely, "'To Protect and to Serve?': An Exploration of Police Conduct in Relation to the Gay, Lesbian, Bisexual, and Transgender Community," *Sexuality and Culture* 11, no. 2 (April 1, 2007): 1–23; Jared Leighton, "'All of Us Are Unapprehended Felons': Gay Liberation, the Black Panther Party, and Intercommunal Efforts Against Police Brutality in the Bay Area," *Journal of Social History* 52, no. 3 (January 1, 2019): 860–885.

21. Nicole Pasulka, "After Pulse Shooting, LGBT Folks of Color Worry About Increased Police Attention," *NPR* (August 3, 2016), https://www.npr.org/sections/codeswitch/2016/08/03/487610257/after-pulse-shooting-lgbt-folks-of-color-worry-about-increased-police-attention; Emma K. Russell, "Carceral Pride: The Fusion of Police Imagery with LGBTI Rights," *Feminist Legal Studies* 26, no. 3 (November 1, 2018): 331–350.

22. Christina B. Hanhardt, *Safe Space: Gay Neighborhood History and the Politics of Violence* (Durham: Duke University Press, 2013), 142, 161; Johan Andersson, "'Wilding' in the West Village: Queer Space, Racism and Jane Jacobs

Hagiography," *International Journal of Urban and Regional Research* 39, no. 2 (2015): 265–283.

23. Matt Baume, "51 Years After Stonewall, Police Raided Two Gay Bars Aiding Protestors," *Them* (June 5, 2020), https://www.them.us/story/police-raided-two-gay-bars-aiding-george-floyd-protestors

24. Christopher B. Stults et al., "Perceptions of Safety Among LGBTQ People Following the 2016 Pulse Nightclub Shooting," *Psychology of Sexual Orientation and Gender Diversity* 4, no. 3 (September 2017): 251–256.

25. Corey Antonio Rose, "Searching for a Kiki: SF's First Black-Owned Gay Bar," *KQED* (June 10, 2022), https://www.kqed.org/arts/13914457/rightnowish-searching-for-a-kiki-sfs-first-black-owned-gay-bar

26. Greggor Mattson, "Are Gay Bars Closing? Using Business Listings to Infer Rates of Gay Bar Closure in the United States, 1977–2019," *Socius* 5 (January 1, 2019), https://doi.org/10.1177/2378023119894832

27. Greggor Mattson, "Style and the Value of Gay Nightlife: Homonormative Placemaking in San Francisco," *Urban Studies* (2015), https://doi.org/10.1177/0042098014555630

28. Theodore Greene, "'You're Dancing on My Seat': Queer Subcultures and the Production of Place in Contemporary Gay Bars," *Subcultures: Studies in Symbolic Interaction* (2022): 137–166.

29. Robert W. Fieseler, *Tinderbox: The Untold Story of the Up Stairs Lounge Fire and the Rise of Gay Liberation* (New York: Liveright, 2018).

30. Mike Gordon, "Gordo's," *Anchorage Press* (July 24, 2014), https://www.anchoragepress.com/news/gordos/article_3049b04d-b46b-5bdc-8110-ce09305e164f.html

31. Caleb Downs, "Police: Man Who Shot 3 on San Antonio's Gay Strip Had Been Kicked out of Bar," *San Antonio News-Express* (October 8, 2018), https://www.mysanantonio.com/news/local/crime/article/SAPD-3-hospitalized-in-drive-by-shooting-outside-13289603.php

32. C. J. Pascoe, *Dude, You're a Fag: Masculinity and Sexuality in High School* (Berkeley and Los Angeles: University of California Press, 2007).

33. Moira Kenney, *Mapping Gay L.A.: The Intersection of Place and Politics* (Philadelphia: Temple University Press, 2001), 24; see also Malcolm Harris, "What's a 'Safe Space'? A Look at the Phrase's 50-Year History," *Splinter* (November 11, 2015),https://splinternews.com/what-s-a-safe-space-a-look-at-the-phrases-50-year-hi-1793852786

34. Harris, "What's a Safe Space?"

35. Brittney C. Cooper, *Beyond Respectability: The Intellectual Thought of Race Women* (Urbana: University of Illinois Press, 2017), 15.

36. Jeffrey DeShawn, *No Safe Space: My Journey from Little Black Boy to Black Gay Man in America* (Jeffrey DeShawn, 2020), 5.

37. Hanhardt, *Safe Space,* 30.

38. Hanhardt, *Safe Space,* 30.

39. Clare Forstie, "'Bittersweet' Emotions, Identities, and Sexualities: Insights from a Lesbian Community Space," in *Selves, Symbols and Sexualities:*

An *Interactionist Anthology,* eds. Thomas S. Weinberg and Staci Newmahr (Thousand Oaks, CA: Sage, 2014), 183–200.

40. *Supergay Detroit* (blog) (February 2008), http://supergaydetroit.blog spot.com/2008/02/

41. Jordan R, "Burnt: Episode 1, Introduction," *YouTube* (December 24, 2011), https://www.youtube.com/watch?v=Cq8SQYwwbJ0

42. Quinlan and Hastings, *The UK Gay Bar Directory,* i.

Chapter 13

1. Juana María Rodríguez, *Sexual Futures, Queer Gestures, and Other Latina Longings* (New York: New York University Press, 2014), 115–116.

2. "Profile of the Unauthorized Population: Fresno, County, CA," *Migration Policy Institute,* https://www.migrationpolicy.org/data/unauthorized -immigrant-population/county/6019

3. Grisanti Valencia, "Undocu-Queers: The Invisible Intersection Between Immigrant and LGBTQ Rights," *Community Alliance* (May 1, 2014), https://fres noalliance.com/undocu-queers-the-invisible-intersection-between-immi grant-and-lgbtq-rights/ Grisanti noted that she'd changed her last name and gained legal status since we spoke.

4. Jesus Cisneros and Christian Bracho, "Undocuqueer Stress: How Safe Are 'Safe' Spaces, and for Whom?" *Journal of Homosexuality* 67, no. 11 (2020): 1491–1511.

5. Katie L. Acosta, "Pulse: A Space for Resilience, A Home for the Brave," *QED: A Journal in GLBTQ Worldmaking* 3, no. 3 (2016): 107–110; Maya Chinchilla, "Church at Night," *GLQ: A Journal of Lesbian and Gay Studies* 24, no. 1 (2018): 3–8; Richard T. Rodríguez, "Beyond Boystown: Latinidad on the Outskirts of Queer Chicago Nightlife," *Latino Studies* 18, no. 2 (June 2020): 277–285; Héctor Carrillo, *Pathways of Desire: The Sexual Migration of Mexican Gay Men* (Chicago: University of Chicago Press, 2018).

6. A pseudonym, for obvious reasons.

7. Rodríguez, *Sexual Futures, Queer Gestures, and Other Latina Longings,* 27.

8. Ramón H. Rivera-Servera, *Performing Queer Latinidad: Dance, Sexuality, Politics* (Ann Arbor: University of Michigan Press, 2012); José Esteban Muñoz, *Disidentifications: Queers of Color and the Performance of Politics* (Minneapolis: University of Minnesota Press, 1999).

9. Rivera-Servera, *Performing Queer Latinidad*; Rodríguez, *Sexual Futures, Queer Gestures, and Other Latina Longings,* 114.

Chapter 14

1. In deference to the bar's main competition for patrons from the free activities of the Great Outdoors, I've taken the geographic definition of the U.S. Fish and Wildlife Service.

2. The conversation with Lady was reproduced from memory, not from a live transcription.

3. Eduardo Bonilla-Silva, *Racism Without Racists: Color-Blind Racism and*

the *Persistence of Racial Inequality in America* (Lanham, MD: Rowman & Little-field, 2009).

4. Loretta Ross, "Opinion: I'm a Black Feminist. I Think Call-Out Culture Is Toxic," *New York Times* (August 17, 2019), https://www.nytimes.com/2019/08/17/opinion/sunday/cancel-culture-call-out.html; Jessica Bennett, "What If Instead of Calling People Out, We Called Them In?" *New York Times* (November 19, 2020), https://www.nytimes.com/2020/11/19/style/loretta-ross-smith-college-cancel-culture.html

5. Linda Alcoff writes, "Certain privileged locations are discursively dangerous." Linda Alcoff, "The Problem of Speaking for Others," *Cultural Critique*, no. 20 (Winter 1991–1992): 5–32, quote on p. 7.

6. Gavin Brown, "Homonormativity: A Metropolitan Concept That Denigrates 'Ordinary' Gay Lives," *Journal of Homosexuality* 59, no. 7 (2012): 1065–1072; Judith Halberstam, *In a Queer Time and Place: Transgender Bodies, Subcultural Lives* (New York: New York University Press, 2005).

Chapter 15

1. America Counts Staff, "Oklahoma: 2020 Census: American Indian and Alaska Native Alone or in Combination," *U.S. Census Bureau* (August 25, 2021), "https://www.census.gov/library/stories/state-by-state/oklahoma-population-change-between-census-decade.html

2. Matthew L. M. Fletcher, "In 5–4 Ruling, Court Dramatically Expands the Power of States to Prosecute Crimes on Reservations," *SCOTUSblog* (blog) (June 29, 2022), https://www.scotusblog.com/2022/06/in-5-4-ruling-court-dramatically-expands-the-power-of-states-to-prosecute-crimes-on-reservations/

3. Dwanna L. McKay, "Oklahoma Is—and Always Has Been—Native Land," *The Conversation* (July 16, 2020), http://theconversation.com/oklahoma-is-and-always-has-been-native-land-142546; Fletcher, "In 5–4 Ruling, Court Dramatically Expands the Power of States to Prosecute Crimes on Reservations."

4. Roxanne Dunbar-Ortiz and Dina Gilio-Whitaker, *"All the Real Indians Died Off": And 20 Other Myths About Native Americans* (Boston: Beacon, 2016).

5. "Two-Spirit" does not always have the hyphen, although that is the most common spelling. When Indigenous people themselves do not use the hyphen, I follow their spelling.

6. Kirsten Matoy Carlson, "Oklahoma State Officials Resist Supreme Court Ruling Affirming Tribal Authority over American Indian Country," *The Conversation* (April 8, 2022), http://theconversation.com/oklahoma-state-officials-resist-supreme-court-ruling-affirming-tribal-authority-over-american-indian-country-175726

7. Qwo-Li Driskill, *Asegi Stories: Cherokee Queer and Two-Spirit Memory* (Tucson: University of Arizona Press, 2016), 5; Jenny L. Davis, "Refusing (Mis)Recognition: Navigating Multiple Marginalization in the US Two Spirit Movement," *Review of International American Studies* 12, no. 1 (2019): 65–86; Mark Rifkin, *When Did Indians Become Straight? Kinship, the History of Sexuality, and Native Sovereignty* (New York: Oxford University Press, 2010).

8. Noé López, "Muxes Have Crossed the Border: Altivas, Celebration, and Walls That Bleed," in *Queer Nightlife*, eds. Kemi Adeyemi, Kareem Khubchandani, and Ramón H. Rivera-Servera (Ann Arbor: University of Michigan Press, 2021), 171–179.

9. Scott Lauria Morgensen, *Spaces Between Us: Queer Settler Colonialism and Indigenous Decolonization* (Minneapolis: University of Minnesota Press, 2011), 168–172.

10. On the diversity among Two-Spirit and Indigenous peoples in North America, see Qwo-Li Driskill et al., eds., *Sovereign Erotics: A Collection of Two-Spirit Literature* (Tucson: University of Arizona Press, 2011). On the continuity between past, present, and future Two-Spirit people, see Kai Pyle, "Naming and Claiming: Recovering Ojibwe and Plains Cree Two-Spirit Language," *TSQ: Transgender Studies Quarterly* 5, no. 4 (November 1, 2018): 574–588; Margaret Robinson, "Two-Spirit Identity in a Time of Gender Fluidity," *Journal of Homosexuality* 67, no. 12 (October 14, 2020): 1675–1690.

11. See Dunbar-Ortiz and Gilio-Whitaker, *"All the Real Indians Died Off."*

12. Sage Chanell, "How Ms. Sage Chanell Learned to Shake Her Shells," *Into* (November 30, 2017), https://www.intomore.com/culture/how-ms-sage -chanell-learned-to-shake-her-shells/

13. I owe a debt in thinking through research ethics to Linda Tuhiwai Smith, *Decolonizing Methodologies: Research and Indigenous Peoples* (London: Zed Books, 2016). I don't claim that this chapter decolonizes anything, though—mere writing doesn't give anybody anything back what was taken.

14. For tools and inspiration, see Qwo-Li Driskill et al., eds., *Queer Indigenous Studies: Critical Interventions in Theory, Politics, and Literature* (Tucson: University of Arizona Press, 2011).

Chapter 16

1. EW Staff, "Best of Eugene 2015–2016," *Eugene Weekly* (November 5, 2015), https://eugeneweekly.com/2015/11/05/best-of-eugene-2015-2016/

2. EW Staff, "Best of Eugene 2015–2016."

3. See, for example, Bonnie J. Morris, *The Disappearing L: Erasure of Lesbian Spaces and Culture* (Albany: SUNY Press, 2016). On transgender and queer feminist objection to lesbian essentialism, see Ann Cvetkovich and Selena Wahng, "Don't Stop the Music: Roundtable Discussion with Workers from the Michigan Womyn's Music Festival," *GLQ: A Journal of Lesbian and Gay Studies* 7, no. 1 (2001): 131–151; Christopher Robinson, "Developing an Identity Model for Transgender and Intersex Inclusion in Lesbian Communities," *Journal of Lesbian Studies* 10, no. 1–2 (July 18, 2006): 181–199; Kath Browne, "Beyond Rural Idylls: Imperfect Lesbian Utopias at Michigan Womyn's Music Festival," *Journal of Rural Studies* 27, no. 1 (January 1, 2011): 13–23.

4. Matthew Denis, "Offering a Spectrum of Services," *Register-Guard* (February 11, 2019).

5. The Wayward Lamb (February 1, 2018), https://www.facebook.com/the waywardlamb/posts/2064712083815497

6. The Wayward Lamb (January 30, 2018), https://www.facebook.com/thewaywardlamb/posts/2063393817280657 The following quotes in this section are comments on the same Facebook post.

7. Meerah Powell, "A Light in the Dark," *Eugene Weekly* (August 9, 2018), https://www.eugeneweekly.com/2018/08/09/a-light-in-the-dark/; Ryan Nguyen, "New Gay Bar Will Open in Eugene After Community Collaboration and Tensions," *Daily Emerald* (November 10, 2018), https://www.dailyemerald.com/news/new-gay-bar-will-open-in-eugene-after-community-collaboration-and-tensions/article_1eeba639-1e58-5578-a821-877cdcf37837.html

8. "Spectrum: Bar | Restaurant | Events," *Spectrum*, https://www.spectrumeugene.com

9. Brady Wakayama, "New Gay Bar to Open in Downtown Eugene," *KEZI News* (May 22, 2018).

Chapter 17

1. Lesbians before the 1970s often referred to their bars as "gay bars"; see Elizabeth Lapovsky Kennedy and Madeline D. Davis, *Boots of Leather, Slippers of Gold: The History of a Lesbian Community* (New York and London: Routledge, 1993); Leslie Feinberg, *Stone Butch Blues* (Ithaca: Firebrand, 1993); Marie Cartier, *Baby, You Are My Religion: Women, Gay Bars, and Theology Before Stonewall* (London and New York: Routledge, 2013); Maxine Wolfe, "Invisible Women in Invisible Places: Lesbians, Lesbian Bars, and the Social Production of People/Environment Relationships," *Architecture and Behavior* 8, no. 2 (1992): 137–158; Greggor Mattson, "Are Gay Bars Closing? Using Business Listings to Infer Rates of Gay Bar Closure in the United States, 1977–2019," *Socius* 5 (January 1, 2019), https://doi.org/10.1177/2378023119894832

2. But not the only places, as attested by theaters, comics, and civic events: Catherine Davy, *Lady Dicks and Lesbian Brothers: Staging the Unimaginable at the WOW Café Theatre* (Ann Arbor: University of Michigan Press, 2010); Sara Warner, *Acts of Gaiety: LGBT Performance and the Politics of Pleasure* (Ann Arbor: University of Michigan Press, 2012); Amy L. Stone, *Queer Carnival: Festivals and Mardi Gras in the South* (New York: New York University Press, 2022).

3. For more on the analysis of this chapter, see Greggor Mattson, "The Impact of Lesbian Bar Ownership on USA Lesbian Bar Geographies: All-Gender/Straight-Integrated LGBTQ Places by Design," *Gender, Place & Culture* (June 1, 2022), https://doi.org/10.1080/0966369X.2022.2080644

4. Bryce J. Renninger, "Grindr Killed the Gay Bar, and Other Attempts to Blame Social Technologies for Urban Development: A Democratic Approach to Popular Technologies and Queer Sociality," *Journal of Homosexuality* 66, no. 12 (October 15, 2019): 1736–1755.

5. Robin, "The State of the Lesbian Bar: San Francisco Toasts to the End of an Era," *Autostraddle* (November 11, 2014), https://www.autostraddle.com/the-state-of-the-lesbian-bar-san-francisco-toasts-to-the-end-of-an-era-262072/

6. Anna Roth, "The Lexington Club Is Closing Because the Mission Has 'Dramatically Changed,'" *SF Weekly* (October 23, 2014), https://archives.sf

weekly.com/foodie/2014/10/23/the-lexington-club-is-closing-because-the
-mission-has-dramatically-changed

7. Jeremy Atherton Lin, *Gay Bar: Why We Went Out* (New York: Little, Brown, 2021), 157.

8. Karin Jaffie, "The History and the Mystery of San Francisco's Wild Side West," *San Francisco Bay Times* (August 24, 2017), http://sfbaytimes.com/hi story-mystery-san-franciscos-wild-side-west/

9. *Wild Side West,* https://www.wildsidewest.com

10. Melissa Anderson, "Why Are All the Lesbian Bars Disappearing?" *Village Voice* (June 21, 2017); Trish Bendix, "Where Did All the Lesbians Go? Reframing the Conversation About Dyke Bars and Nightlife," *Into* (December 13, 2017), https://www.intomore.com/culture/where-did-all-the-lesbians-go -reframing-the-conversation-about-dyke-bars-and-nightlife/; Krista Burton, "I Want My Lesbian Bars Back," *New York Times* (April 14, 2017); Sascha Cohen, "What Comes After the Death of the Lesbian Bar?" *Vice* (July 26, 2016); Ryan Kost, "Last Call for City's Last Lesbian Bar," *San Francisco Chronicle* (April 18, 2015); Mary Emily O'Hara, "Lesbian Bars Are Nearly Extinct and This Is Their Eulogy," *The Daily Dot* (September 25, 2015); Ellena Rosenthal, "Who Crushed the Lesbian Bars?" *Willamette Week* (November 30, 2016); JD Samson and Broadly Staff, "The Last Lesbian Bars," *Broadly* (October 22, 2015); Erika Star, "On the Death of Lesbian Bars," *The Frisky* (August 19, 2013).

11. "The Lesbian Bar Project," https://www.lesbianbarproject.com/ (as of September 7, 2022).

12. Mattson, "Are Gay Bars Closing?"

13. Mattson, "Are Gay Bars Closing?"

14. Lou Chibbaro Jr., "Lesbian Bar Project to the Rescue," *Los Angeles Blade* (August 19, 2021), https://www.losangelesblade.com/2021/08/19/lesbian-bar -project-to-the-rescue/

15. Mattson, "Are Gay Bars Closing?"

16. A. Finn Enke, *Finding the Movement: Sexuality, Contested Space, and Feminist Activism* (Durham: Duke University Press, 2007).

17. Kathy Jack, the co-manager of lesbian bar Sue Ellen's in Dallas, suggested this. See Mattson, "The Impact of Lesbian Bar Ownership on USA Lesbian Bar Geographies"; see also Beth E. Schneider and Nancy E. Stoller, *Women Resisting AIDS: Feminist Strategies of Empowerment* (Philadelphia: Temple University Press, 1995); Simon Watney, "Lesbian and Gay Studies in the Age of AIDS," in *Lesbian and Gay Studies: A Critical Introduction,* eds. Sally Munt and Andy Medhurst (London: Cassell, 1997), 368–384.

18. Clare Forstie, "'Bittersweet' Emotions, Identities, and Sexualities: Insights from a Lesbian Community Space," in *Selves, Symbols and Sexualities: An Interactionist Anthology,* eds. Thomas S. Weinberg and Staci Newmahr (Thousand Oaks, CA: Sage, 2014), 183–200.

19. Kennedy and Davis, *Boots of Leather, Slippers of Gold*; Feinberg, *Stone Butch Blues*; Gary L. Atkins, *Gay Seattle: Stories of Exile and Belonging* (Seattle: University of Washington Press, 2003), 59.

20. Ann Cvetkovich, *Depression: A Public Feeling* (Durham: Duke University Press Books, 2012), 68; Juana María Rodríguez, *Sexual Futures, Queer Gestures, and Other Latina Longings* (New York: New York University Press, 2014), 121.

21. Felice Newman, "Why I'm Not Dancing," in *Lavender Culture*, eds. Karla Jay and Allen Young (New York: Jove, 1978), 140–145; Sy Adler and Johanna Brenner, "Gender and Space: Lesbians and Gay Men in the City," *International Journal of Urban and Regional Research* 16, no. 1 (1992): 24–34; Julie A. Podmore and Line Chamberland, "Entering the Urban Frame: Early Lesbian Activism and Public Space in Montréal," *Journal of Lesbian Studies* 19, no. 2 (April 3, 2015): 192–211; Alexis Clements, *All We've Got* (Women Make Movies, 2019), https://www.wmm.com/catalog/film/all-weve-got/

22. Deborah Goleman Wolf, *The Lesbian Community* (Berkeley: University of California Press, 1979); Enke, *Finding the Movement*; Alexandra Diva Ketchum, "'Say "Hi" from Gaia': Women's Travel Guides and Lesbian Feminist Community Formation in the Pre-Internet Era (1975–1992)," *Feminist Media Studies* (September 18, 2019): 1–17.

23. Arlene Stein, *Sex and Sensibility: Stories of a Lesbian Generation* (Berkeley: University of California Press, 1997); Bonnie J. Morris, *The Disappearing L: Erasure of Lesbian Spaces and Culture* (Albany: SUNY Press, 2016); Jen Jack Gieseking, *A Queer New York: Geographies of Lesbians, Dykes, and Queers* (New York: New York University Press, 2020).

24. Enke, *Finding the Movement*; Morris, *The Disappearing L*.

25. Japonica Brown-Saracino, "From Situated Space to Social Space: Dyke Bar Commemoration as Reparative Action," *Journal of Lesbian Studies* 24, no. 3 (2020): 1–15; Japonica Brown-Saracino, "The Afterlife of Identity Politics: Gentrification, Critical Nostalgia, and the Commemoration of Lost Dyke Bars," *American Journal of Sociology* 126, no. 5 (March 1, 2021): 1017–1066.

26. Mark Casey, "De-Dyking Queer Space(s): Heterosexual Female Visibility in Gay and Lesbian Spaces," *Sexualities* 7, no. 4 (November 1, 2004): 446–461; Jaime Hartless, "'They're Gay Bars, but They're Men Bars': Gendering Questionably Queer Spaces in a Southeastern US University Town," *Gender, Place & Culture* 25, no. 12 (December 2, 2018): 1781–1800.

27. Alex D. Ketchum, "Lost Spaces, Lost Technologies, and Lost People: Online History Projects Seek to Recover LGBTQ Spatial Histories," *Digital Humanities Quarterly* 14, no. 3 (2020); National Park Service, *LGBTQ America: A Theme Study of Lesbian, Gay, Bisexual, Transgender and Queer History* (Washington DC: Department of the Interior, 2016).

28. Anonymous, "London Lesbian Bars," *Lost Womyn's Space* (blog) (January 3, 2016), lostwomynsspace.blogspot.com; Anonymous, "Exhale Bar & Grill," *Lost Womyn's Space* (May 5, 2013), lostwomynsspace.blogspot.com; Anonymous, "Lick Club," *Lost Womyn's Space* (May 24, 2011), lostwomynsspace.blogspot.com; Anonymous, "Pi Bar," *Lost Womyn's Space* (September 10, 2013), lostwomynsspace.blogspot.com.

29. Anonymous, "Prism Bar and Grill," *Lost Womyn's Space* (October 30, 2011), lostwomynsspace.blogspot.com

30. Anonymous, "London Lesbian Bars," *Lost Womyn's Space* (January 3, 2016), lostwomynsspace.blogspot.com

31. Anonymous, "Exhale Bar & Grill," *Lost Womyn's Space* (May 5, 2013), lostwomynsspace.blogspot.com

32. Anonymous, "Six Degrees," *Lost Womyn's Space* (September 16, 2011), lostwomynsspace.blogspot.com

33. Anonymous, "Club Metro," *Lost Womyn's Space* (March 8, 2014), lostwomynsspace.blogspot.com; Anonymous, "The Dalloway," *Lost Womyn's Space* (March 8, 2015), lostwomynsspace.blogspot.com

34. Marke B., "Why SF's Iconic Dyke Bar, the Lexington Club, Is Closing," *48 Hills* (October 23, 2014), https://48hills.org/2014/10/lexington-club-closing-owner-says-higher-rent-gentrification-gender-inequality-hurt-iconic-lesbian-bar/#:~:text=We%20are%20closing%20because%20we,queer%20women%20living%20in%20it.

35. HalCall, "Perfect Neighborhood Bar," comment on Wild Side West, *Gay Cities* (n.d.), https://sanfrancisco.gaycities.com/bars/47-wild-side-west

36. MissionBernal comment in Todd Lappin, "Is Wild Side West Now San Francisco's Last Lesbian Bar?" *Bernalwood* (October 28, 2014), https://bernalwood.com/2014/10/28/is-wild-side-west-now-san-franciscos-last-lesbian-bar/

37. Marke B., "With Virgil's Closure, SF Loses Another Great Queer Space," *48 Hills* (February 24, 2021), https://48hills.org/2021/02/with-virgils-closure-sf-loses-another-great-queer-space/

38. Hartless, "'They're Gay Bars, but They're Men Bars.'"

Chapter 18

1. Some readers asked about the name: I never asked any of the owners about the names! How dumb of me! Gay bar names range from the banal to the bizarre, and each one has a story. That story will have to be told by someone else, particularly someone who finds out the story behind Mable Peabody's Beauty Supply and Chainsaw Repair. On lesbian bar numbers, see Greggor Mattson, "Are Gay Bars Closing? Using Business Listings to Infer Rates of Gay Bar Closure in the United States, 1977–2019," *Socius* 5 (January 1, 2019), https://doi.org/10.1177/2378023119894832

2. Anna Lvovsky, *Vice Patrol: Cops, Courts, and the Struggle over Urban Gay Life Before Stonewall* (Chicago and London: University of Chicago Press, 2021), 158.

3. Charlotte Canning, *The Most American Thing in America: Circuit Chautauqua as Performance* (Iowa City: University of Iowa Press, 2005).

4. Jesse McKinley, "Heard the One About Jamestown? State Bets Comedy Can Spark a Revival," *New York Times* (September 5, 2017), https://www.nytimes.com/2017/09/05/nyregion/national-comedy-center-jamestown.html

5. Esther Newton, *My Butch Career: A Memoir* (Durham: Duke University Press, 2018), 241.

6. I should have asked whether this was a racist *nom de guerre* or a racist appellation for an Indigenous person, or both, or something else.

7. Scott E. Branton and Cristin A. Compton, "There's No Such Things as a Gay Bar: Co-Sexuality and the Neoliberal Branding of Queer Spaces," *Management Communication Quarterly* 25, no. 1 (2021): 95.

Chapter 19

1. Trudy Ring, "'Christian' Foundation Is Huge Funder of Anti-LGBTQ Hate Groups," *Advocate* (March 19, 2019), https://www.advocate.com/religion/2019/3/19/christian-foundation-huge-funder-anti-lgbtq-hate-groups

2. Carol Mason, *Oklahomo: Lessons in Unqueering America* (Albany: SUNY Press, 2015).

3. M. V. Lee Badgett, "Beyond Biased Samples: Challenging the Myths on the Economic Status of Lesbians and Gay Men," *Homo Economics: Capitalism, Community, and Lesbian and Gay Life*, eds. Amy Gluckman and Betsy Reed (New York and London: Routledge, 1997), 65–71; Emma Mishel, "Discrimination Against Queer Women in the US Workforce: A Résumé Audit Study," *Socius* 2 (2016), https:doi.org/10.1177/2378023115621316

4. Greggor Mattson, "The Impact of Lesbian Bar Ownership on USA Lesbian Bar Geographies: All-Gender/Straight-Integrated LGBTQ Places by Design," *Gender, Place & Culture* (June 1, 2022), https://doi.org/10.1080/0966369X.2022.2080644

5. Moira Kenney, *Mapping Gay L.A.: The Intersection of Place and Politics* (Philadelphia: Temple University Press, 2001); The Roestone Collective, "Safe Space: Towards a Reconceptualization," *Antipode* 46, no. 5 (2014): 1346–1365; Brittney Cooper, "Stop Mocking 'Safe Spaces': What the Mizzou & Yale Backlash Is Really About," *Salon* (November 18, 2015), https://www.salon.com/2015/11/18/what_the_mizzou_yale_backlash_is_really_about_the_right_of_white_people_to_engage_in_racial_recklessness/; Matthew Feinberg and Robb Willer, "Moral Reframing: A Technique for Effective and Persuasive Communication Across Political Divides," *Social and Personality Psychology Compass* 13, no. 12 (2019): e12501.

6. Arlene Stein, *Sex and Sensibility: Stories of a Lesbian Generation* (Berkeley: University of California Press, 1997); A. Finn Enke, *Finding the Movement: Sexuality, Contested Space, and Feminist Activism* (Durham: Duke University Press, 2007); Jen Jack Gieseking, *A Queer New York: Geographies of Lesbians, Dykes, and Queers* (New York: New York University Press, 2020); Japonica Brown-Saracino, *How Places Make Us: Novel LBQ Identities in Four Small Cities* (Chicago: University of Chicago Press, 2017); Mattson, "The Impact of Lesbian Bar Ownership on USA Lesbian Bar Geographies."

7. Brown-Saracino, *How Places Make Us*; Mattson, "The Impact of Lesbian Bar Ownership on USA Lesbian Bar Geographies."

8. Joey L. Mogul, Andrea J. Ritchie, and Kay Whitlock, eds., *Queer (In)Justice* (Boston: Beacon, 2012); Eric A. Stanley, Dean Spade, and Queer (In)Justice, "Queering Prison Abolition, Now?" *American Quarterly* 64, no. 1 (2012):

115–127; Ali Greey, "Queer Inclusion Precludes (Black) Queer Disruption: Media Analysis of the Black Lives Matter Toronto Sit-in During Toronto Pride 2016," *Leisure Studies* 37, no. 6 (November 2, 2018): 662–676.

9. Gavin Brown, "Homonormativity: A Metropolitan Concept That Denigrates 'Ordinary' Gay Lives," *Journal of Homosexuality* 59, no. 7 (2012): 1065–1072.

Chapter 20

1. E. Patrick Johnson, *Black. Queer. Southern. Women.: An Oral History* (Chapel Hill: University of North Carolina Press, 2018), 21; E. Patrick Johnson, *Honeypot: Black Southern Women Who Love Women* (Durham: Duke University Press, 2019).

2. On the rarity of spaces for Black lesbians even in big cities, see Nikki Lane, "All the Lesbians Are White, All the Villages Are Gay, but Some of Us Are Brave: Intersectionality, Belonging, and Black Queer Women's Scene Space in Washington DC," in *Lesbian Geographies: Gender, Power, and Place*, eds. Kath Browne and Eduarda Ferreira (London and New York: Routledge, 2016), 235–258; Kemi Adeyemi, "The Practice of Slowness: Black Queer Women and the Right to the City," *GLQ: A Journal of Lesbian and Gay Studies* 25, no. 4 (October 1, 2019): 545–567.

3. Not that its patrons necessarily identify as "lesbian"; among the diverse Black lesbian communities in the United States, many other terms are often preferred. Mignon R. Moore, *Invisible Families: Gay Identities, Relationships, and Motherhood Among Black Women* (Berkeley and Los Angeles: University of California Press, 2011), 22.

4. Jerry Mitchell, "Controversial HB 1523 Now Mississippi's Law of Land," *Clarion-Ledger* (June 22, 2017), https://www.clarionledger.com/story/news/2017/ 06/22/controversial-hb-1523-now-mississippis-law-land/419941001/; Samantha Allen, "SCOTUS Lets Mississippi's HB 1523, America's Most Anti-LGBT Law, Stay in Place," *The Daily Beast* (January 11, 2018), https://www.thedailybeast.com/ scotus-lets-mississippis-hb-1523-americas-most-anti-lgbt-law-stay-in-place

5. "Pine Belt Pride 2019 to Be Celebrated in Hattiesburg," *WJTV* (September 22, 2019), https://www.wjtv.com/news/pine-belt-pride-2019-to-be-celebra ted-in-hattiesburg/

6. James H. Sanders, Karen Hutzel, and Jennifer M. Miller, "White Folk in Black Spaces," *Journal of Cultural Research in Art Education* 27 (2009): 132; Elijah Anderson, *Black in White Space: The Enduring Impact of Color in Everyday Life* (Chicago: University of Chicago Press, 2022).

7. Cathy J. Cohen, *The Boundaries of Blackness: AIDS and the Breakdown of Black Politics* (Chicago: University of Chicago Press, 1999).

8. On coming out and familial relations among LGBTQ+ communities of color, see Carlos Ulises Decena, *Tacit Subjects: Belonging and Same-Sex Desire Among Dominican Immigrant Men* (Durham: Duke University Press, 2011); Moore, *Invisible Families*.

9. Nikki Lane, *The Black Queer Work of Ratchet: Race, Gender, Sexuality, and the (Anti) Politics of Respectability* (Cham, Switzerland: Palgrave Macmillan, 2019).

10. Adeyemi, "The Practice of Slowness"; Lane, "All the Lesbians Are White, All the Villages Are Gay, but Some of Us Are Brave"; Rochella Thorpe, "'A House Where Queers Go': African-American Lesbian Nightlife in Detroit, 1940–1975," in *Inventing Lesbian Cultures in America*, ed. Ellen Lewin (Boston: Beacon, 1996), 40–61.

11. Marlon M. Bailey, *Butch Queens up in Pumps: Gender, Performance, and Ballroom Culture in Detroit* (Ann Arbor: University of Michigan Press, 2013).

12. Moore, *Invisible Families*; Valerie Q. Glass, "'We Are with Family': Black Lesbian Couples Negotiate Rituals with Extended Families," *Journal of GLBT Family Studies* 10, no. 1–2 (January 1, 2014): 79–100; Johnson, *Black. Queer. Southern. Women.*

13. Mignon R. Moore, "Lipstick or Timberlands? Meanings of Gender Presentation in Black Lesbian Communities," *Signs* 32, no. 1 (September 1, 2006): 113–139; Laura Lane-Steele, "Studs and Protest-Hypermasculinity: The Tomboyism Within Black Lesbian Female Masculinity," *Journal of Lesbian Studies* 15, no. 4 (2011): 480–492.

14. Shaka McGlotten, *Virtual Intimacies: Media, Affect, and Queer Sociality* (Albany: SUNY Press, 2013).

Chapter 21

1. Julie A. Podmore, "Gone 'Underground'? Lesbian Visibility and the Consolidation of Queer Space in Montréal," *Social & Cultural Geography* 7 (August 2006): 595–625; Bonnie J. Morris, *The Disappearing L: Erasure of Lesbian Spaces and Culture* (Albany: SUNY Press, 2016); Jen Jack Gieseking, *A Queer New York: Geographies of Lesbians, Dykes, and Queers* (New York: New York University Press, 2020); Kristin Esterberg, *Lesbian & Bisexual Identities* (Philadelphia: Temple University Press, 1997); Catherine J. Nash, "Trans Experiences in Lesbian and Queer Space," *Canadian Geographer / Le Géographe Canadien* 55, no. 2 (2011): 192–207; Clare Forstie, "'Bittersweet' Emotions, Identities, and Sexualities: Insights from a Lesbian Community Space," in *Selves, Symbols and Sexualities: An Interactionist Anthology,* eds. Thomas S. Weinberg and Staci Newmahr (Thousand Oaks, CA: Sage, 2014), 183–200.

2. Morris, *The Disappearing L*, 2.

3. Danika Worthington, "Blush and Blu: The Last Lesbian Bar Standing in Denver," *Denver Post* (blog) (June 11, 2017), https://www.denverpost.com/2017/06/11/blush-and-blu-the-last-lesbian-bar-in-denver/; Nic Austin, "How Denver's Blush & Blu Survives as a Last Remaining Lesbian Bar," *Advocate* (September 28, 2021), https://www.advocate.com/exclusives/2021/9/28/how-denvers-blush-blu-survives-last-remaining-lesbian-bar

4. Worthington, "Blush and Blu"; "Blush & Blu," *blushbludenver.com* (July 15, 2017); "All Humans Welcome," *Characters of Colfax* (blog) (April 3, 2018), https://charactersofcolfax.com/all-humans-welcome/

5. devworker1, "Cocktail Queens: Breaking Bar Standards at Blush & Blu," *OUT FRONT* (blog) (September 7, 2017), https://www.outfrontmagazine.com/cocktail-queens-breaking-bar-standards-blush-blu/

6. "Blush & Blu," *Lesbian Bar Project,* https://www.lesbianbarproject.com/blush-blu

7. Gabrielle Bye, "Blush & Blu Is One of the Last Lesbian Bars Left in the Country," *Westword* (May 18, 2021), https://www.westword.com/restaurants/blush-and-blu-is-one-of-the-last-remaining-lesbian-bars-in-the-country-11971873

8. Mark T. Fillmore and Jessica Weafer, "Alcohol Impairment of Behavior in Men and Women," *Addiction* 99, no. 10 (2004): 1237–1246.

9. Bye, "Blush & Blu Is One of the Last Lesbian Bars Left in the Country."

10. For more on drag kings, see Jae Basiliere, "Staging Dissents: Drag Kings, Resistance, and Feminist Masculinities," *Signs* 44, no. 4 (June 1, 2019): 979–1001; Katie Horowitz, *Drag, Interperformance, and the Trouble with Queerness* (London and New York: Routledge, 2019).

11. Tiney Ricciardi, "Denver Is Home to One of Just 21 Lesbian Bars in the U.S.; Here's Why It Matters," *Denver Post* (June 24, 2021), https://www.denverpost.com/2021/06/24/blush-blu-denver-lesbian-bars/

12. "Best LGBTQ Bar: Blush & Blu Denver," *Westword* (2021), https://www.westword.com/best-of/2021/arts-and-entertainment/best-lgbtq-bar-11960244

13. Tiney Ricciardi, "Denver's Only Lesbian Bar Is Being Sued for Racial Discrimination, Unfair Pay," *Denver Post* (November 16, 2021), https://www.denverpost.com/2021/11/16/blush-blu-lawsuit-racial-discrimnation-unfair-wages/

14. Ricciardi, "Denver's Only Lesbian Bar Is Being Sued for Racial Discrimination, Unfair Pay."

15. A. Finn Enke, *Finding the Movement: Sexuality, Contested Space, and Feminist Activism* (Durham: Duke University Press, 2007).

Chapter 22

1. Interview and site visit conducted by the incomparable Tory Sparks.

2. Allison Phillips and KatieBeth, "Betz Boenning, Owner of Walkers Pint & Lex Stath," *We ARE MKE* (podcast) (April 7, 2020), https://wearemke.libsyn.com/betz-boenning-owner-of-walkers-pint-lex-stath

3. "Most to Least Segregated Metro Regions in 2020: According to 2020 Census Data," *Other & Belonging Institute,* https://belonging.berkeley.edu/most-least-segregated-metro-regions-2020

4. Elly-Jean Nielsen, "Lesbian Camp: An Unearthing," *Journal of Lesbian Studies* 20, no. 1 (January 2, 2016): 116–135; Ann Cvetkovich, *An Archive of Feelings: Trauma, Sexuality, and Lesbian Public Cultures* (Durham: Duke University Press, 2003).

5. Staff writers, "Milwaukee All-Star: Walker's Pint Owner Bet-z Boenning," *On Milwaukee* (December 6, 2015), https://onmilwaukee.com/articles/betzpintallstar

6. Molly Snyder, "Where Have All the Lesbian Bars Gone?" *On Milwaukee* (June 3, 2021), https://onmilwaukee.com/articles/lesbianbarsdisappear

7. Snyder, "Where Have All the Lesbian Bars Gone?"

8. Bonnie J. Morris, *The Disappearing L: Erasure of Lesbian Spaces and Culture* (Albany: SUNY Press, 2016); Jen Jack Gieseking, *A Queer New York: Geographies of Lesbians, Dykes, and Queers* (New York: New York University Press, 2020).

9. A. Finn Enke, *Finding the Movement: Sexuality, Contested Space, and Feminist Activism* (Durham: Duke University Press, 2007).

Chapter 23

1. Andrew Childs, "Hyper or Hypo-Masculine? Re-Conceptualizing 'Hyper-Masculinity' Through Seattle's Gay, Leather Community," *Gender, Place & Culture* 23, no. 9 (September 1, 2016): 1315–1328; Joseph RG DeMarco, "Power and Control in Gay Strip Clubs," *Journal of Homosexuality* 53, no. 1–2 (2007): 111–127; Peter Hennen, "Bear Bodies, Bear Masculinity: Recuperation, Resistance, or Retreat?" *Gender and Society* 19, no. 1 (February 2005): 25–43.

2. Martin P. Levine, *Gay Macho: The Life and Death of the Homosexual Clone*, ed. and introduction by Michael Kimmel (New York: New York University Press, 1998).

3. Étienne Meunier and Jeffrey Escoffier, "Gay Collective Sex in New York City from the Late 1800s to Today," in *The Gayborhood: From Sexual Liberation to Cosmopolitan Spectacle,* eds. Christopher T. Conner and Daniel Okamura (Lanham, MD: Rowman & Littlefield, 2021), 85–105.

4. Jason Orne, *Boystown: Sex and Community in Chicago* (Chicago: University of Chicago Press, 2017), 54.

5. Greggor Mattson, "Gay Bars and the Impact of the COVID-19 Pandemic," *SocArXiv* (June 16, 2021), https://doi.org/10.31235/osf.io/4uw6j

6. Nara Schoenberg, "Northalsted Chamber Drops Boystown Name for Neighborhood," *Chicago Tribune* (September 23, 2020), https://www.chicago tribune.com/lifestyles/ct-life-boystown-name-change-tt-09232020-20200923 -wv2z5wyounau3owtjvcc6ac4dy-story.html

7. "About Us—Jackhammer," https://jackhammerchicago.com/about-us

8. William L. Leap, ed., *Public Sex / Gay Space* (New York: Columbia University Press, 1999).

9. Orne, *Boystown*.

10. "Menergy," originally by Patrick Cowley and released in 1981, was re-released posthumously with vocals by Sylvester in 1984 on ERC Records but licensed from Megatone Records. See also Joshua Gamson, *The Fabulous Sylvester: The Legend, the Music, the Seventies in San Francisco* (New York: Henry Holt, 2006).

11. Orne, *Boystown*.

12. Illinois Liquor Control Commission, *Local Liquor Commissioner's Handbook* (Springfield: State of Illinois, March 2019), 25–26.

13. John Rechy, *The Sexual Outlaw: A Documentary* (New York: Grove, 1977); Rusty Barrett, *From Drag Queens to Leathermen: Language, Gender, and Gay Male Subcultures* (New York: Oxford University Press, 2017).

14. Supporters of this view include Samuel R. Delaney, *Times Square Red, Times Square Blue* (New York: New York University Press, 1999); Alex Espinoza, *Cruising: An Intimate History of a Radical Pastime* (Los Angeles, The Unnamed Press, 2019); and Orne, *Boystown*. Rejectors of this view include Priyank Jindal, "Sites of Resistance or Sites of Racism?" in *That's Revolting! Queer Strategies for Resisting Assimilation*, ed. Mattilda Bernstein Sycamore (Berkeley: Soft Skull, 2008), 39–46; Eddie Gamboa, "Pedagogies of the Dark: Making Sense of Queer Nightlife," in *Queer Nightlife*, eds. Kemi Adeyemi, Kareem Khubchandani, and Ramón H. Rivera-Servera (Ann Arbor: University of Michigan Press, 2021), 91–100; C. Winter Han, *Racial Erotics: Gay Men of Color, Sexual Racism, and the Politics of Desire* (Seattle: University of Washington Press, 2021).

15. Amin Ghaziani, *There Goes the Gayborhood?* (Princeton: Princeton University Press, 2015), 249; see also Lauren Berlant and Michael Warner, "Sex in Public," *Critical Inquiry* 24, no. 2 (1998): 547–566.

16. Martin P. Levine, ed., *Gay Men: The Sociology of Male Homosexuality* (New York: HarperCollins, 1979), 155.

17. Greggor Mattson, "Are Gay Bars Closing? Using Business Listings to Infer Rates of Gay Bar Closure in the United States, 1977–2019," *Socius* 5 (January 1, 2019), https://doi.org/10.1177/2378023119894832

18. Lisa Duggan, "The New Homonormativity: The Sexual Politics of Neoliberalism," in *Materializing Democracy*, eds. Russ Castronovo and Dana D. Nelson (Durham: Duke University Press, 2002), 175–194; see also the critique by Gavin Brown, "Homonormativity: A Metropolitan Concept That Denigrates 'Ordinary' Gay Lives," *Journal of Homosexuality* 59, no. 7 (2012): 1065–1072.

19. Ela Przybylo, *Asexual Erotics: Intimate Readings of Compulsory Sexuality* (Columbus: Ohio State University Press, 2019).

20. Mike Miksche, "In an Era of Closing Leather Bars and Harness-Wearing Poseurs, Where Are the Real Leather Men?" *Slate* (June 29, 2017), https://slate.com/human-interest/2017/06/with-leather-bars-closing-and-poseurs-copying-the-aesthetic-where-are-real-leather-men.html; Edward Siddons, "Why Is the Gay Leather Scene Dying?" *The Guardian* (October 4, 2018), https://www.theguardian.com/lifeandstyle/2018/oct/04/why-is-gay-leather-scene-dying

21. Everyone disagrees about the old guard, but a definitive statement is Guy Baldwin, "The Old Guard: Classical Leather Culture Revisited," *Leatherati* (September 27, 2011), https://leatherati.com/the-old-guard-classical-leather-culture-revisited-4fdc796aa25

22. Staci Newmahr, "Rethinking Kink: Sadomasochism as Serious Leisure," *Qualitative Sociology* 33, no. 3 (September 1, 2010): 313–331.

23. Darren Langdridge and Jamie Lawson, "The Psychology of Puppy Play: A Phenomenological Investigation," *Archives of Sexual Behavior* 48, no. 7 (October 1, 2019): 2201–2215.

24. Alex Ross, *Wagnerism: Art and Politics in the Shadow of Music* (New York: Farrar, Straus and Giroux, 2020), 633.

25. See, for example, https://bearsimdisappointedin.tumblr.com/post/ 30884286992/bear-rape-culture/

26. Greggor Mattson, "The Impact of Lesbian Bar Ownership on USA Lesbian Bar Geographies: All-Gender/Straight-Integrated LGBTQ Places by Design," *Gender, Place & Culture* (June 1, 2022), https://doi.org/10.1080/096636 9X.2022.2080644

27. Orne, *Boystown*.

28. Kate Sosin, "Bar Installs Gender Policy After Complaint," *Windy City Times* (January 12, 2011), https://www.windycitytimes.com/lgbt/Bar-installs -gender-policy-after-complaint/30138.html

29. Andy Armano, "James Trycha," *Out Clique* (blog) (October 31, 2020), https://www.outclique.com/james-tyrcha/

30. See, for example, Mickey Keating, "Chicago's Jackhammer Nightclub Accused of Transphobia," *Instinct* (March 7, 2019), https://instinctmagazine .com/chicagos-jackhammer-nightclub-accused-of-transphobia/

31. "Men's Room IML with DJ Harvey," *RA* (May 26, 2017), https://ra.co/ events/951348

32. Dan Jakes, "Forget IHOP, 'Chicago's Best Worst Drag Show' at Jackhammer Is the Place to Be at 2 AM on a Monday," *Chicago Reader* (November 15, 2018), https://chicagoreader.com/arts-culture/forget-ihop-chicagos-best -worst-drag-show-at-jackhammer-is-the-place-to-be-at-2-am-on-a-monday/

33. Jake Wittich, "Andersonville Bar Owners Purchase Jackhammer Complex, Saving Iconic LGBTQ Bar from Closure," *Windy City Times* (October 10, 2018), https: //www.windycitytimes.com/lgbt/Andersonville-bar-owners-purchase -Jackhammer-Complex-saving-iconic-LGBTQ-bar-from-closure/64370.html

34. "Local Bar Owners Strike Deal to Save Jackhammer," *Go Pride* (October 10, 2018), https://chicago.gopride.com/news/article.cfm/articleid/986353 29#:~:text=Chicago%2C%20IL%20%2D%20Owners%20of%20The,maintain% 20brand%20continuity%20and%20legacy

Chapter 24

1. See Peter Hennen, "Bear Bodies, Bear Masculinity: Recuperation, Resistance, or Retreat?" *Gender and Society* 19, no. 1 (February 2005): 25–43.

2. Nick McGlynn, "Bearspace: Experiences of Fat GBQ Men in Spaces of the UK's Bear Community" (University of Brighton, 2022), https://blogs. brighton.ac.uk/ctsg/2022/02/02/bearspace-report/; Jason Whitesel, *Fat Gay Men: Girth, Mirth, and the Politics of Stigma* (New York: New York University Press, 2014).

3. Keith Garcia, "Popular Gay Bar The Wrangler Moving to Five Points This Summer," *Westword* (April 7, 2016), https://www.westword.com/restau rants/popular-gay-bar-the-wrangler-moving-to-five-points-this-summer-77 81429

4. Kristen Leigh Painter, "Ruling: Denver's Wrangler Bar Discriminated When It Turned Away Gay Man Dressed in Drag," *Denver Post* (August 4, 2014),

https://www.denverpost.com/2014/08/04/ruling-denvers-wrangler-bar-dis criminated-when-it-turned-away-gay-man-dressed-in-drag/

5. Kristen Leigh Painter, "Denver Bar Customer Leads Boycott After Being Turned Away While in Drag," *Denver Post* (September 19, 2013), https://www .denverpost.com/2013/09/19/denver-bar-customer-leads-boycott-after-being -turned-away-while-in-drag/

6. Painter, "Denver Bar Customer Leads Boycott After Being Turned Away While in Drag."

7. Sadie Gurman, "Colorado: Bar Discriminated Against Man in Drag," *AP News* (August 4, 2014), https://apnews.com/article/4d4358f35f9a4fc38530459ff 8f6ecb7

8. Gurman, "Colorado: Bar Discriminated Against Man in Drag,"

9. Associated Press, "Gayborhood Racism Is Long-Standing, Philadelphia Report Says," *NBC News* (January 23, 2017), https://www.nbcnews.com/fea ture/nbc-out/gayborhood-racism-long-standing-philadelphia-report-says-n7 11081

10. Allison Taylor, "'But Where Are the Dates?' Dating as a Central Site of Fat Femme Marginalisation in Queer Communities," *Psychology & Sexuality* 13, no. 1 (January 2, 2022): 57–68.

11. Danika Worthington, "Longtime Gay Bar Denver Wrangler Is Closing Its Doors After More Than 20 Years," *Denver Post* (May 14, 2018), https:// theknow.denverpost.com/2018/05/14/denver-wrangler-closing/184506/

12. Denny Patterson, "Denver Sweet Is Where the Bears Meet," *Out Front* (July 8, 2020), https://www.outfrontmagazine.com/denver-sweet-is-where-the-bears-meet/

13. Patterson, "Denver Sweet Is Where the Bears Meet."

Chapter 25

1. "What Is a Gay Eagle Bar—And Are They Right for Me?" *Queer in the World* (January 23, 2019), https://queerintheworld.com/gay-eagle-bar/

2. Kate Drabinski, "Iconic Baltimore Gay Bar The Eagle Is Finally Back— and Revamped," *Baltimore Sun* (February 7, 2017), https://www.baltimoresun .com/citypaper/bcp-020817-eats-and-drinks-the-eagle-20170207-story.html; Brandon Weigel and Ethan McLeod, "Iconic Leather Bar the Baltimore Eagle Has Closed amid Alleged Business Disputes," *Baltimore Fishbowl* (July 27, 2018), https://baltimorefishbowl.com/stories/iconic-leather-bar-the-balti more-eagle-has-closed-amid-alleged-business-disputes/

3. Steve Charing, "Baltimore Eagle Set to Take Flight," *Washington Blade* (January 11, 2017), https://www.washingtonblade.com/2017/01/11/baltimore -eagle-set-take-flight/

4. David Hudson, "Iconic Eagle Bar Set to Re-Open After Four-Year Clo- sure," *Gay Star News* (December 16, 2016), https://www.gaystarnews.com/arti cle/baltimore-eagle-bar-open-four-year/

5. Drabinski, "Iconic Baltimore Gay Bar The Eagle Is Finally Back—and Revamped."

6. @NihilSegniter, *Twitter* (7:48 AM July 26, 2018).

7. Wesley Case, "New Baltimore Eagle Still Soars," *Baltimore Sun* (July 21, 2017), https://digitaledition.baltimoresun.com/tribune/article_popover.aspx ?guid=a858d8aa-058c-4ccd-a6d5-be8837ddcd4c

8. Drabinski, "Iconic Baltimore Gay Bar The Eagle Is Finally Back—and Revamped."

9. Ethan McLeod, "Former Baltimore Eagle Operators Opening Their Own Club, Night Shift 2.0," *Baltimore Fishbowl* (September 12, 2019), https:// baltimorefishbowl.com/stories/former-baltimore-eagle-operators-opening -their-own-club-night-shift-2-0/. See also Sameer Rao, "Meet 7 of Baltimore's Baddest Drag Queens (and One King)," *Baltimore Sun* (January 13, 2020), https: //www.baltimoresun.com/entertainment/bs-fe-baltimores-baddest-drag -queens-20191212-20200113-otxab3xfjvcbdnaqhzos3yfday-story.html

10. Mike Miksche, "In an Era of Closing Leather Bars and Harness-Wearing Poseurs, Where Are the Real Leather Men?" *Slate* (June 29, 2017), https://slate .com/human-interest/2017/06/with-leather-bars-closing-and-poseurs-copying -the-aesthetic-where-are-real-leather-men.html; Edward Siddons, "Why Is the Gay Leather Scene Dying?" *The Guardian* (October 4, 2018), https://www.the guardian.com/lifeandstyle/2018/oct/04/why-is-gay-leather-scene-dying

11. Michael K. Lavers, "Baltimore Neighborhood's Gentrification Sparks Tension," *Washington Blade* (August 16, 2017), https://www.washingtonblade. com/2017/08/16/baltimore-lgbt-neighborhoods-gentrification-sparks-tension/

12. Raye Weigel, "We Are Kinda Unbreakable," *Baltimore Sun* (September 26, 2017), https://www.baltimoresun.com/citypaper/bcpnews-we-are-kinda -unbreakable-20170926-htmlstory.html

13. Weigel, "We Are Kinda Unbreakable."

14. Weigel, "We Are Kinda Unbreakable."

15. Weigel, "We Are Kinda Unbreakable."

16. John Riley, "Exclusive: The Internal Fighting That Brought Down the Baltimore Eagle," *Metro Weekly* (July 30, 2018), https://www.metroweekly.com /2018/07/exclusive-the-internal-fighting-that-brought-down-the-baltimore -eagle/

17. Ed Gunts, "Baltimore Eagle Owners Seek to Keep Liquor License in the Family, Future of the Club Remains Murky," *Baltimore Fishbowl* (November 27, 2018), https://baltimorefishbowl.com/stories/baltimore-eagle-owners -seek-to-keep-liquor-license-in-the-family-future-of-the-club-remains -murky/; Chris Kaltenbach, "Baltimore Eagle Bar Closes amid Internal Disputes; Owner Pledges to Reopen," *Baltimore Sun* (July 26, 2018), https://www .baltimoresun.com/entertainment/bs-fe-baltimore-eagle-20180726-story. html; Riley, "Exclusive"; Weigel and McLeod, "Iconic Leather Bar the Baltimore Eagle Has Closed amid Alleged Business Disputes."

18. Riley, "Exclusive."

Chapter 26

1. One reader asked for fact checking on this point, and all I can say is: I don't know of any older leather bars that have been uninterruptedly open without moving locations while remaining a leather bar.

2. Ken Schneck, *LGBTQ Cleveland: Images of America* (Charleston: Arcadia, 2018), 35.

3. Evan MacDonald, "Cleveland Club Where Two Shot, Two Stabbed Among Bars Approved for All-Star Week Late-Night Waivers," *Cleveland.com* (July 8, 2019), https://www.cleveland.com/crime/2019/07/cleveland-club-where-two-shot-two-stabbed-among-bars-approved-for-all-star-week-late-night-waivers.html

4. Greggor Mattson, "Before It Was Hingetown," in *Cleveland Neighborhood Guidebook*, eds. the staff of *Belt Magazine* (Cleveland: Belt Publishing, 2016), 53–56.

5. All quotes from the organizations' websites and social media as of July 2021. For more on the charity-raising parodic sorority of drag nuns, see Melissa M. Wilcox, *Queer Nuns: Religion, Activism, and Serious Parody* (New York: New York University Press, 2018).

6. Patrick Cooley, "Cleveland's Gay Bars Evolve in Age of Greater Tolerance," *Cleveland.com* (March 28, 2017), https://www.cleveland.com/entertainment/2017/03/clevelands_gay_bars_evolve_in.html

7. John Petkovic, "Gay Cleveland Through the Decades: The Clubs, Queens and Music That Brought Gay Culture into the Mainstream," *Cleveland Plain Dealer* (June 25, 2014), https://www.cleveland.com/bars/2014/06/gay_cleveland_through_the_deca.html

8. Petkovic, "Gay Cleveland Through the Decades."

9. The Stallion—Leather Stallion Saloon (June 4, 2020), https://www.facebook.com/permalink.php?story_fbid=3107002719343648&id=104975149546435

10. Ken Schneck, "We Say Goodbye to Bounce Nightclub Hinge Lounge," *Cleveland Magazine* (January 5, 2018), https://clevelandmagazine.com/in-the-cle/articles/we-say-goodbye-to-bounce-nightclub-hinge-lounge

11. Unicorn Motorcycle Club, http://www.unicorn-mc.org/index.php/homepage

12. Greggor Mattson, "Are Gay Bars Closing? Using Business Listings to Infer Rates of Gay Bar Closure in the United States, 1977–2019," *Socius* 5 (January 1, 2019), https://doi.org/10.1177/2378023119894832; Greggor Mattson, "Gay Bars and the Impact of the COVID-19 Pandemic," *SocArXiv* (June 16, 2021), https://doi.org/10.31235/osf.io/4uw6j

13. Unicorn Motorcycle Club.

14. Tyler Baldor, "Acquainted Strangers: Thwarted Interaction in Digitally Mediated Urban Gay Bars," *Social Problems* 69, no. 1 (2022): 58–73.

Chapter 27

1. Marlena Williams, "Stripping in Oregon," *Oregon Encyclopedia* (January 20, 2021), https://www.oregonencyclopedia.org/articles/stripping_in_oregon /; Andrew D. Jankowski, "The (Almost) Universal Guide to Enjoying Portland's Strip Clubs," *Vanguard* (blog) (February 8, 2017), https://psuvanguard .com/almost-universal-guide-to-enjoying-portland-strip-clubs/

2. Jason Orne, *Boystown: Sex and Community in Chicago* (Chicago: University of Chicago Press, 2017).

3. Fiona Buckland, *Impossible Dance: Club Culture and Queer World-Making* (Middletown, CT: Wesleyan University Press, 2002).

4. Byron Beck, "Stag PDX to Open in Old Town," *Go Local PDX* (May 1, 2015), http://m.golocalpdx.com/business/sneak-peek-stag-pdx-to-open-in -old-town

5. Sylvia Rodemeyer, "Stag Is One of the West Coast's Only Gay Strip Clubs," *Willamette Week* (June 9, 2018), https://www.wweek.com/bars/2018/06 /09/stag-is-one-of-the-west-coasts-only-gay-strip-clubs/

6. Alex Zielinski, "Gender Bender," *Portland Mercury* (March 22, 2012), https: //www.portlandmercury.com/portland/gender-bender/Content?oid=5809569; Alex Zielinski, "Silverado's Take on Inequal Entry Fees," *Portland Mercury* (March 22, 2012), http://blogtown.portlandmercury.com/BlogtownPDX/ar chives/2012/03/22/silverados-take-on-inequal-entry-fees

7. Zielinski, "Silverado's Take on Inequal Entry Fees."

8. Jankowski, "The (Almost) Universal Guide to Enjoying Portland's Strip Clubs."

9. Lizzy Acker, "Stag: Bar Review: Buck Naked," *Willamette Week* (June 9, 2015), https://www.wweek.com/portland/article-24856-stag-bar-review.html

10. I couldn't get in touch with him to register his reactions to our interview. People have the right to grow and change, even if that makes me an overprotective Pollyanna. I thus redact his last name, even though he signed an informed consent form allowing me to use his full name.

11. Jack Rushall, "So You're Queer, but You Don't Drink? Here's Where to Meet People in Portland," *Willamette Week* (September 8, 2017), https://www.wweek.com /bars/2017/09/08/so-youre-queer-but-you-dont-drink-heres-where-to-meet-people/

12. Bernadette Barton, *Stripped: More Stories from Exotic Dancers*, completely revised and updated (New York: New York University Press, 2017).

13. Barton, *Stripped.*

14. Omar Ali Mushtaq, "Erotic Capital and Queer Men of Color," in *The Gayborhood: From Sexual Liberation to Cosmopolitan Spectacle*, eds. Christopher T. Conner and Daniel Okamura (Lanham, MD: Rowman & Littlefield, 2021), 125–142.

15. tonotherapper, https://www.instagram.com/p/B5Er1OQn08u/

16. queerpartypdx, https://www.instagram.com/p/B6Rk-00BP7S/

17. nikkilev78, https://www.instagram.com/nikkilev78/

18. nikkilev78, https://www.instagram.com/p/BxIq7n1hKOg/

19. Elise Herron, "Sex-Positive Portland Is Creating More Space for Transgen-

der Strippers, but It Still Has Some Work to Do," *Willamette Week* (June 11, 2019), https://www.wweek.com/culture/2019/06/11/sex-positive-portland-is-creating -more-space-for-transgender-strippers-but-it-still-has-some-work-to-do/

20. Stag PDX, https://www.facebook.com/stagpdx/photos/a.447002282124 783/1372746072883728/

21. Herron, "Sex-Positive Portland Is Creating More Space for Transgender Strippers."

22. Herron, "Sex-Positive Portland Is Creating More Space for Transgender Strippers."

23. Herron, "Sex-Positive Portland Is Creating More Space for Transgender Strippers."

24. alexiscampbellstarr, Stag PDX (April 25, 2019), https://www.instagram .com/p/BwsG27wBJuI/

25. Andrew Jankowski, "An Overview of Portland's LGBTQ+ Nightlife for the Newcomer," *Portland Mercury* (June 6, 2019), https://www.portlandmercury .com/queer-issue-2019/2019/06/06/26594597/an-overview-of-portlands-lgbtq -nightlife-for-the-newcomer

Chapter 28

1. Greg Elmer, Sabrina Ward-Kimola, and Anthony Glyn Burton, "Crowd-funding During COVID-19: An International Comparison of Online Fundraising," *First Monday* (October 16, 2020), https://doi.org/10.5210/fm.v25i11.10869

2. Kavish Harjai, "Last Black-Owned Gay Bar in New York City Is Rallying to Survive COVID-19," *Now This News* (June 30, 2020), https://nowthisnews.com/ news/gay-bar-alibi-lounge-in-new-york-city-is-rallying-to-survive-covid-19

3. Lou Delaney, "The Founder of Harlem's First Black-Owned Gay Bar on Saving Queer Spaces," *Complex* (June 4, 2021), https://www.complex.com/ style/alibi-lounge-pride-2020

4. Michael Musto, "Gay Bar Owner Discusses Recent Arson Attacks, the Resilience of Harlem," *Logo TV News*, (July 10, 2019), http://www.newnownext .com/harlem-gay-bar-alexi-minko-alibi-lounge/07/2019/

5. Martin F. Manalansan, *Global Divas: Filipino Gay Men in the Diaspora* (Durham: Duke University Press, 2003); Lionel Cantú, *The Sexuality of Migration: Border Crossings and Mexican Immigrant Men*, eds. Nancy A. Naples and Salvador Vidal-Ortiz (New York: New York University Press, 2009); Fatima El-Tayeb, *European Others: Queering Ethnicity in Postnational Europe* (Minneapolis: University of Minnesota Press, 2011); Jin Haritaworn, *Queer Lovers and Hateful Others: Regenerating Violent Times and Places* (London: Pluto, 2015).

6. Matt Tracy, "Harlem Gay Bar Alibi Lounge Burglarized Again," *Gay City News* (July 29, 2020), https://gaycitynews.com/harlem-gay-bar-alibi-lounge -burglarized-again/

7. Erika Adams, "Alibi Lounge, One of the City's Only Black-Owned LGBTQ Bars, Is in Another Fight for Survival," *Eater New York* (March 23, 2021), https:// ny.eater.com/2021/3/23/22346390/harlem-alibi-lounge-fundraising-lease-re newal

8. Gwen Aviles, "Business Owner Fights to Save 'Last LGBTQIA+ Black Club in NYC,'" *NBC News* (February 17, 2019), https://www.nbcnews.com/feature/nbc-out/business-owner-fights-save-last-lgbtqia-black-club-nyc-n972296

9. Tim Teeman, "New York City LGBT Bar Owner's 'Relief' as Rainbow Flag Burning Suspect Is Caught," *The Daily Beast* (July 9, 2019), https://www.thedailybeast.com/new-york-city-lgbt-bar-owners-relief-as-rainbow-flag-burning-suspect-is-caught

10. Greggor Mattson, "Are Gay Bars Closing? Using Business Listings to Infer Rates of Gay Bar Closure in the United States, 1977–2019," *Socius* 5 (January 1, 2019), https://doi.org/10.1177/2378023119894832; Greggor Mattson, "Gay Bars and the Impact of the COVID-19 Pandemic," *SocArXiv* (June 16, 2021), https://doi.org/10.31235/osf.io/4uw6j

11. Jamal Jordan, "'The Energy Was Just Indescribable': Club Langston Didn't Go Quietly," *New York Times* (September 5, 2019), https://www.nytimes.com/2019/09/05/nyregion/club-langston-nyc.html

12. "Out & Open: Hear Their Stories," *Absolut,* https://www.absolut.com/us/out-and-open/

13. Ron Lee, "Lambda Lounge Provides Safe Space for Harlem's LGBTQ+ Community," *Spectrum News NY1* (June 28, 2021), https://www.ny1.com/nyc/all-boroughs/pride-month/2021/06/27/lambda-lounge-provides-safe-space-for-harlem-s-lgbtq--community

14. Erica Rose, personal communication (July 7, 2022).

15. https://www.gofundme.com/f/thisisitbar; Piet Levy, "Drag Superstar Trixie Mattel Now Co-Owner of This Is It!, Oldest LGBTQ+ Bar in Wisconsin," *Milwaukee Journal Sentinel* (February 2, 2021), https://www.jsonline.com/story/entertainment/2021/02/02/drag-superstar-trixie-mattel-now-co-owner-it-oldest-lgbtq-bar-wisconsin/4290883001/

16. Chris A. Barcelos, "'Bye-Bye Boobies': Normativity, Deservingness and Medicalisation in Transgender Medical Crowdfunding," *Culture, Health & Sexuality* 21, no. 12 (December 2, 2019): 1394–1408.

17. Trena M. Paulus and Katherine R. Roberts, "Crowdfunding a 'Real-Life Superhero': The Construction of Worthy Bodies in Medical Campaign Narratives," *Discourse, Context & Media* 21 (March 1, 2018): 64–72; Nora Kenworthy, "Like a Grinding Stone: How Crowdfunding Platforms Create, Perpetuate, and Value Health Inequities," *Medical Anthropology Quarterly* 35, no. 3 (2021): 327–345.

18. Alexia Arani, "Mutual Aid and Its Ambivalences: Lessons from Sick and Disabled Trans and Queer People of Color," *Feminist Studies* 46, no. 3 (2020): 653–662; Barcelos, "'Bye-Bye Boobies.'"

Chapter 29

1. On queer history in Roanoke, there is no better source than the excellent work by Samantha Rosenthal, *Living Queer History: Remembrance and Belonging in a Southern City* (Chapel Hill: University of North Carolina Press, 2021). The Park hardly registers in it, however.

2. Sarah McConnell, "How to Go Clubbing," *With Good Reason* (podcast) (February 8, 2019), https://www.withgoodreasonradio.org/episode/how-to-go -clubbing/

3. Mason Adams, "Roanoke's Gay Bar Scene Will Never Be the Same," *Vice* (June 27, 2017), https://www.vice.com/en_us/article/pay778/roanokes-gay -bar-scene-will-never-be-the-same; Rachel Barton, "Walking Tour: Gentrification and Queer Erasure in Roanoke, Virginia," *Notches* (April 27, 2017), http: //notchesblog.com/2017/04/27/walking-tour-gentrification-and-queer-era sure-in-roanoke-virginia/

4. Tiffany Holland, "Owner Donates The Park Dance Club to Roanoke Pride," *Roanoke Times* (June 8, 2015), https://www.roanoke.com/news/local/ owner-donates-the-park-dance-club-to-roanoke-pride/article_f0c04048-e329 -5622-831a-90f99f5ac878.html; Tiffany Holland, "The Park Dance Club in Roanoke Comes Back Stronger Than Ever," *Roanoke Times* (April 19, 2015), https:// www.roanoke.com/news/local/the-park-dance-club-in-roanoke-comes-back -stronger-than-ever/article_aa65c680-6f70-559f-b017-c123dac38f67.html

5. Cass Adair, "How to Go Clubbing," *With Good Reason* (podcast) (February 8, 2019), https://www.withgoodreasonradio.org/episode/how-to-go-club bing/

6. Richard Tate, "Two Sides of a Town," *Advocate* (November 7, 2000); "Editorial: The Other Stonewall," *Roanoke Times* (June 28, 2019), https://www. roanoke.com/opinion/editorials/editorial-the-other-stonewall/article_e8d5 6265-bb40-5285-8ee9-84e9f57c1866.html

7. Adams, "Roanoke's Gay Bar Scene Will Never Be the Same."

Chapter 30

1. Suzi Nash, "Ellen Braun: Getting Schooled on Longtime State College Staple," *Philadelphia Gay News* (August 13, 2015), https://epgn.com/2015/08/13/ ellen-braun-getting-schooled-on-longtime-state-college-staple/; Greggor Mattson, "Small-City Gay Bars, Big-City Urbanism," *City & Community* 19, no. 1 (2020): 76–97.

2. Kevin Briggs, "How Music Has Driven the Evolution of Chumley's in Downtown State College," *Centre Daily Times* (January 10, 2019), https://www .centredaily.com/entertainment/this-weekend/article224124180.html

3. Amin Ghaziani, *There Goes the Gayborhood?* (Princeton: Princeton University Press, 2015).

4. Briggs, "How Music Has Driven the Evolution of Chumley's in Downtown State College."

5. Peter Hennen, *Faeries, Bears, and Leathermen: Men in Community Queering the Masculine* (Chicago: University of Chicago Press, 2008).

6. Will Fellows and Helen P. Branson, *Gay Bar: The Fabulous, True Story of a Daring Woman and Her Boys in the 1950s* (Madison: University of Wisconsin Press, 2010).

Chapter 31

1. David Bauer, "Lords of an Underground Empire," *D Magazine* (June 1979), https://www.dmagazine.com/publications/d-magazine/1979/june/lords-of-an-underground-empire/; David Taffet, "The Over 30 Club: Caven Enterprises," *Dallas Voice* (May 16, 2014), https://dallasvoice.com/30-club-caven-enterprises/

2. Karen S. Wisely, "The 'Dallas Way' in the Gayborhood: The Creation of a Lesbian, Gay, Bisexual, and Transgender Community in Dallas, Texas, 1965–1986," master's thesis, University of North Texas, 2011, https://digital.library.unt.edu/ark:/67531/metadc103411/

3. Ilene Jacobs, "Ten LGBTQ-Friendly Clubs and Bars That Should Be on Your Radar," *10Best* (September 12, 2018), https://www.10best.com/destinations/texas/dallas/nightlife/gay-clubs/

4. "RVA 2019 Winners: Nightlife," *Dallas Voice* (2019), https://dallasvoice.com/rva-2019-nightlife-results/

5. See Greggor Mattson, "The Impact of Lesbian Bar Ownership on USA Lesbian Bar Geographies: All-Gender/Straight-Integrated LGBTQ Places by Design," *Gender, Place & Culture* (June 1, 2022), https://doi.org/10.1080/0966369X.2022.2080644

6. "RVA 2019 Winners: Nightlife."

7. "Station 4," *Dallas Morning News*, https://www.dallasnews.com/place/cGVnYXN1czpwbGFjZQ-NTkyOQ-TlRreU9R/Station-4/

8. Tammye Nash, "Dallas City Council Approves PegasusAblon Development," *Dallas Voice* (May 13, 2021), https://dallasvoice.com/dallas-city-council-approves-pegasusablon-development/

9. David Taffet, "Caven to Partner with Developer in New Residential/Retail Space on Cedar Springs," *Dallas Voice* (November 11, 2020), https://dallasvoice.com/caven-to-partner-with-developer-on-land-behind-bars/

10. Greggor Mattson, "Bar Districts as Subcultural Amenities," *City, Culture and Society* 6, no. 1 (2015): 1–8.

11. Rosin Saez, "Can Developer Mike Ablon's Oak Lawn Towers Keep the LGBTQ Neighborhood Intact?" *D Magazine* (November 20, 2020), http://www.dmagazine.com/frontburner/2020/11/can-developer-mike-ablons-oak-lawn-towers-keep-the-lgbtq-neighborhood-intact/

12. Saez, "Can Developer Mike Ablon's Oak Lawn Towers Keep the LGBTQ Neighborhood Intact?"

13. Bianca Montes, "Mike Ablon Details His Plans for Oak Lawn—His Most Ambitious Project Yet," *D Magazine* (January 19, 2022), https://www.dmagazine.com/publications/d-ceo/2022/january-february/mike-ablons-most-ambitious-project-yet/

14. Saez, "Can Developer Mike Ablon's Oak Lawn Towers Keep the LGBTQ Neighborhood Intact?"

15. Saez, "Can Developer Mike Ablon's Oak Lawn Towers Keep the LGBTQ Neighborhood Intact?"

16. The Gayborhood Neighbors Association, "Not the Only Choice," *Dallas Voice* (April 2, 2021), https://dallasvoice.com/not-the-only-choice/

17. The Gayborhood Neighbors Association, "Not the Only Choice."

18. The Diva, "The Dallas LGBTQ+ Community Needs Your Help to Save the Gayborhood," *Drag Star Diva* (February 28, 2021), https://dragstardiva. com/2021/02/the-dallas-lgbtq-community-needs-your-help-to-save-the -gayborhood/

Chapter 32

1. Giulia Heyward and Melissa Gray, "The Pandemic Is Hurting Gay and Lesbian Bars. The Consequences for the Community Could Be Devastating," *CNN* (November 22, 2020), https://www.cnn.com/2020/11/22/business/gay -lesbian-bars-covid-consequences-trnd/index.html; Nico Lang, "Gay Bars Bet on Virtual Happy Hours to Save Them from Extinction," *Vice* (April 15, 2020), https://www.vice.com/en_us/article/qjdy8q/gay-bars-bet-on-virtual-happy -hours-to-save-them-from-extinction; Liam Stack, "Can Gay Bars, an Anchor of N.Y.C. Nightlife, Survive the Pandemic?" *New York Times* (June 20, 2020), https://www.nytimes.com/2020/06/20/nyregion/nyc-gay-bars-pride.html

2. Portions of this chapter adapted from Greggor Mattson, "Shuttered by the Coronavirus, Many Gay Bars— Already Struggling—Are Now on Life Support," *The Conversation* (April 14, 2020), https://theconversation.com/shutter ed-by-the-coronavirus-many-gay-bars-already-struggling-are-now-on-life -support-135167. Used with permission.

3. Greggor Mattson, "Gay Bars and the Impact of the COVID-19 Pandemic," *SocArXiv* (June 16, 2021), https://doi.org/10.31235/osf.io/4uw6j

4. Amanda Kludt and Brenna Houck, "Restaurants and Bars Shuttered Across the U.S. in Light of Coronavirus Pandemic," *Eater* (March 15, 2020), https://www .eater.com/2020/3/15/21180761/coronavirus-restaurants-bars-closed-new-york-la -chicago

5. Austin R. Anderson and Eric Knee, "Queer Isolation or Queering Isolation? Reflecting upon the Ramifications of COVID-19 on the Future of Queer Leisure Spaces," *Leisure Sciences* 43, no. 1–2 (2021): 118–124; see also Eric Knee and Austin R. Anderson, "Queer Politics, the Gay Bar, and Hapless Victimhood During COVID-19: A Brief Response to Burns (2021) *Queerness as/and Political Attunement*," *Leisure Sciences* (May 11, 2021), https://doi.org/10.1080/0149 0400.2021.1919254

6. Nico Lang, "LGBTQ Party Scene Confronts 'Devastating' Coronavirus Crisis," *The Daily Beast* (March 21, 2020), https://www.thedailybeast.com/ lgbtq-party-scene-confronts-devastating-coronavirus-crisis

7. "Small Businesses Say They're Still Waiting for COVID-19 Relief Funds," *Morning Edition: NPR* (April 9, 2020), https://www.npr.org/2020/04/09/ 830474620/small-businesses-say-theyre-still-waiting-for-covid-19-relief -funds

8. Christopher Rugaber, "Gig Workers, Self-Employed Face Delays in Jobless Aid," *USA Today* (April 9, 2020), https://www.usatoday.com/story/money/ 2020/04/09/coronavirus-gig-workers-self-employed-delays-jobless-aid/512675 1002/

9. Lily Janiak, "S.F. Board of Supervisors Creates Music and Entertainment Venue Recovery Fund," *Datebook* (blog) (February 19, 2021), https://datebook.sfchronicle.com/entertainment/s-f-board-of-supervisors-creates-music-and-entertainment-venue-recovery-fund

10. Nolan Hicks, "NYC Lawmakers Push for Big Apple 'Drag Laureate,'" *New York Post* (October 26, 2021), https://nypost.com/2021/10/26/nyc-lawmakers-push-for-big-apple-drag-laureate/

11. "Support CT Rule Allowing Bars & Restaurants to Sell Beer/Liquor/Wine During COVID-19," *Change.org*, https://www.change.org/p/ned-lamont-support-connecticut-law-allowing-bars-restaurants-to-sell-beer-liquor-during-covid-19

12. Daniel Hernandez, "A Gay L.A. Nightclub Is Live-Streaming a Drag and Go-Go Show. How It Supports Performers," *Los Angeles Times* (March 22, 2020), https://www.latimes.com/entertainment-arts/story/2020-03-19/gay-nightlife-club-cobra-stream-performances-relief-fund

13. Phil Hall, "Norwalk's Troupe429 LGBTQ Bar Reopens as Pop-up Record Store," *Westfair Communications* (August 7, 2020), https://westfaironline.com/127245/norwalks-troupe429-lgbtq-bar-reopens-as-pop-up-record-store/; Robin Kish, "Troupe429, Iconic Connecticut Gay Bar, Is Staying Alive Through Music—Literally," *GO Mag* (August 13, 2020), http://gomag.com/article/troupe429-iconic-connecticut-gay-bar-is-staying-alive-through-music-literally/; Erin Kayata, "COVID Closed Norwalk LGBTQ Bar. But the Dance Floor Is Back—as a Record Store," *The Hour* (August 17, 2020), https://www.thehour.com/news/coronavirus/article/COVID-closed-Norwalk-LGBTQ-bar-But-the-dance-15488945.php; Staff reports, "Norwalk Record Enthusiasts Plan Record Store Day Celebration," *CT Post* (September 25, 2020), https://www.ctpost.com/news/article/Troupe429-celebrates-Record-Store-Day-in-Norwalk-15596722.php

14. https://recordstoreday.com/Store/23418; Staff reports, "Norwalk Record Enthusiasts Plan Record Store Day Celebration."

15. "RSVP to Record Store Gay! Troupe429 in Norwalk, CT" (2020), https://www.facebook.com/events/721676355231704/721676365231703/?active_tab=about

16. Lindsay Dawson, Ashley Kirzinger, and Jennifer Kates, "The Impact of the COVID-19 Pandemic on LGBT People," *Kaiser Family Foundation* (March 11, 2021), https://www.kff.org/coronavirus-covid-19/poll-finding/the-impact-of-the-covid-19-pandemic-on-lgbt-people/; Kevin C. Heslin and Jeffrey E. Hall, "Sexual Orientation Disparities in Risk Factors for Adverse COVID-19–Related Outcomes, by Race/Ethnicity—Behavioral Risk Factor Surveillance System, United States, 2017–2019," *Morbidity and Mortality Weekly Report* 70 (February 5, 2021), https://doi.org/10.15585/mmwr.mm7005a1

17. Peter Kusnic, "Cleveland's Gay Bars Fought to Survive the Pandemic. Will Patrons Return?" *The Buckeye Flame* (March 3, 2022), https://thebuckeyeflame.com/2022/03/03/cleveland-gay-bars/

18. "New Review for Troupe429," https://www.instagram.com/p/Bk0wn pHAmO2/

Chapter 33

1. "A History of the National Archives Building, Washington, DC," *National Archives* (last reviewed June 27, 2022), https://www.archives.gov/about/history/building.html

2. Diana Taylor, *The Archive and the Repertoire: Performing Cultural Memory in the Americas* (Durham: Duke University Press, 2003), 16.

3. For this metaphor of "growing sideways" to describe the growth of LGBT children in light of heterosexist expectations for "growing up," see Kathryn Bond Stockton, *The Queer Child, or Growing Sideways in the Twentieth Century* (Durham: Duke University Press, 2009); E. Patrick Johnson, *No Tea, No Shade: New Writings in Black Queer Studies* (Durham: Duke University Press, 2016).

4. Ann Cvetovich asks us to consider how LGBT public culture constitutes an archive and argues that it affords a foundation for community, public recognition, and political rights: Ann Cvetkovich, *An Archive of Feelings: Trauma, Sexuality, and Lesbian Public Cultures* (Durham: Duke University Press, 2003). Historians rightfully dispute her late arrival to the world of archives and her lack of distinction between physical and metaphorical archives.

5. See the consecration by Martin B. Duberman, *Stonewall: The Definitive Story of the LGBTQ Rights Uprising That Changed America* (New York: Dutton, 1993).

6. "A History of the National Archives Building, Washington, DC"; Marc Stein, *The Stonewall Riots: A Documentary History* (New York: New York University Press, 2019), 2.

7. Stein, *The Stonewall Riots*, 2. The only autobiography of a midcentury gay bar owner is a straight woman's: Will Fellows and Helen P. Branson, *Gay Bar: The Fabulous, True Story of a Daring Woman and Her Boys in the 1950s* (Madison: University of Wisconsin Press, 2010).

8. Partially adapted from Greggor Mattson, "The Stonewall Riots Didn't Start the Gay Rights Movement," *JSTOR Daily* (June 12, 2019). Used with permission. The first to call Stonewall "the first" may have been Dick Leitsch, the executive director of the Mattachine Society of New York; see Stein, *The Stonewall Riots*, 78.

9. Much of this section relies heavily on the brilliant work of Elizabeth A. Armstrong and Suzanna M. Crage, "Movements and Memory: The Making of the Stonewall Myth," *American Sociological Review* 71, no. 5 (October 1, 2006): 724–751. It, in turn, relies heavily on the iconic John D'Emilio, *Sexual Politics, Sexual Communities* (Chicago: University of Chicago Press, 1998 [orig. 1983]).

10. Christopher Agee, "Gayola: Police Professionalization and the Politics of San Francisco's Gay Bars, 1950–1968," *Journal of the History of Sexuality* 15, no. 3 (2006): 462–489.

11. Susan Stryker, *Transgender History* (New York: Seal, 2008); Christina B. Hanhardt, *Safe Space: Gay Neighborhood History and the Politics of Violence* (Durham: Duke University Press, 2013), 73–78.

12. Armstrong and Crage, "Movements and Memory."

13. Armstrong and Crage, "Movements and Memory."

14. Simon Hall, "The American Gay Rights Movement and Patriotic Protest," *Journal of the History of Sexuality* 19, no. 3 (2010): 536–562.

15. Marc Stein, *City of Sisterly and Brotherly Loves: Lesbian and Gay Philadelphia, 1945–1972* (Chicago: University of Chicago Press, 2000).

16. Emily K. Hobson, *Lavender and Red: Liberation and Solidarity in the Gay and Lesbian Left* (Oakland: University of California Press, 2016).

17. Armstrong and Crage, "Movements and Memory."

18. Martin Meeker, "Behind the Mask of Respectability: Reconsidering the Mattachine Society and Male Homophile Practice, 1950s and 1960s," *Journal of the History of Sexuality* 10, no. 1 (2001): 78–116.

19. Carolyn Steedman, *Dust: The Archive and Cultural History* (New Brunswick: Rutgers University Press, 2002), 4.

20. David Carter, *Stonewall: The Riots That Sparked the Gay Revolution* (New York: Macmillan, 2004).

21. Katherine McFarland Bruce, *Pride Parades: How a Parade Changed the World* (New York: New York University Press, 2016); for example, Document 77 in Stein, *The Stonewall Riots*.

22. Carter, *Stonewall*.

23. Armstrong and Crage, "Movements and Memory."

24. Bruce, *Pride Parades*; C. J. Janovy, *No Place Like Home: Lessons in Activism from LGBT Kansas* (Lawrence: University Press of Kansas, 2019).

25. Armstrong and Crage, "Movements and Memory," 740.

26. Armstrong and Crage, "Movements and Memory," 724.

27. Obama White House, "Announcing the Stonewall National Monument," *YouTube* (June 24, 2016), https://www.youtube.com/watch?v=ywtvJy XDWkk

28. "Celebrating the New Stonewall National Monument," *U.S. Department of the Interior* (last edited September 29, 2021), https://www.doi.gov/photos/celebrating-new-stonewall-national-monument

29. Park ranger at Stonewall National Monument, email to the author (March 3, 2022); Congressional Research Service, "National Monuments and the Antiquities Act" (updated July 11, 2022), https://sgp.fas.org/crs/misc/R41330.pdf; National Park Service, "Foundation Document: Stonewall National Monument New York" (last updated June 24, 2021), https://www.nps.gov/ston/foundation-document.htm

30. As advertised on their "Friday Night Dance Party" between 2018 and 2020.

31. Steedman, *Dust*, 7.

32. National Park Service, "Foundation Document."

33. Steedman, *Dust*, 10.

34. Stein, *The Stonewall Riots*; Jason Baumann and the New York Public Library, eds., *The Stonewall Reader* (New York: Penguin, 2019).

35. See David M. Halperin, *How to Be Gay* (Cambridge, MA: Belknap, 2012), 21–24.

36. Danielle C. Skeehan, "Archive," *Early American Studies* 16, no. 4 (2018): 584–590.

37. Steedman, *Dust*.

38. Mary Emily O'Hara, "The Stonewall Inn Refused Entrance to a Blind Person," *Them* (June 6, 2018), https://www.them.us/story/stonewall-inn -refused-entrance-to-a-blind-person

39. Carolyn Steedman, "The Space of Memory: In an Archive," *History of the Human Sciences* 11, no. 4 (November 1, 1998): 67.

40. Stein, *The Stonewall Riots*, 17–18.

41. See, for example, "The History of Pride Part 2: Don't Forget the Leaders of the Movement," *Response for Teens: JCFS Chicago* (n.d.), https://www.jcfs .org/response/blog/history-pride-part2; Grant Rindner, "No One Knows Who Started the Stonewall Rebellion, but These Leaders Were Key," *Oprah Daily* (May 13, 2021), https://www.oprahdaily.com/life/a36319161/stonewall-riot -leaders/; Shane O'Neill, "Who Threw the First Brick at Stonewall? Let's Argue About It," *New York Times* (May 31, 2019), https://www.nytimes.com/2019/05/ 31/us/first-brick-at-stonewall-lgbtq.html

42. Jason Baumann and the New York Public Library, eds., "Sylvia Rivera, from Interview with Eric Marcus," in *The Stonewall Reader*, 141–147. See also Document 70 in Stein, *The Stonewall Riots*. There are many prejudices that influenced the reception of Rivera's testimonies; see Lawrence La Fountain-Stokes, "The Life and Times of Trans Activist Sylvia Rivera," in *Critical Dialogues in Latinx Studies: A Reader*, eds. Ana Y. Ramos-Zayas and Mérida M. Rúa (New York: New York University Press, 2021), 241–253.

43. Stein, *The Stonewall Riots*.

44. Duberman, *Stonewall*.

45. Document 82 in Stein, *The Stonewall Riots*. He does include bricks among a summary of items possibly thrown on page 5.

46. Chrysanthemum Tran, "When Remembering Stonewall, We Need to Listen to Those Who Were There," *Them* (June 11, 2018), https://www.them.us /story/who-threw-the-first-brick-at-stonewall; O'Neill, "Who Threw the First Brick at Stonewall?"

47. Jason Baumann and the New York Public Library, eds., "Marsha P. Johnson and Randy Wicker, from Interview with Eric Marcus," in *The Stonewall Reader*, 128–135.

48. Stein, *The Stonewall Riots*, 3.

49. Stein, *The Stonewall Riots*, 1.

50. Steedman, "The Space of Memory," 77.

51. In an influential formulation, José Muñoz defines "queer" as a "hori-

zon of futurity" that does not yet exist but that we yearn towards. See José Esteban Muñoz, *Cruising Utopia: The Then and There of Queer Futurity* (New York: New York University Press, 2009).

Chapter 34

1. Portions of this essay adapted from Greggor Mattson, "Learning from Pulse, Listening to Latinx Queers," *The Society Pages* (blog) (July 27, 2017), https://thesocietypages.org/specials/learning-from-pulse-listening -to-la tinx-queers/

2. Michael Levenson, "Congress Backs National Memorial Designation for Former Pulse Nightclub Site," *New York Times* (June 16, 2021), https://www. nytimes.com/2021/06/16/us/pulse-nightclub-shooting-memorial.html

3. Audre Lorde, "The Uses of Anger (Fall 1981)," *Women's Studies Quarterly* 25, no. 1/2 (1997): 278–285; bell hooks, *Killing Rage: Ending Racism* (New York: Henry Holt, 1995).

4. @DonnieHinkle, https://twitter.com/DonnieHinkle/status/741928763517112 322; Mathew Rodriguez, "Orlando's Gay Latino Community Describes Pulse Nightclub in Their Own Words," *Mic* (June 18, 2016), https://www.mic.com/articles/1464 57/orlando-s-gay-latino-community-describes-pulse-nightclub-in-their-own -words

5. Lucas Grindley, "Attacking Any Gay Bar Is a Hate Crime," *Advocate* (June 13, 2016), http://www.advocate.com/commentary/2016/6/13/attacking-any-gay-bar-hate -crime

6. Dan Avery, "Vice President Joe Biden Addresses Orlando, Anti-LGBT Laws, At Logo Trailblazer Honors Special," *Logo TV News* (June 24, 2016), http: //www.newnownext.com/vice-president-joe-biden-addresses-orlando-anti -lgbt-laws-at-logo-trailblazer-honors-special/06/2016/

7. Pulse Orlando, https://www.facebook.com/pulseorlando/posts/101549 38990430031

8. @OrlandoPolice, https://twitter.com/orlandopolice/status/7419314003 92249344?lang=en

9. Mattson, "Post-Orlando Truth for You."

10. Go read his memoir! Marco Wilkinson, *Madder: A Memoir in Weeds* (Minneapolis: Coffee House Press, 2021).

11. "Letter: Father of Christopher Leinonen Speaks Out," *Detroit News* (June 13, 2016), https://www.detroitnews.com/story/news/local/detroit-city/ 2016/06/13/letter-father-christopher-leinonen-speaks/85850766/

12. Elyssa Cherney, "Prosecutor Suspended After Facebook Comments About Pulse Shooting," *Orlando Sentinel* (June 17, 2016), https://www.orlando sentinel.com/news/breaking-news/os-prosecutor-suspended-pulse-com ments-20160617-story.html

13. Jennicet Gutiérrez et al., "Systemic Violence: Reflections on the Pulse Nightclub Massacre," in *The Unfinished Queer Agenda After Marriage Equality*, eds. Angela Jones, Joseph Nicholas DeFilippis, and Michael W. Yarbrough (London and New York: Routledge, 2018), 20–34.

14. See, for example, Leah Donnella, "What Queer Muslims Are Saying About the Orlando Shooting," *Code Switch: NPR* (June 13, 2016), https://www.npr.org/sections/codeswitch/2016/06/13/481853353/what-queer-muslims-are-saying-about-the-orlando-shooting; Orie Givens, "How One Queer Muslim Activist Combats Islamophobia After Orlando," *Advocate* (June 20, 2016), http://www.advocate.com/religion/2016/6/20/how-one-queer-muslim-activist-combats-islamophobia-after-orlando

15. President Barack Obama, "Remarks by the President in a Statement to the Press," *The White House* (June 16, 2016), https://obamawhitehouse.archives.gov/the-press-office/2016/06/16/remarks-president-statement-press

16. Steven W. Thrasher, "Latino Community Mourns Pulse Shooting Victims: '90% Were Hispanic,'" *The Guardian* (June 14, 2016), https://www.theguardian.com/us-news/2016/jun/14/latino-hispanic-orlando-shooting-victims

17. "El Club Gay Pulse Celebraba Una 'Noche Latina' Cuando Ocurrió La Matanza En Orlando," *Univision* (June 12, 2016), https://www.univision.com/noticias/masacre-en-orlando/el-club-gay-pulse-celebraba-una-noche-latina-cuando-ocurrio-la-matanza-en-orlando

18. Thrasher, "Latino Community Mourns Pulse Shooting Victims."

19. Allan Bérubé, "How Gay Stays White and What Kind of White It Stays," in *The Making and Unmaking of Whiteness*, eds. B. B. Rasmussen et al. (Durham: Duke University Press, 2001), 234–265; M. A Hunter, "All the Gays Are White and All the Blacks Are Straight: Black Gay Men, Identity, and Community," *Sexuality Research and Social Policy* 7, no. 2 (2010): 81–92.

20. Juana María Rodríguez, "Voices: Gay Clubs Let Us Embrace Queer Latinidad, Let's Affirm This," *NBC News* (June 16, 2016), https://www.nbcnews.com/storyline/orlando-nightclub-massacre/voices-lgbt-clubs-let-us-embrace-queer-latinidad-let-s-n593191; see also Juana María Rodríguez, *Queer Latinidad: Identity Practices, Discursive Spaces* (New York: New York University Press, 2003).

21. Justin Torres, "In Praise of Latin Night at the Queer Club," *Washington Post* (June 13, 2016), https://www.washingtonpost.com/opinions/in-praise-of-latin-night-at-the-queer-club/2016/06/13/e841867e-317b-11e6-95c0-2a6873031302_story.html

22. @mathewrodriguez, https://twitter.com/mathewrodriguez/status/741976928266129408?lang=en

23. Rodríguez, "Voices."

24. Salvador Vidal-Ortiz, "Queer-Orlando-América—Feminist Reflections," *The Society Pages* (June 17, 2016), https://thesocietypages.org/feminist/2016/06/17/queer-orlando-america/

25. Arun Kundnani, *The Muslims Are Coming! Islamophobia, Extremism, and the Domestic War on Terror* (London: Verso, 2014); Kumar Rao et al., "Equal Treatment? Measuring the Legal and Media Responses to Ideologically Motivated Violence in the United States," *Institute for Social Policy & Understanding* (April 2018), https://www.imv-report.org

26. Jin Haritaworn, *Queer Lovers and Hateful Others: Regenerating Violent Times and Places* (London: Pluto, 2015).

27. Rea Carey and Farhana Khera, "Muslims & LGBTs: We Are One Family," *Advocate* (June 15, 2016), http://www.advocate.com/commentary/2016/6/15/muslims-lgbts-we-are-one-family; Donnella, "What Queer Muslims Are Saying About the Orlando Shooting."

28. Pete Williams et al., "Gunman Omar Mateen Described as Belligerent, Racist, 'Toxic,'" *NBC News* (June 13, 2016), https://www.nbcnews.com/story line/orlando-nightclub-massacre/terror-hate-what-motivated-orlando-night club-shooter-n590496

29. Melissa Jeltsen, "Everyone Got the Pulse Massacre Story Completely Wrong," *HuffPost* (April 5, 2018), https://www.huffpost.com/entry/noor -salman-pulse-massacre-wrong_n_5ac29ebae4b04646b6454dc2

30. Jane Coaston, "New Evidence Shows the Pulse Nightclub Shooting Wasn't About Anti-LGBTQ Hate," *Vox* (April 5, 2018), https://www.vox.com/policy-and-politics/2018/4/5/17202026/pulse-shooting-lgbtq-trump-terror -hate

31. Tim Fitzsimons, "What Really Happened That Night at Pulse," *NBC News* (June 12, 2018), https://www.nbcnews.com/feature/nbc-out/what-really -happened-night-pulse-n882571

32. Christina B. Hanhardt, "Safe Space Out of Place," *QED: A Journal in GLBTQ Worldmaking* 3, no. 3 (2016): 121–125; Haritaworn, *Queer Lovers and Hateful Others*; Doug Meyer, "Resisting Hate Crime Discourse: Queer and Intersectional Challenges to Neoliberal Hate Crime Laws," *Critical Criminology* 22, no. 1 (March 1, 2014): 113–125; Doug Meyer, "Interpreting and Experiencing Anti-Queer Violence: Race, Class, and Gender Differences Among LGBT Hate Crime Victims," *Race, Gender & Class* 15, no. 3/4 (2008): 262–282.

33. Coaston, "New Evidence Shows the Pulse Nightclub Shooting Wasn't About Anti-LGBTQ Hate."

34. Nico Lang, "'I Did the Shooting': Pulse Gunman's 911 Calls Released," *Advocate* (November 1, 2016), http://www.advocate.com/crime/2016/11/01/i -did-shooting-pulse-gunmans-911-calls-released

35. Coaston, "New Evidence Shows the Pulse Nightclub Shooting Wasn't about Anti-LGBTQ Hate."

36. Holly Randell-Moon, "Mediations of Security, Race, and Violence in the Pulse Nightclub Shooting: Homonationalism in Anti-Immigration Times," *GLQ: A Journal of Lesbian and Gay Studies* 28, no. 1 (January 1, 2022): 1–28.

37. Micaela J. Díaz-Sánchez, "*Bailando*: 'We Would Have Been There,'" *QED: A Journal in GLBTQ Worldmaking* 3, no. 3 (2016): 154–156.

38. Jacob Ogles, "Making Plans for a Pulse Memorial," *Advocate* (September 11, 2017), https://www.advocate.com/society/2017/9/11/making-plans -pulse-memorial

39. Paul Brinkmann, "'We Needed This,' Pulse Shooting Survivor Says at Fundraiser," *Orlando Sentinel* (June 23, 2016), https://www.orlandosentinel. com/news/pulse-orlando-nightclub-shooting/os-pulse-fundraising-event -coverage-20160623-story.html

40. Cheryl Corley, "Orlando Club Hosts Dance Party Nearly 2 Weeks After Deadly Mass Shooting," *Morning Edition: NPR* (June 24, 2016), https://www.npr.org/2016/06/24/483337005/orlando-club-reopens-after-49-patrons-were-killed-in-deadliest-u-s-shooting

41. Jacob Ogles, "The Story Behind Pulse's Unclaimed Victim," *Advocate* (June 8, 2017), http://www.advocate.com/crime/2017/6/08/story-behind-pulses-unclaimed-victim

42. JD Doyle, "Memorials Held in Mary's Patio & OutBack," *Houston LGBT History* (n.d.), https://www.houstonlgbthistory.org/houston-marys-memorials.html

43. "Barbara Poma: More Than 'Just Another Gay Club,'" *Internet Archive: Wayback Machine,* https://web.archive.org/web/20160612041305/http://www.pulseorlandoclub.com/about-barbara-poma

44. Zachary Blair, "10 Alternatives to an On-Site Pulse Memorial and Museum," *Zachary Blair* (blog) (July 19, 2019), https://www.zachary-blair.com/post/10-alternatives-to-a-pulse-memorial-and-museum

45. Blair, "10 Alternatives to an On-Site Pulse Memorial and Museum."

46. Lorde, "The Uses of Anger"; Douglas Crimp, "Mourning and Militancy," *October* 51 (1989): 3–18; Jennifer Tyburczy, "Orlando and the Militancy of Queer Mourning," *QED: A Journal in GLBTQ Worldmaking* 3, no. 3 (2016): 142–146.

47. Lawrence La Fountain-Stokes, "Queer Puerto Ricans and the Burden of Violence," *QED: A Journal in GLBTQ Worldmaking* 3, no. 3 (2016): 99–102. Here he echoes hooks, *Killing Rage.*

48. Gutiérrez et al., "Systemic Violence."

49. Eun Kyung Kim, "Orlando Nightclub Owner Describes Moment She Heard About Massacre," *Today* (June 14, 2016), https://www.today.com/news/orlando-nightclub-owner-describes-moment-she-heard-about-massacre-t98136

50. President Joseph Biden, "Remarks by President Biden in Bill Signing of H.R. 49 to Designate the National Pulse Memorial into Law," *The White House* (June 25, 2021), https://www.whitehouse.gov/briefing-room/speeches-remarks/2021/06/25/remarks-by-president-biden-in-bill-signing-of-h-r-49-to-designate-the-national-pulse-memorial-into-law/

Chapter 35

1. Camden Miller and Alex Bitterman, "Commemorating Historically Significant Gay Places Across the United States," in *The Life and Afterlife of Gay Neighborhoods: Renaissance and Resurgence,* eds. Alex Bitterman and Daniel Baldwin Hess (Cham, Switzerland: Springer, 2021), 339–370; Amin Ghaziani, *There Goes the Gayborhood?* (Princeton: Princeton University Press, 2015).

2. Brenden Shucart, "Preserving LGBT History Means Saving These Spaces," *Advocate* (July 19, 2017), https://www.advocate.com/current-issue/2017/7/19/preserving-lgbt-history-means-saving-these-spaces

3. Greggor Mattson, "Style and the Value of Gay Nightlife: Homonorma-

tive Placemaking in San Francisco," *Urban Studies* (2015), https://doi.org/10
.1177/0042098014555630; Greggor Mattson, "Bar Districts as Subcultural
Amenities," *City, Culture and Society* 6, no. 1 (2015): 1–8.

4. Jason Orne, *Boystown: Sex and Community in Chicago* (Chicago: University of Chicago Press, 2017).

5. Bill Eppridge and Paul Welch, "Homosexuality in America," *Life* (June
26, 1964).

6. Gayle S. Rubin, "The Miracle Mile: South of Market and Gay Male
Leather, 1962–1997," in *Reclaiming San Francisco*, ed. James Brook (San Francisco: City Lights, 1998), 247–272.

7. Gayle Rubin, "Requiem for the Valley of the Kings," *Southern Oracle* (Fall
1989), https://sfleatherdistrict.org/wp-content/uploads/2021/04/Rubin
-Requiem-for-VoK.pdf

8. Rubin, "The Miracle Mile"; Nan Alamilla Boyd, *Wide-Open Town: A His-
tory of Queer San Francisco to 1965* (Berkeley and Los Angeles: University of
California Press, 2005); see also Paul Groth, *Living Downtown: The History of
Residential Hotels in the United States* (Berkeley and Los Angeles: University of
California Press, 1994).

9. See Ghaziani, *There Goes the Gayborhood?*

10. Rubin, "The Miracle Mile"; see also Stephen O. Murray, "The Promiscuity Paradigm, AIDS, and Gay Complicity with the Remedicalization of Homosexuality," in *American Gay*, ed. Stephen O. Murray (Chicago: University of
Chicago Press, 1996), 99–125.

11. Michael Flanagan, "Live from the Stud!—Etta James, Sylvester and
More—When Live Music First Ruled Folsom Street," *Bay Area Reporter* (September 19, 2018), https://www.ebar.com/bartab/barchive//265586

12. Flanagan, "Live from the Stud!" Sylvester's biographer used he/him
pronouns for Sylvester. See Joshua Gamson, *The Fabulous Sylvester: The
Legend, the Music, the Seventies in San Francisco* (New York: Henry Holt, 2006).

13. Gamson, *The Fabulous Sylvester.*

14. Mark Freeman, "The Stud: Decade by Decade," *Passed and Present:
Me-Anderings You-Beentheres* (blog) (August 5, 2020), https://markhfreeman
.wordpress.com/the-stud-decade-by-decade/

15. Freeman, "The Stud."

16. Tony Bravo, "Trannyshack Updates Name to T-Shack as Terms, Times
Change," *SFGate* (May 22, 2014), https://www.sfgate.com/performance/article
/Trannyshack-updates-name-to-T-Shack-as-terms-5499509.php

17. These are all from memory and without notes: I wasn't always a bar
researcher, and I wasn't always sober in the bars.

18. John Ferrannini, "SOMA Developers Work with Leather District as
Hearing Nears," *Bay Area Reporter* (August 19, 2020), https://www.ebar.com/
news/news//296191

19. Jay Barmann, "Endangered SoMa Bar The Stud Gets Legacy Business
Status," *SFist* (November 29, 2016), https://sfist.com/2016/11/29/endangered_
soma_bar_the_stud_gets_l/

20. Mattson, "Style and the Value of Gay Nightlife."

21. The Collective's membership has shifted over time; it was eighteen in mid-2020.

22. Queerty, "San Francisco Stories: Honey Mahogany," *YouTube* (January 28, 2020), https://www.youtube.com/watch?v=kZvHeL7BFrg

23. Legacy Business, https://legacybusiness.org/

24. Miller and Bitterman, "Commemorating Historically Significant Gay Places across the United States."

25. Brenden Shucart, "Protecting Queer Spaces," *The Fight Magazine*, (July 31, 2018), https://thefightmag.com/2018/07/protecting-queer-spaces/

26. Ferrannini, "SOMA Developers Work with Leather District as Hearing Nears."

27. Ferrannini, "SOMA Developers Work with Leather District as Hearing Nears."

28. Shucart, "Protecting Queer Spaces."

29. Shucart, "Protecting Queer Spaces."

30. Liz Highleyman, "Leather Cultural District Cuts Ribbon," *Bay Area Reporter* (June 13, 2018), https://www.ebar.com/news/news//261295

31. Marke B., "The Stud Closes Its Location—to Save Itself for the Future," *48 Hills* (May 20, 2020), https://48hills.org/2020/05/the-stud-closes-its-location -in-order-to-save-itself-for-the-future/

32. Greggor Mattson, "Gay Bars and the Impact of the COVID-19 Pandemic," *SocArXiv* (June 16, 2021), https://doi.org/10.31235/osf.io/4uw6j

33. John Ferrannini, "Haney's Office Hopeful Nightlife Fund Can Start in March," *Bay Area Reporter* (February 24, 2021), https://www.ebar.com/news/ news//302325

34. Greggor Mattson, "Shuttered by the Coronavirus, Many Gay Bars— Already Struggling—Are Now on Life Support," *The Conversation* (April 14, 2020), https://theconversation.com/shuttered-by-the-coronavirus-many-gay-bars -already-struggling-are-now-on-life-support-135167

35. Chelsea Donovan, "Iconic Hershee Bar, Oldest Lesbian Bar in Nation, Will Reopen in Norfolk," *WTKR* (July 1, 2021), https://www.wtkr.com/news/ iconic-hershee-bar-oldest-lesbian-bar-in-nation-will-reopen-in-norfolk

36. Andrew Roberts, "Demolition of Buildings That Housed Norfolk's Iconic Hershee Bar Begins," *Outwire757* (August 12, 2019), https://outwire757 .com/demolition-of-buildings-that-housed-norfolks-iconic-hershee-bar -begins/; Eric Hause, "The Mystical, Magical, Triumphant Return of Annette Stone," *Outwire757* (June 23, 2021), https://outwire757.com/the-mystical -magical-triumphant-return-of-annette-stone/ [[continue]]

37. Matt Hennie, "Iconic Gay Bar Atlanta Eagle to Close, Plans New Location for 2021," *Project Q Atlanta* (October 9, 2020), https://www.projectq.us/ iconic-gay-bar-atlanta-eagle-to-close-after-33-years/; Josh Green, "Friction over Atlanta Eagle, Kodak Building Historic Preservation Continues," *Urbanize Atlanta* (May 12, 2021), https://urbanize.city/atlanta/post/eagle-midtown -kodak-lgbtq-historic-preservation; Jonathan Raymond, "Famed Atlanta Gay

Bar Given Boost with Historical Landmark Designation," *11Alive,* (January 14, 2021), https://www.11alive.com/article/news/local/atlanta-eagle-lgbtq-bar-historical-landmark-designation/85-51915e3b-47a6-4c8c-99c4-dc468c87 86b5

38. Matthew S. Bajko, "San Francisco Supervisors Back Leather District Sidewalk Markers," *Bay Area Reporter* (April 6, 2021), https://www.ebar.com/news/latest_news//303723

39. Jack Coffin, "Plateaus and Afterglows: Theorizing the Afterlives of Gayborhoods as Post-Places," in *The Life and Afterlife of Gay Neighborhoods,* 371.

40. Jim Provenzano, "Online Extra: The Stud's Closure Ends an Era, for Now," *Bay Area Reporter* (May 21, 2020), https://www.ebar.com/bartab/bars//292533

Chapter 36

1. Greggor Mattson, "Are Gay Bars Closing? Using Business Listings to Infer Rates of Gay Bar Closure in the United States, 1977–2019," *Socius* 5 (January 1, 2019), https://doi.org/10.1177/2378023119894832; Greggor Mattson, "Gay Bars and the Impact of the COVID-19 Pandemic," *SocArXiv* (June 16, 2021), https://doi.org/10.31235/osf.io/4uw6j

2. D. W. Smith, "Barriers to Risk Reduction in a Southern Community," in *Biobehavioral Control of AIDS,* ed. David G. Ostrow (New York: Irvington, 1987), 121–123.

3. Michael Brown et al., "The Gay Bar as a Place of Men's Caring," in *Masculinities and Place,* eds. Andrew Gorman-Murray and Peter Hopkins, *Masculinities and Place* (London and New York: Routledge, 2014), 299–315; Fiona Buckland, *Impossible Dance: Club Culture and Queer World-Making* (Middletown, CT: Wesleyan University Press, 2002).

4. Maureen Dowd, "For Victims of AIDS, Support in a Lonely Siege," *New York Times* (December 5, 1983), https://www.nytimes.com/1983/12/05/nyregion/for-victims-of-aids-support-in-a-lonely-siege.html

5. T. J. Honnen and C. L. Kleinke, "Prompting Bar Patrons with Signs to Take Free Condoms," *Journal of Applied Behavior Analysis* 23, no. 2 (1990): 215–217.

6. See, for example, Ralph J. DiClemente and John L. Peterson, eds., *Preventing AIDS: Theories and Methods of Behavioral Interventions* (Boston: Springer, 2013); Alan E. Kazdin, *Behavior Modification in Applied Settings,* 7th ed. (Long Grove, IL: Waveland, 2012); Tamar C. Renaud et al., "The Free Condom Initiative: Promoting Condom Availability and Use in New York City," *Public Health Reports* 124, no. 4 (July 1, 2009): 481–489.

7. Tammi Jo Honnen, "Prompting Bar Patrons with Signs to Take Free Condoms," *UAA Student Showcase Journal: Recognizing Excellence* 5, no. 1 (1990): 125–128.

8. Franklin B. Krohn and Laura M. Milner, "The AIDS Crisis: Unethical Marketing Leads to Negligent Homicide," *Journal of Business Ethics* 8, no. 10 (1989): 773–780.

9. Steven D. Pinkerton et al., "Cost-Effectiveness of a Community-Level HIV Risk Reduction Intervention," *American Journal of Public Health* 88, no. 8 (1998): 1239–1242; Jeffrey A. Kelly et al., "Community AIDS/HIV Risk Reduction: The Effects of Endorsements by Popular People in Three Cities," *American Journal of Public Health* 82, no. 11 (1992): 1483–1489; Centers for Disease Control and Prevention, "Popular Opinion Leader (POL): A Community AIDS/HIV Risk Reduction Program for Gay Men," *CDC* (last reviewed January 21, 2020), https://www.cdc.gov/hiv/research/interventionresearch/rep/packages/pol.html

10. Leon McKusick et al., "Reported Changes in the Sexual Behavior of Men at Risk for AIDS, San Francisco, 1982–84: The AIDS Behavioral Research Project," *Public Health Reports* 100, no. 6 (1985): 622–629.

11. Robert B. Hays and John L. Peterson, "HIV Prevention for Gay and Bisexual Men in Metropolitan Cities," in *Preventing AIDS,* 267–296; Karen Trocki and Laurie Drabble, "Bar Patronage and Motivational Predictors of Drinking in the San Francisco Bay Area: Gender and Sexual Identity Differences," *Journal of Psychoactive Drugs* 40, supp. no. 5 (November 1, 2008): 345–356.

12. "I thank Chris Barcelos for this point. See, for example, Ian Warwick et al., "Context Matters: The Educational Potential of Gay Bars Revisited," *AIDS Education and Prevention* 15, no. 4 (August 2003): 320–333.

13. Craig Pittman, "Mortician Guilty of Revealing AIDS List," *Tampa Bay Times* (April 30, 1997), https://www.tampabay.com/archive/1997/04/30/mortician-guilty-of-revealing-aids-list/

14. United Press International, "Man May Lose Job over AIDS List Release," *UPI* (October 10, 1996) (accessed June 4, 2016), https://www.upi.com/Archives/1996/10/10/Man-may-lose-job-over-AIDS-list-release/5928844920000/; John Gallagher, "Confidentially Speaking," *Advocate* (November 26, 1996): 33.

15. Liza S. Rovniak et al., "Engaging Community Businesses in Human Immunodeficiency Virus Prevention: A Feasibility Study," *American Journal of Health Promotion* (May 1, 2010), https://doi.org/10.4278/ajhp.080721-ARB-129

16. Renaud et al., "The Free Condom Initiative."

17. Renaud et al., "The Free Condom Initiative."

18. Michalina A. Montaño et al., "Changes in Sexual Behavior and STI Diagnoses Among MSM Initiating PrEP in a Clinic Setting," *AIDS and Behavior* 23, no. 2 (February 1, 2019): 548–555.

19. Vanita Salisbury, "One of the Country's Best Gay Bars Is Hiding in Alaska," *Thrillist* (August 25, 2021), https://www.thrillist.com/travel/nation/mad-myrnas-anchorage-alaska-best-gay-bars

20. RJ Johnson, "A Raven in Winter," *Anchorage Press* (March 15, 2018), https://www.anchoragepress.com/prismpress/a-raven-in-winter/article_8a22f546-28be-11e8-93af-bbc406596b02.html

21. RJ Johnson, "Penguins and Ravens: Changing of the Guard in the Local Gay Bar Scene," *Anchorage Press* (January 17, 2019), https://www.anchoragepress.com/prismpress/changing-of-the-guard-in-the-local-gay-bar-scene/article_9e29d48a-1a83-11e9-8355-d7ad98bb3fa6.html

22. Johnson, "Penguins and Ravens: Changing of the Guard in the Local Gay Bar Scene."

23. Cathy J. Cohen, *The Boundaries of Blackness: AIDS and the Breakdown of Black Politics* (Chicago: University of Chicago Press, 1999); Irene S. Vernon, *Killing Us Quietly: Native Americans and HIV/AIDS* (Lincoln and London: University of Nebraska Press, 2001); Jafari S. Allen, *There's a Disco Ball Between Us: A Theory of Black Gay Life* (Durham: Duke University Press, 2022).

24. Russ Reno, "110 Photos of 7 Fully Packed Days of Alaska Pride," *Advocate* (June 20, 2018), https://www.advocate.com/pride/2018/6/20/110-photos-7 -fully-packed-days-alaska-pride

25. https://www.instagram.com/p/BzEy_jlhR_W/

Chapter 37

1. Eric Cervini, *The Deviant's War: The Homosexual vs. the United States of America* (New York: Farrar, Straus and Giroux, 2021).

2. Derek S. Hyra, *Race, Class, and Politics in the Cappuccino City* (Chicago and London: University of Chicago Press, 2017). See also Theodore Greene's forthcoming book from Columbia University Press, *Not in MY Gayborhood: Gay Neighborhoods and the Rise of the Vicarious Citizen*.

3. Staff reports, "Best of Gay D.C. XVII," *Washington Blade* (October 18, 2018),https://www.washingtonblade.com/2018/10/18/best-of-gay-d-c-xvii/; Austa Somvichian-Clausen, "Be Queer Right Here at DC's Best LGBTQ Bars and Parties," *Thrillist* (March 12, 2020), https://www.thrillist.com/drink/ washington-dc/best-gay-bars-in-dc; Jessica Sidman, "How Do Non-Gay Bars Become Gay Destinations?" *Washington City Paper* (June 4, 2015), http://wash ingtoncitypaper.com/article/332653/how-do-non-gay-bars-become-gay-desti nations/

4. Adriana Brodyn and Amin Ghaziani, "Performative Progressiveness: Accounting for New Forms of Inequality in the Gayborhood," *City & Community* 17, no. 2 (2018): 307–329.

5. Benjamin Kampler and Catherine Connell, "The Post-Gay Debates: Competing Visions of the Future of Homosexualities," *Sociology Compass* 12, no. 12 (2018): e12646; Amin Ghaziani, "There Goes the Gayborhood?" *Contexts* 9, no. 4 (2010): 64–66; Amin Ghaziani, "Post-Gay Collective Identity Construction," *Social Problems* 58, no. 1 (February 1, 2011): 99–125.

6. Staff reports, "Best of Gay D.C. XVII"; Theodore Greene, "The Whiteness of Queer Urban Placemaking," in *The Gayborhood: From Sexual Liberation to Cosmopolitan Spectacle*, eds. Christopher T. Conner and Daniel Okamura (Lanham, MD: Rowman & Littlefield, 2021), 143–158.

7. Gavin Brown, "Cosmopolitan Camouflage: (Post-) Gay Space in Spital-fields, East London," in *Cosmopolitan Urbanism*, ed. Jon Binnie (London and New York: Routledge, 2006), 130–45; Juan Miguel Kanai and Kai Kent-tamaa-Squires, "Remaking South Beach: Metropolitan Gayborhood Trajecto-ries Under Homonormative Entrepreneurialism," *Urban Geography* 36, no. 3 (2015): 385–402; Toby Lea, John De Wit, and Robert Reynolds, "'Post-Gay' Yet?

The Relevance of the Lesbian and Gay Scene to Same-Sex Attracted Young People in Contemporary Australia," *Journal of Homosexuality* 62, no. 9 (2015): 1264–1285.

8. A good place to start would be Jane Ward, *Not Gay: Sex Between Straight White Men* (New York: New York University Press, 2015).

9. Benjamin Kampler and Catherine Connell, "The Post-Gay Debates: Competing Visions of the Future of Homosexualities," *Sociology Compass* 12, no. 12 (2018): e12646.

10. Kampler and Connell, "The Post-Gay Debates."

11. Ryan Stillwagon and Amin Ghaziani, "Queer Pop-Ups: A Cultural Innovation in Urban Life," *City & Community* 18, no. 3 (September 1, 2019): 874–895.

12. Erin O'Hare, "Escafé Has Served as a Gathering Spot for Many Different Groups," *C-VILLE Weekly* (February 14, 2018), https://www.c-ville.com/escafe-served-gathering-spot-many-different-groups/

13. Erin Petenko, "Fox Market Is Vermont's 1st LGBTQ+ Bar in 15 Years. What Took So Long?" *VTDigger* (April 3, 2022), https://vtdigger.org/2022/04/03/fox-market-is-vermonts-1st-lgbtq-bar-in-15-years-what-took-so-long/

14. Brock Keeling, "Gay Bar Death: Kok to Become Driftwood," *SFist* (February 8, 2013), https://sfist.com/2013/02/08/kok_to_become_driftwood/. See also Greggor Mattson, "Style and the Value of Gay Nightlife: Homonormative Placemaking in San Francisco," *Urban Studies* (2015), https://doi.org/10.1177/0042098014555630

15. The lone exception is Melissa Kravitz, "The Drag Queen Burger Joint That's Planning World Domination," *Bon Appétit* (July 10, 2017), https://www.bonappetit.com/story/hamburger-marys-restaurant

16. Michael Mackie, "By the Numbers: Hamburger Mary's Kansas City," *In Kansas City* (February 14, 2019), https://www.inkansascity.com/eat-drink/restaurants/by-the-numbers-hamburger-marys-kansas-city/

17. Jordyn Pari, "Ypsilanti's Tower Inn Combining with Hamburger Mary's in Dual-Concept Restaurant," *MLive* (January 6, 2022), https://www.mlive.com/news/ann-arbor/2022/01/ypsilantis-tower-inn-combining-with-hamburger-marys-in-dual-concept-restaurant.html

18. https://www.hamburgermarys.com/franchise/

19. David M. Halperin, *How to Be Gay* (Cambridge, MA: Belknap, 2012).

20. Devlyn Camp, "Hamburger Mary's, Chicago's All-Ages Queer Burger Bar, Made Drag a Family Affair," *Them* (December 21, 2020), https://www.them.us/story/hamburger-marys-chicago-queer-spaces-covid-19

21. Dr. Shannon Caramiello, "Hamburger Mary's Ybor City More Than Just a Restaurant," *Institute for LGBT Health & Wellbeing* (blog) (February 25, 2019), http://www.instituteforlgbthealth.org/1/category/hamburger-marys

22. Kravitz, "The Drag Queen Burger Joint That's Planning World Domination."

23. Halperin, *How to Be Gay*, 448.

24. Theodore Greene, "'You're Dancing on My Seat': Queer Subcultures

and the Production of Place in Contemporary Gay Bars," *Subcultures: Studies in Symbolic Interaction* (2022): 137–166; Ryan Stillwagon and Amin Ghaziani, "Queer Pop-Ups: A Cultural Innovation in Urban Life," *City & Community* 18, no. 3 (September 1, 2019): 874–895; Mary L. Gray, *Out in the Country: Youth, Media, and Queer Visibility in Rural America*, vol. 2 (New York: New York University Press, 2009). See also Clare Forstie's forthcoming *Queering the Midwest: Forging LGBTQ Community* from New York University Press.

25. Greggor Mattson, "Small-City Gay Bars, Big-City Urbanism," *City & Community* 19, no. 1 (2020): 76–97. See also Greene's forthcoming, *Not in MY Gayborhood*.

26. See the diverse accounts in S. Renée Bess and Lee Lynch, eds., *Our Happy Hours: LGBT Voices from the Gay Bars* (Sardinia, Ohio: Flashpoint, 2017), and also Lucas Hilderbrand's forthcoming book from Duke University Press, *The Bars Are Ours: Histories and Cultures of Gay Bars in America, 1960 and After*.

27. Brenden Shucart, "Preserving LGBT History Means Saving These Spaces," *Advocate* (July 19, 2017), https://www.advocate.com/current-issue/2017/7/19/preserving-lgbt-history-means-saving-these-spaces

Index

A Man's World (Cleveland). *See* Man's World

AAPI. *See* Asian Americans and Pacific Islanders

AAPI-helmed or -focused gay bars: Denver Sweet, 219; insideOUT, 96-105; N'Touch, 85; Wang Chung's, 79-87; The Web (NYC), 85

ACT-UP, 309

activism: of bar owners, 15, 101, 108, 255, 296; Black Lives Matter, 108, 121; of drag queens, 70, 101; around gay bars, 43, 53, 106, 175, 207, 227, 254, 316; around HIV/AIDS, 309, 312, 329; pre-Stonewall, 43, 172, 293-94; Stonewall uprising and, 292, 294-95; Two-Spirit, 142, 145; undocu-queer, 126, 128; violence against, 3. *See also* Harvey Milk

\aut\ BAR (Ann Arbor): in 1996, 21–23; in 2017, 22–23; AIDS activism, 23–24; bookstore and, 22, 23, 24–25, 27; brunches, 24; change at, 25–26, 31; closure of, 27; community center and, 23, 24; drag events, 25–26; map, ix; opening of, 23; pandemic and, 27; straight-friendly, 332

Ablon, Mike (developer), 277–78

Adair, Cass (journalist), 261

Adelman, Jason (owner), 18

African Americans. *See* Black people

ageism, 21, 104, 360n17. *See also* \aut\ BAR (Ann Arbor); older patrons

agender people, 16

AIDS activism: \aut\ BAR (Ann Arbor) and, 23–24; bars supporting, 52; queer bars and, 148; The Raven (Anchorage), 319–26; The Stud (San Francisco), 312–13. *See also* ACT-UP, HIV/AIDS

Aistrake, Mark (patron), 307

Akbar (Los Angeles), 256

Alabama: B-Bob's (Mobile); Cabaret Club Dothan, 72; Gabriel's Downtown, 300

Alaska: Gordo's (Anchorage), 122; Jade Room, 321; Mad Myrna's, 324; The Raven (Anchorage), viii, 300, 319–26; The Village, 321, 324

Alaska Thunderfuck 5000 (drag artist), 73. *See also* Ru Girls (RPDR)

Alaskan AIDS Assistance Associations (Four A's), 325

alcohol, 59 93, 94, 104, 125, 141, 225, 228, 259, 332; abuse of, 16, 43, 123; doing research around, 274; gay bars without, 15; and Indigenous people, 140-42; regulation of, 39, 107, 119, 126, 205, 276, 284; and women, 162, 190-1;

Alibi Lounge (NYC), ix, 252–57

Alibi's (Oklahoma City), viii, 172–78

Alig, Michael (promoter), 14

Allbee, Nate (owner), 313, 314, 336

The Alley (Chicago), 205–6, 209–10. *See also* Jackhammer

Alter, Ilya (owner), 330

alternative lifestyle bars, 7, 75

alternatives to gay bars, 16. *See also* bathhouses; bookstores; coffeehouses; dining; house parties; pop up parties. *See also* nonalcoholic socializing

Alyssa Edwards (drag artist), 278. *See also* Ru Girls (RPDR)

ambivalence: about crowdfunding, 256–57; about decline in gay bars, 13–14; about gay bars, 16–20, 17; about role of straight people, 12, 24, 50; ambivalent politics, 59; defined, 13; of owners, 35; queer people and, 16–17; of racial camp 79–87, 354n1. *See also* ageism; change; rebranding

Amy (friend), 231, 332

Anhedonia Delight (drag artist), 233

anger. *See* rage

Anita Manager (drag artist), 285

Ann Arbor, 23, 118, 321. *See also* \aut\ BAR

anti-Semitism, 246

anxiety, 14, 118, 203, 205, 231

apps. *See* cell phones; dating apps

Appalachia, 7, 258, 263, 335

Arabs, 118, 301

archipelago, as metaphor, 30, 346n1, 352n5

archive, queer, 70, 290-2, 294, 296, 297-300

Ardina (drag artist), 69

Arkansas: C4 (Fayetteville, AR), 76; gay resort community of Eureka Springs, 64; Kinkead's (Fort Smith), 74; lack of lesbian bars in, 173; LGBTQ+ equality in, 28

Armstrong, Elizabeth A. (academic), 389n9, 12, 13, 14, 17, 23, 25, 26; 349n38

asexuality, 16, 207, 377n19

asthma, 14, 325

Asian Americans and Pacific Islanders (AAPI) 79–87, 122. *See also* AAPI-helmed or -focused gay bars

assumptions: about dating apps, 28; about gentrification, 28; about Great Recession, 28; about LGBTQ+ acceptance, 28; challenging, 28–29; about urban LGBTQ+ people, 35. *See also* Garlow's (Gun Barrel City)

Avendaño, Grisanti (activist), 126, 129-30, 365n3

B-Bob's Downtown (Mobile, AL), 74

Baker, Ezra (friend), 281

Bieschke, Marke. *See* Marke B.

bachelorettes, 102, 109, 240, 241

The Backstreet (Roanoke, VA), 262–63

Horse (Oakland); Wild Side West (San Francisco), viii, 157–65, 200

cafés. *See* coffeeshops; dining

calling out / calling in, 137, 365n4

Camas (Washington), 15, 239;

cameras in gay bars, 205, 237,

camp humor, 38, 70, 74, 79, 85, 103, 139, 157, 198-99, 297, 329, 331, 332-34. *See also* Hamburger Mary's; lesbian camp; racial camp; Wang Chung's (Honolulu)

Campbell-McDaniel, Krystal (owner), 173–78

carding policies, 43, 121, 125-7, 244

Carl's-The Saloon (Reno), 78

Carrillo, Héctor (academic), 98, 359n4-6, 11; 365n5

Caven, Frank (owner), 273, 274, 275–76

Caven Enterprises (Dallas), viii, 272–79

cell phones 4, 19, 21, 26, 45, 60, 63, 64, 91, 144, 148, 158, 204, 205, 218, 222-23, 224, 226, 236, 299, 305. *See also* dating apps

Central Oklahoma Two-Spirit Society (COTSS), 140–41, 142, 145

chain restaurants: compared to gay bars 232; as competition to gay bars, 66, 217; as LGBTQ+ spaces, 16. *See also* Hamburger Mary's

Chanell, Sage (activist), 142–44, 145–46

Chang, Danny (owner), 80–85, 87, 336

change: accounting for, 6, 21; aging and, 22–23, 25–26; celebration of, 3; in LGBTQ+ life, 16, 23, 35, 41; youth and, 35

charities, 2, 22-23, 27, 151, 164, 197, 220, 232, 274, The Baltimore Eagle, 224; Club Xclusive (Hattiesburg) and, 185–86; donation of a gay bar as, 259; Garlows (Gun Barrel City)

and, 33-34, 256, 257; gay bars supporting, 33–34, 52; The Park (Roanoke), 259, 263

Charles, RuPaul. *See* RuPaul

Chavez, Jay (manager), 72

Chekaldin, Dmitri "Dima" (owner), 328–31, 334–35

Chez Est (Hartford, CT), 59

Chicago, 35, 72-74, 88, 110-11, 196, 294-95, 334; Black-owned gay bars, 85, 179; The Hole, 205–6, 209; Jackhammer, 202, 204–5, 209–10, 283; Touché, 205

Chi Chiz (NYC), 121

Christopher Street Liberation Day, 294

Chumley's (State College, PA), ix, 264–71, 332

cigarettes. *See* smoking

cissexism, 77. *See also* transphobia

The City Nightclub (Portland, OR), viii, 14–15, 20

Clark, Calvin (owner), 255

Clarke, Kris (friend), 125–26

Cleveland: Bounce (gay dance club), 2, 234; Burton's Soul Food, 2; Club Cleveland, 2; Crossover, 2; Dean Rufus House of Fun, 2; drag performance in, 2, 233–34; gayborhoods and, 2, 3–4; Leather Stallion, ix, 71, 230–38, 302; A Man's World, xvi, xvi, 1-5, 9-10, 86, 231-32; Ohio City Café, 2; The Tool Shed, 2; value of drag queens from, 76, 354n18; Vibe (Cleveland), 232

Cleveland Leather Awareness Weekend (CLAW), 2, 18, 232

Cleveland Mr. Leather, 2

Club Bunns (Baltimore), 218

Club Cabaret (Hickory, NC), 65

Club Chico (Los Angeles County), viii, 88–98, 285

Club Cleveland (gay bathhouse), 2

Club Cobra (Los Angeles County), viii, 88–98, 285

15-16, 43, 163, 194, 247; by
Wrangler (Denver), 213, 215-16
discrimination against LGBTQ+
people: economic, 257; by
Mississippi state law, 180
disidentification, racial camp as,
354n1
disinvestment, 5
diversity of queer people, 1, 13–14.
46, 48, 54, 80, 92, 98, 145, 174, 191-
92, 232, 270, 282, 312, 336
DJs: as celebrities, 273, 275; as
ghosts, 287; as gig workers,
283; as interviewees 6, 53; as
necessary entertainment, 25, 45,
61, 103, 193, 234, 296; inclusion
and, 149, 169-70, 198, 217, 220, 271;
livestreaming, 277, 284-85; music
discrimination of, 86, 122, 169-70;
as bar owners, 219, 314, 316
DJ Code Villain 284
DJ Deanne, 277
DJ El Concentido, 277
DJ Genesiis, 277
DJ Linkx, 284
DJ OMG Yaaas Queen. See Nicholas
Ruiz
DJ Shawna, 198
DJ Sinna-G, 220
DJ Mateo, 273
Dominguez, Michael (manager),
235–38
Don't Ask, Don't Tell policy, 23, 330
doorman / doorperson. See bouncer
Dorian Society (Seattle), 43
Double Header (Seattle), 46
drag kings, 51–52, 71, 72, 76, 108,
113, 149, 193, 374n10
drag performance: \aut\ BAR (Ann
Arbor), 25; at The Baltimore
Eagle, 224-25; cisgender women
as performers, 108; in Cleveland,
2, 233–34; at Garden of Allah,
40; at Garlow's (Gun Barrel City,
TX), 31; increasing focus on, 45;

at Independence Place (Cape
Girardeau, MO), 69–78; at Leather
Stallion (Cleveland), 233–34;
proliferation of, 71; as queer,
149; range of, 70–71; at Sneakers
(Jameston, NY), 168; at Splash
Bar Florida (Panama City Beach),
61–63, 68; at Stonewall National
Monument, 296; The Stud (San
Francisco), 313; as transgender
art form, 70;Troupe429 (Norwalk,
CT), 282. See also drag queens
drag queens: Ardina, 69; as activists,
299, 315; Anhedonia Delight,
233; bearded, 77; The Baltimore
Eagle, 224–25; COVID-19 support
for, 284–85, 286; data collection
from, 6, 8; as essential to
business, 63, 71-72, 242, 285; faux,
108; fees for, 70; fundraising by,
33–34, 70–71, 193; at Garden of
Allah, 45; Hamburger Mary's Bar
& Grill and, 333; heckling by, 45;
gay male hostility toward, 213-14;
as influencers, 33–34, 73; and
leather and kink community, 225,
232, 234; lesbian views of, 163,
168, 195; memorable, 17, 19, 21,
70, 233, 313; migrations of, 30, 33,
72-73, 102, 112, 333; Pretty Belle,
110–12; as professionals, 69–70;
straight patronage of, 74–75. See
also Ru Girls (RPDR)
drama: of drag queens, 33; lack of,
31, 132, 192; of patrons, 262; of
queer bar ownership. See Blush
& Blu (Denver); of social media,
50, 184
dress codes: discrimination via,
43, 216; in leather bars, 166, 216,
222-23;
drugging, 52, 121
drugs, 3, 4, 19, 62, 65, 119, 123, 144,
170-1, 191, 227. See also alcohol,
marijuana

333; in Seattle, 38, 46; Shaw (Washington, DC), 327, 329; Soma (San Francisco), 311-12, 315, 317; Walker's Point (Milwaukee), 156, 195; in Washington, DC, 6, 46, 329; in West Hollywood, 89, 95, 334; Wilton Manors (FL), 229. *See also* Amin Ghaziani, Theodore Greene

gay-friendly straight bars, 4, 15, 18, 68, 111, 217, 296, 328, 332, 335

gay literature, 25, 350n50. *See also* Damron Guide

gay marriage, *see* same-sex marriage

gay men, bars for, 161, 203, 207, 212-13; desire for mixed LGBTQ+ spaces, 24, 40, 297; and drag, 70, 74; and gayborhoods, 97, 104; gentrification and, 3, 311; and HIV/AIDS, 312, 319, 321, 325, and lesbian spaces, 160, 180, 198; politics of, 231, 245, 319; privileges of, 16, 30; on slurs, 134; and racism, 80, 82; and straight spaces, 217; on straight women in gay bars, 119-20

gay strip clubs: general comments on, 183, 203, 209; Silverado (Portland, OR), 239, 240–41; The Stag PDX (Portland), viii, 239–47; straight, 198, 330.

gender binary rejection, 7, 48, 162

gender fluidity, 141, 367n5

gender identity: gay bar exclusion and, 16. *See also* transgender gay bar exclusion

gender nonbinary people, 16, 135, 140, 145, 159–60, 162; advertising featuring, 228; dancers, 244, 245; equality demands for, 9; inclusion of, 268, 282; integration with, 165, 189, 190; sexy community and, 209.

genderqueer, 18, 216, 220, 312

gentrification, 47, 98, 118, 191, 227, 277, 327, 329; as influenced by gay bars, 4-5, 277, 311, 313, 347n8; gay bars pushed out by, 4, 8–9, 28, 36, 158, 222, 343n17, 344n10; mistakenly identified, 5; policies to address, 315

George Floyd protests, 121, 233, 255, 363n23

Georgia: Columbus, 73; research companion Ezra Baker, 281; Sister Louisa's Church (It's a Glory Hole) (Athens), 332; Sister Louisa's Church of the Living Room & Ping Pong Emporium... Come on in, Precious! (Atlanta), 332

Ghaziani, Amin (academic), 245n16, 19; 346n1, 351n3, 352n8, 5; 358n1, 359n1, 360n13, 1; 376n15; 385n3; 395n1, 9; 399n4, 5

Gieseking, Jack (academic), 110, 158, 338, 346n1, 352n5, 359n6, 370n23

Gilmore, Jason (owner), 75, 259

Girl Bar (Chicago), 196

Girton, Moe (owner), 99

Gladys, The Nosy Neighbor (Denver), 72

go-go dancers, 62, 104, 204, 240, 272-73, 283, 285, 313. *See also* strippers

Gonzales, Natalie (patron), 307

González-Torres, Félix (artist), 320

Good Time Lounge (Denison, TX), 160

Gordo's (Anchorage), 122

Gormley, Quinn (activist), 53

Gossip Grill (San Diego), 96, 99, 103

government IDs. *See also* EDACTED unidentified bar (Fresno); carding

Graham, Colin, (owner) 147–52, 153

Great Recession, 28, 35, 91

Green, Mary (owner), 166–71, 200

Greene, Theo (academic), 53, 54, 345n16, 346n1, 351n13, 356n24, 28; 357n1; 358n15; 359n3, 6, 9, 10, 12; 364n28; 399n2, 6; 401n24, 25

Latinidad, 304, 306, 309, 356n27; 357n29; 357n1

Latinx-owned gay bars: \aut\ BAR (Ann Arbor, MI), 21-27; Club Chico (Los Angeles), 89–95; Club Cobra (Los Angeles County), 89–95; Club FAB (Fresno), 88; New Jalisco Bar (Los Angeles), 85; Troupe429 (Norwalk, CT), ix, 280-88

Latinx people: activists, 44, 299; artists, 77; DACA and, 128–30; dance clubs for, 90, 95; diversity of, 128-29, 304, 306; events by, 148; in gay bars, 120, 122; gay bars for, 85-86, 88-89, 122; geographies of, 125-26, 190, 303-04, 315; marginalization of, 86, 299; music, 246, 269; politics of, 86, 89, 95; Pulse (Orlando), 303–4. *See also* undocuqueer stress

law enforcement. *See* police

leather bars, 47–55, 71, 202–5, 209–10, 223, 230–38, 283, 380n1. *See also* The Baltimore Eagle, Jackhammer (Chicago), kink bars

leather events, 2, 18, 49, 109, 110, 128, 332. *See also* kink events

Leather Stallion (Cleveland), ix, 71, 230–38, 302

Le Bistro (Hattiesburg, MS), 322

Legacy Business Program (San Francisco), 315, 316

legal issues: against bars, 194; in Colorado, 214, 216; crossdressing law, 97, 216; cruisy bars and, 225; Defense of Marriage Act, 330; defining bars, 125; Don't Ask, Don't Tell policy, 23; human rights codes and, 149; from hyper-policing of Black communities, 184; liquor laws, 260; marijuana legalization, 45; in Mississippi, 180-81; against police harassment of gay bars,

43; raids and, 121, 293; regarding checking ID, 126, 244; restriction of alcohol on reservations, 140; strippers and, 234, 239; The Stud (San Francisco) and, 317; Supreme Court cases, 172; in Virginia, 350n49

Leitsch, Dick (activist), 389n8

Lentz, Stacy (owner), 292, 296–99

Leonard, Steve (owner), 207

Lesbian Bar Project, 159, 160–61, 177, 188–89, 194, 255, 256, 277

lesbian bars, 9; attracting customers, 179, 187; closure of, 161–62, 344n4; definitions of, 15, 157, 159-61, 163, 188, 200; lesbian dislike for, 166, 168, 171; drama of queer bar ownership, 188, 194; evolution of, 195, 200; referenced as gay bars, 368n1; gay men in, 168, 330; gayborhoods and, 162; scarcity of, 156, 157, 165; Sisters (Portland, ME), 350n1; as straight friendly, 172-73, 177–78, 196; straight patrons and, 174, 177; Sue Ellen's (Dallas), 273–74; violence and, 122, 184; as women's-only spaces, 16, 42. *See also* lesbian-owned bars

lesbian-owned bars. *See* Alibi's (Oklahoma City); Blush & Blu (Denver); Bum Bum Bar (NYC), 160; Club Xclusive (Hattiesburg); Easy Street Tavern (Southwest region); Flavor+Attic (Baltimore), 160; Good Time Lounge (Denison); Herz (Mobile); Nobody's Darling (Chicago); Sneakers (Jamestown); Sue Ellen's (Dallas); Q Bar (Greensboro), 160; Pirate's Cove (Pueblo), 160; Squiggy's (Binghamton), 160; Walker's Pint (Milwaukee); Wild Side West (San Francisco)

Maine: Blackstones (Portland), ix, 12, 47, 47–55, 49, 71, 256; research in 9; Sisters (Portland), 350n1

MaineTransNet, 52

managers: Bayliss, 273–74; Braun, 264–71; Chavez, 72; Currie, 12, 48–55; data collection from, 6, 8, 88, 335; Jack, 275–76, 369n17; Jay, 225; Kam, 241, 246–47; Keup, 209–10; King, 222–29; manager model, 314; May, 71; Nicole, 242–43, 245; people of color, 98; Quion, 98, 101; Robison, 33; on running a bar, 61; Ryan, 314, 316; Shumaker, 75; Smith, 260; straight managers, 75, 246–47; on straight patrons, 102; on televised drag shows, 76; transgender, 98

A Man's World (Cleveland): closure of, xvi, 1, 3–4, 5, 232; Leather Stallion and, 231–32; longing for, 9–10; map, ix; neighborhood of, 2, 3–4; racist remarks at, 86

Marie's Crisis, (NYC) 285

marijuana: and bars, 4, 191, 185; legalization of, 9, 45, 191

Marke B. (owner), 164, 316

marketing: cynicism of, 308; degree in, 260; diversity and, 101, 103; via drag, 107; via firms, 226, 297; via political involvement, 32–33

Mary's Tavern (Denver), 39

Maryland: The Baltimore Eagle, ix, 221–29; Club Bunns, 218; Flavor+Attic (Baltimore), 160; The Hippo, 221, 224-25

masculinity, 49, 85, 123, 203, 207, 213, 220-21, 245, 311; female, 183. *See also* butch, toxic masculinity

Masher, Joe (entrepreneur), 285

Massachusetts, bar in Springfield, 7. *See also* Boston, Provincetown

Matson, George (owner), 312

Mattachine Society, 43, 293

The Max (Omaha), 131

May, Gary (owner), 71

May, Reuben A. Buford (academic), 86, 356n26,

Mayflower Lounge (Oklahoma City), 40

McClymond, Terry (bartender), 26

McDaniel, Tiffany (owner), 173–78

McRae, Jon (owner), 332

Meeting House (Chicago), 283

Menard, Justin (owner), 59

"Menergy" (1981 record) (Cowley), 376n10

"Menergy" (1984 record) (Sylvester), 376n10

Menjo's (Detroit), 300

men's bars, 7 *See also* cruisy men's bars

Mercury, Freddie (artist), 52

methodology: book structure, 9; data collection, 7–10; ethics, 136-37; research background, 5–6; strategy, 6, 8

metronormativity, 35, 346n5,

Michael (owner), 241–47

Michigan: Ann Arbor, 23, 118, 321; House of Chanel (Detroit), 70; Menjo's (Detroit), 300; R&R Saloon (Detroit), 118–19, 124; Saugatuck, 64. *See also* \aut\ BAR; R&R Saloon

middle class, *see* social class

Midwest: Alibi's (Oklahoma City), 172–78; Belle's Basix (Cedar Rapids, IA), 107, 110–13; Black-owned gay bars, 85; Blush & Blu (Denver), 188–94; closures in, 4; college towns, 17; data collection from, 6–7, 8; The Hole (Chicago), 205–6, 209; House of Chanel (Detroit), 70; Independence Place (Cape Girardeau, MO), 69–78; Iowa as, 110-11; Jackhammer (Chicago), 202, 204–5, 209–10, 283; Leather Stallion (Cleveland), ix, 71, 230–38, 302; premier lesbian bar of, 196; Menjo's (Detroit), 300; R House (Toledo), 72; R&R Saloon (Detroit), 118–19, 124; redevelopment and displacement in, 3–5; Studio 13 (Iowa City, IA), 107, 107–10, 112–13; Touché (Chicago), 205; Walker's Pint (Milwaukee), 195–200; Wrangler (Denver), 213–19. *See also* \aut\ BAR; Illinois, Missouri, Ohio

military, U.S., 26, 39, 45, 80, 84, 306. *See also* Don't Ask, Don't Tell policy

Milk, Harvey (activist), 44

Millennials and gay bars, 8, 60, 235

Milstead, Chris, (owner) 332

Milwaukee, Walker's Pint (Milwaukee), 195–200

Mineshaft (NYC), 208

Minko, Alexi (owner), 252–57

Minnesota, as patrons of Iowa bars, 109

Minogue, Kylie (artist), 336

Minten, Randy (owner), 219

misogyny, 16, 44, 84, 120, 133, 157, 163, 168, 196-97, 207, 362n10

Mississippi: Black Sheep's Café & Speakeasy (Hattiesburg), 71; Club Xclusive (Hattiesburg, MS), ix, 179–87, 181; Joey's on the Beach (Biloxi), 322; Le Bistro (Hattiesburg), 322

Missouri: Equality Rocks (Joplin), 4, 68; Hamburger Mary's (Kansas City), 333; Independence Place (Cape Girardeau), 58, 69–78

mobile phones. *See* cell phones

Molnar, Brian (owner), 232

monuments: AIDS and, 319–21, 325–26; designations of, 301, 309; gay bars as, 258, 286, 290, 291, 299-302, 307, 308, 327; municipal landmarks, 310, 317-18. *See also* AIDS activism; Dacha (Washington, D. C.);

post-gay places; Pulse (Orlando); The Raven (Anchorage); The Stonewall Inn (NYC); The Stud (San Francisco); Troupe429 (Norwalk, CT)

Moody, Chris (friend), 21-22

Moore, Mignon (academic), 373n3, 374n13

MTV, 15

Muñoz, José Esteban (academic), 69; definition of queer, 391n51

music, African, 253; ambient, 104; as atmosphere, 14, 22, 103, 127, 197, 205; as attraction, 25, 160; Black, 246; Bollywood, 87; country, 261; EDM, 260; house, 261, 313; quality of, 18; rap, 136, 169-70; Spanish-language, 89, 126, 129, 246; as status, 20. *See also* live music

Muslims: discrimination against, 233, 305; queer, 302-3, 305

Myers, Ken (owner), 231–33, 235

My Sister's Room (Atlanta), 71

National Independent Venue Association, 283

Native Americans. *See* Indigenous peoples

Nebraska, The Max (Omaha), 131; as patrons of Iowa bars, 109; research in, 8, 338

Nevada: Carl's-The Saloon, 78; Faces (Reno), 75; research in, 8, 338

New Beginnings (Johnson City, TN), 335

Newell, Chris (owner), 72

New Jalisco Bar (Los Angeles), 85

New Jersey: Paradise (Asbury Park), 88

Newman, Felice (author), 43

New York: Alibi Lounge (NYC), 252–57; Bum Bum Bar (NYC), 160; Chi Chiz (NYC), 121; Club Langston (NYC), 255-56; Julius' (NYC) 293; Lambda Lounge

259; and sexual orientation, 257; and upscale aesthetics, 2-3, 20, 104, 182, 240;

social media, 26, 50–51, 64, 101, 103, 137, 151, 184–85, 220, 223, 225–26, 282, 284, 298, 302; Facebook, 8, 50–54, 64, 73, 111, 112, 151–52, 163, 180, 216, 232–33, 237, 282, 285, 302, 303; Instagram, 73, 76, 83, 91, 95, 101, 104, 282, 284, 325; Snapchat, 64, 282; TikTok, 104; Twitter, 282. *See also* technology

SoFo Tap (Chicago), 283

Sokol, Marty (owner), 89–95

Solomon, Ricky (owner), 256

SoMa gayborhood (San Francisco), 310–15

Sorg, Jeff (owner), 269–70

The South: alcohol politics of, 66; The Backstreet (Roanoke, VA), 262–63; B-Bobs (Mobile, AL), 74; Black chosen families of, 183; Black Sheep's Café & Speakeasy (Hattiesburg, MS), 71–72, 182, 183; Bolt (Lafayette, LA), 59; C4 (Fayetteville, AR), 76; Cabaret Club Dothan (AL), 72; Café Lafitte in Exile (New Orleans), 40; Club Cabaret (Hickory, NC), 65; Club Xclusive (Hattiesburg, MS), ix, 179–87; Corky's Lounge (Monroe, LA), 322; Crystal's Downtown (Lake Charles, LA), 71; data collection from, 6, 7; 131–38; drag performance in 70-71; Equality Rocks (Joplin, MO), 4, 68; Escafé (Charlottesville, VA), 86, 331; Eureka Springs (AR), 64; Freddie's Beach Bar (Arlington, VA), 177; Gabriel's Downtown (Mobile, AL), 300; gay bars and, 67; Herz (Mobile, AL), 179; Independence Place (Cape Girardeau, MO), 58, 69–78; Kinkead's (Fort Smith, AR), 74; LGBTQ+ acceptance in,

6; My Sister's Room (Atlanta), 71; O. Henry's (Asheville, NC), 9; The Park Dance Club (Roanoke, VA), ix, 75, 258–64, 314; pretty gay not-gay bars of, 332; racism and sexism of, 181; research in, 7; Q Bar (Greensboro, NC), 160; UpStairs Lounge (New Orleans), 122. *See also* Florida; Georgia; Texas

South Carolina, 6

South Dakota, 6

Southside Speakeasy (Salem, OR), 69

Southwest region, viii, 131–38

Sparks, Tory (coauthor), 6, 8, 29, 31, 58, 107, 119, 161–62, 199, 272–75, 334, 360, 375n1

Spears, Britney (artist), 5, 282

Spector-Bishop, Jack (research assistant), 8, 88, 89, 91, 94

Spectrum (Eugene, OR), 152–53

Splash Bar Florida (Panama City Beach, FL), ix, 59–68

Squiggy's (Binghamton, NY), 160

The Stable (Providence, RI), 207

The Stag PDX (Portland, OR), viii, 239–47

Stath, Lex (bartender), 198–200

Station 4 (Dallas), *see* S4

Stein, Marc (academic), 299, 349n46, 388n6, 389n7-8, 15, 21; 390n34, 40, 42, 43; 381n45, 48, 49

Stewart, Katie (patron), 109

Stigma, 35, 67, 142-43, 217, 220, 354n5, 356n20, 363n18, 378n2,

STIs (sexually transmitted infections), 67, 320. *See also* HIV/AIDS, public health services

The Stonewall Inn (NYC), ix, 41, 256, 290, 291–300, 308

The Stonewall National Monument, 295-96, 380n27, 28, 29

The Stonewall Riots, 29, 42, 389n8, 391n45

stories: assumptions within, 28;